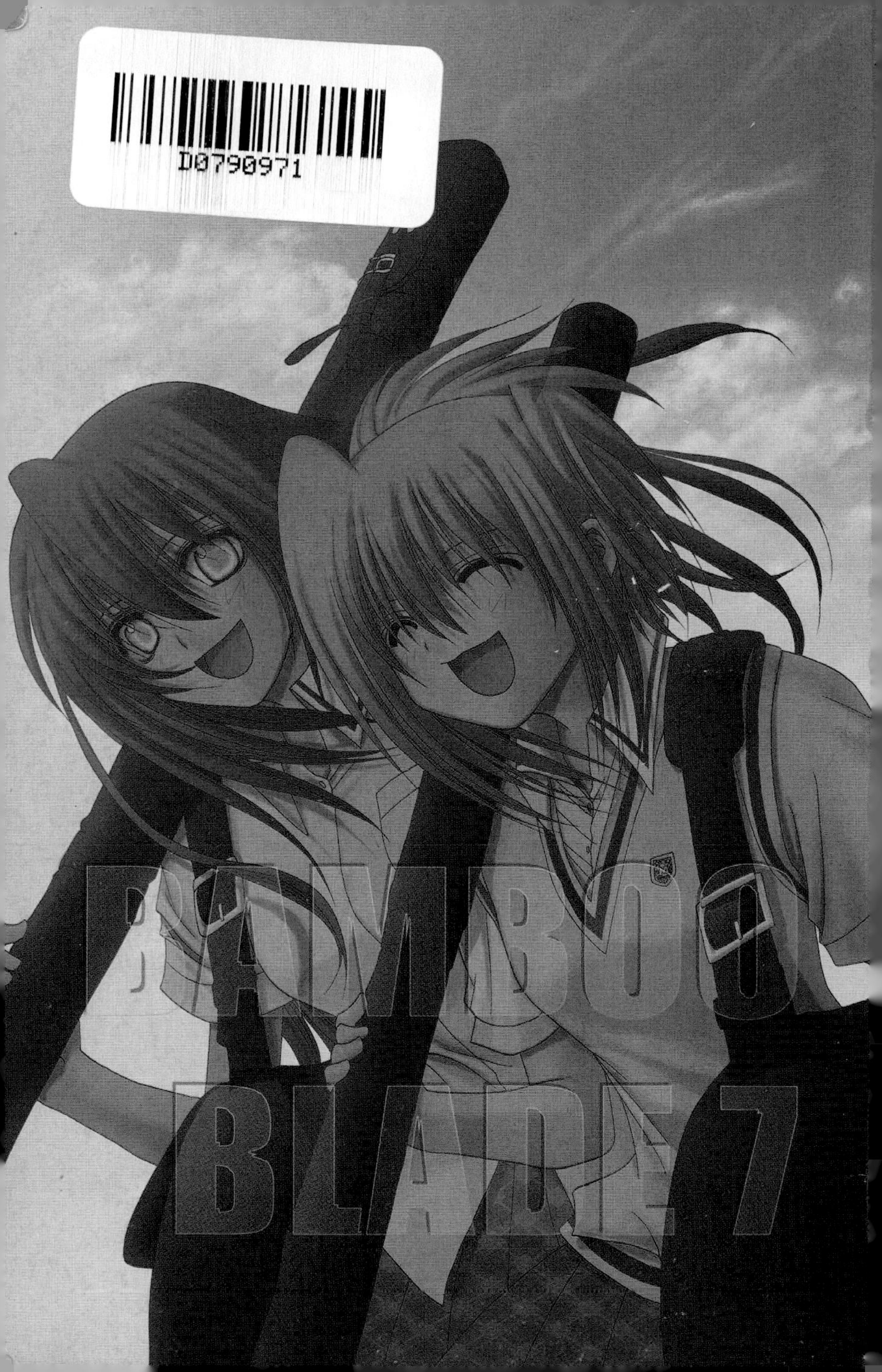
BAMBOO
BLADE 7

BAMBOO BLADE 7
CONTENTS

Story: Masahiro Totsuka / Art: Aguri Igarashi

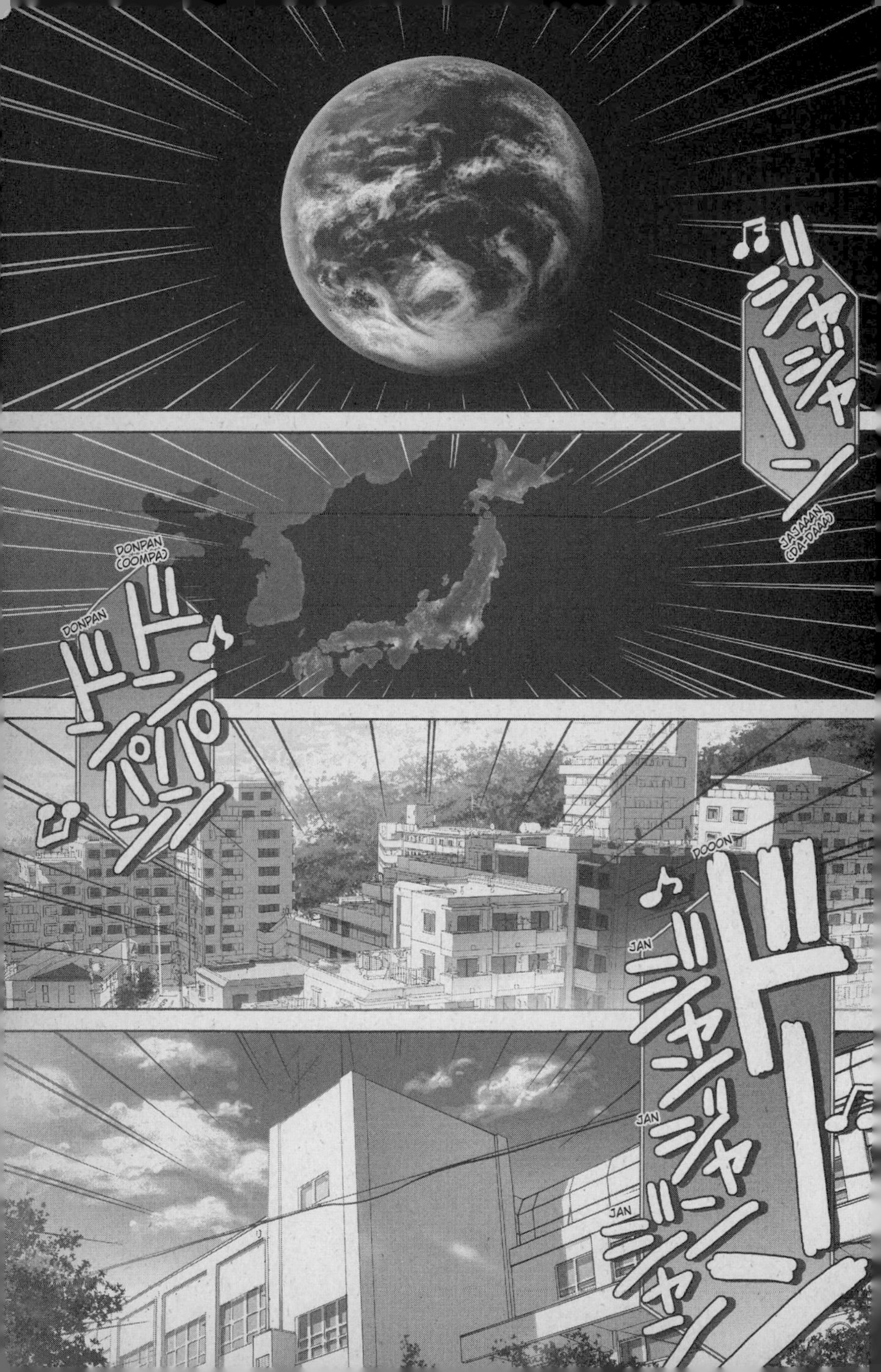
JAJAAN (DA-DAA)
DONPAN (OOMPA)
DONPAN
DOOON
JAN
JAN
JAN

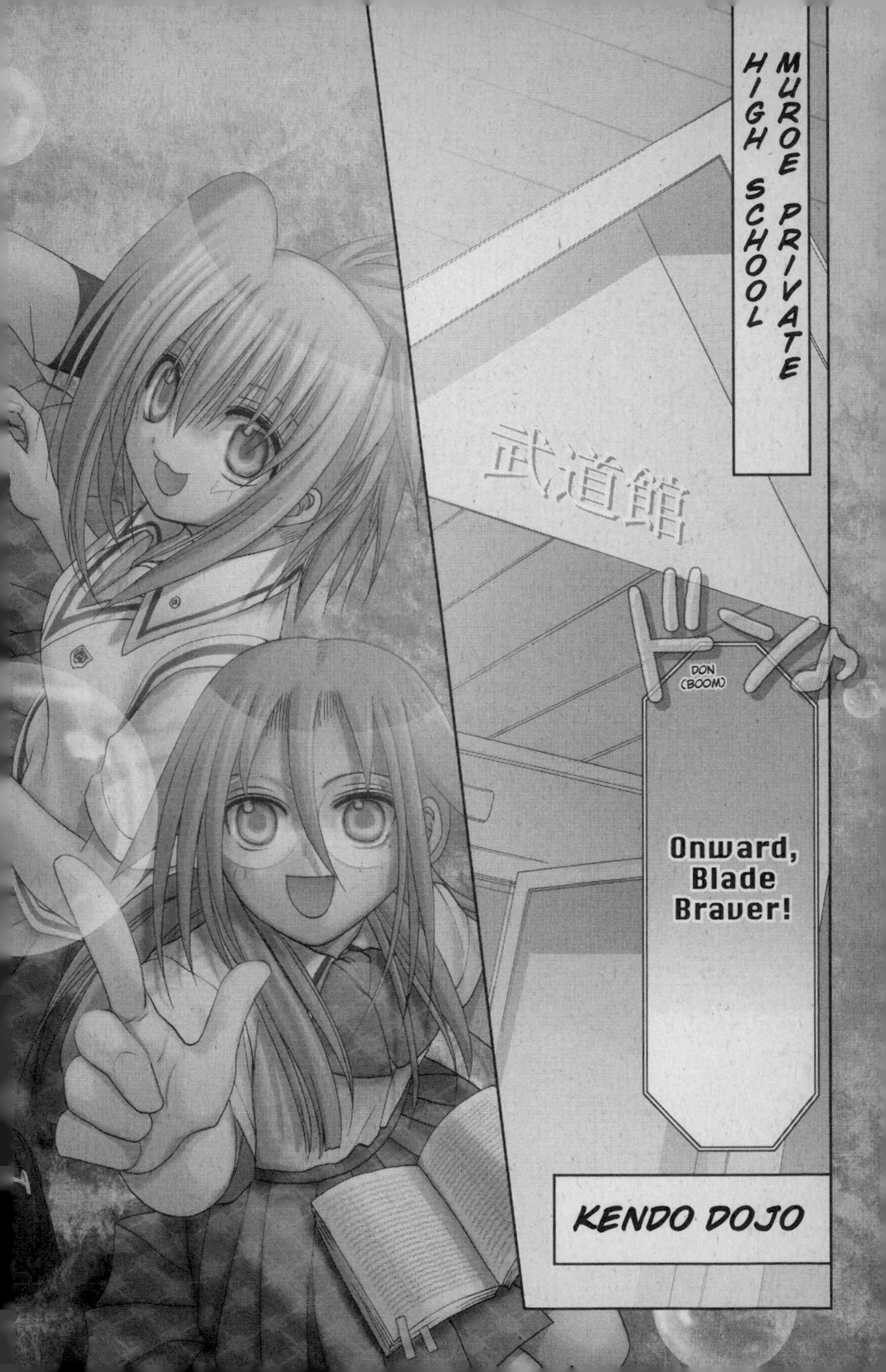
MUROE PRIVATE HIGH SCHOOL
武道館
ドーン
DON (BOOM)
Onward, Blade Braver!
KENDO DOJO

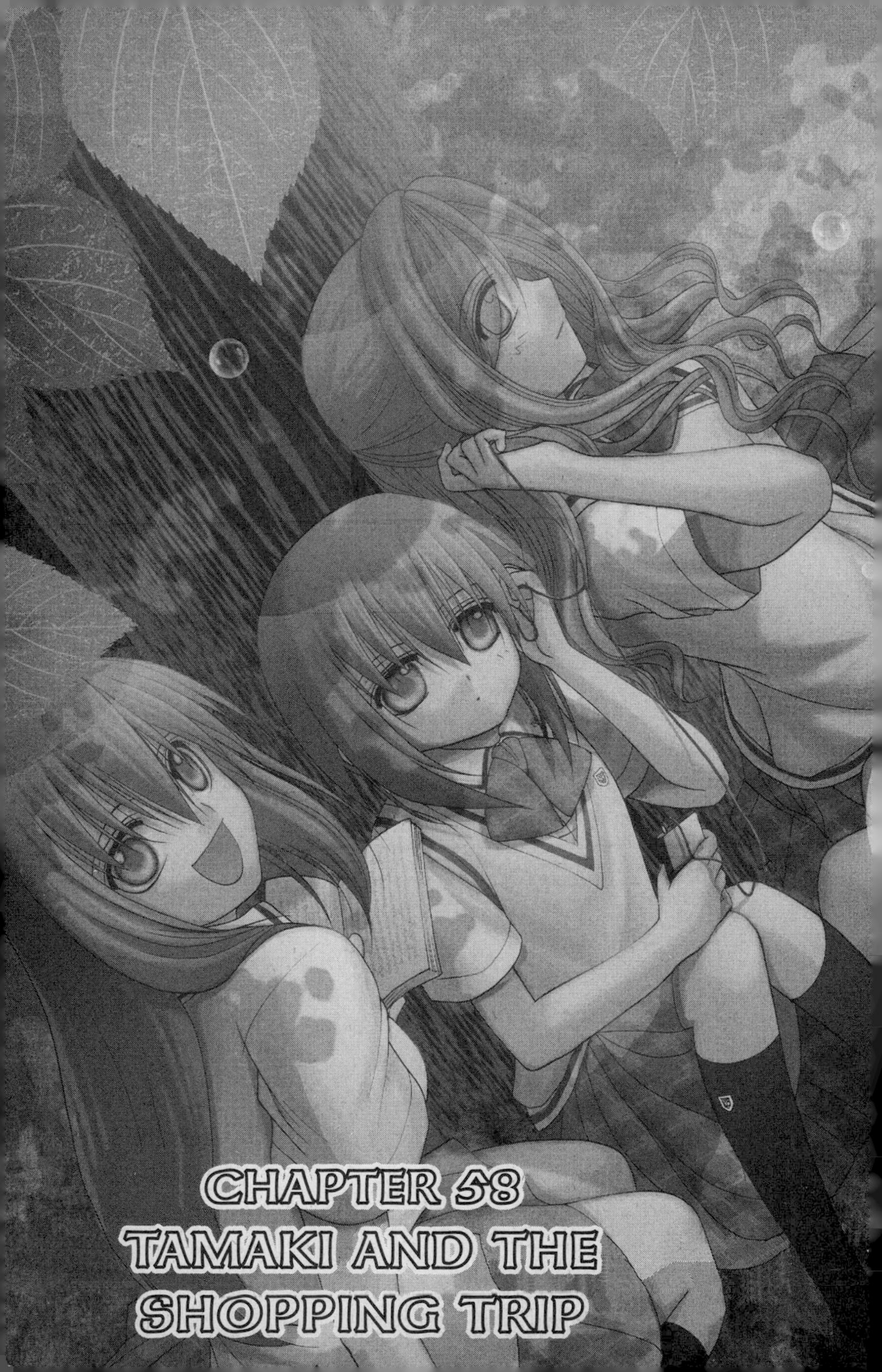
CHAPTER 58
TAMAKI AND THE
SHOPPING TRIP

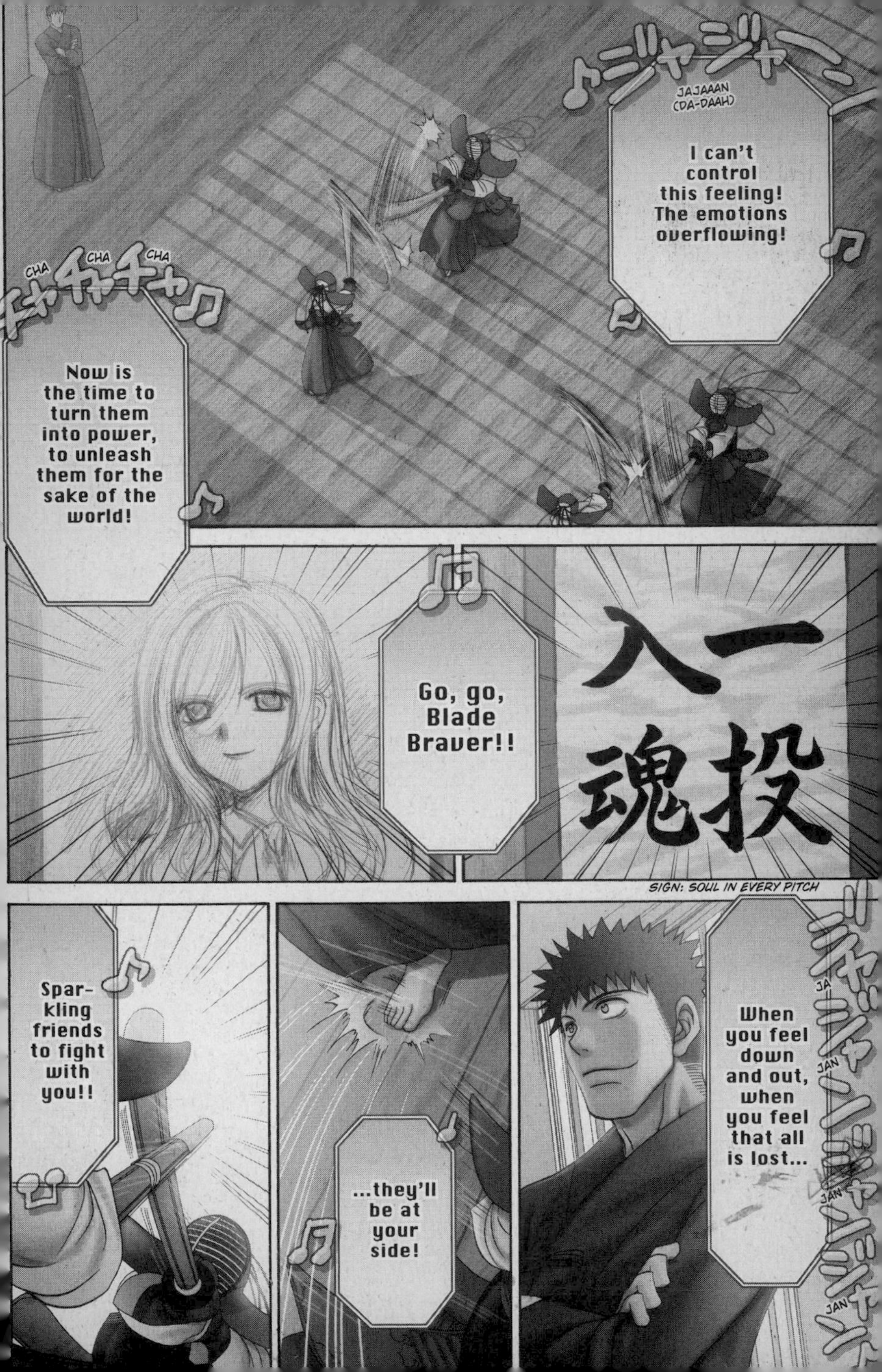
JAJAAAN (DA-DAAH)
I can't control this feeling! The emotions overflowing!
CHA CHA CHA
Now is the time to turn them into power, to unleash them for the sake of the world!
一投入魂
SIGN: SOUL IN EVERY PITCH
Go, go, Blade Braver!!
JA JAN JAN JAN
When you feel down and out, when you feel that all is lost...
...they'll be at your side!
Spar-kling friends to fight with you!!

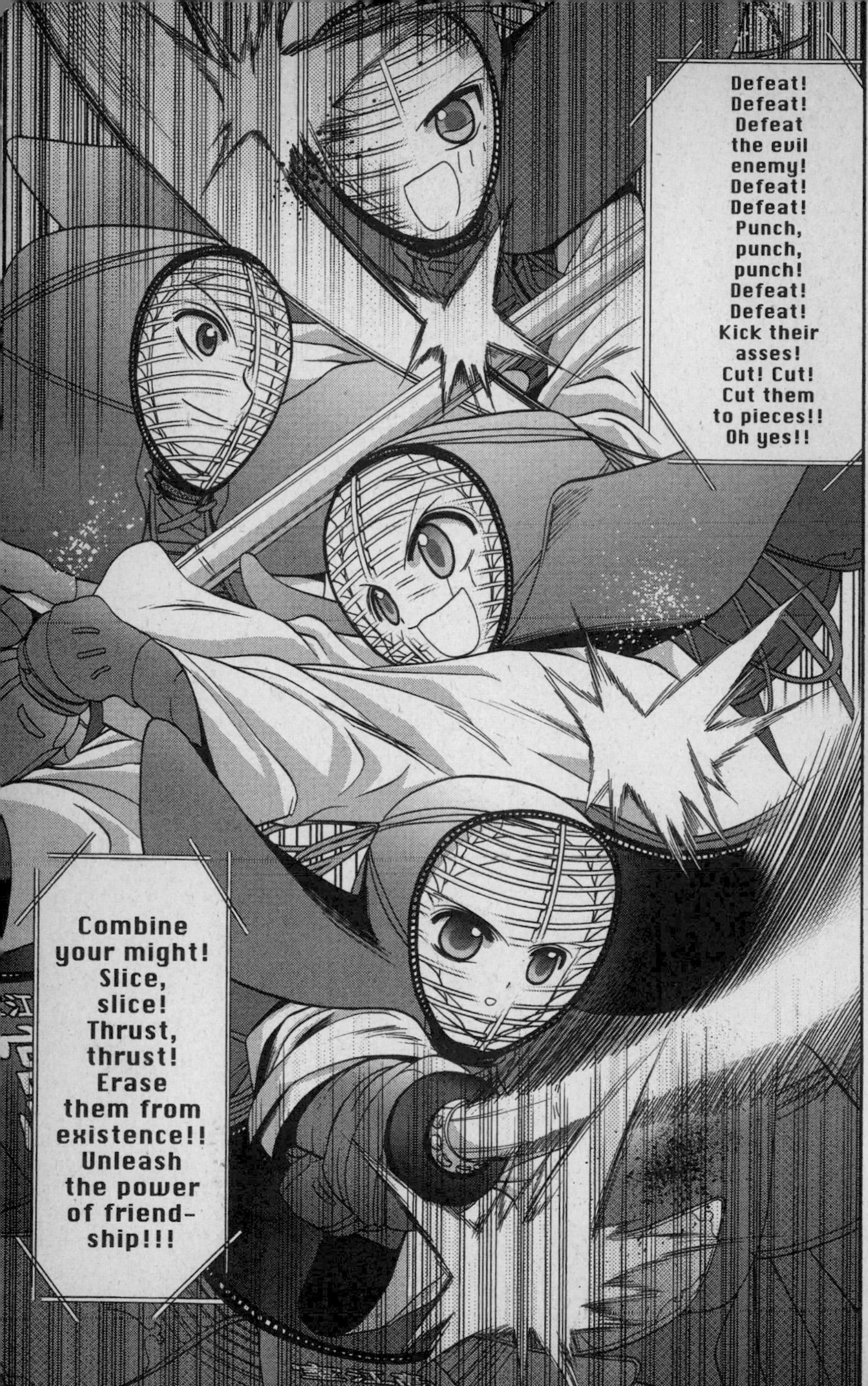
Defeat! Defeat! Defeat the evil enemy! Defeat! Defeat! Punch, punch, punch! Defeat! Defeat! Kick their asses! Cut! Cut! Cut them to pieces!! Oh yes!!
Combine your might! Slice, slice! Thrust, thrust! Erase them from existence!! Unleash the power of friend-ship!!!

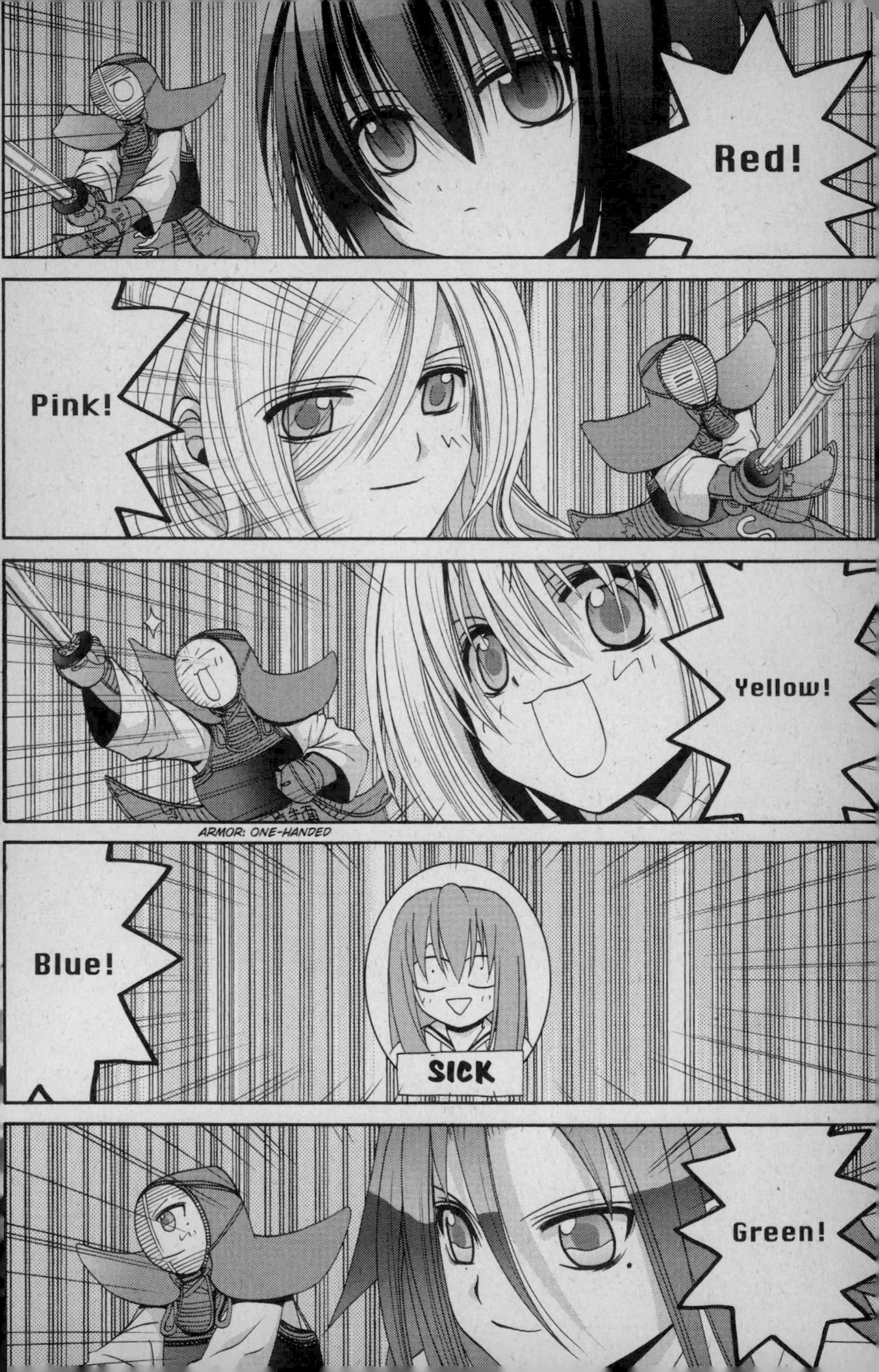

Red!
Pink!
Yellow!
ARMOR: ONE-HANDED
Blue!
SICK
Green!

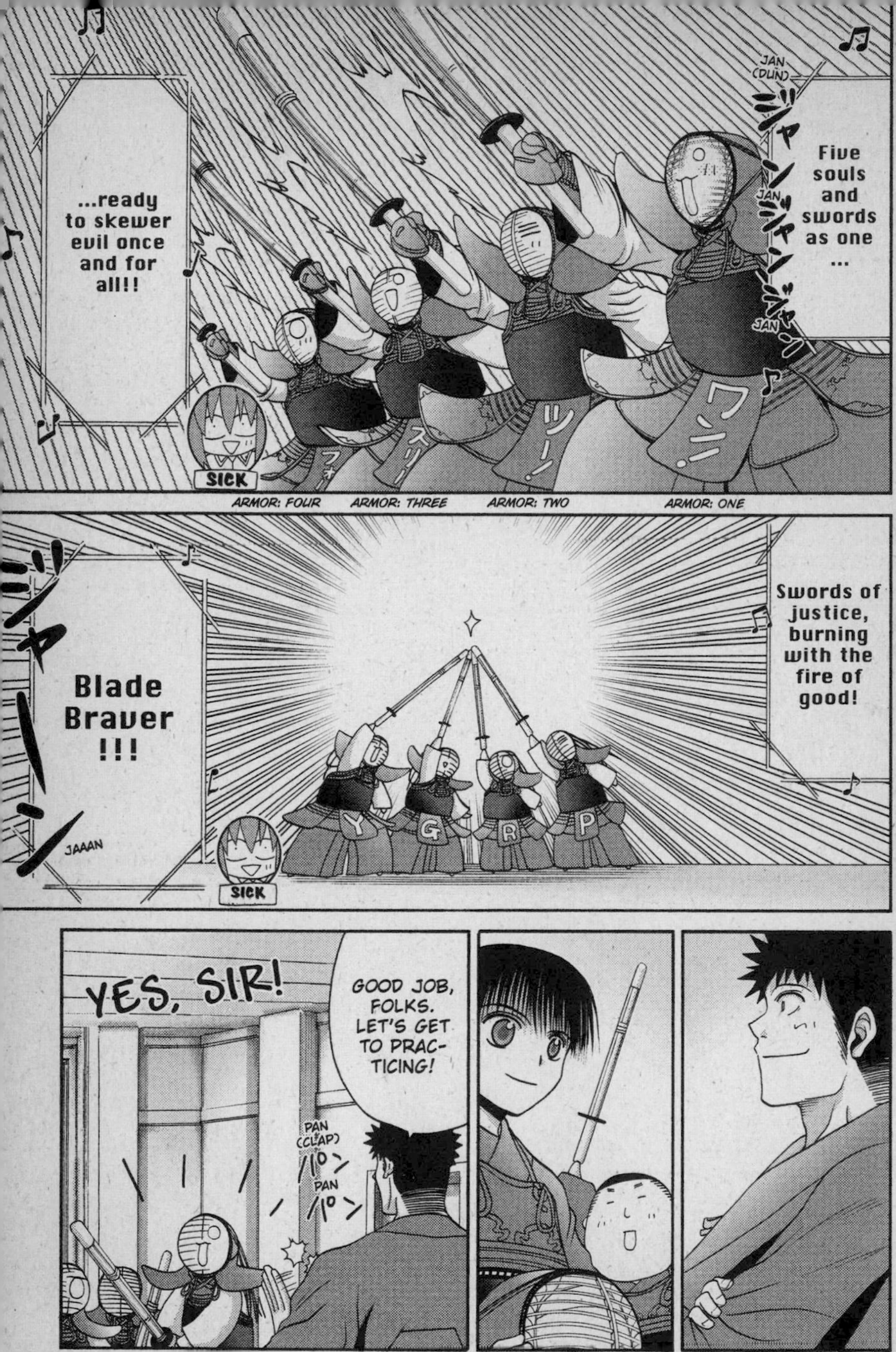
JAN (DUN)
ジャンジャンジャン
JAN
JAN
Five souls and swords as one ...
ワン
ツー
スリー
フォ
...ready to skewer evil once and for all!!
SICK
ARMOR: ONE
ARMOR: TWO
ARMOR: THREE
ARMOR: FOUR
Swords of justice, burning with the fire of good!
Y
G
R
P
SICK
Blade Braver !!!
ジャーン
JAAAN
GOOD JOB, FOLKS. LET'S GET TO PRAC-TICING!
PAN (CLAP)
パン
PAN
パン
YES, SIR!

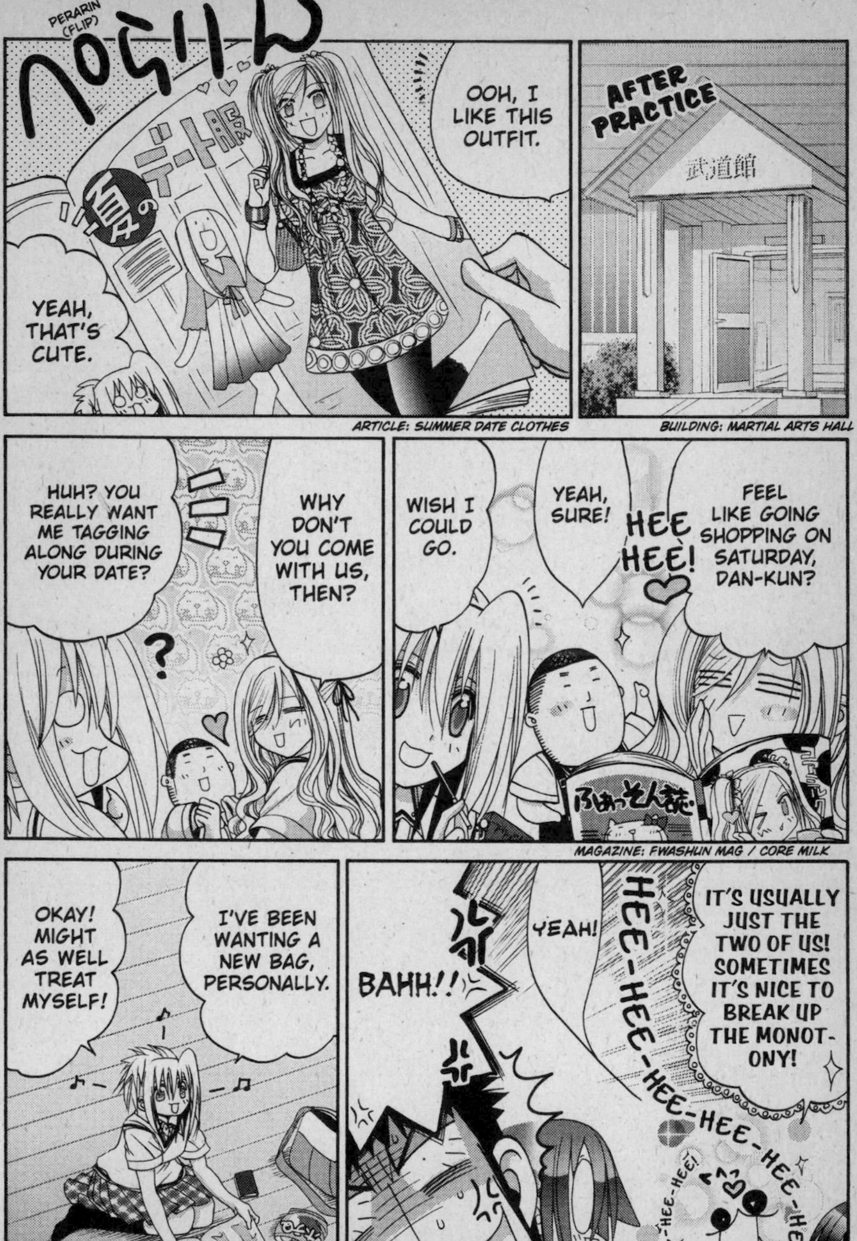

AFTER PRACTICE
武道館
BUILDING: MARTIAL ARTS HALL
ぺらりん
PERARIN (FLIP)
OOH, I LIKE THIS OUTFIT.
夏のデート服
YEAH, THAT'S CUTE.
ARTICLE: SUMMER DATE CLOTHES
FEEL LIKE GOING SHOPPING ON SATURDAY, DAN-KUN?
HEE HEE!
YEAH, SURE!
WISH I COULD GO.
ふぁっそん誌
MAGAZINE: FWASHUN MAG / CORE MILK
WHY DON'T YOU COME WITH US, THEN?
HUH? YOU REALLY WANT ME TAGGING ALONG DURING YOUR DATE?
IT'S USUALLY JUST THE TWO OF US! SOMETIMES IT'S NICE TO BREAK UP THE MONOT-ONY!
HEE-HEE-HEE-HEE-HEE-HEE-HEE-HEE-HEE!
YEAH!
BAHH!!
I'VE BEEN WANTING A NEW BAG, PERSONALLY.
OKAY! MIGHT AS WELL TREAT MYSELF!

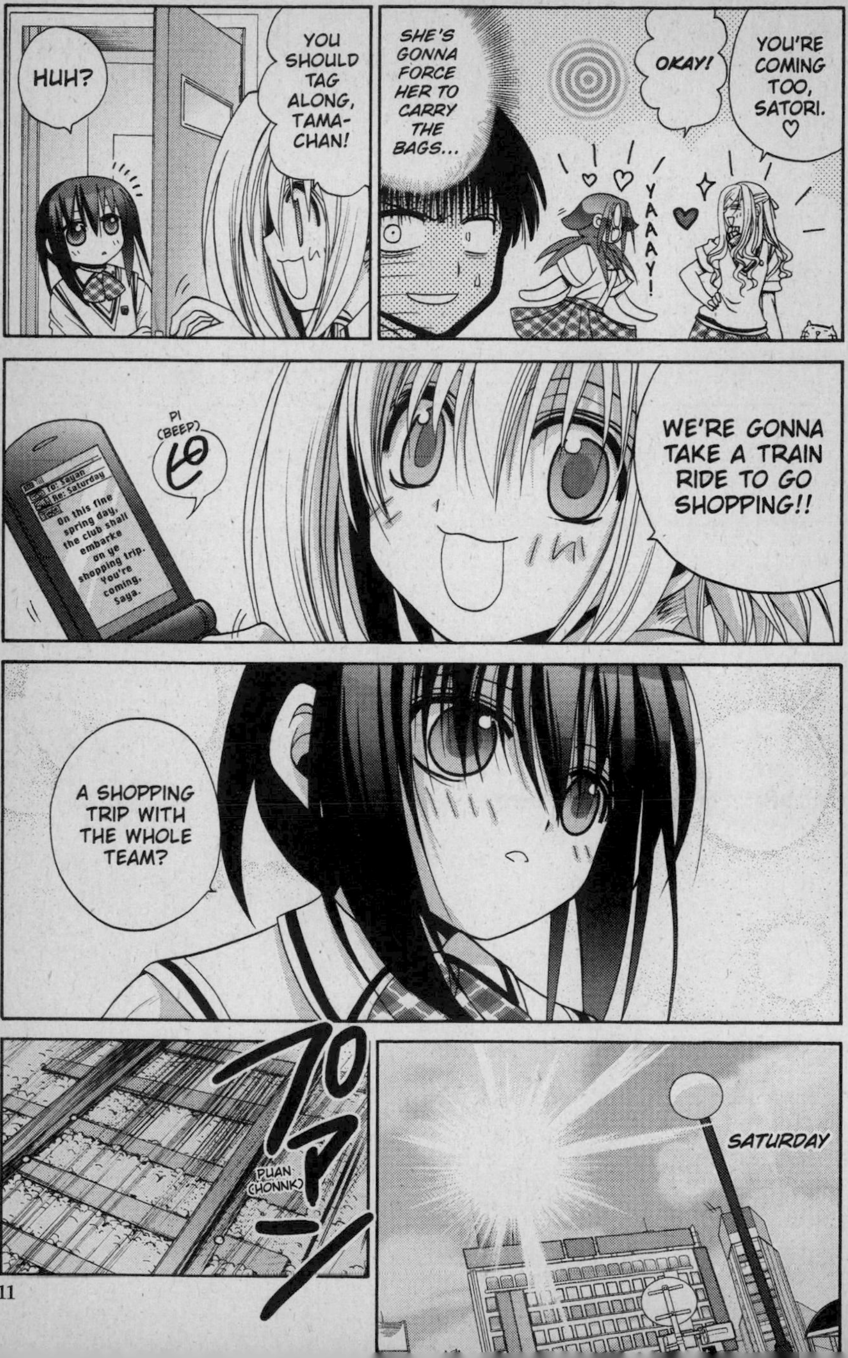
YOU'RE COMING TOO, SATORI. ♡
OKAY!
YAAAY!
SHE'S GONNA FORCE HER TO CARRY THE BAGS...
YOU SHOULD TAG ALONG, TAMA-CHAN!
HUH?
WE'RE GONNA TAKE A TRAIN RIDE TO GO SHOPPING!!
PI (BEEP)
ぴ
To: Sayan
Re: Saturday
On this fine spring day, the club shall embarke on ye shopping trip. You're coming, Saya.
A SHOPPING TRIP WITH THE WHOLE TEAM?
SATURDAY
PUAN (HONNK)
プァン

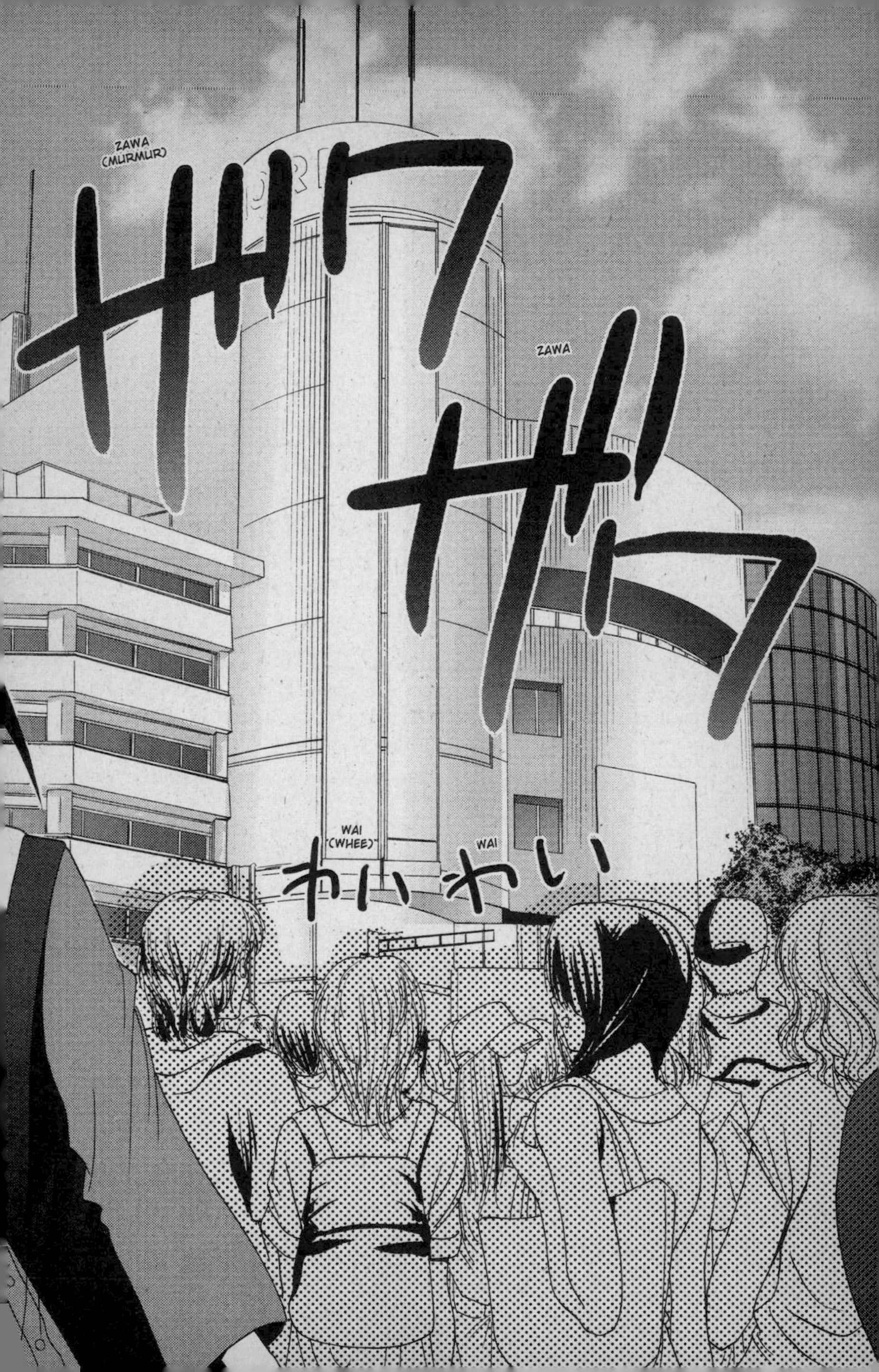
ザワ
ZAWA (MURMUR)
ザワ
ZAWA
わいわい
WAI "(WHEE)"
WAI

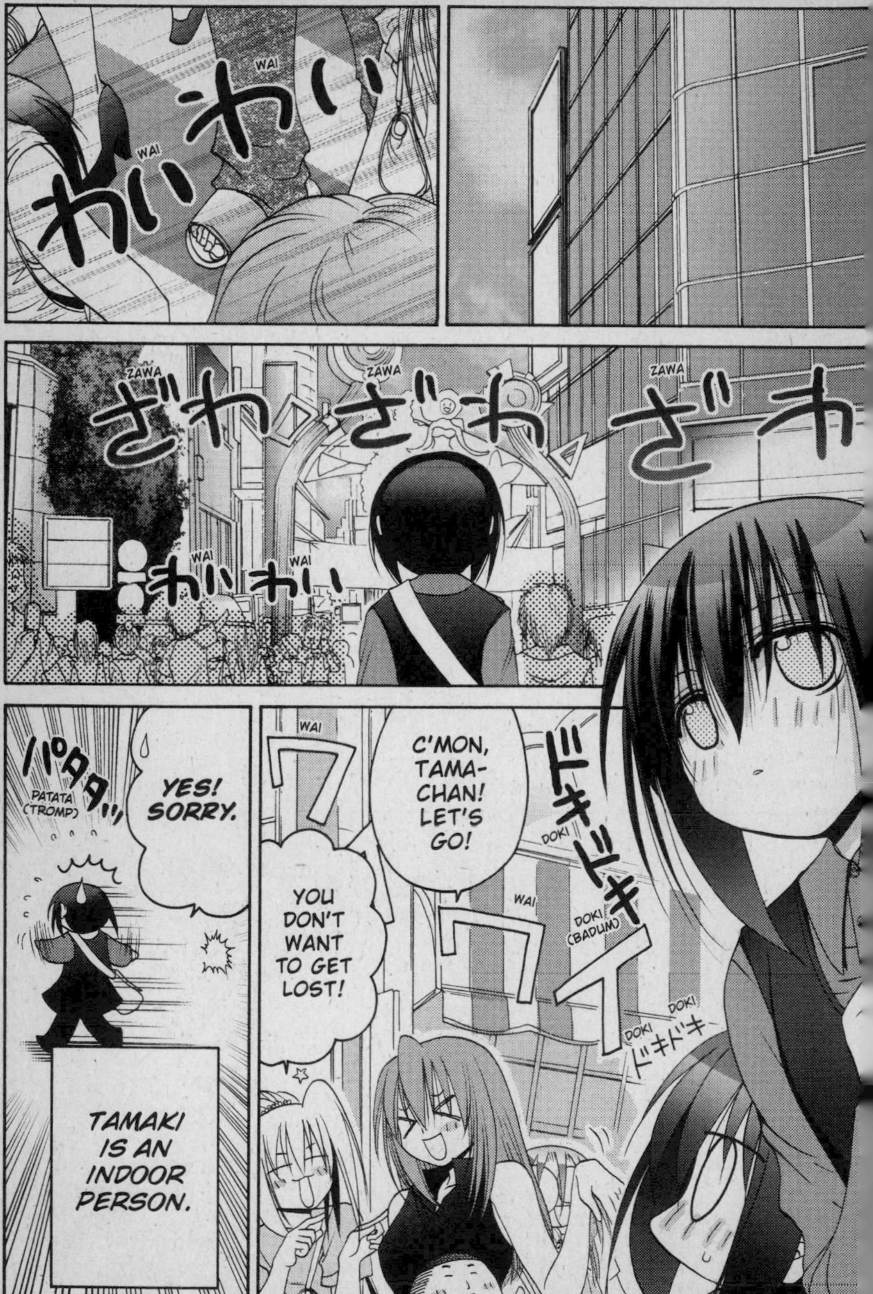
わいわい
WAI
WAI
ざわざわざわ
ZAWA
ZAWA
ZAWA
わいわい
WAI
WAI
ドキドキ
DOKI
DOKI (BADUM)
C'MON, TAMA-CHAN! LET'S GO!
ワイ
WAI
WAI
YOU DON'T WANT TO GET LOST!
ドキドキ
DOKI
DOKI
YES! SORRY.
パタタッ
PATATA (TROMP)
TAMAKI IS AN INDOOR PERSON.

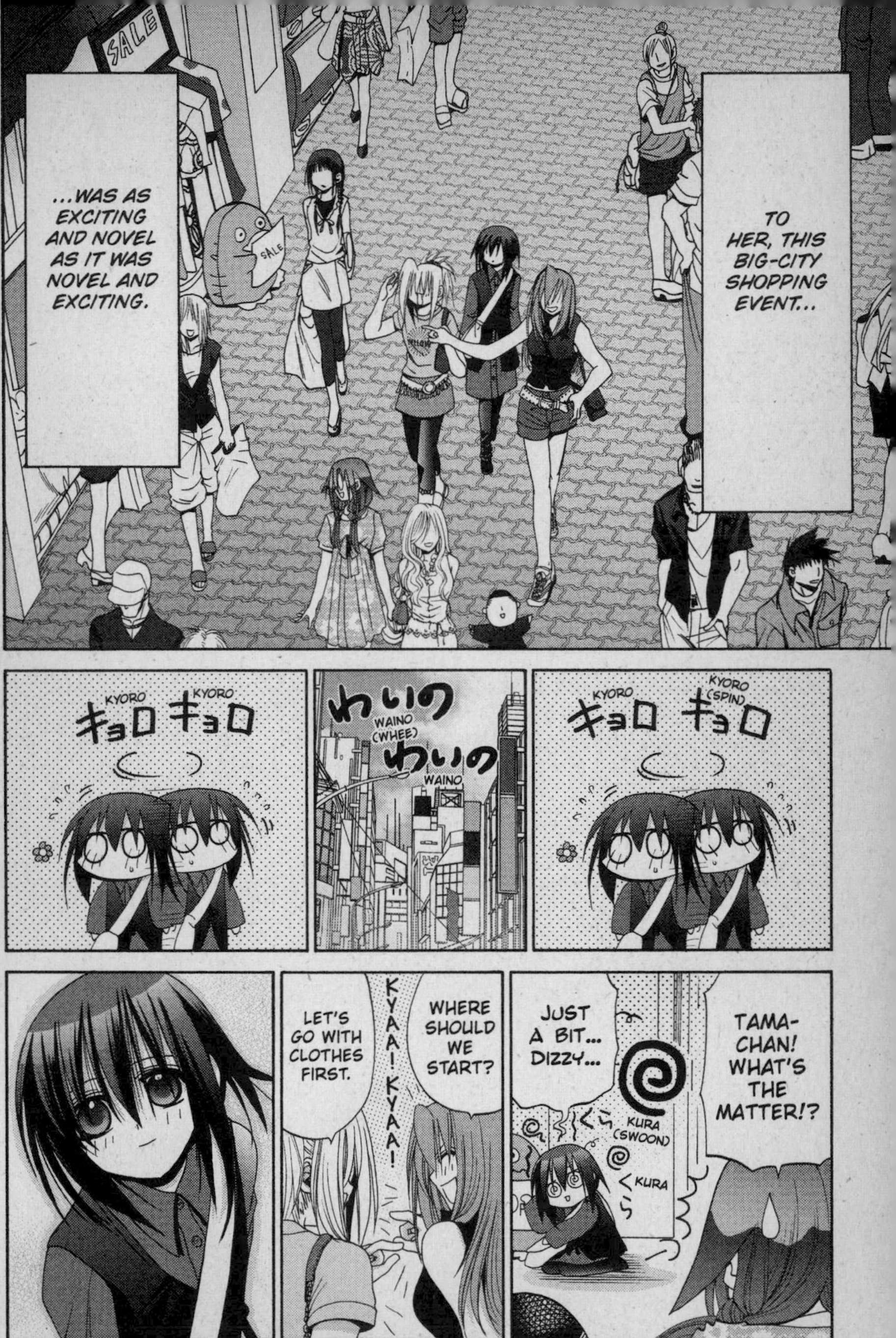
TO HER, THIS BIG-CITY SHOPPING EVENT...
...WAS AS EXCITING AND NOVEL AS IT WAS NOVEL AND EXCITING.
SALE
SALE
キョロ キョロ
KYORO KYORO (SPIN)
わいの わいの
WAINO (WHEE) WAINO
キョロ キョロ
KYORO KYORO
TAMA-CHAN! WHAT'S THE MATTER!?
JUST A BIT... DIZZY...
くら くら
KURA (SWOON) KURA
WHERE SHOULD WE START?
KYAA! KYAA!
LET'S GO WITH CLOTHES FIRST.

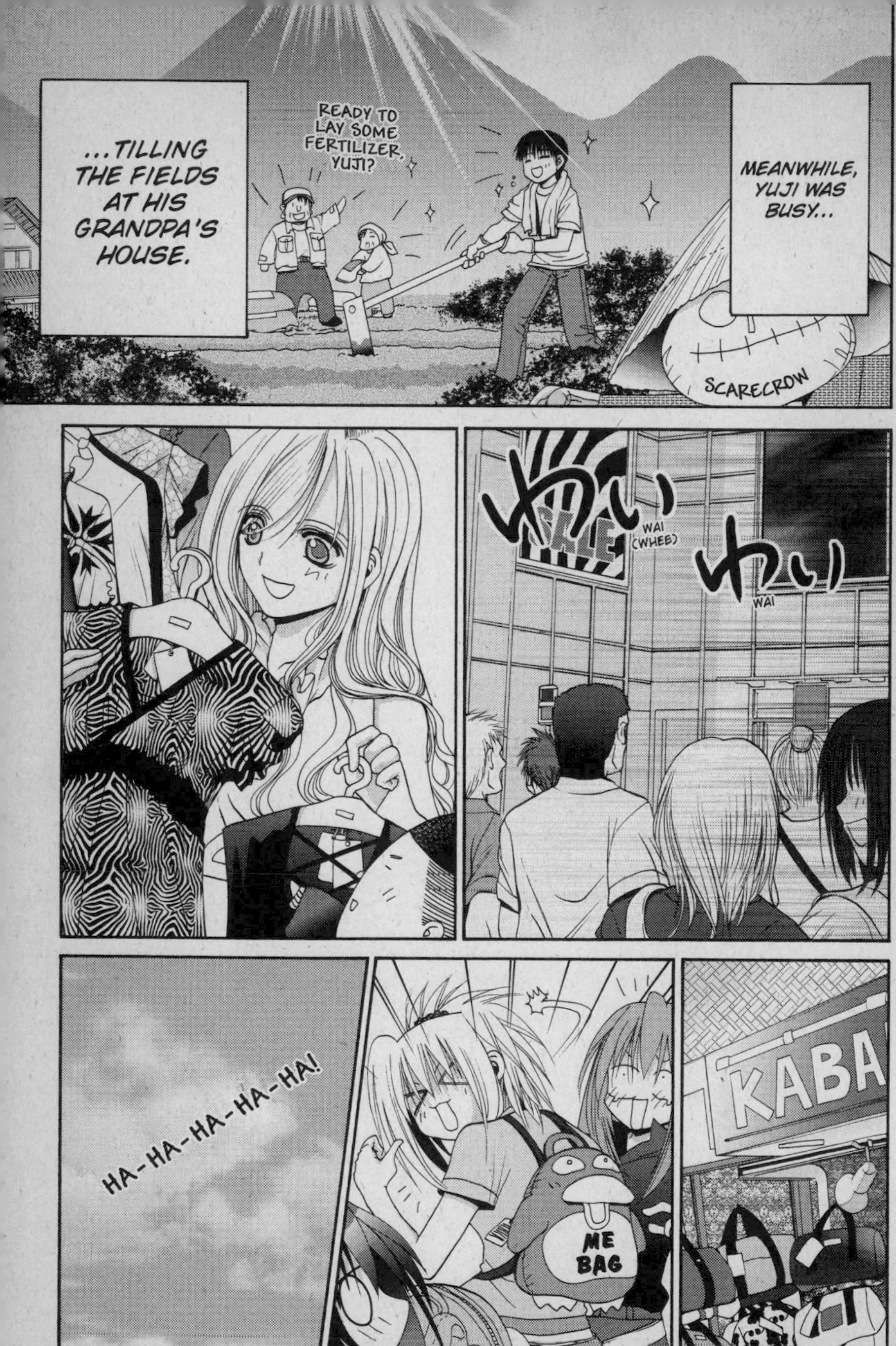
MEANWHILE, YUJI WAS BUSY...
READY TO LAY SOME FERTILIZER, YUJI?
...TILLING THE FIELDS AT HIS GRANDPA'S HOUSE.
SCARECROW
WAI (WHEE)
WAI
KABA
ME BAG
HA-HA-HA-HA-HA!

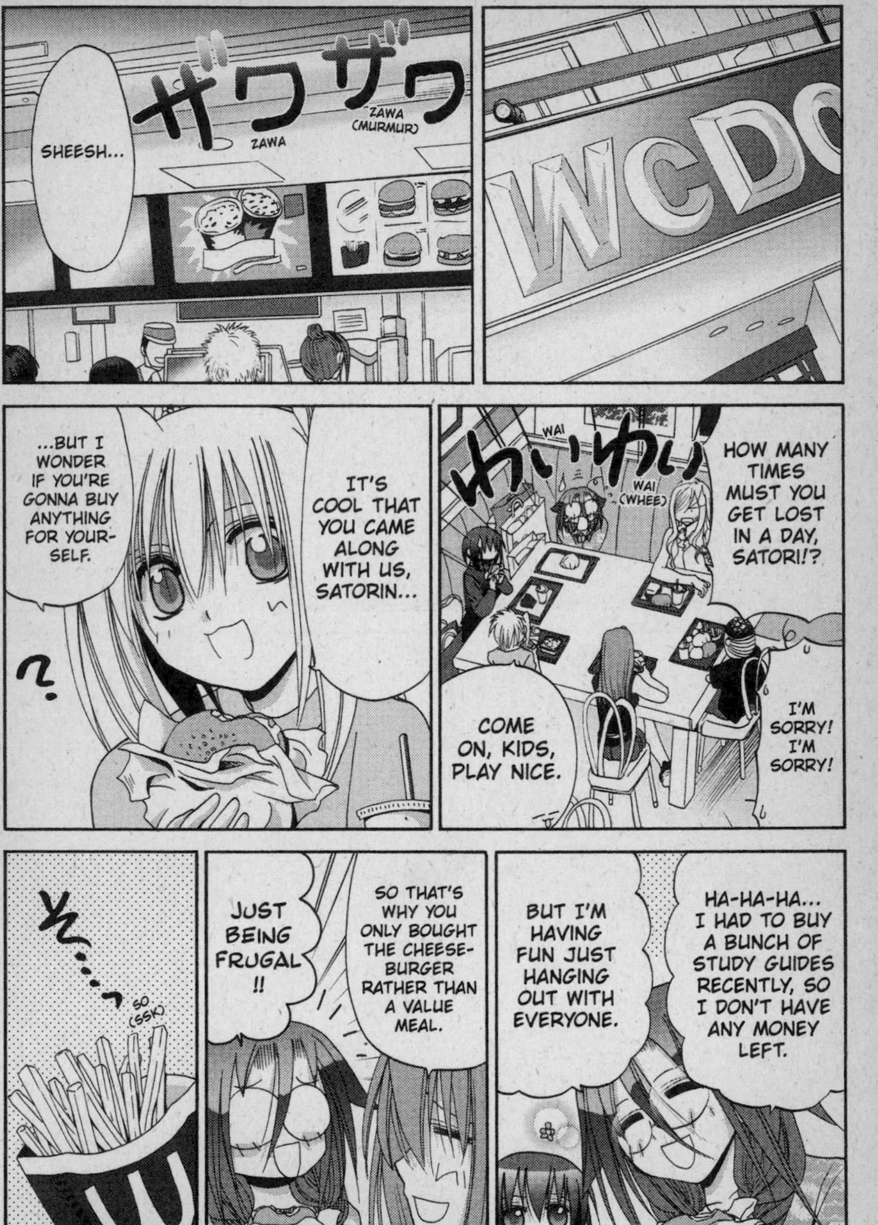

ザワザワ
ZAWA
ZAWA (MURMUR)
SHEESH...
わいわい
WAI
WAI (WHEE)
HOW MANY TIMES MUST YOU GET LOST IN A DAY, SATORI!?
I'M SORRY! I'M SORRY!
COME ON, KIDS, PLAY NICE.
IT'S COOL THAT YOU CAME ALONG WITH US, SATORIN...
...BUT I WONDER IF YOU'RE GONNA BUY ANYTHING FOR YOUR-SELF.
?
HA-HA-HA... I HAD TO BUY A BUNCH OF STUDY GUIDES RECENTLY, SO I DON'T HAVE ANY MONEY LEFT.
BUT I'M HAVING FUN JUST HANGING OUT WITH EVERYONE.
SO THAT'S WHY YOU ONLY BOUGHT THE CHEESE-BURGER RATHER THAN A VALUE MEAL.
JUST BEING FRUGAL !!
そ...
SO (SSK)

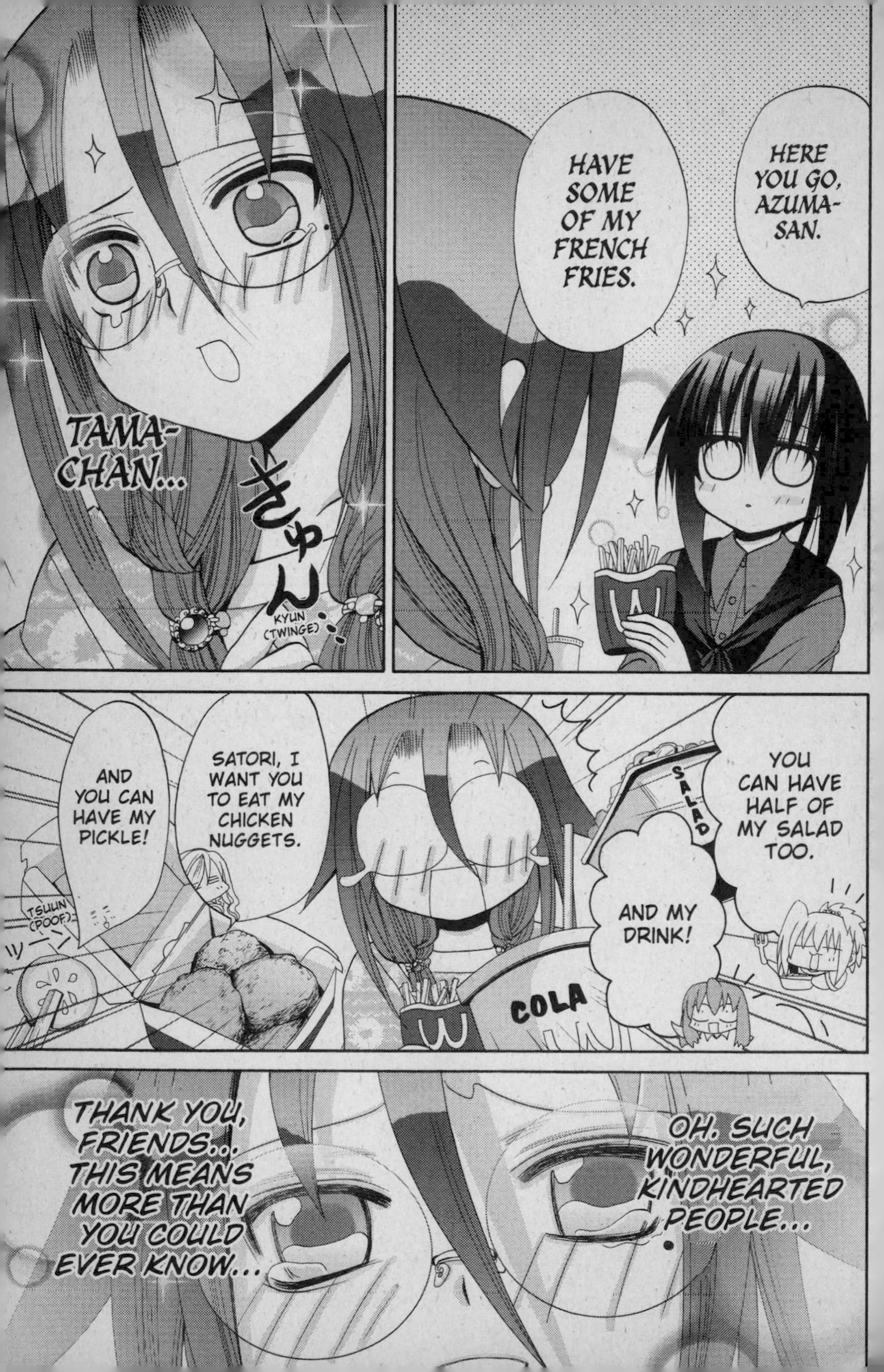
HERE YOU GO, AZUMA-SAN.
HAVE SOME OF MY FRENCH FRIES.
TAMA-CHAN...
きゅん
KYUN (TWINGE)
YOU CAN HAVE HALF OF MY SALAD TOO.
SALAD
AND MY DRINK!
COLA
SATORI, I WANT YOU TO EAT MY CHICKEN NUGGETS.
AND YOU CAN HAVE MY PICKLE!
TSUUN (POOF)
OH. SUCH WONDERFUL, KINDHEARTED PEOPLE...
THANK YOU, FRIENDS... THIS MEANS MORE THAN YOU COULD EVER KNOW...

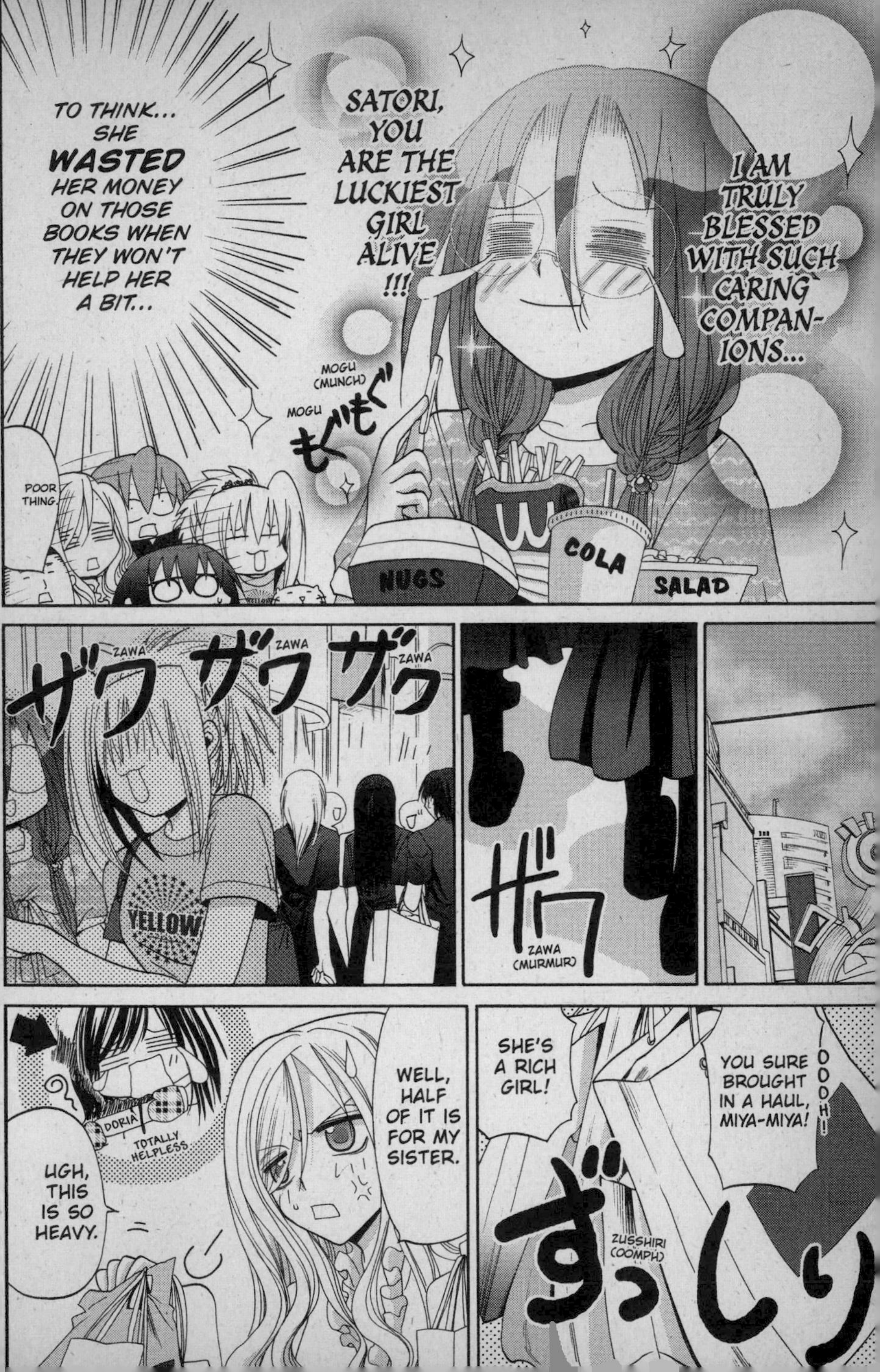
I AM TRULY BLESSED WITH SUCH CARING COMPANIONS...
SATORI, YOU ARE THE LUCKIEST GIRL ALIVE!!!
TO THINK... SHE WASTED HER MONEY ON THOSE BOOKS WHEN THEY WON'T HELP HER A BIT...
MOGU (MUNCH) MOGU
NUGS
COLA
SALAD
POOR THING.
ZAWA (MURMUR)
ZAWA ZAWA ZAWA
YELLOW
OOOH!
YOU SURE BROUGHT IN A HAUL, MIYA-MIYA!
SHE'S A RICH GIRL!
ZUSSHIRI (OOMPH)
WELL, HALF OF IT IS FOR MY SISTER.
DORIA
TOTALLY HELPLESS
UGH, THIS IS SO HEAVY.

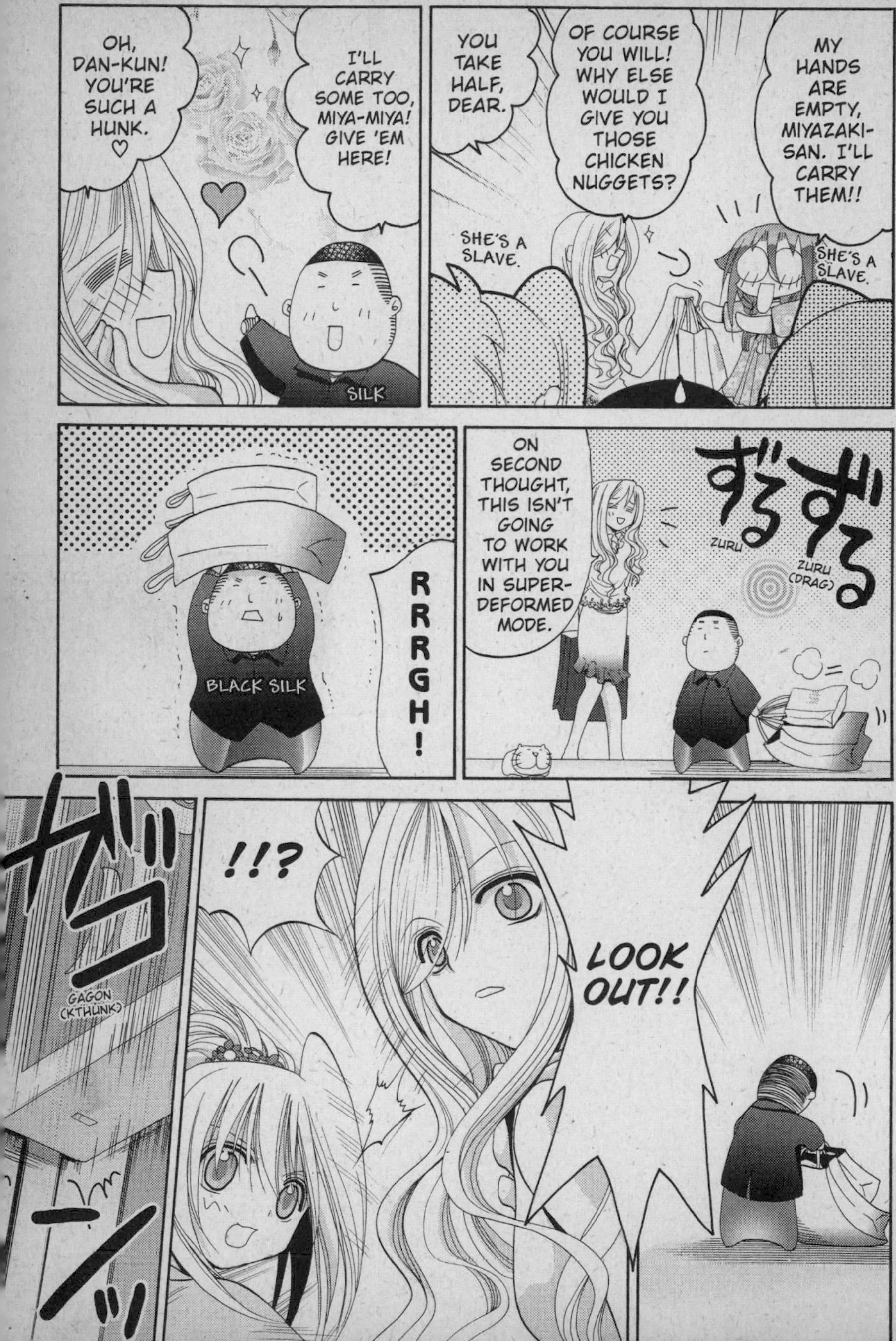
MY HANDS ARE EMPTY, MIYAZAKI-SAN. I'LL CARRY THEM!!
OF COURSE YOU WILL! WHY ELSE WOULD I GIVE YOU THOSE CHICKEN NUGGETS?
YOU TAKE HALF, DEAR.
SHE'S A SLAVE.
SHE'S A SLAVE.
I'LL CARRY SOME TOO, MIYA-MIYA! GIVE 'EM HERE!
OH, DAN-KUN! YOU'RE SUCH A HUNK. ♡
SILK
ずるずる
ZURU
ZURU (DRAG)
ON SECOND THOUGHT, THIS ISN'T GOING TO WORK WITH YOU IN SUPER-DEFORMED MODE.
RRRGH!
BLACK SILK
LOOK OUT!!
!!?
GAGON (KTHUNK)

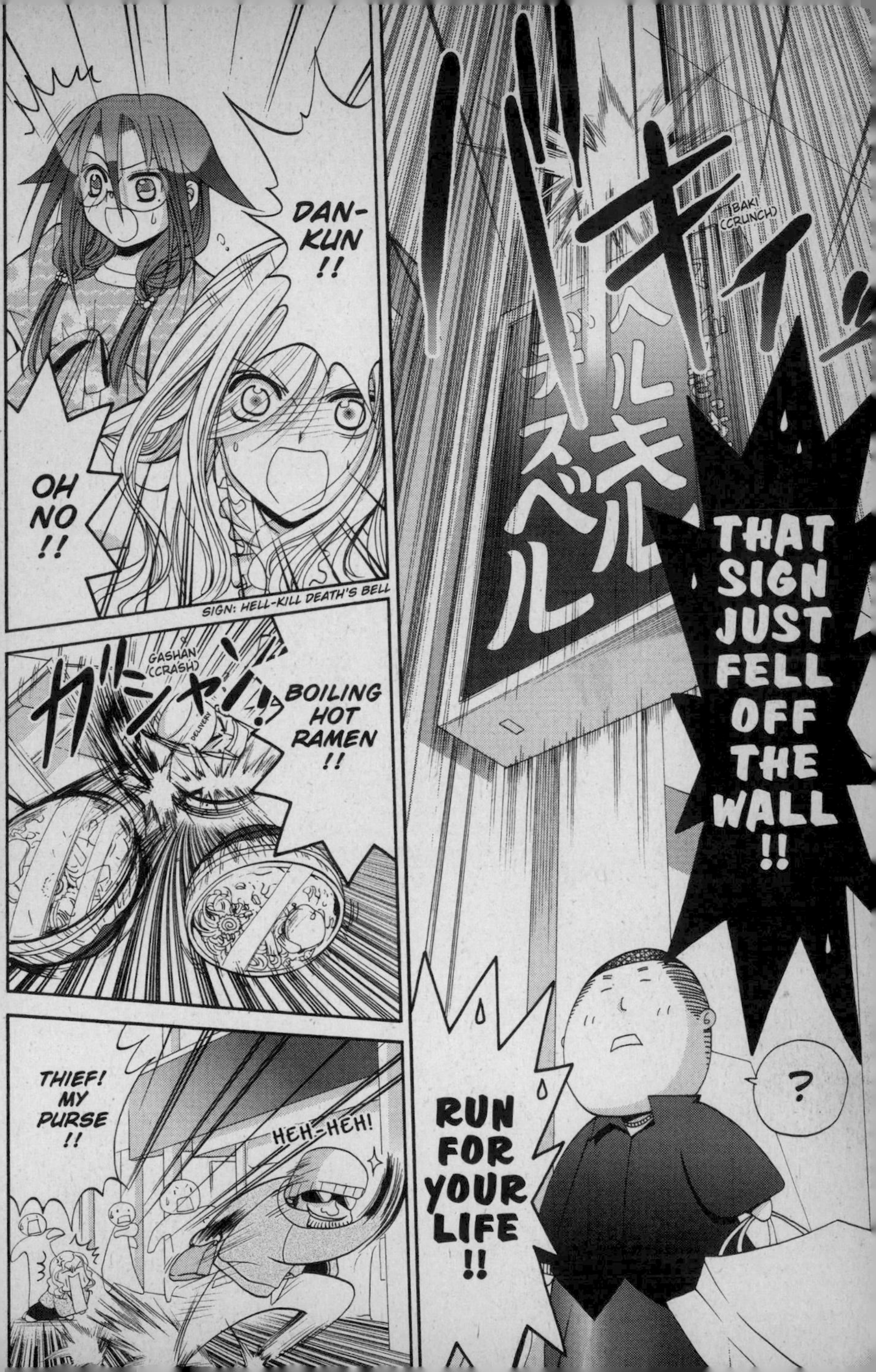
BAKI (CRUNCH)
THAT SIGN JUST FELL OFF THE WALL !!
?
RUN FOR YOUR LIFE !!
DAN-KUN !!
OH NO !!
SIGN: HELL-KILL DEATH'S BELL
GASHAN (CRASH)
BOILING HOT RAMEN !!
DELIVERY
THIEF! MY PURSE !!
HEH-HEH!

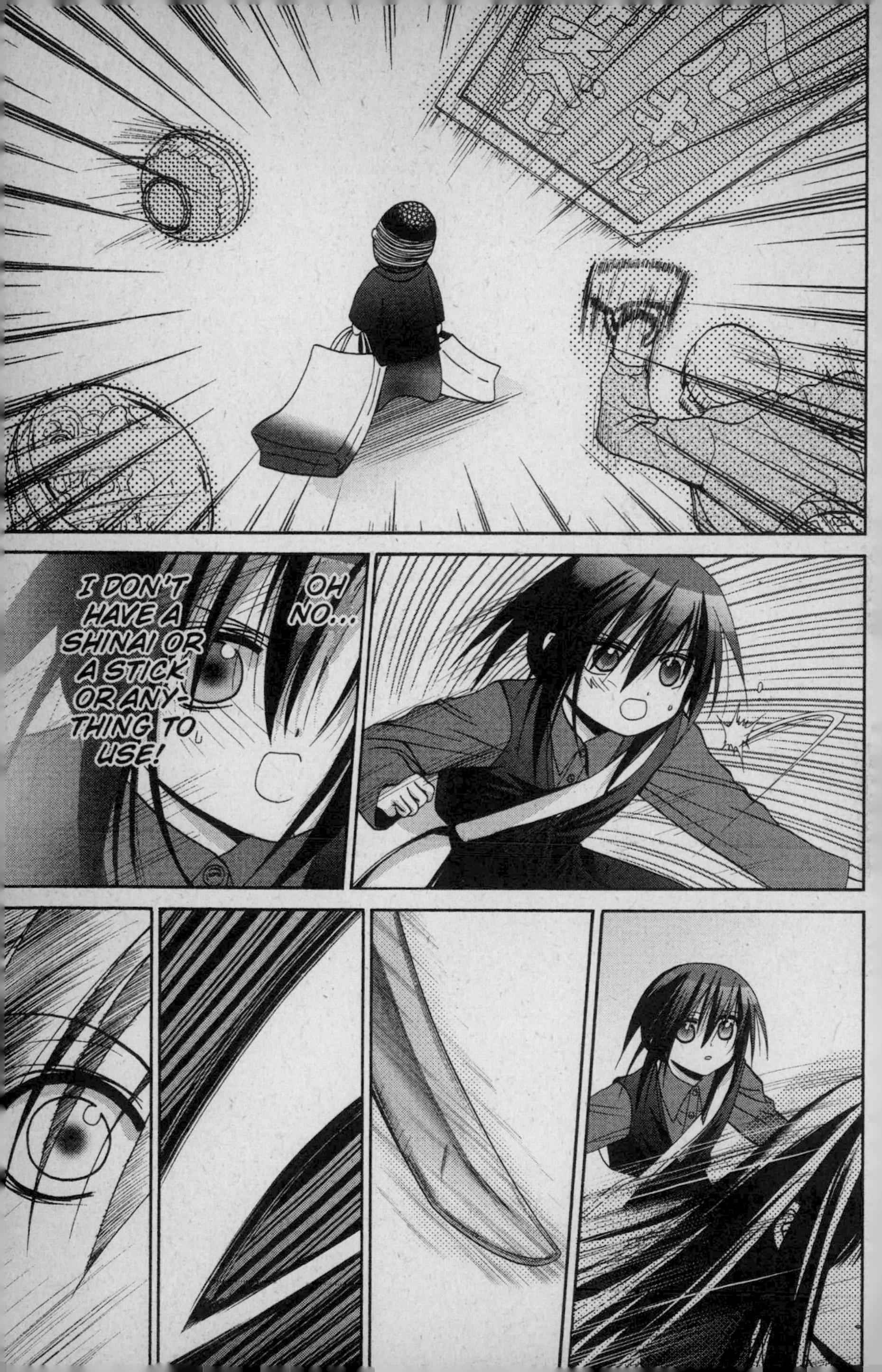
OH NO...
I DON'T HAVE A SHINAI OR A STICK OR ANY-THING TO USE!

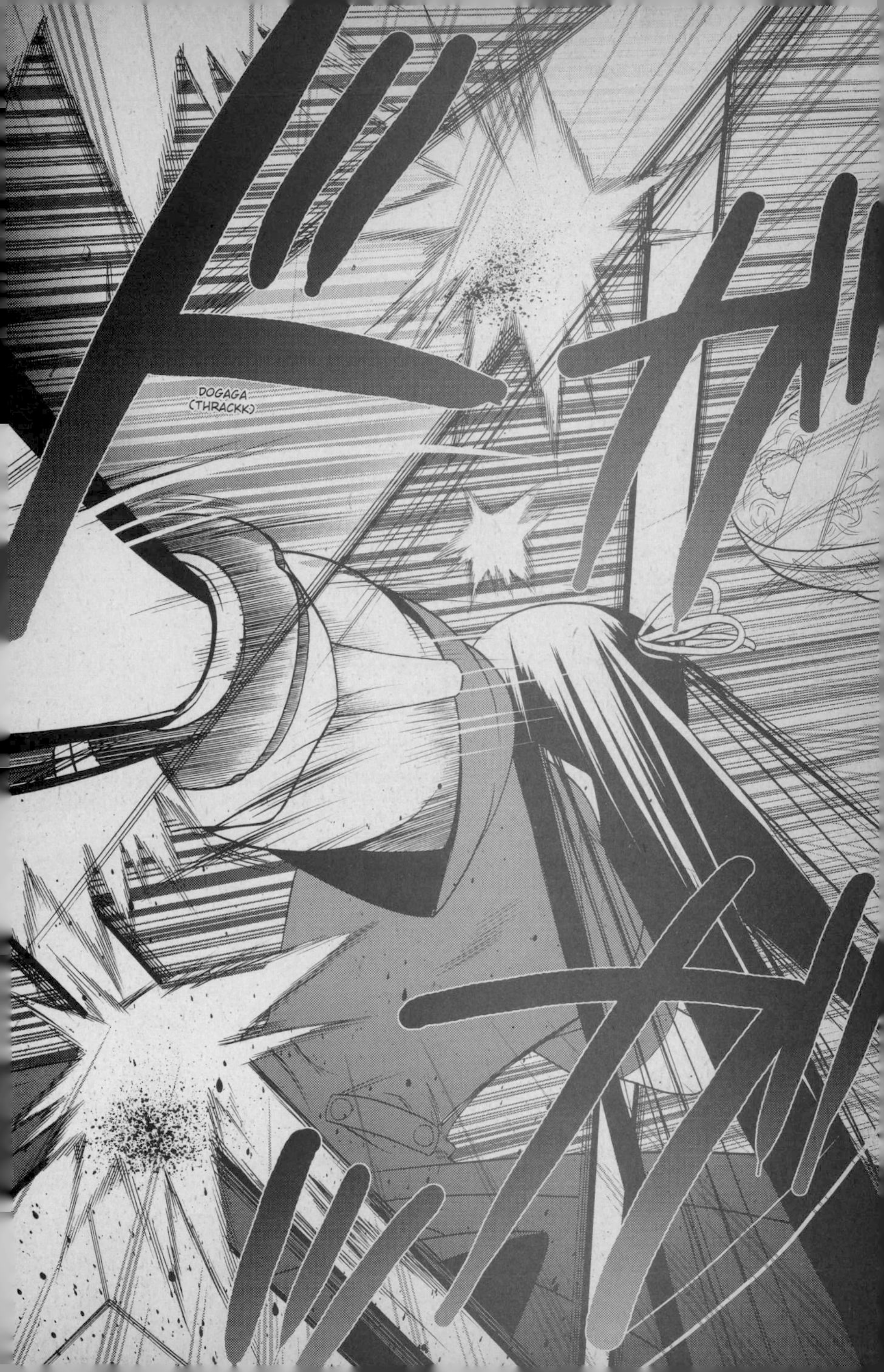
DOGAGA
(THRACKK)

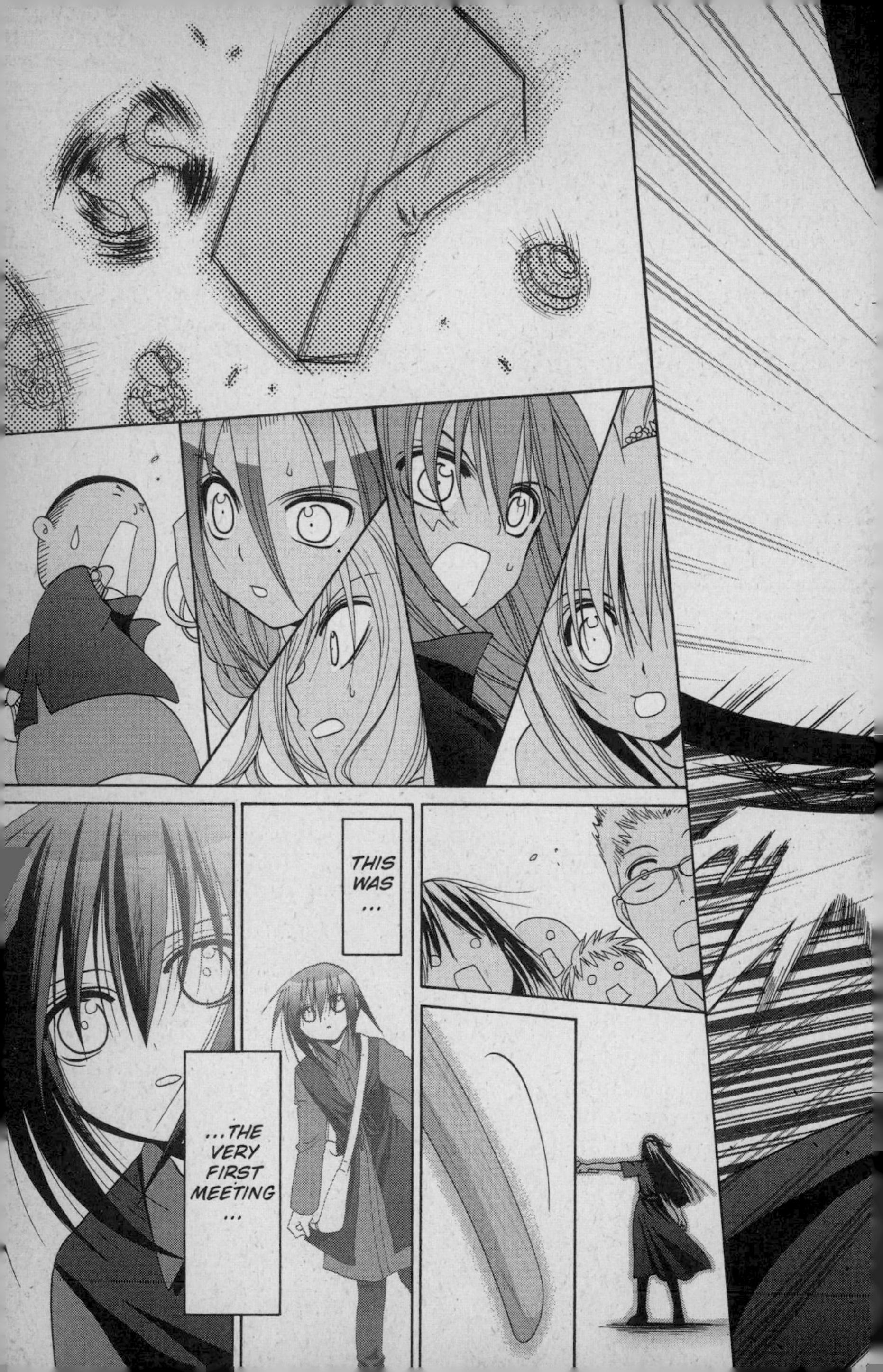
THIS WAS ...
...THE VERY FIRST MEETING ...

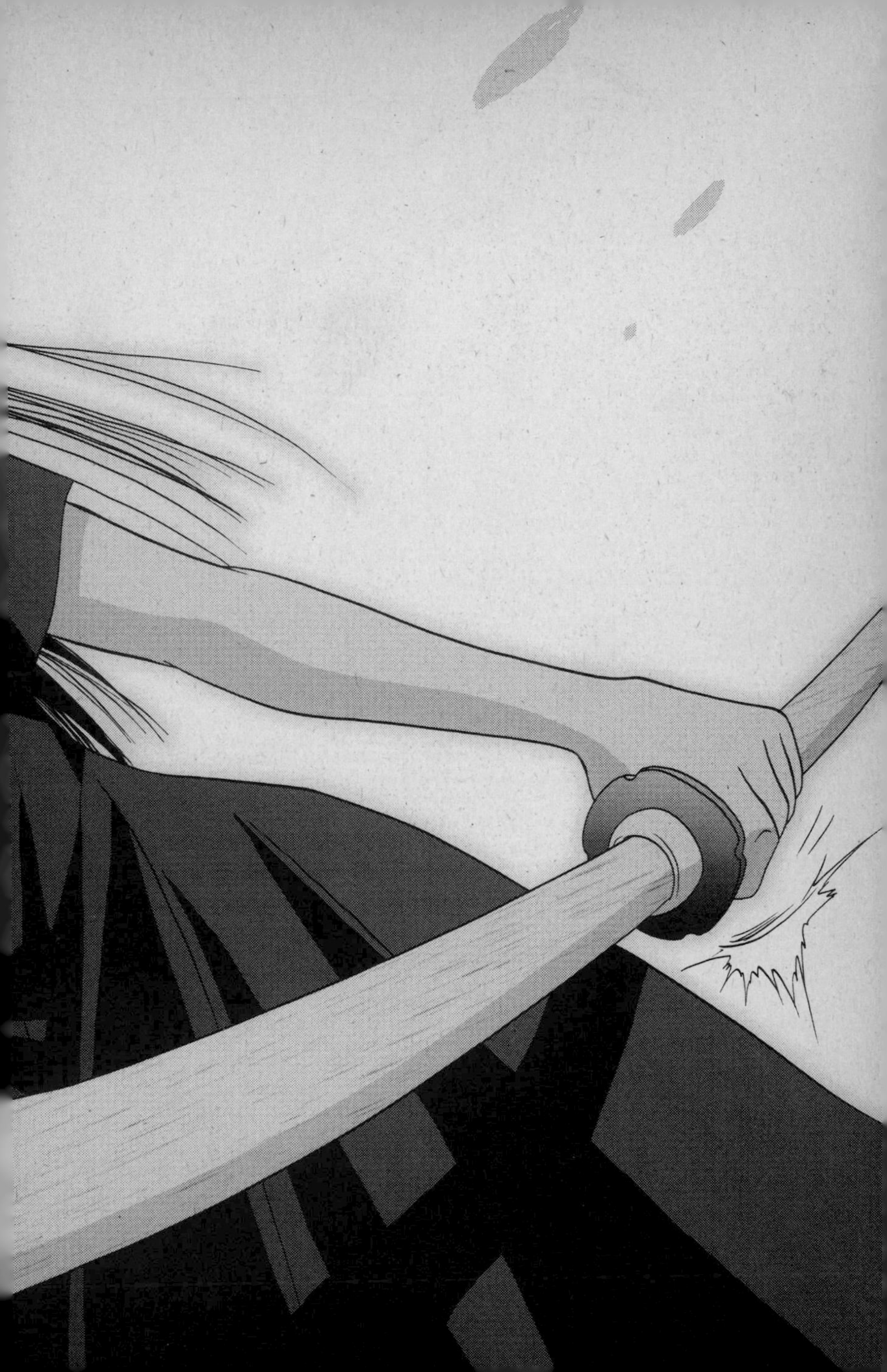

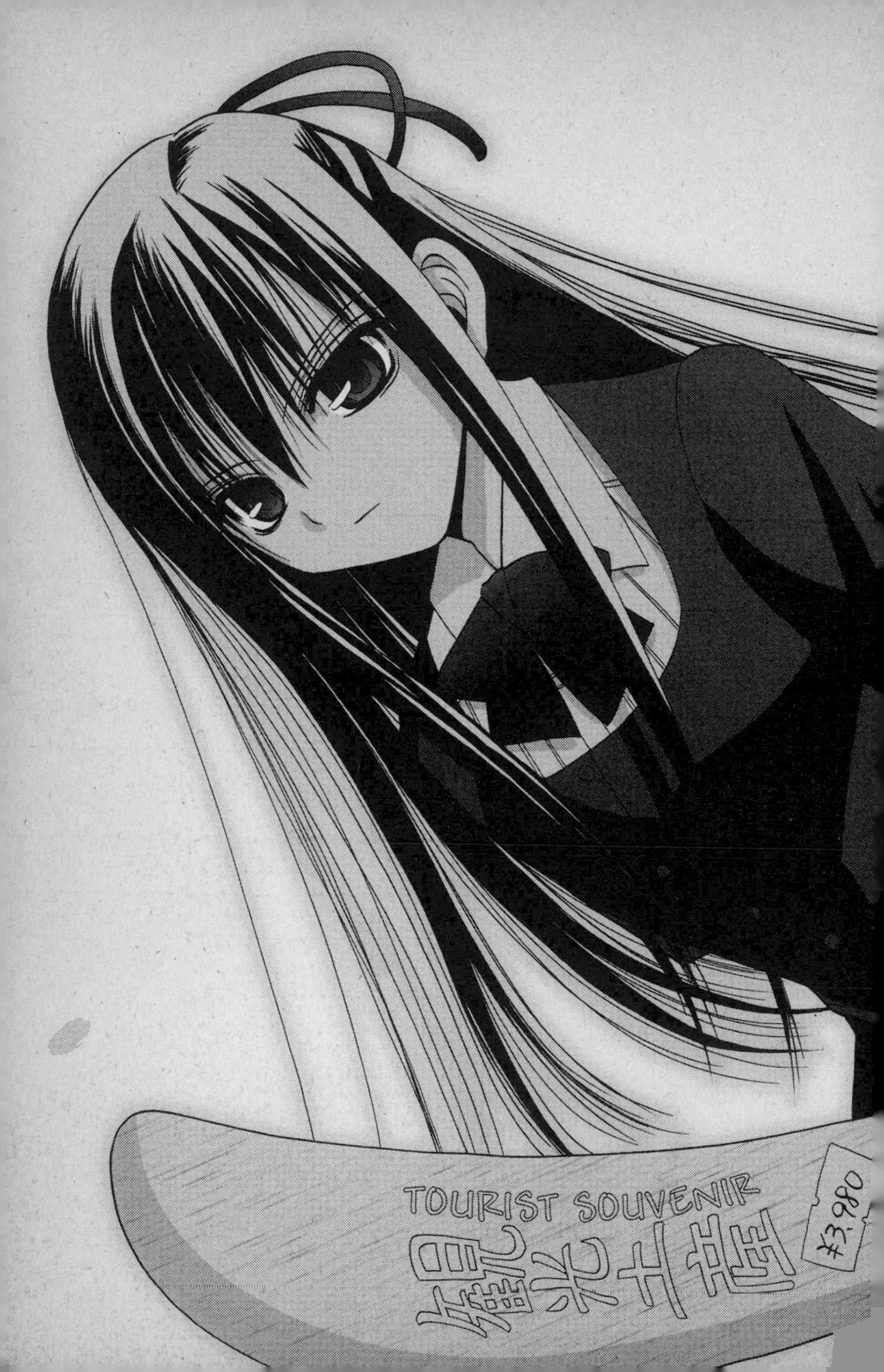
TOURIST SOUVENIR
¥3,980

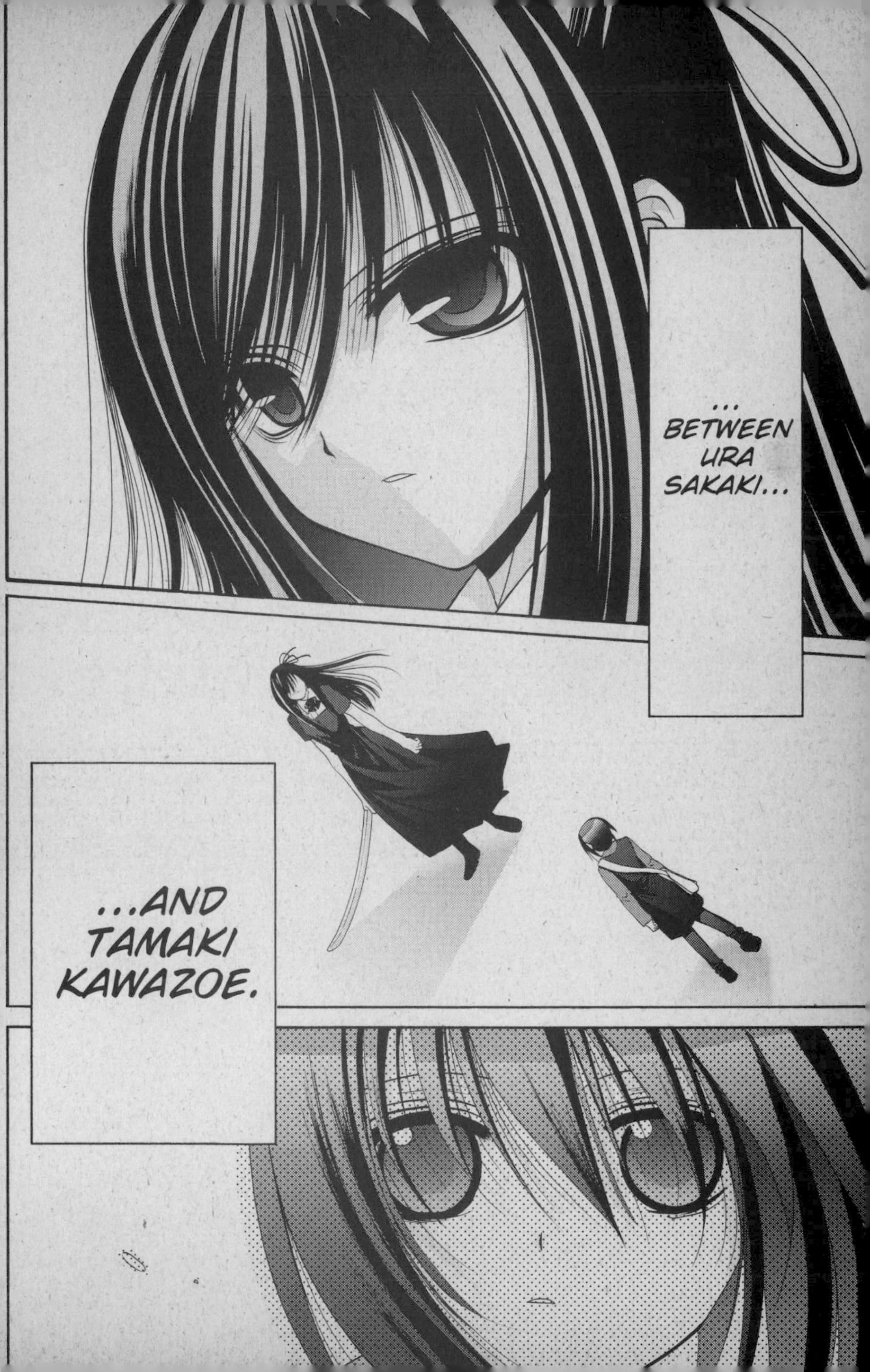
...
BETWEEN
URA
SAKAKI...
...AND
TAMAKI
KAWAZOE.

BAMBOO BLADE

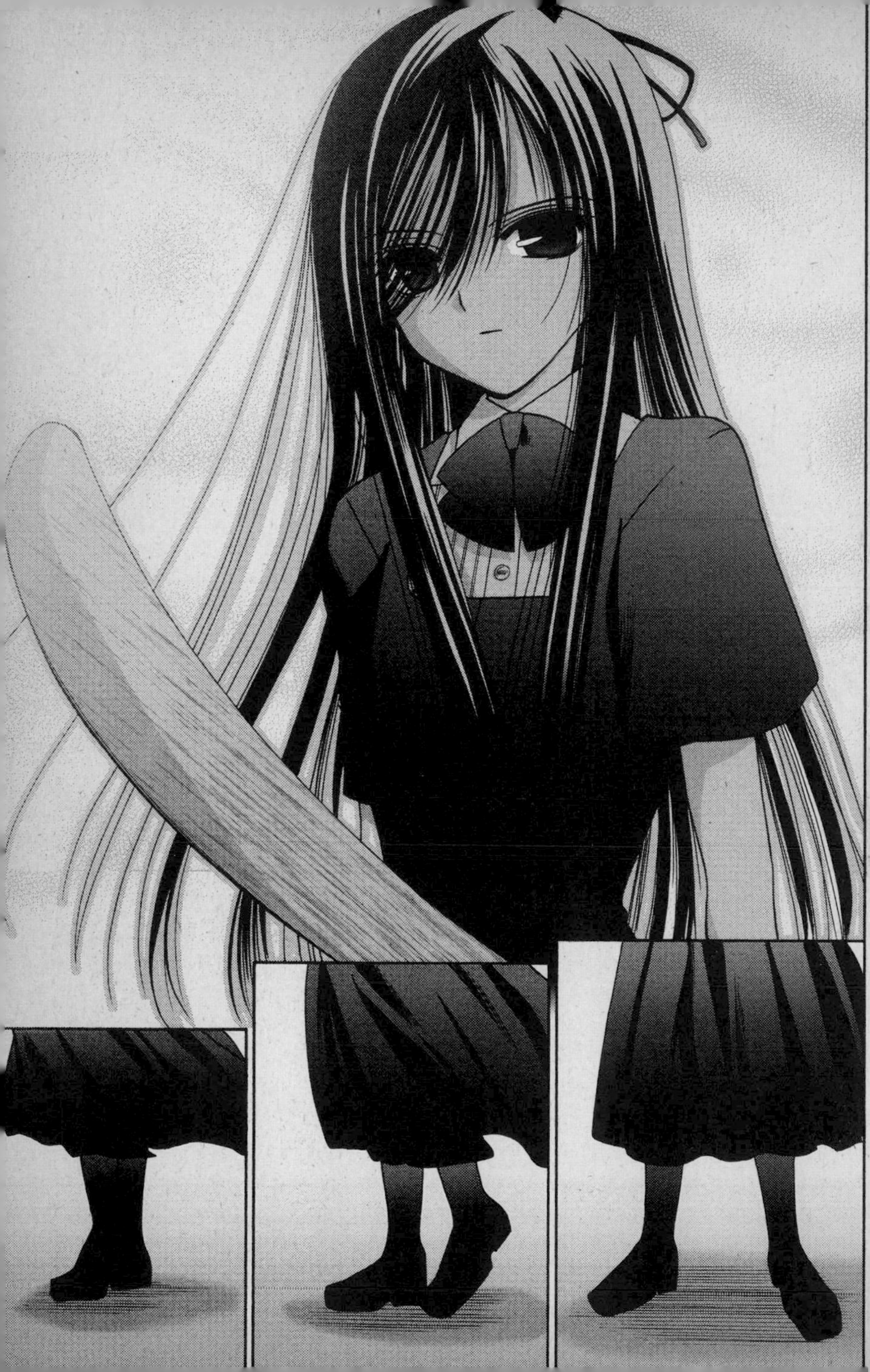

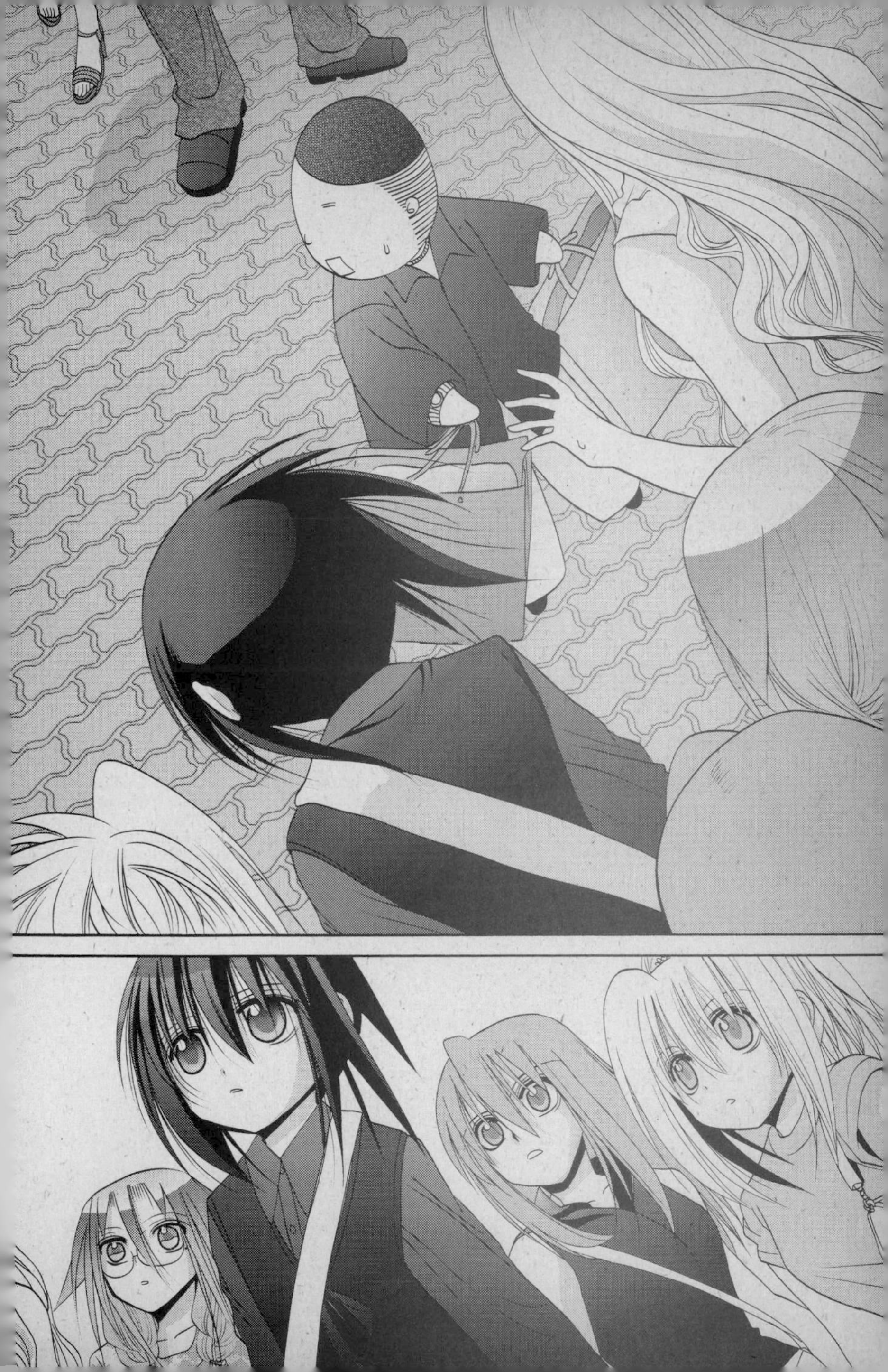

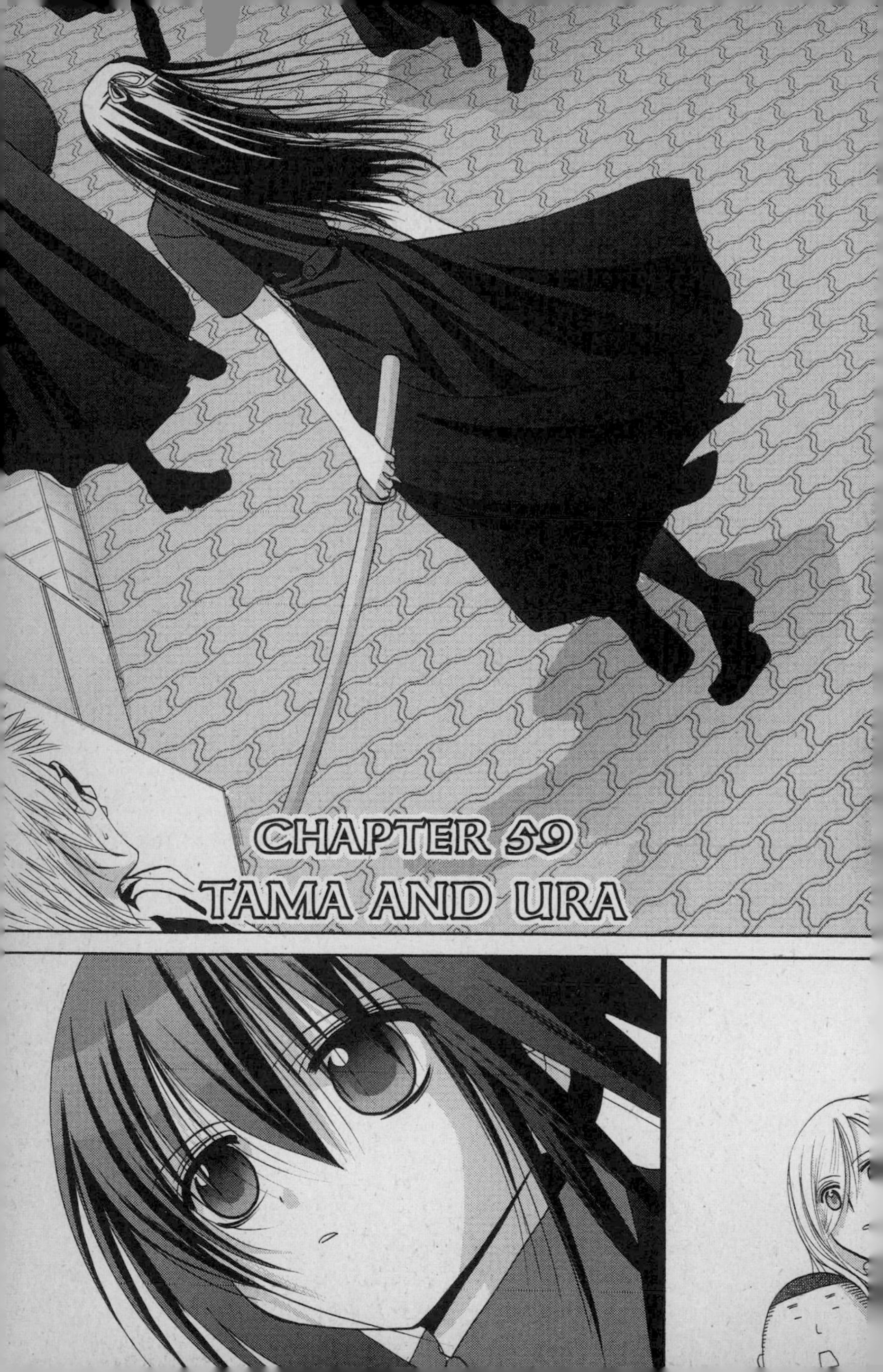
CHAPTER 59
TAMA AND URA

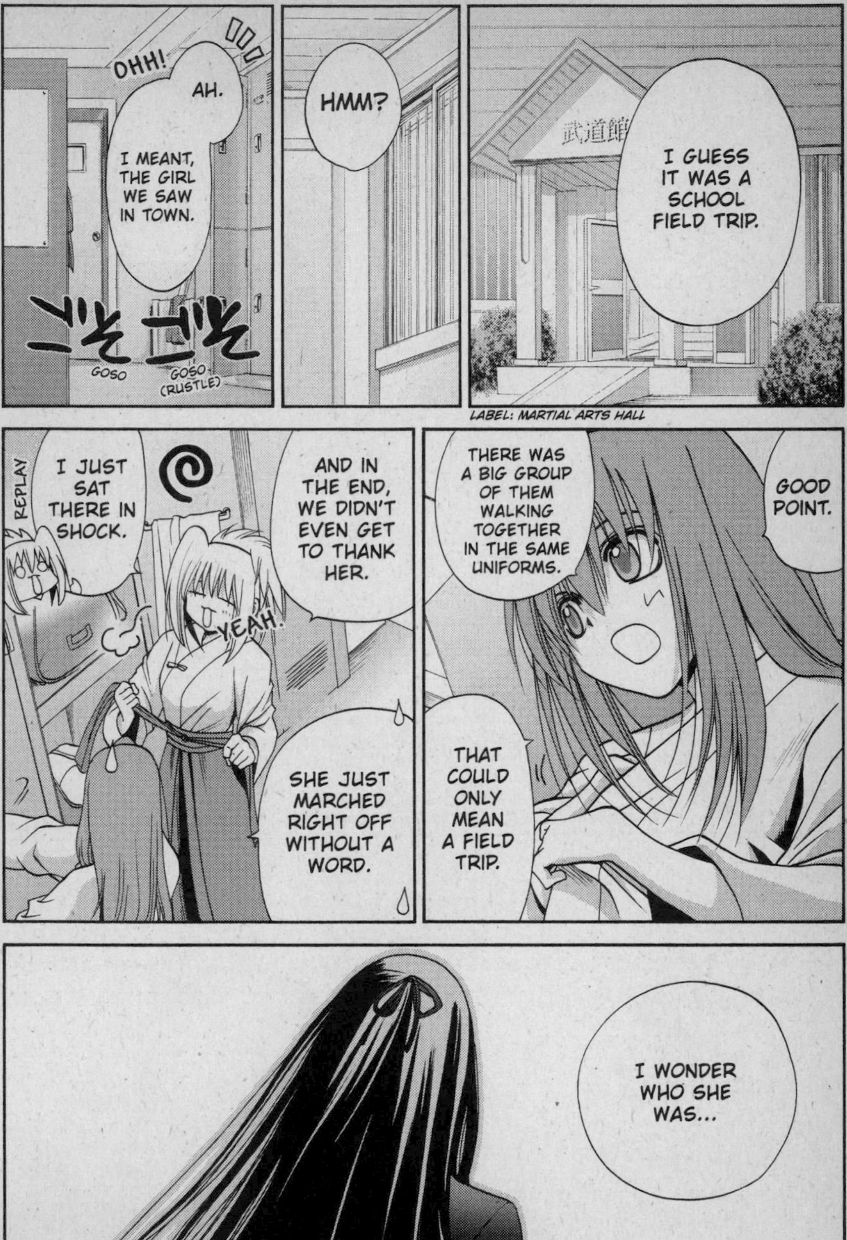
武道館
I GUESS IT WAS A SCHOOL FIELD TRIP.
LABEL: MARTIAL ARTS HALL
HMM?
OHH!
AH.
I MEANT, THE GIRL WE SAW IN TOWN.
ごそごそ
GOSO GOSO (RUSTLE)
GOOD POINT.
THERE WAS A BIG GROUP OF THEM WALKING TOGETHER IN THE SAME UNIFORMS.
THAT COULD ONLY MEAN A FIELD TRIP.
AND IN THE END, WE DIDN'T EVEN GET TO THANK HER.
SHE JUST MARCHED RIGHT OFF WITHOUT A WORD.
YEAH.
I JUST SAT THERE IN SHOCK.
REPLAY
I WONDER WHO SHE WAS...

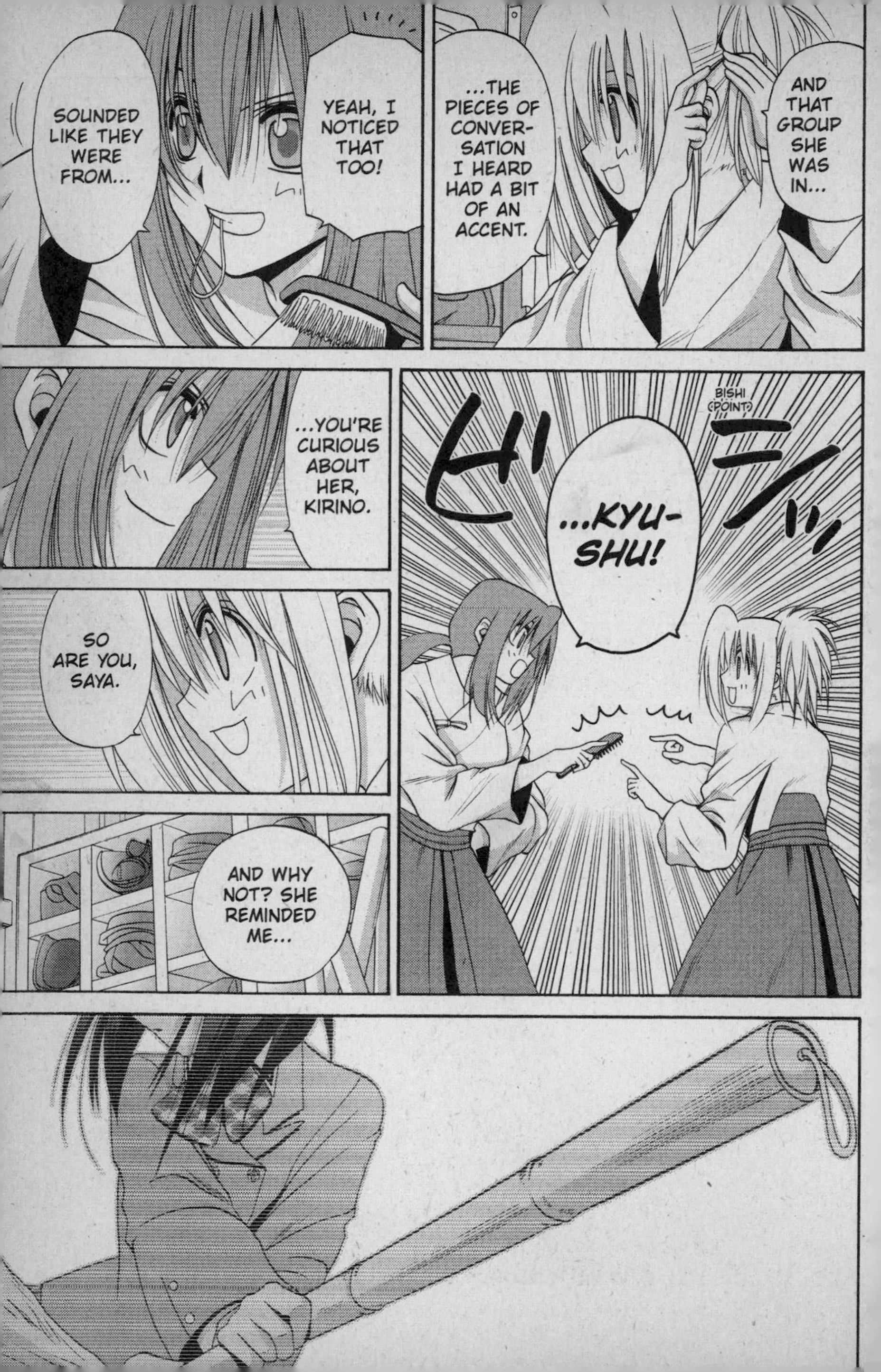
AND THAT GROUP SHE WAS IN...
...THE PIECES OF CONVER-SATION I HEARD HAD A BIT OF AN ACCENT.
YEAH, I NOTICED THAT TOO!
SOUNDED LIKE THEY WERE FROM...
BISHI (POINT)
...KYU-SHU!
...YOU'RE CURIOUS ABOUT HER, KIRINO.
SO ARE YOU, SAYA.
AND WHY NOT? SHE REMINDED ME...

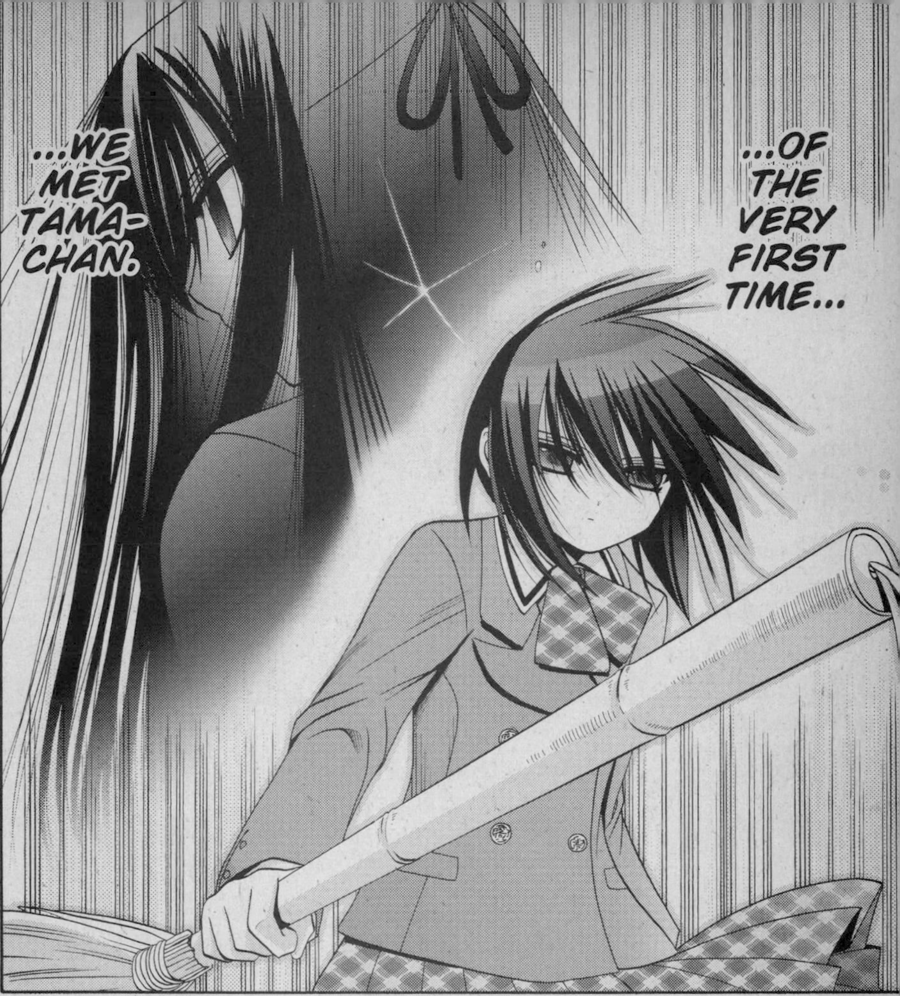
...OF THE VERY FIRST TIME...
...WE MET TAMA-CHAN.

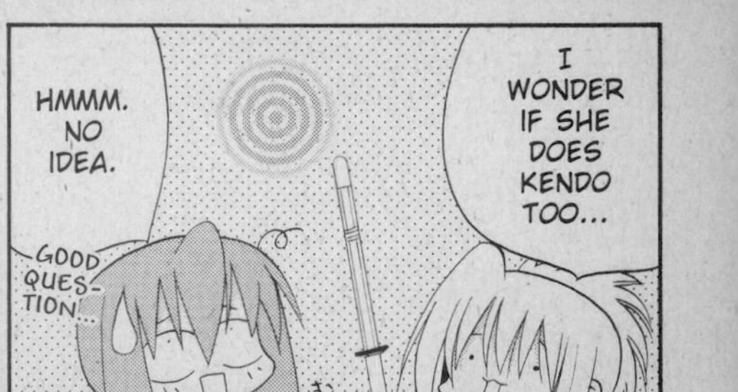
I WONDER IF SHE DOES KENDO TOO...
HMMM. NO IDEA.
GOOD QUESTION...

SFX: MUNI (PULL) MUNI

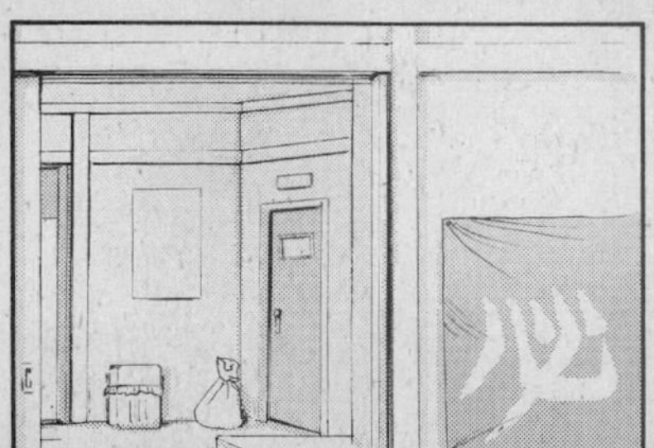
必

LABEL: VICTORY

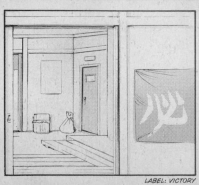

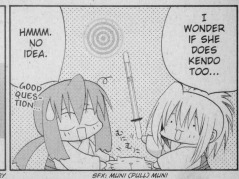

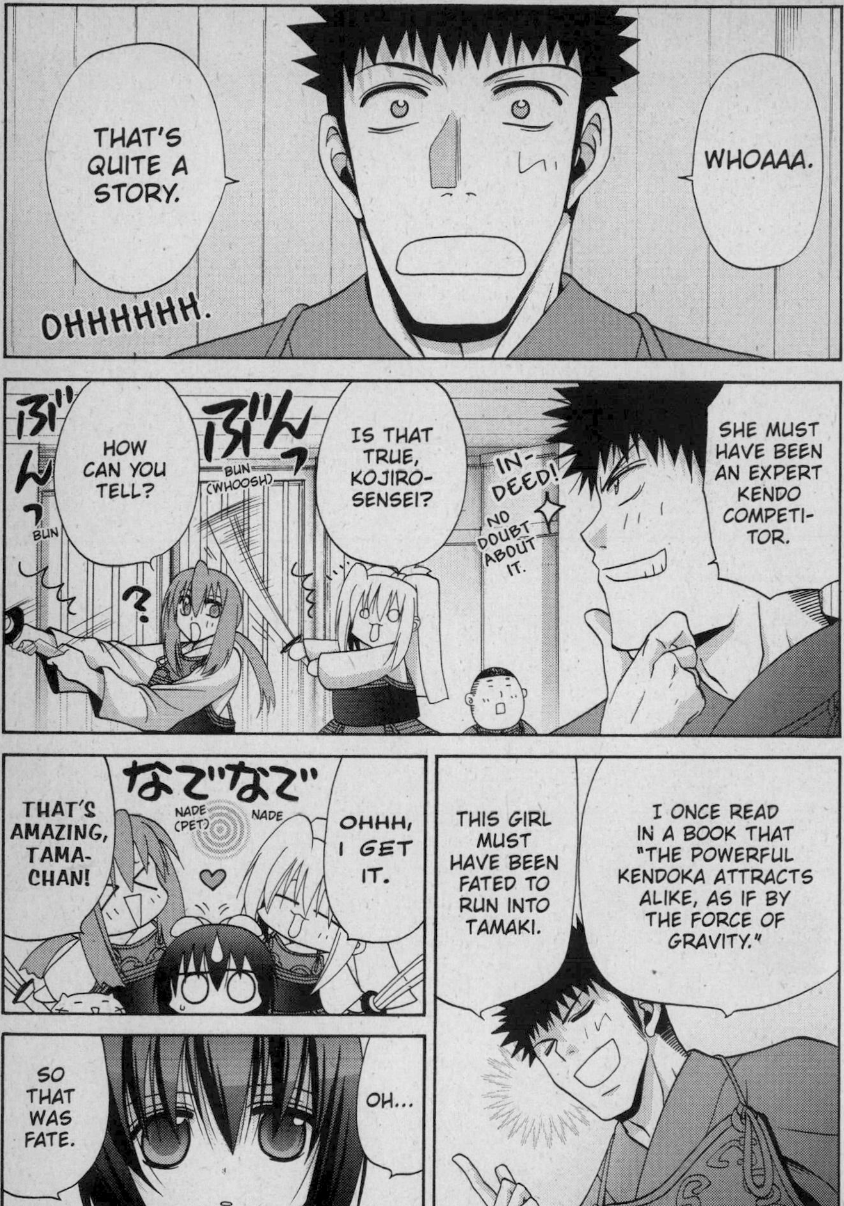

WHOAAA.
THAT'S QUITE A STORY.
OHHHHHH.
SHE MUST HAVE BEEN AN EXPERT KENDO COMPETI-TOR.
IN-DEED!
NO DOUBT ABOUT IT.
IS THAT TRUE, KOJIRO-SENSEI?
ぶんっ
BUN (WHOOSH)
HOW CAN YOU TELL?
ぶんっ
BUN
I ONCE READ IN A BOOK THAT "THE POWERFUL KENDOKA ATTRACTS ALIKE, AS IF BY THE FORCE OF GRAVITY."
THIS GIRL MUST HAVE BEEN FATED TO RUN INTO TAMAKI.
OHHH, I GET IT.
なでなで
NADE (PET)
NADE
THAT'S AMAZING, TAMA-CHAN!
OH...
SO THAT WAS FATE.
ぼー
BOOO (DUHH)

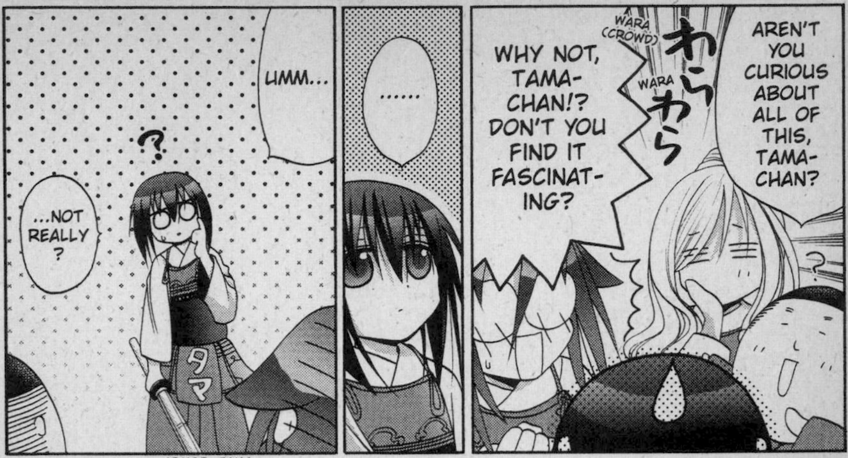
AREN'T YOU CURIOUS ABOUT ALL OF THIS, TAMA-CHAN?
WARA (CROWD)
わら
WARA
わら
WHY NOT, TAMA-CHAN!? DON'T YOU FIND IT FASCINATING?
?
......
UMM...
?
...NOT REALLY ?
タマ

ARMOR: TAMA

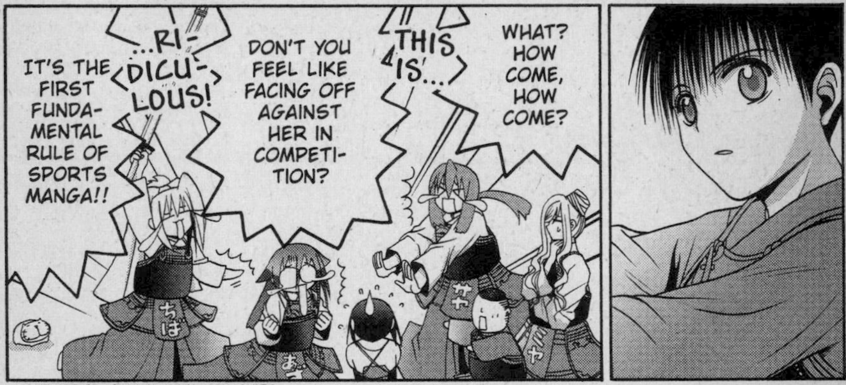
WHAT? HOW COME, HOW COME?
THIS IS...
DON'T YOU FEEL LIKE FACING OFF AGAINST HER IN COMPETITION?
...RIDICULOUS!
IT'S THE FIRST FUNDAMENTAL RULE OF SPORTS MANGA!!
ミヤ
サヤ
ちば

ARMOR (R-L): MIYA, SAYA, AZU, CHIBA

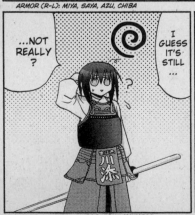

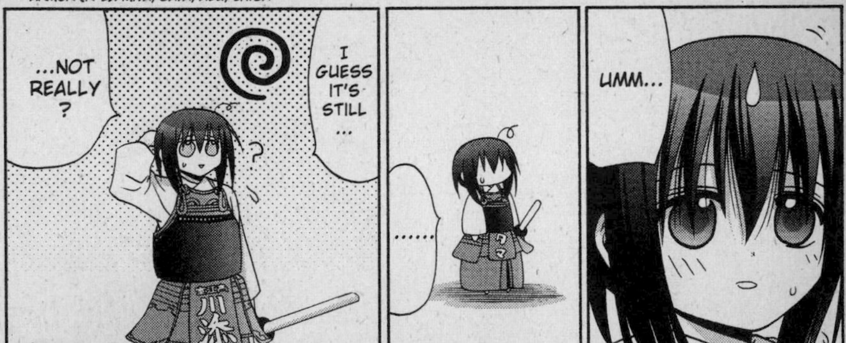
UMM...
......
タマ
I GUESS IT'S STILL ...
?
...NOT REALLY ?
川添

LABEL: MUROE HIGH - KAWAZOE

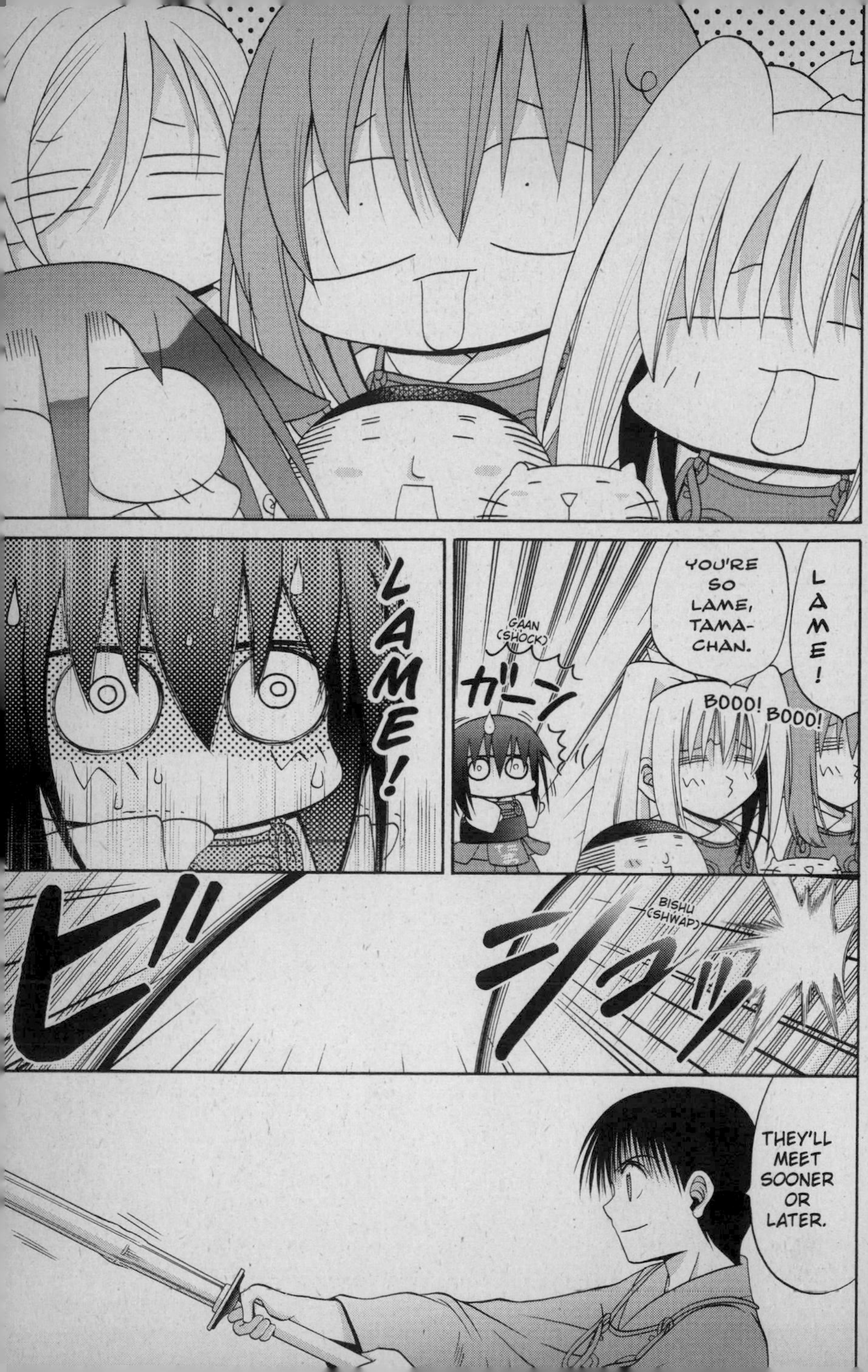
LAME!
YOU'RE SO LAME, TAMA-CHAN.
BOOO! BOOO!
GAAN (SHOCK)
ガーン
LAME!
BISHU (SHWAP)
ビシュッ
THEY'LL MEET SOONER OR LATER.

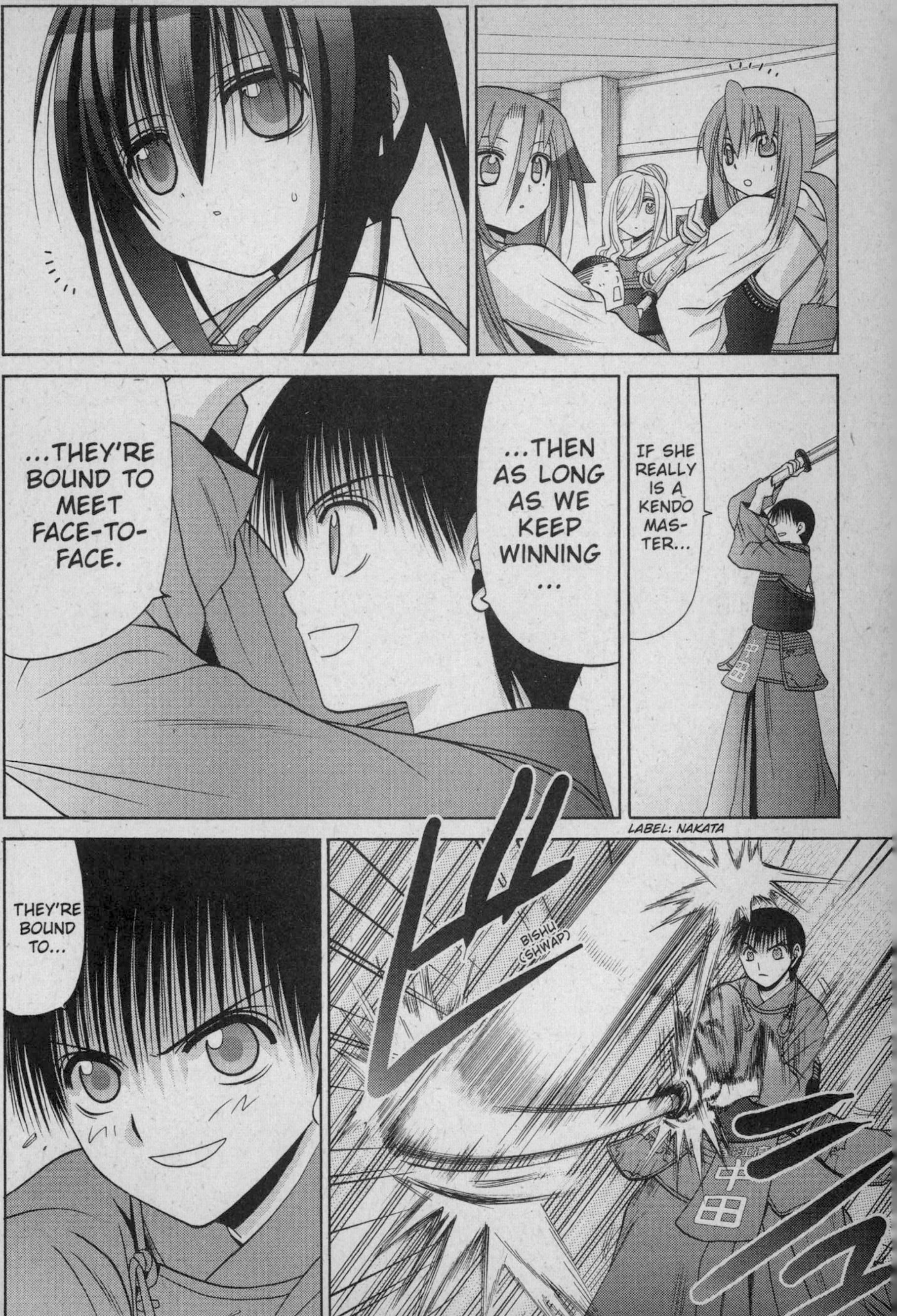
IF SHE REALLY IS A KENDO MASTER...
...THEN AS LONG AS WE KEEP WINNING...
...THEY'RE BOUND TO MEET FACE-TO-FACE.
LABEL: NAKATA
BISHU (SHWAP)
THEY'RE BOUND TO...

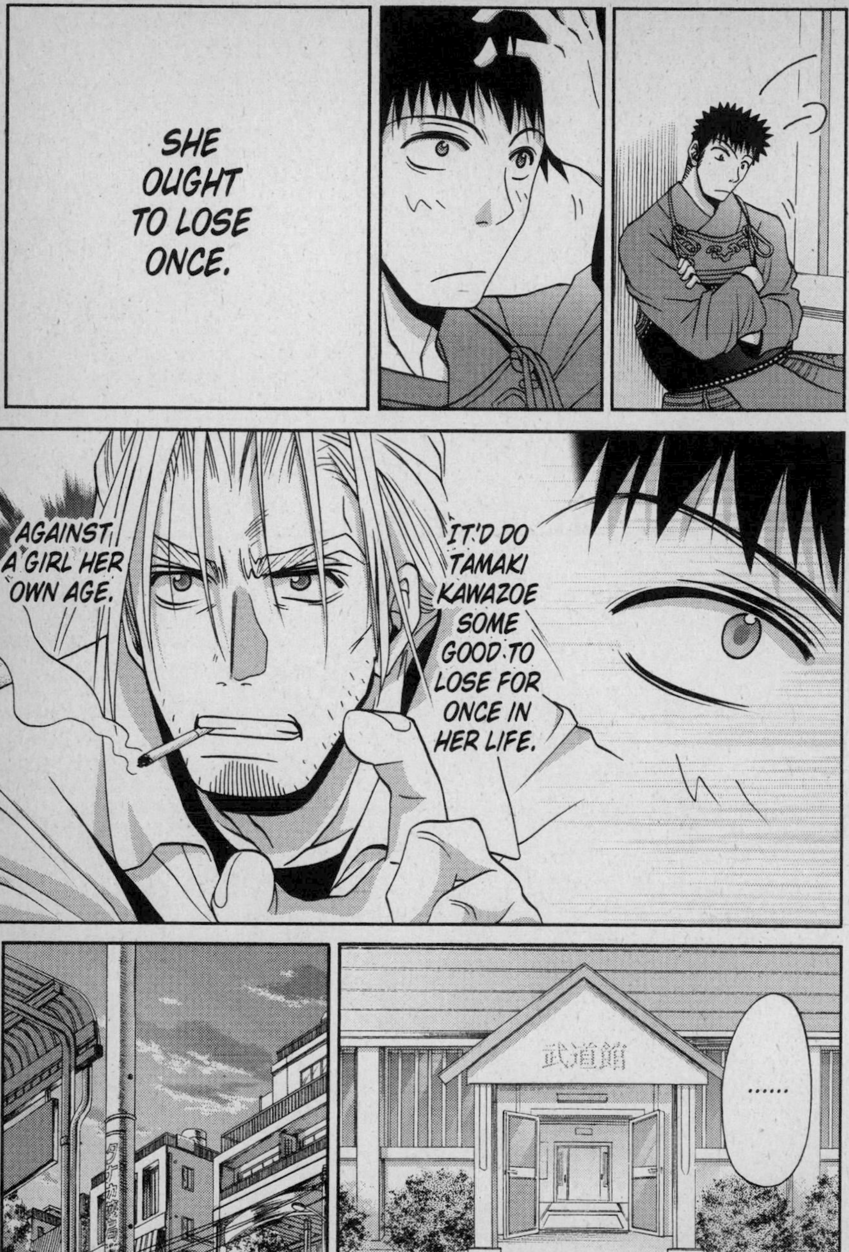
SHE OUGHT TO LOSE ONCE.
IT'D DO TAMAKI KAWAZOE SOME GOOD TO LOSE FOR ONCE IN HER LIFE.
AGAINST A GIRL HER OWN AGE.
武道館
......
LABEL: TANAKA PHARMACY

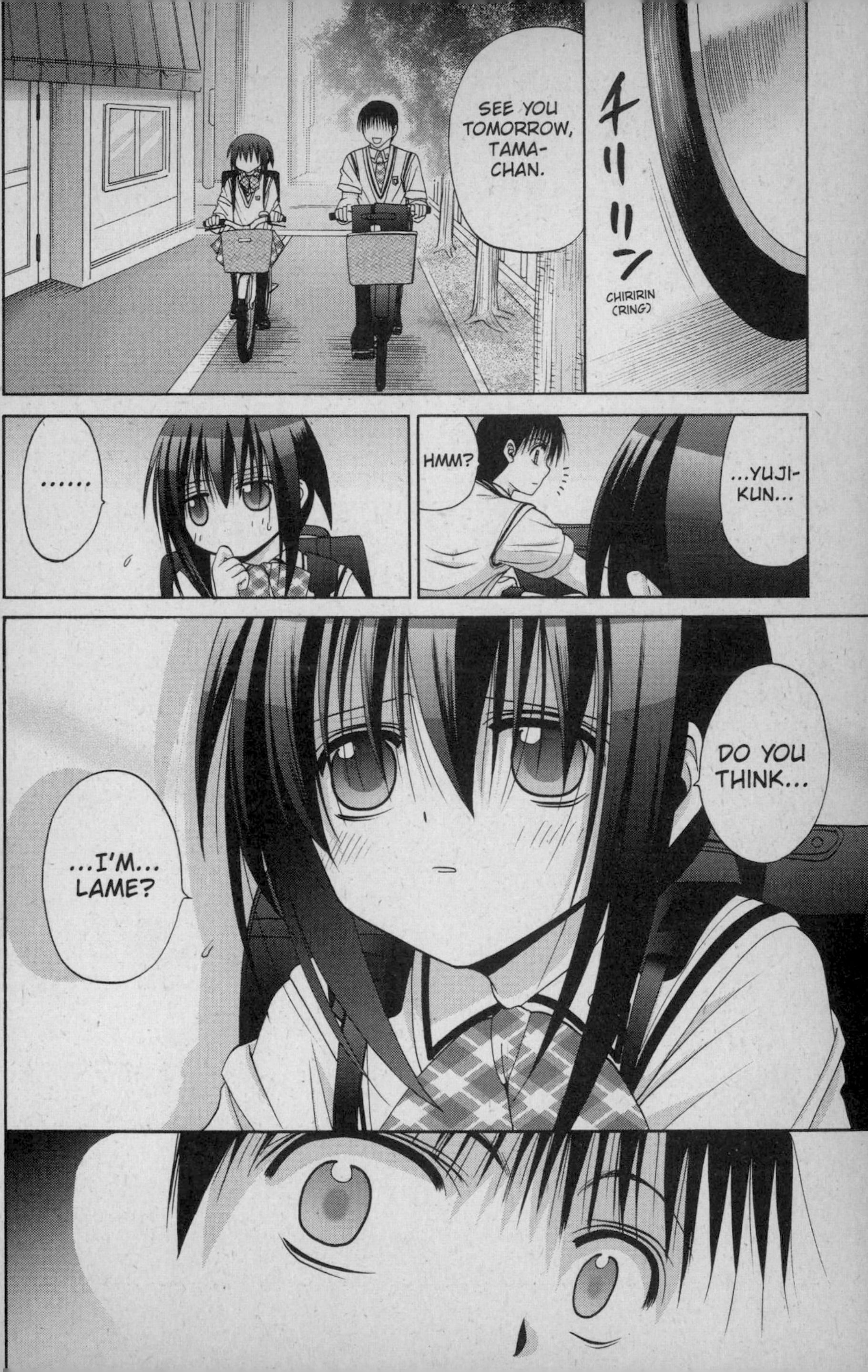
チリリン
CHIRIRIN (RING)
SEE YOU TOMORROW, TAMA-CHAN.
...YUJI-KUN...
HMM?
......
DO YOU THINK...
...I'M... LAME?

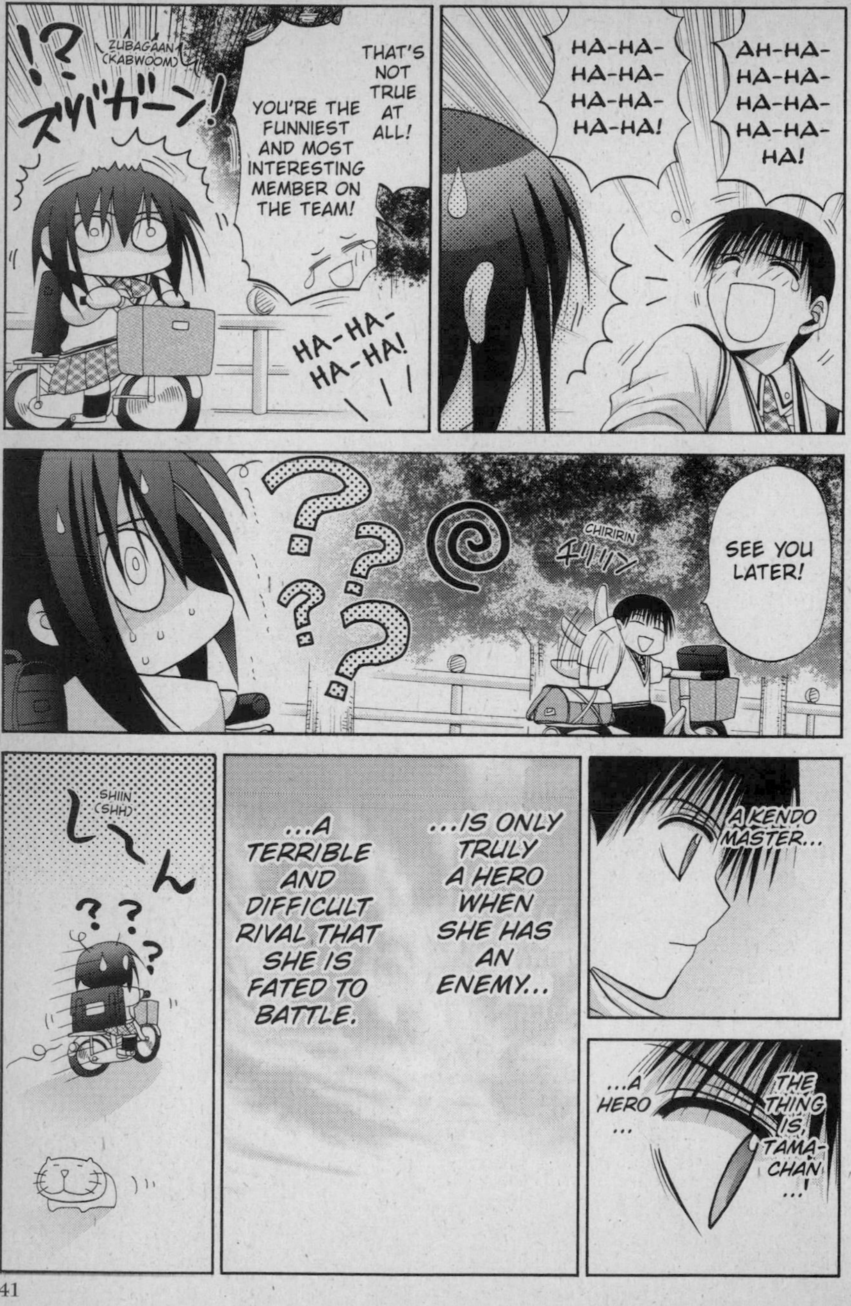
AH-HA-HA-HA-HA-HA-HA-HA-HA!
HA-HA-HA-HA-HA-HA-HA-HA!
THAT'S NOT TRUE AT ALL!
YOU'RE THE FUNNIEST AND MOST INTERESTING MEMBER ON THE TEAM!
ZUBAGAAN (KABWOOM)
!?
ズバガーン!
HA-HA-HA-HA!
SEE YOU LATER!
CHIRIRIN
チリリン
A KENDO MASTER...
THE THING IS, TAMA-CHAN...!
...A HERO...
...IS ONLY TRULY A HERO WHEN SHE HAS AN ENEMY...
...A TERRIBLE AND DIFFICULT RIVAL THAT SHE IS FATED TO BATTLE.
SHIIN (SHH)
し～ん

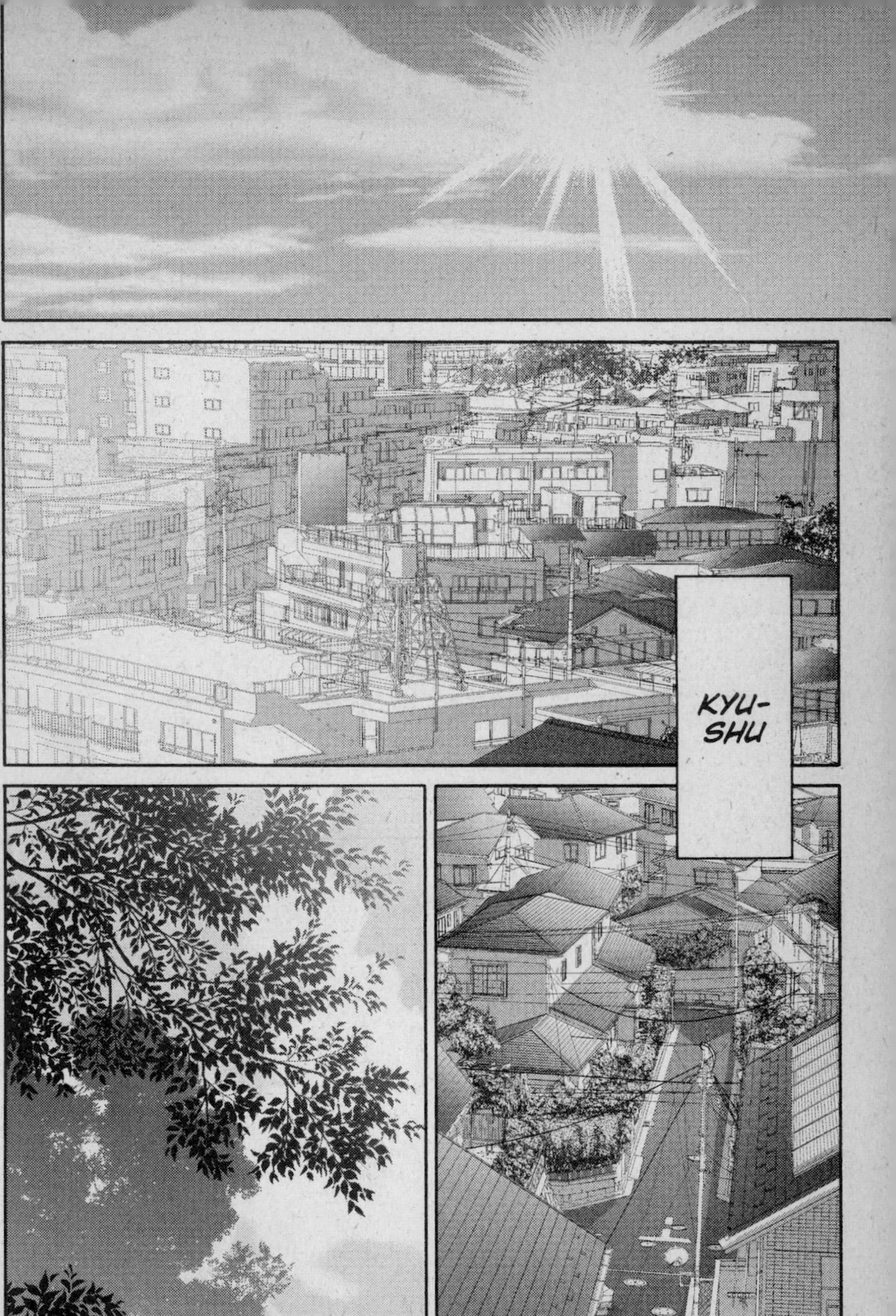
KYU-SHU

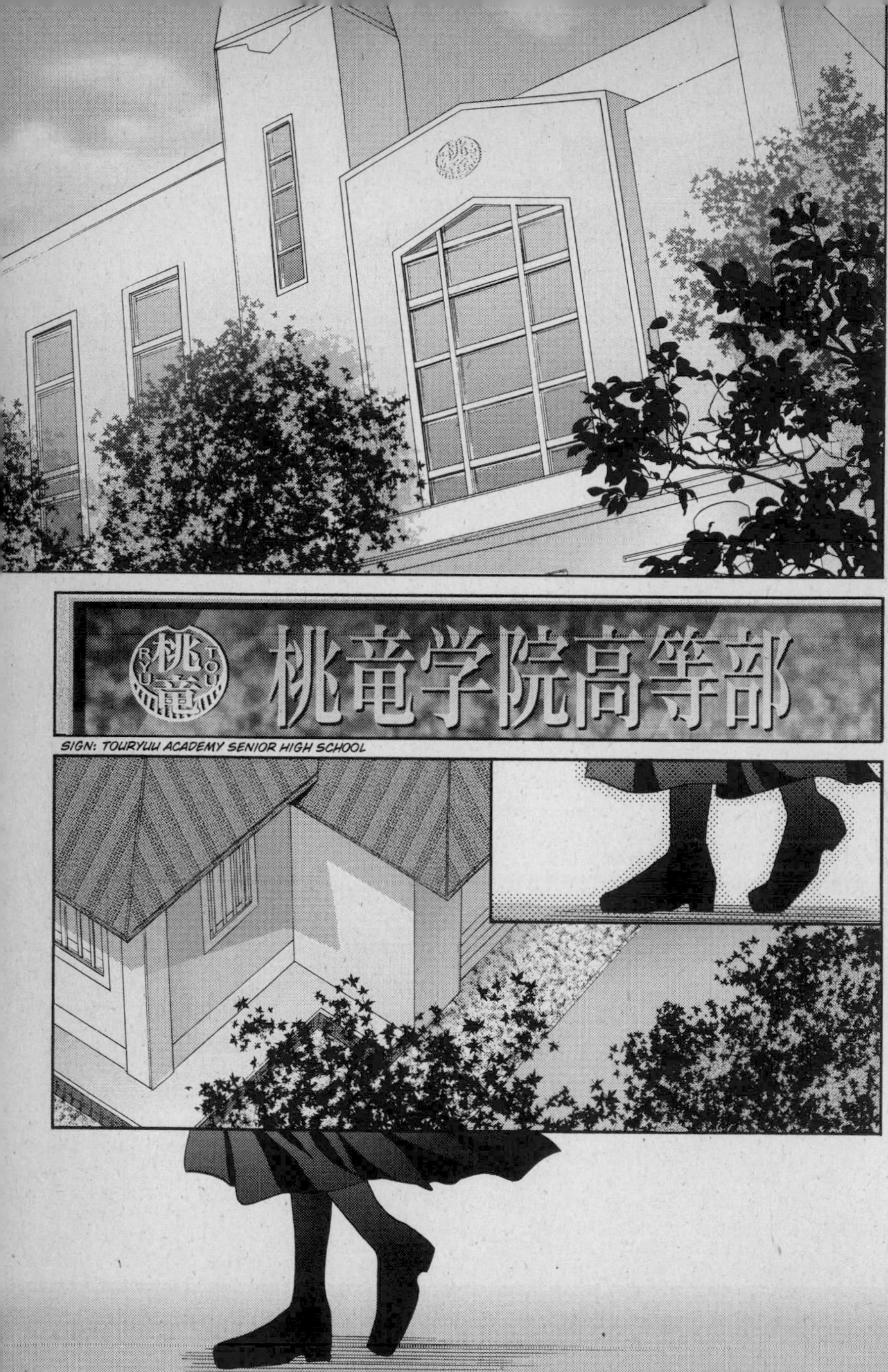
桃竜学院高等部
SIGN: TOURYUU ACADEMY SENIOR HIGH SCHOOL

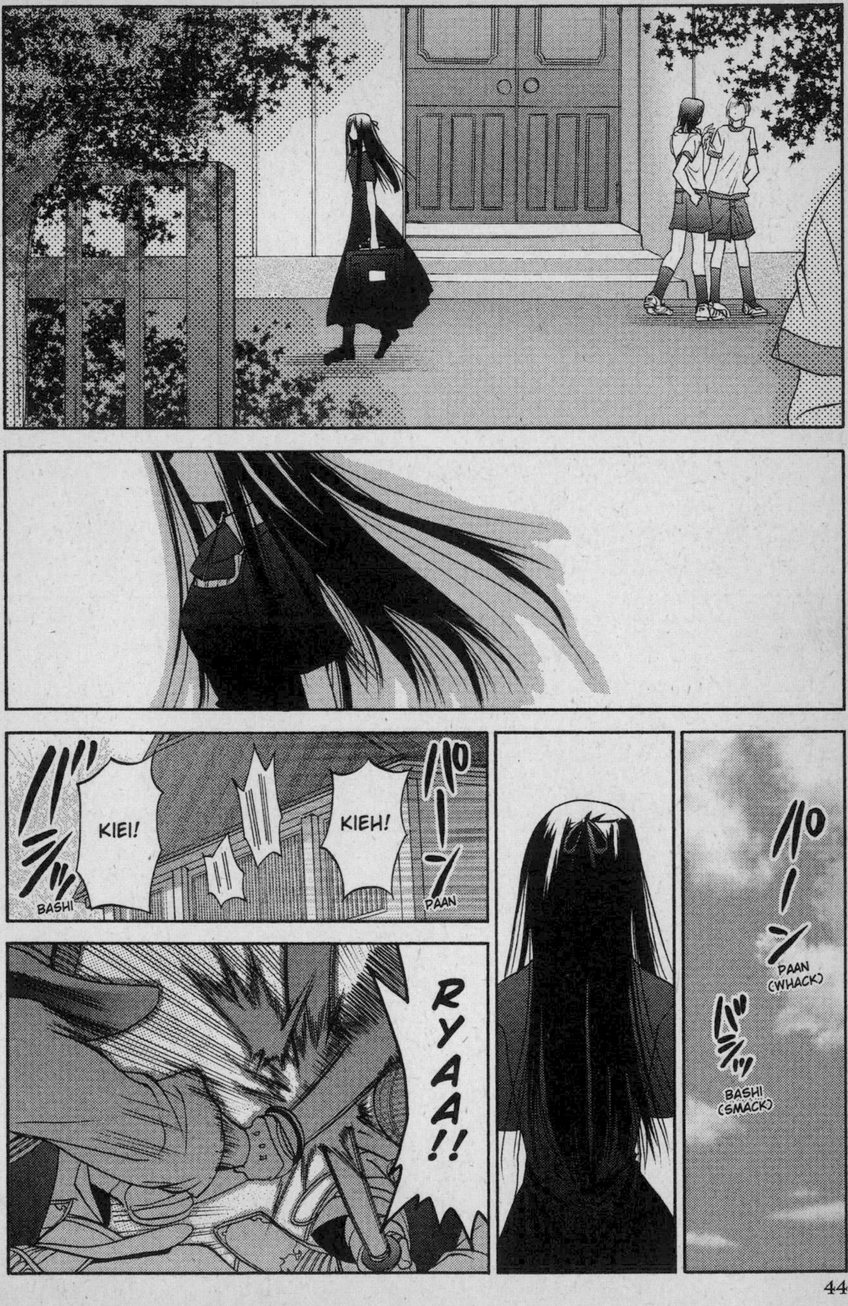

PAAN (WHACK)
BASHI (SMACK)
PAAN
KIEH!
KIEI!
BASHI
RYAA!!

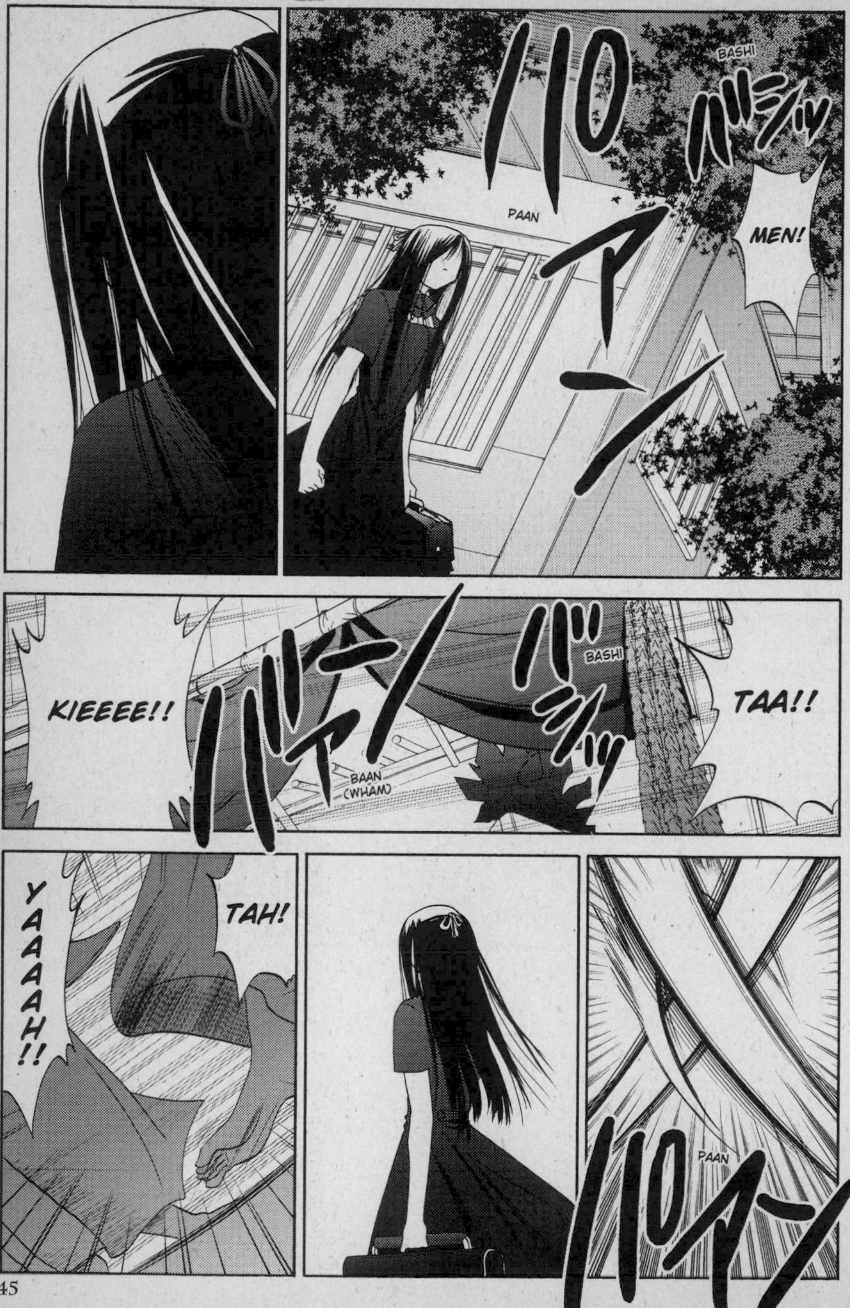
BASHI
MEN!
PAAN
TAA!!
BASHI
BAAN
(WHAM)
KIEEEE!!
PAAN
TAH!
YAAAAAH!!

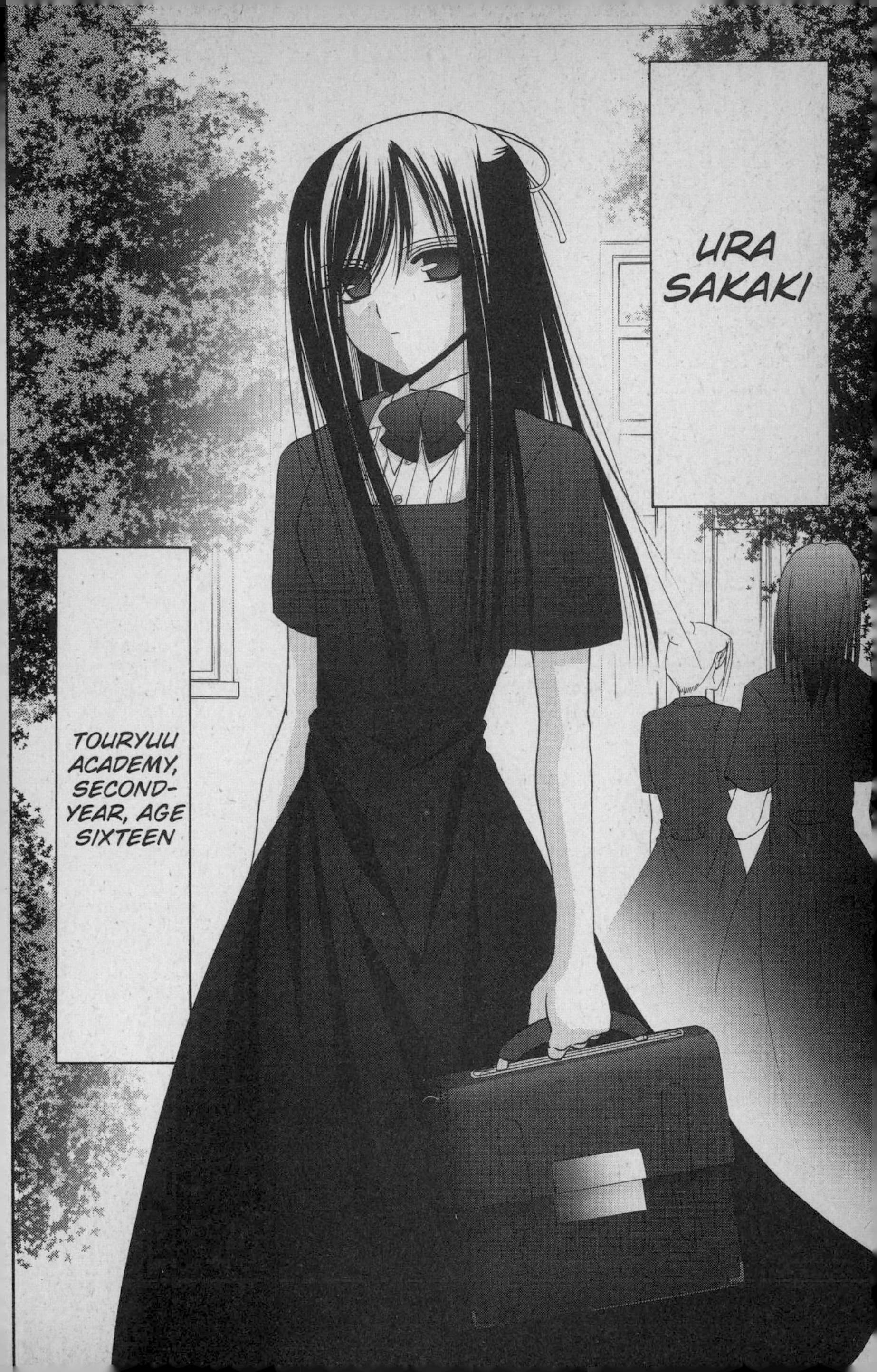
URA SAKAKI
TOURYUU ACADEMY, SECOND-YEAR, AGE SIXTEEN

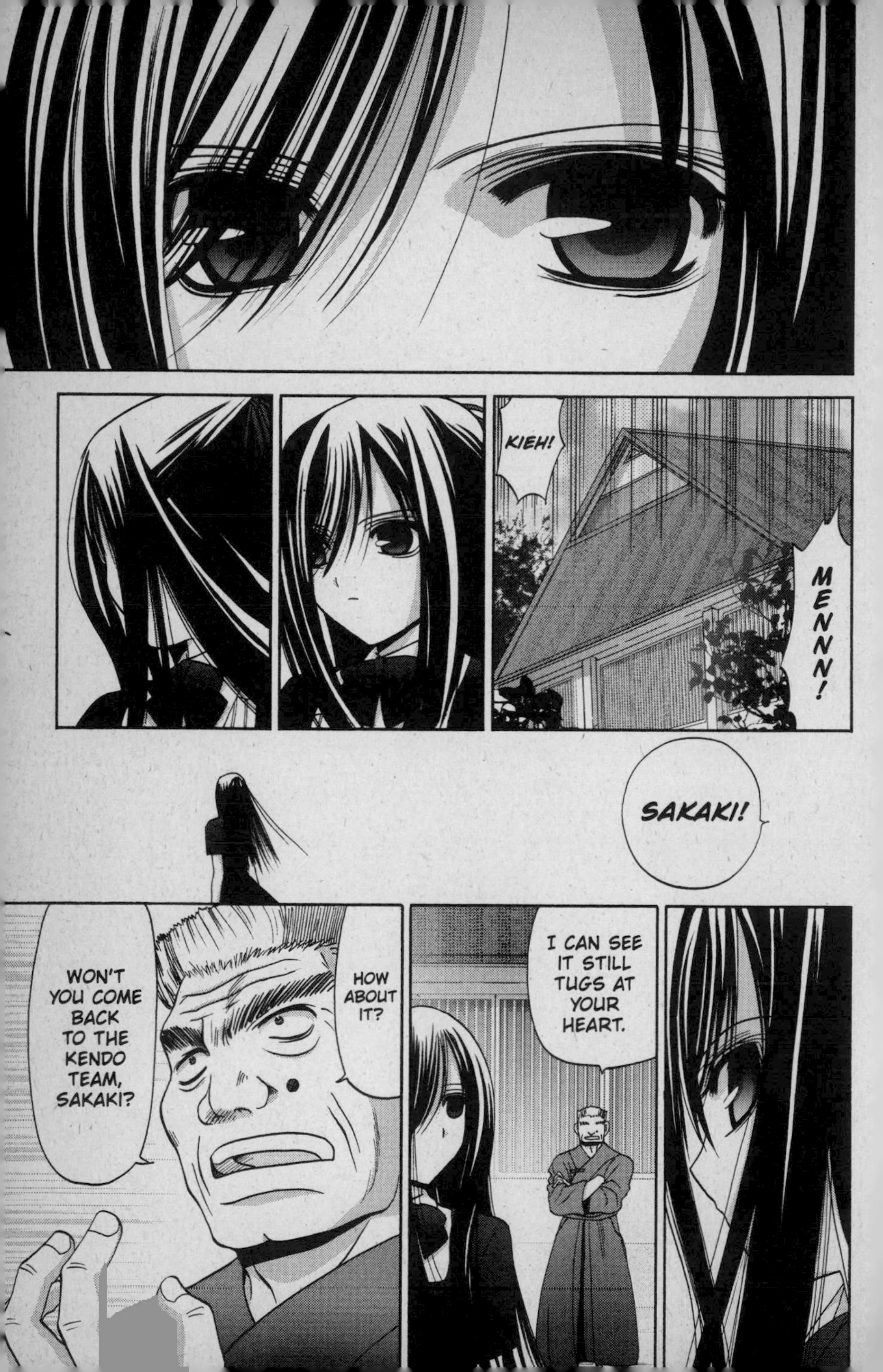
KIEH!
MENNNN!
SAKAKI!
I CAN SEE IT STILL TUGS AT YOUR HEART.
HOW ABOUT IT?
WON'T YOU COME BACK TO THE KENDO TEAM, SAKAKI?

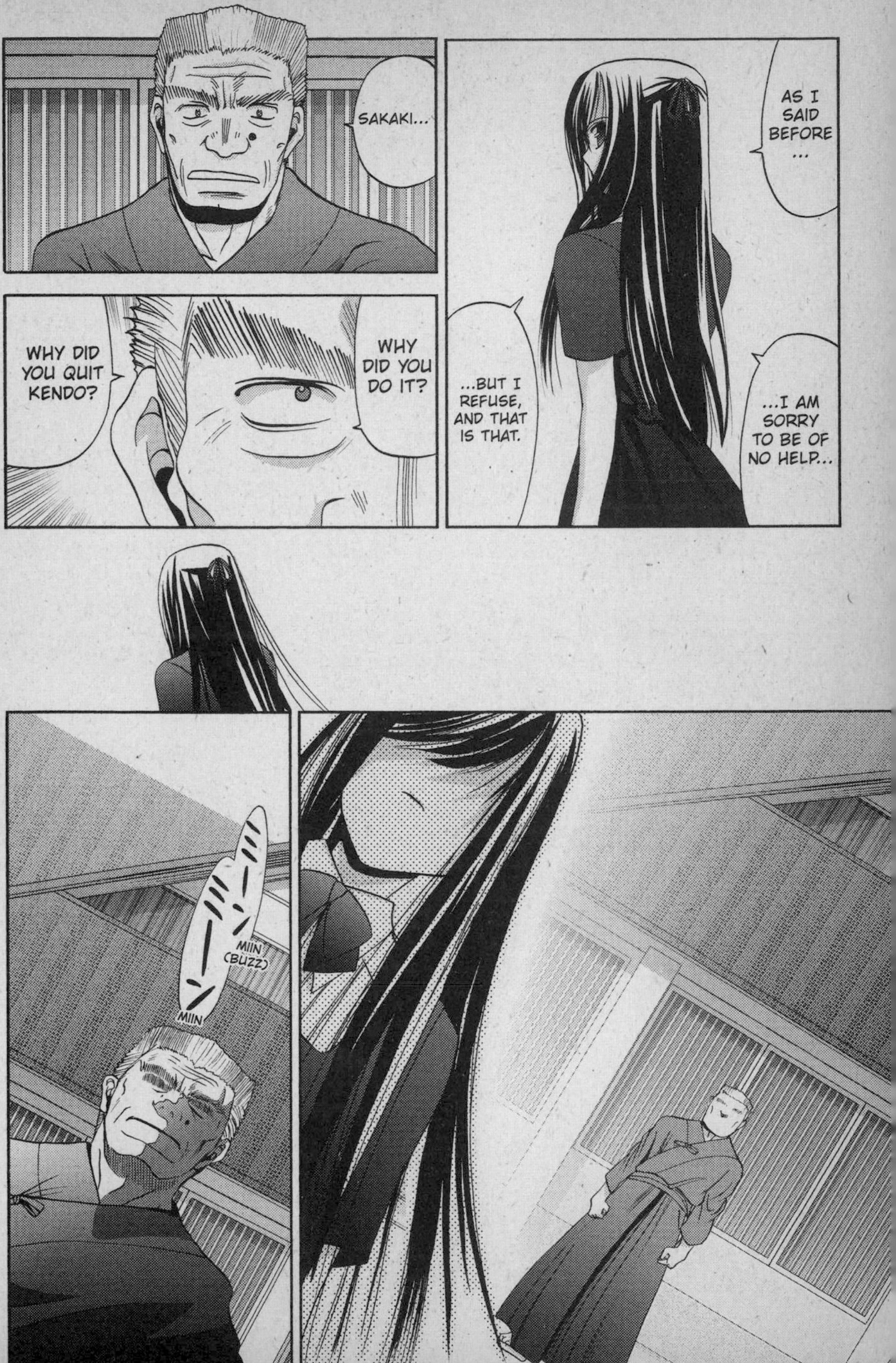
AS I SAID BEFORE ...
...I AM SORRY TO BE OF NO HELP...
...BUT I REFUSE, AND THAT IS THAT.
SAKAKI...
WHY DID YOU DO IT?
WHY DID YOU QUIT KENDO?
MIIN (BUZZ)
MIIN

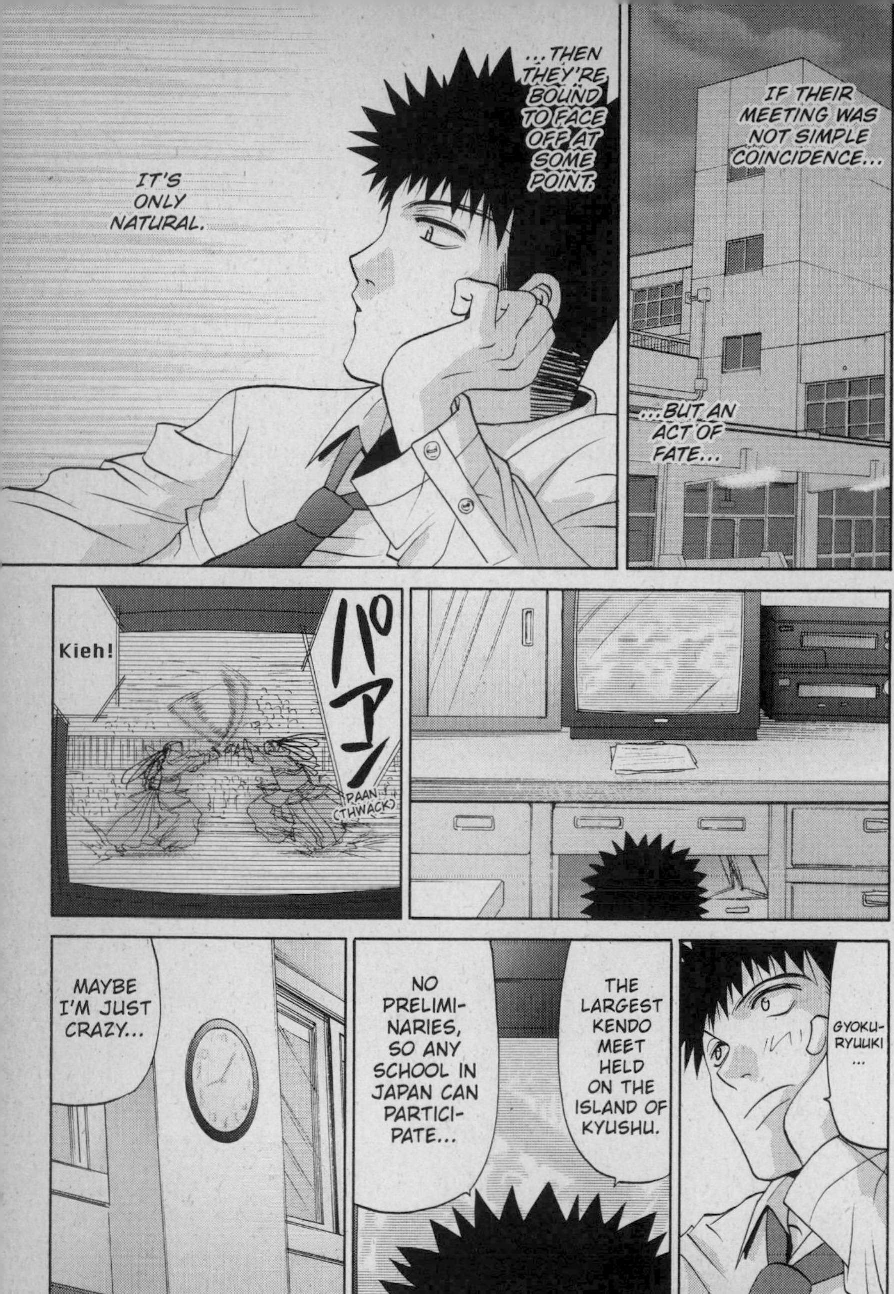
IF THEIR MEETING WAS NOT SIMPLE COINCIDENCE...
...BUT AN ACT OF FATE...
...THEN THEY'RE BOUND TO FACE OFF AT SOME POINT.
IT'S ONLY NATURAL.
パアン
PAAN (THWACK)
Kieh!
GYOKU-RYUUKI...
THE LARGEST KENDO MEET HELD ON THE ISLAND OF KYUSHU.
NO PRELIMI-NARIES, SO ANY SCHOOL IN JAPAN CAN PARTICI-PATE...
MAYBE I'M JUST CRAZY...

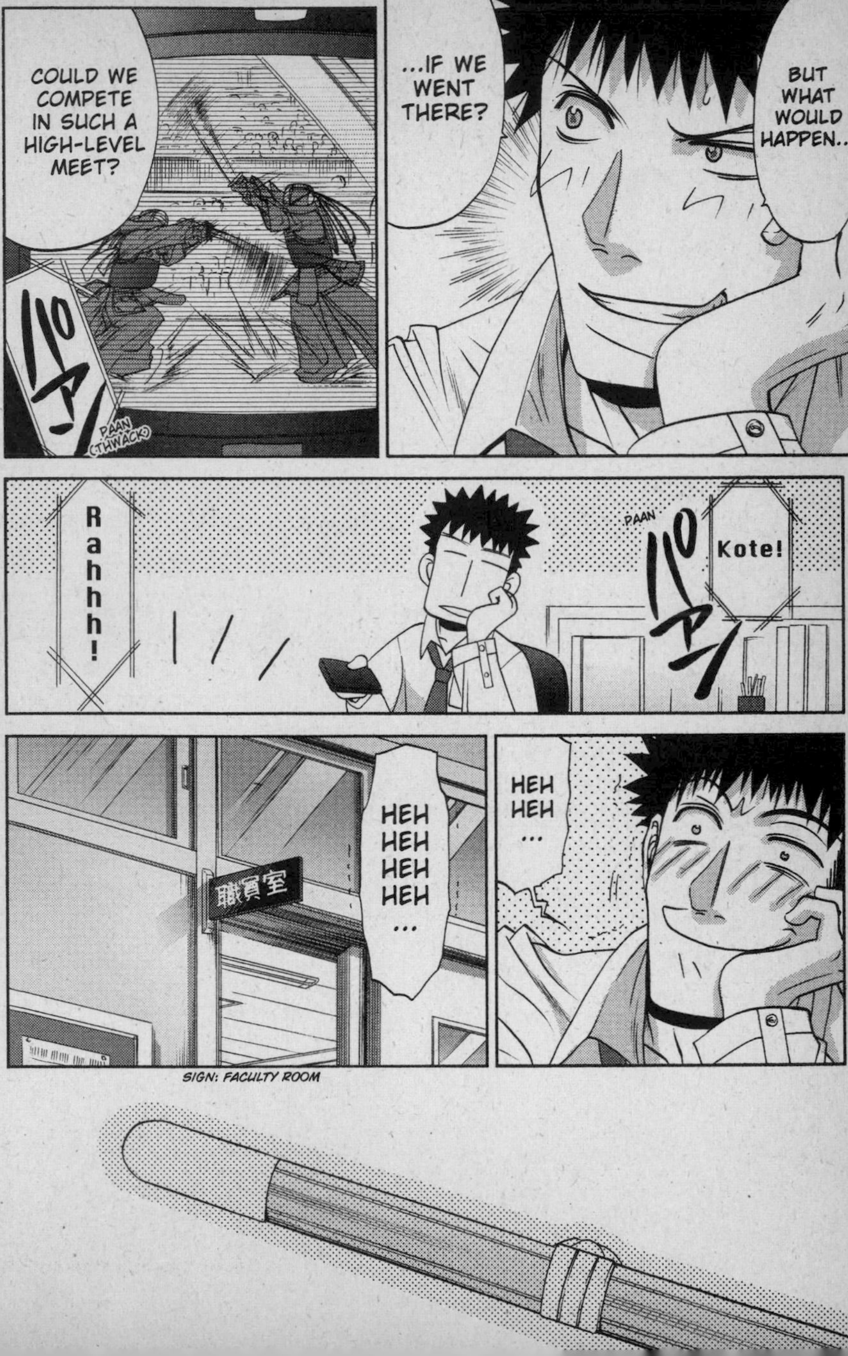
BUT WHAT WOULD HAPPEN...
...IF WE WENT THERE?
COULD WE COMPETE IN SUCH A HIGH-LEVEL MEET?
パァン
PAAN (THWACK)
Kote!
パァン
PAAN
Rahhhh!
HEH HEH ...
HEH HEH HEH HEH ...
職員室
SIGN: FACULTY ROOM

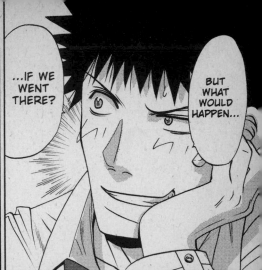

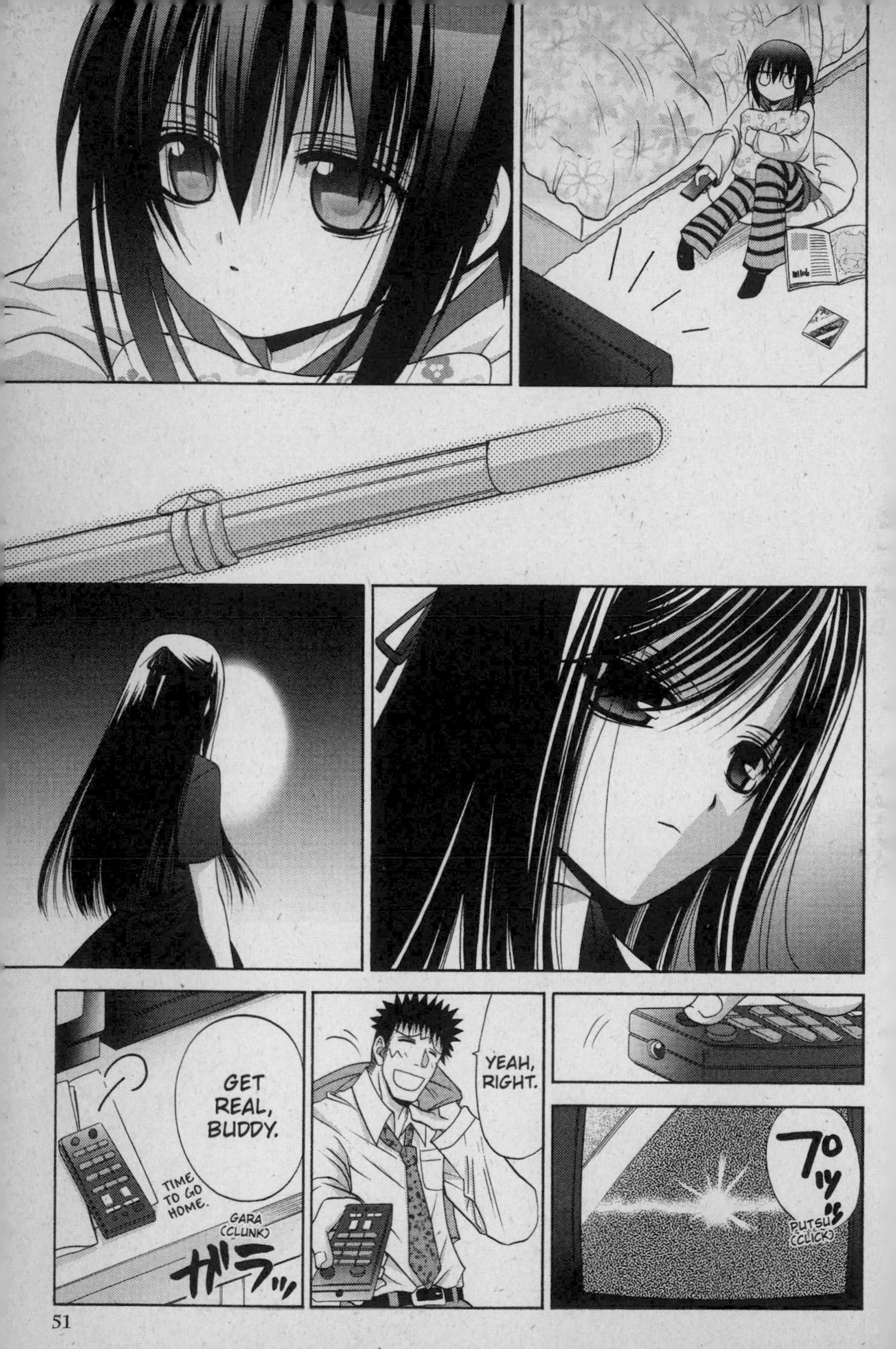
プッ
PUTSU (CLICK)
YEAH, RIGHT.
GET REAL, BUDDY.
TIME TO GO HOME.
GARA (CLUNK)
ガラッ

BAMBOO BLADE

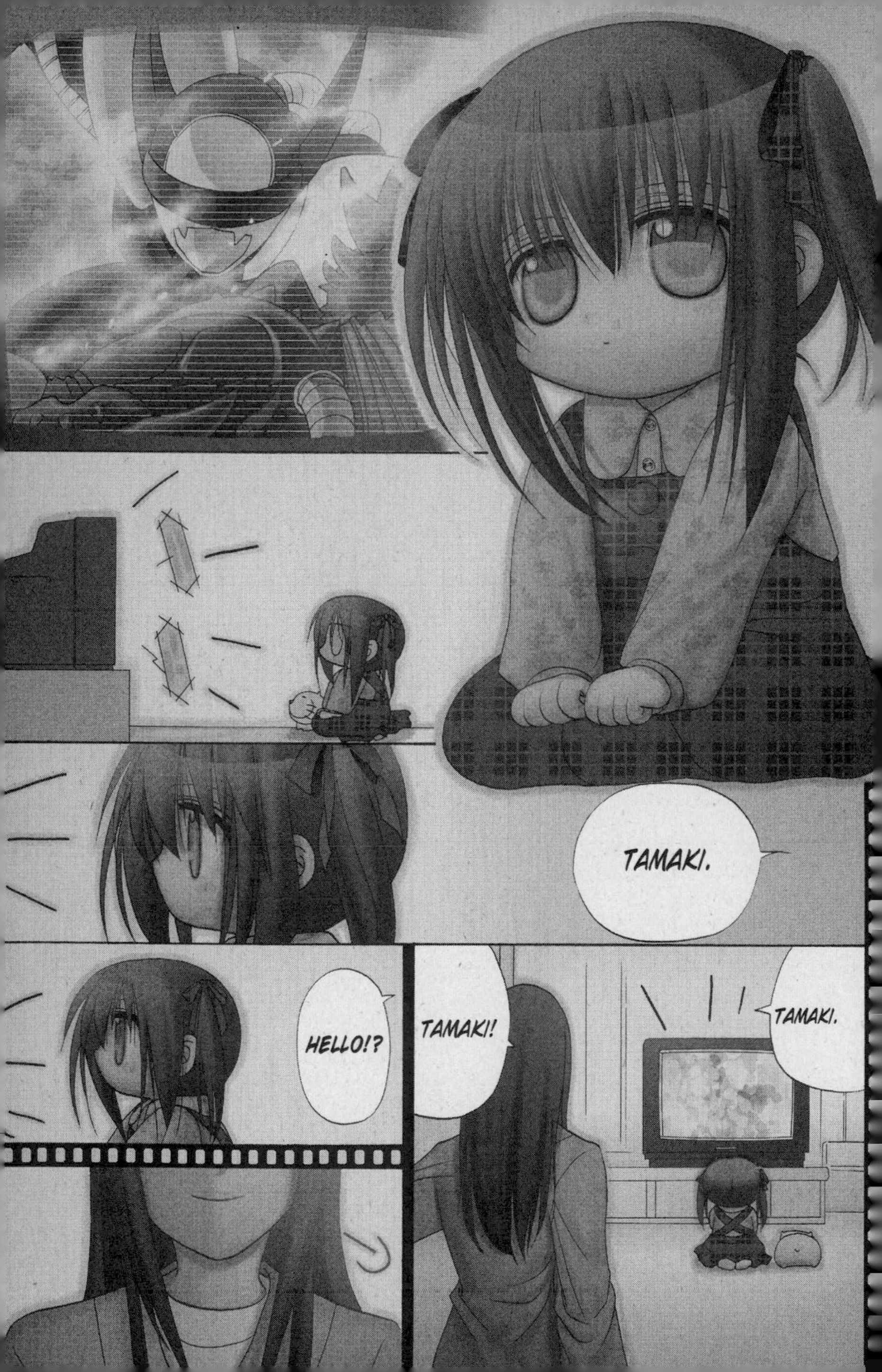
TAMAKI.
TAMAKI.
TAMAKI!
HELLO!?

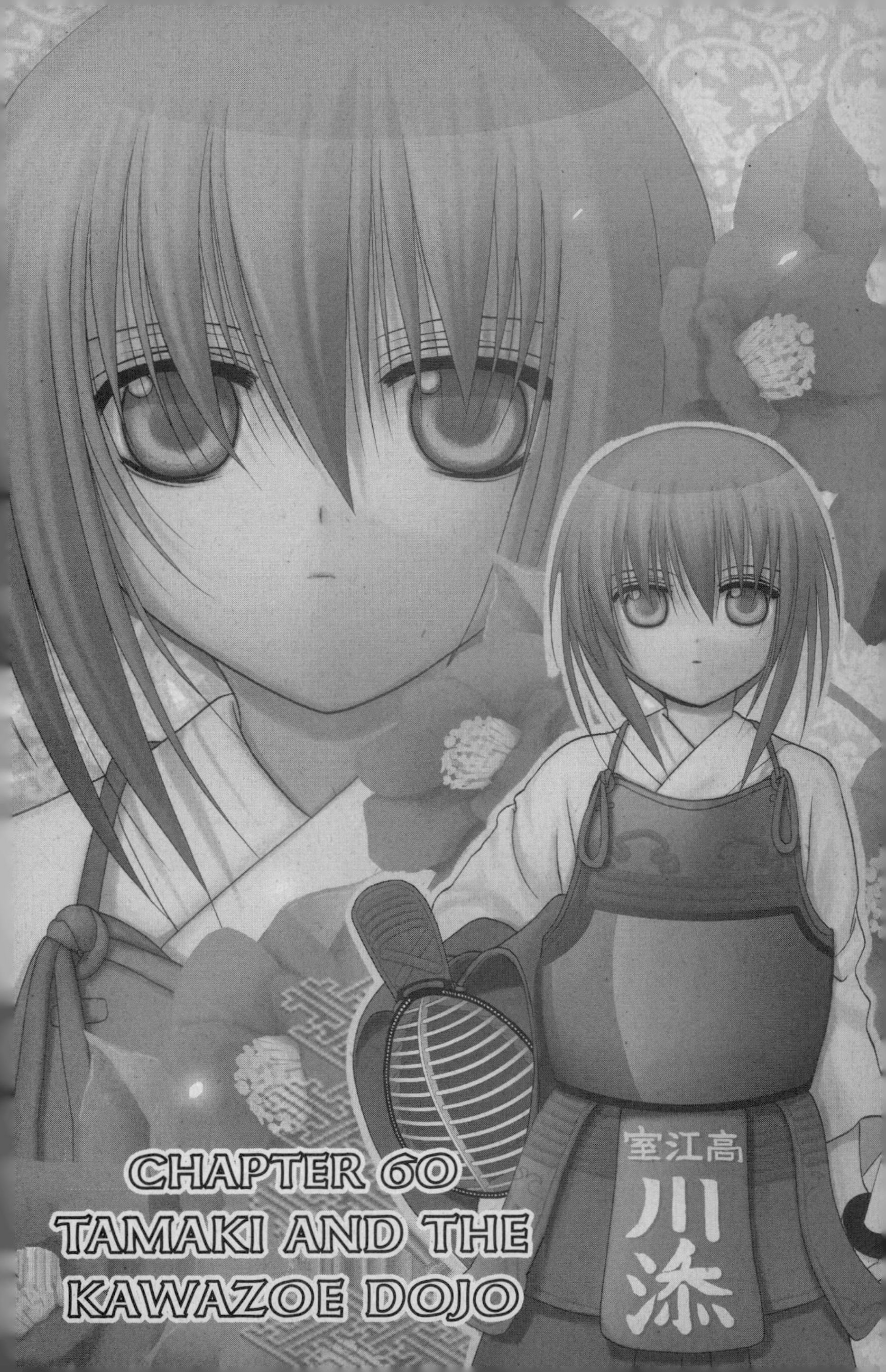
CHAPTER 60
TAMAKI AND THE KAWAZOE DOJO
室江高
川添

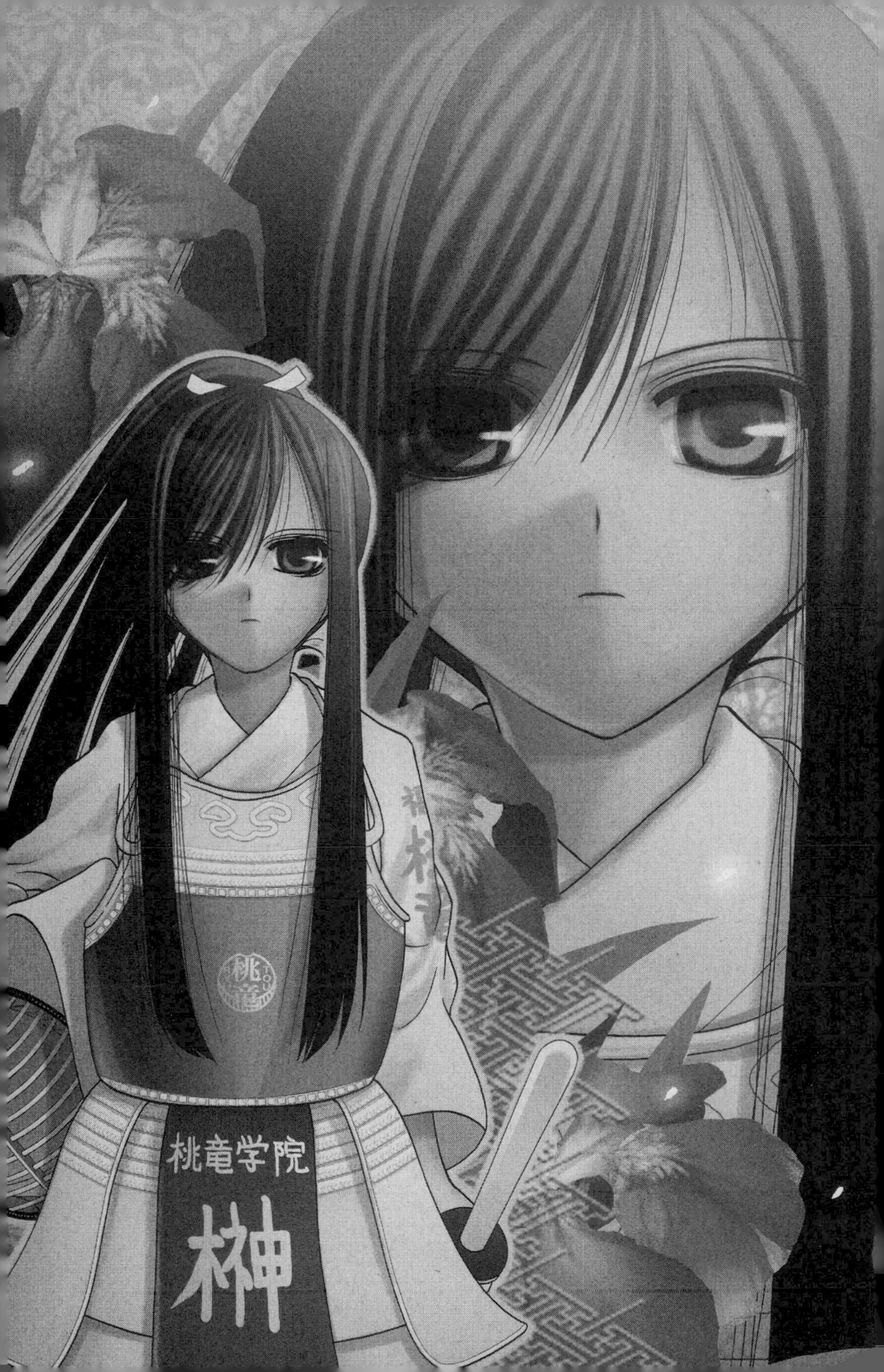
桃竜学院
榊

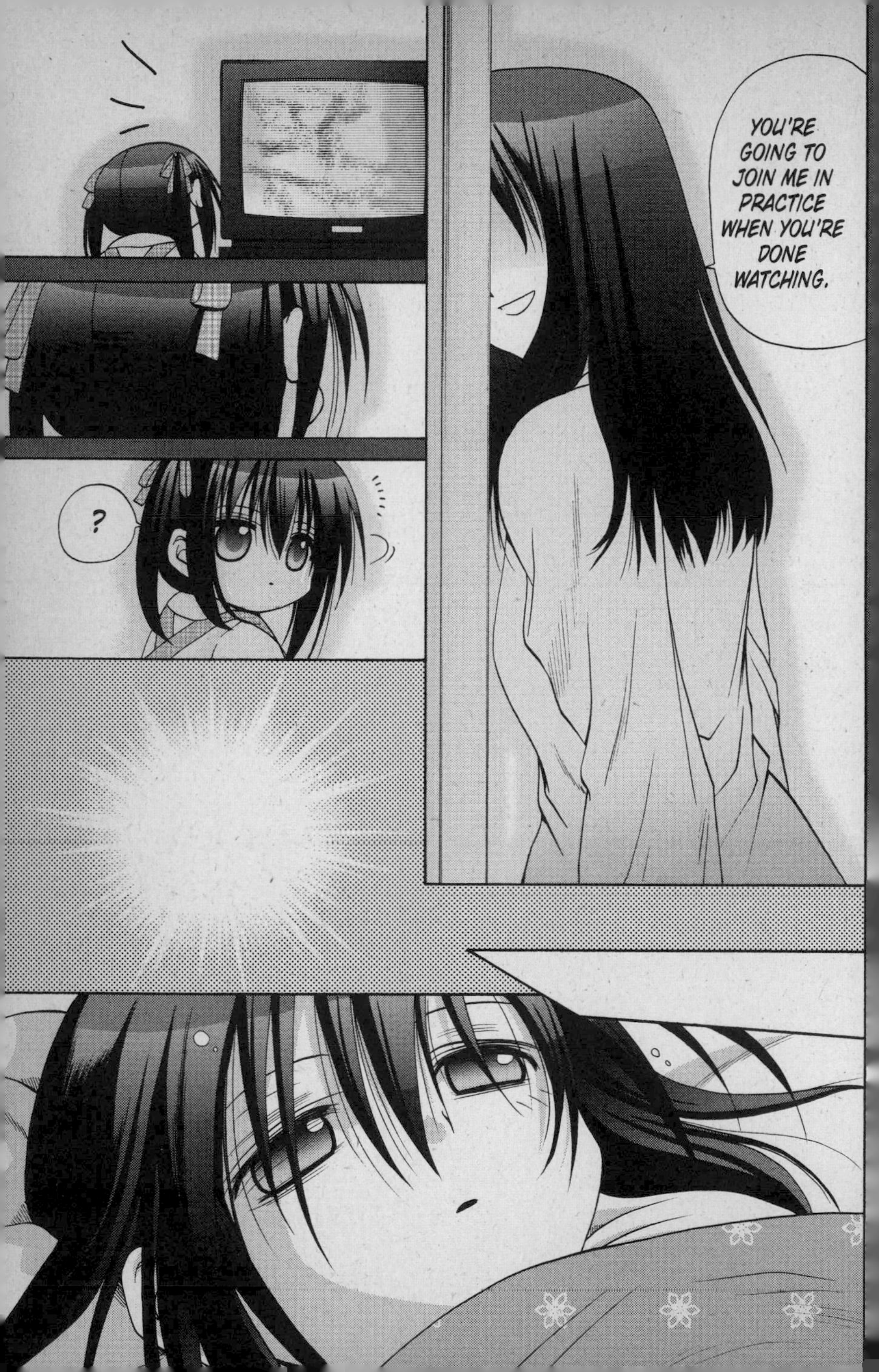
YOU'RE GOING TO JOIN ME IN PRACTICE WHEN YOU'RE DONE WATCHING.
?

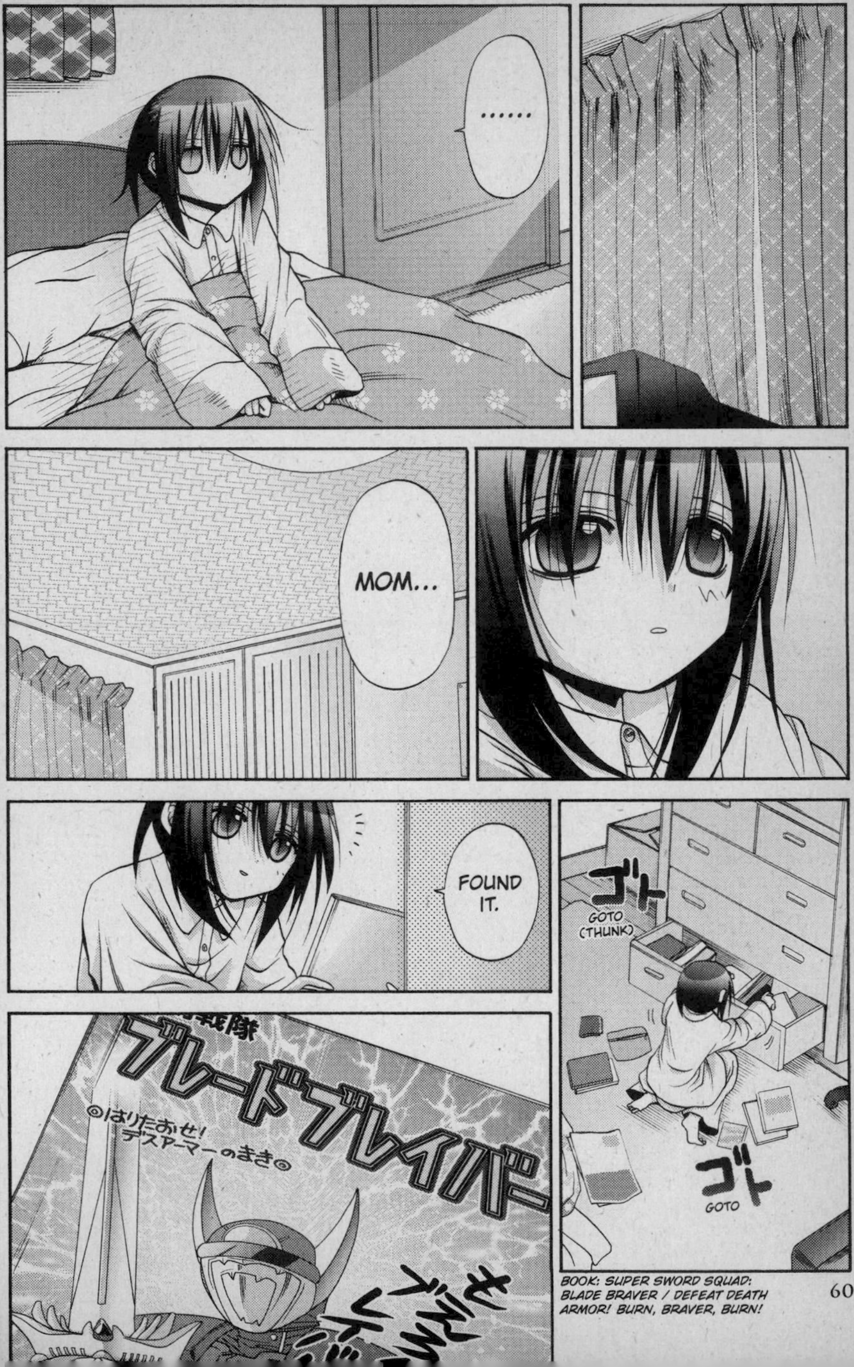
......
MOM...
ゴト
GOTO (THUNK)
ゴト
GOTO
FOUND IT.
ブレードブレイバー
◎はりたおせ! デスアーマーのまき◎
BOOK: SUPER SWORD SQUAD: BLADE BRAVER / DEFEAT DEATH ARMOR! BURN, BRAVER, BURN!

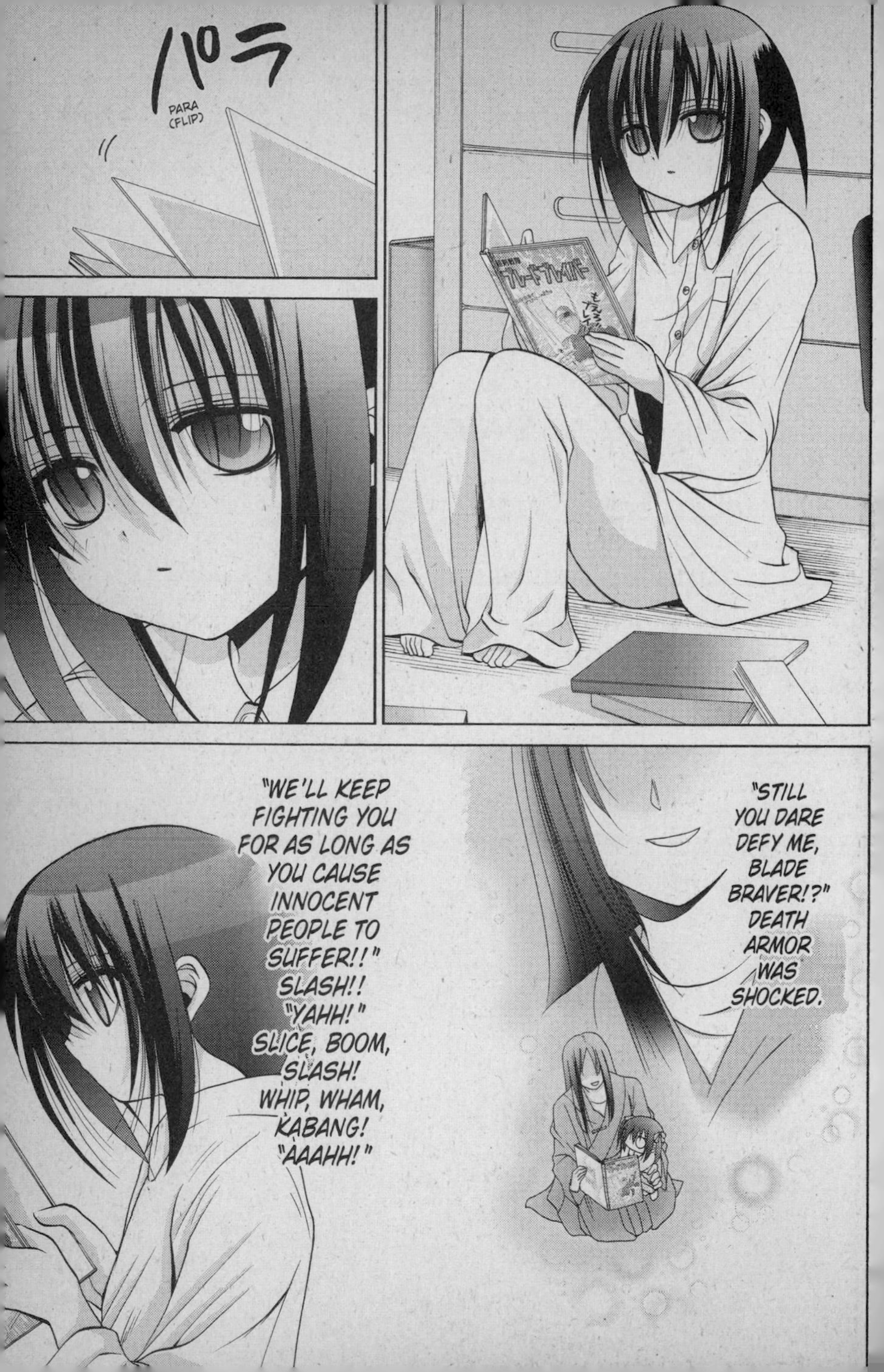
パラ
PARA (FLIP)
"STILL YOU DARE DEFY ME, BLADE BRAVER!?" DEATH ARMOR WAS SHOCKED.
"WE'LL KEEP FIGHTING YOU FOR AS LONG AS YOU CAUSE INNOCENT PEOPLE TO SUFFER!!" SLASH!! "YAHH!" SLICE, BOOM, SLASH! WHIP, WHAM, KABANG! "AAAHH!"

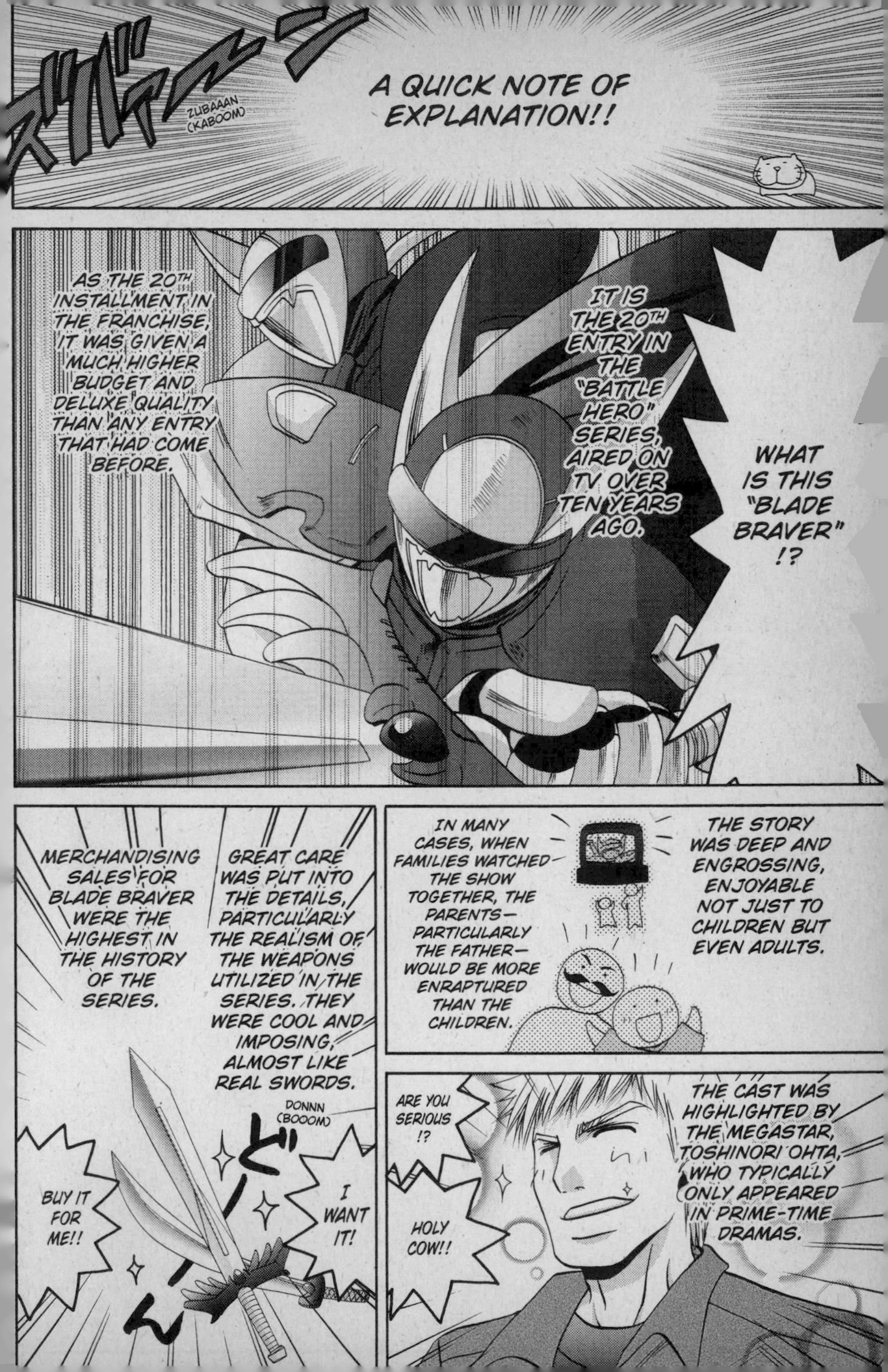
A QUICK NOTE OF EXPLANATION!!
ZUBAAAN (KABOOM)
WHAT IS THIS "BLADE BRAVER"!?
IT IS THE 20TH ENTRY IN THE "BATTLE HERO" SERIES, AIRED ON TV OVER TEN YEARS AGO.
AS THE 20TH INSTALLMENT IN THE FRANCHISE, IT WAS GIVEN A MUCH HIGHER BUDGET AND DELUXE QUALITY THAN ANY ENTRY THAT HAD COME BEFORE.
THE STORY WAS DEEP AND ENGROSSING, ENJOYABLE NOT JUST TO CHILDREN BUT EVEN ADULTS.
IN MANY CASES, WHEN FAMILIES WATCHED THE SHOW TOGETHER, THE PARENTS—PARTICULARLY THE FATHER—WOULD BE MORE ENRAPTURED THAN THE CHILDREN.
THE CAST WAS HIGHLIGHTED BY THE MEGASTAR, TOSHINORI OHTA, WHO TYPICALLY ONLY APPEARED IN PRIME-TIME DRAMAS.
ARE YOU SERIOUS!?
HOLY COW!!
GREAT CARE WAS PUT INTO THE DETAILS, PARTICULARLY THE REALISM OF THE WEAPONS UTILIZED IN THE SERIES. THEY WERE COOL AND IMPOSING, ALMOST LIKE REAL SWORDS.
MERCHANDISING SALES FOR BLADE BRAVER WERE THE HIGHEST IN THE HISTORY OF THE SERIES.
DONNN (BOOOM)
I WANT IT!
BUY IT FOR ME!!

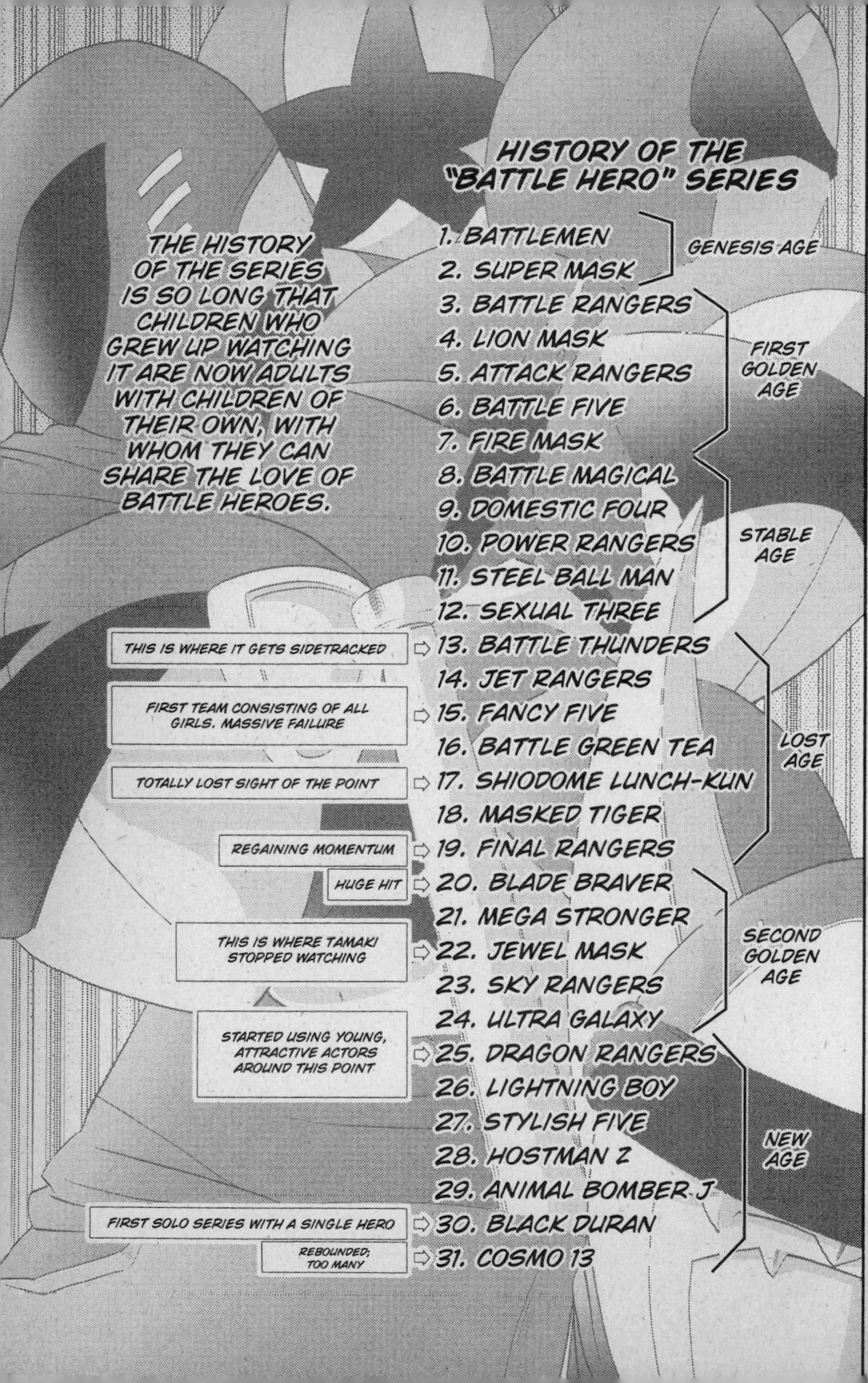
HISTORY OF THE "BATTLE HERO" SERIES
1. BATTLEMEN
2. SUPER MASK
GENESIS AGE
3. BATTLE RANGERS
4. LION MASK
5. ATTACK RANGERS
6. BATTLE FIVE
7. FIRE MASK
FIRST GOLDEN AGE
8. BATTLE MAGICAL
9. DOMESTIC FOUR
10. POWER RANGERS
11. STEEL BALL MAN
12. SEXUAL THREE
STABLE AGE
13. BATTLE THUNDERS
THIS IS WHERE IT GETS SIDETRACKED
14. JET RANGERS
15. FANCY FIVE
FIRST TEAM CONSISTING OF ALL GIRLS. MASSIVE FAILURE
16. BATTLE GREEN TEA
17. SHIODOME LUNCH-KUN
TOTALLY LOST SIGHT OF THE POINT
18. MASKED TIGER
19. FINAL RANGERS
REGAINING MOMENTUM
LOST AGE
20. BLADE BRAVER
HUGE HIT
21. MEGA STRONGER
22. JEWEL MASK
THIS IS WHERE TAMAKI STOPPED WATCHING
23. SKY RANGERS
24. ULTRA GALAXY
SECOND GOLDEN AGE
25. DRAGON RANGERS
STARTED USING YOUNG, ATTRACTIVE ACTORS AROUND THIS POINT
26. LIGHTNING BOY
27. STYLISH FIVE
28. HOSTMAN Z
29. ANIMAL BOMBER J
30. BLACK DURAN
FIRST SOLO SERIES WITH A SINGLE HERO
31. COSMO 13
REBOUNDED; TOO MANY
NEW AGE
THE HISTORY OF THE SERIES IS SO LONG THAT CHILDREN WHO GREW UP WATCHING IT ARE NOW ADULTS WITH CHILDREN OF THEIR OWN, WITH WHOM THEY CAN SHARE THE LOVE OF BATTLE HEROES.

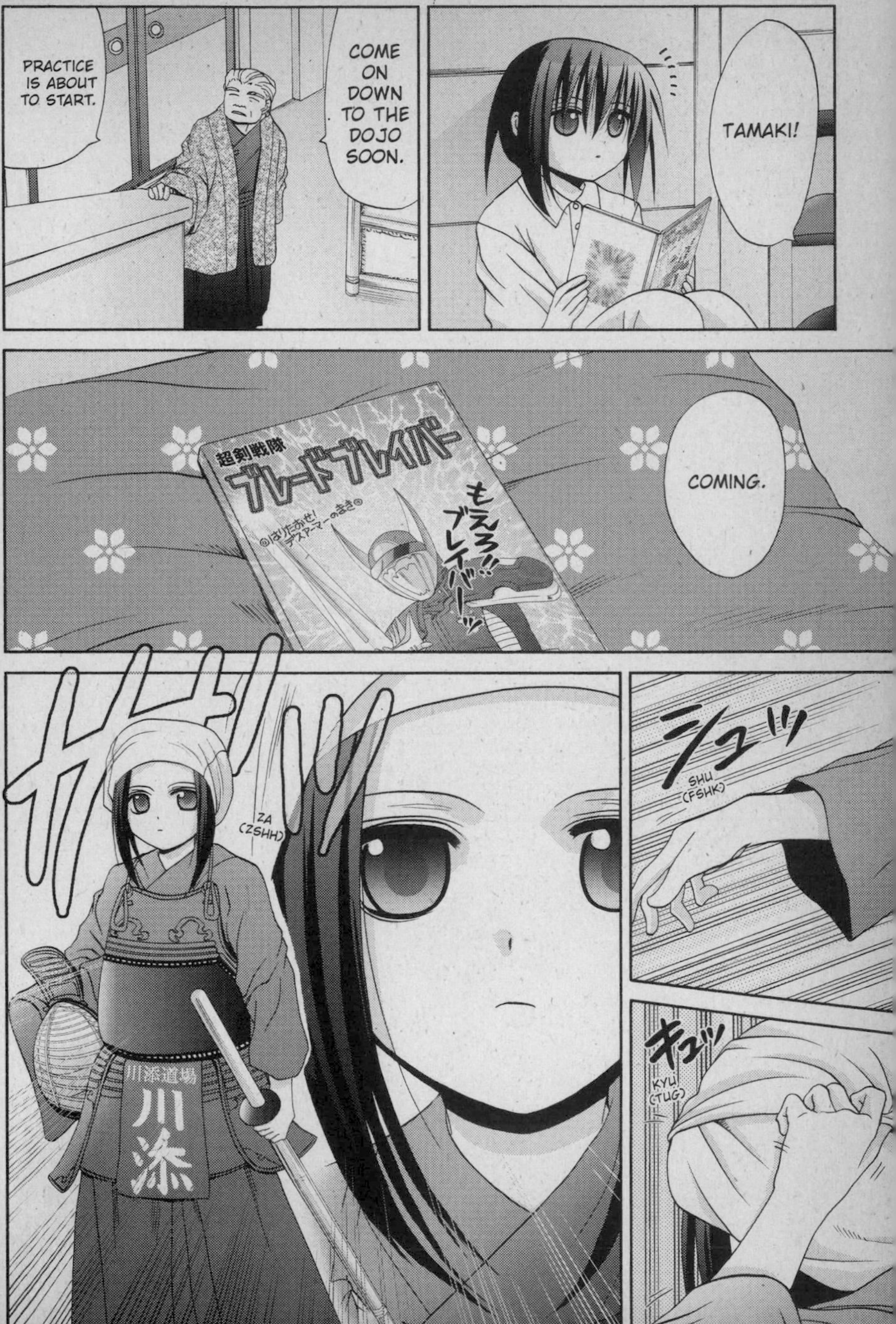
TAMAKI!
COME ON DOWN TO THE DOJO SOON.
PRACTICE IS ABOUT TO START.
COMING.
超剣戦隊
ブレードブレイバー
◎はりたおせ！デスアーマーのまき◎
もえろブレイバー!!
シュッ
SHU (FSHK)
キュッ
KYU (TUG)
ザッ
ZA (ZSHH)
川添道場
川添

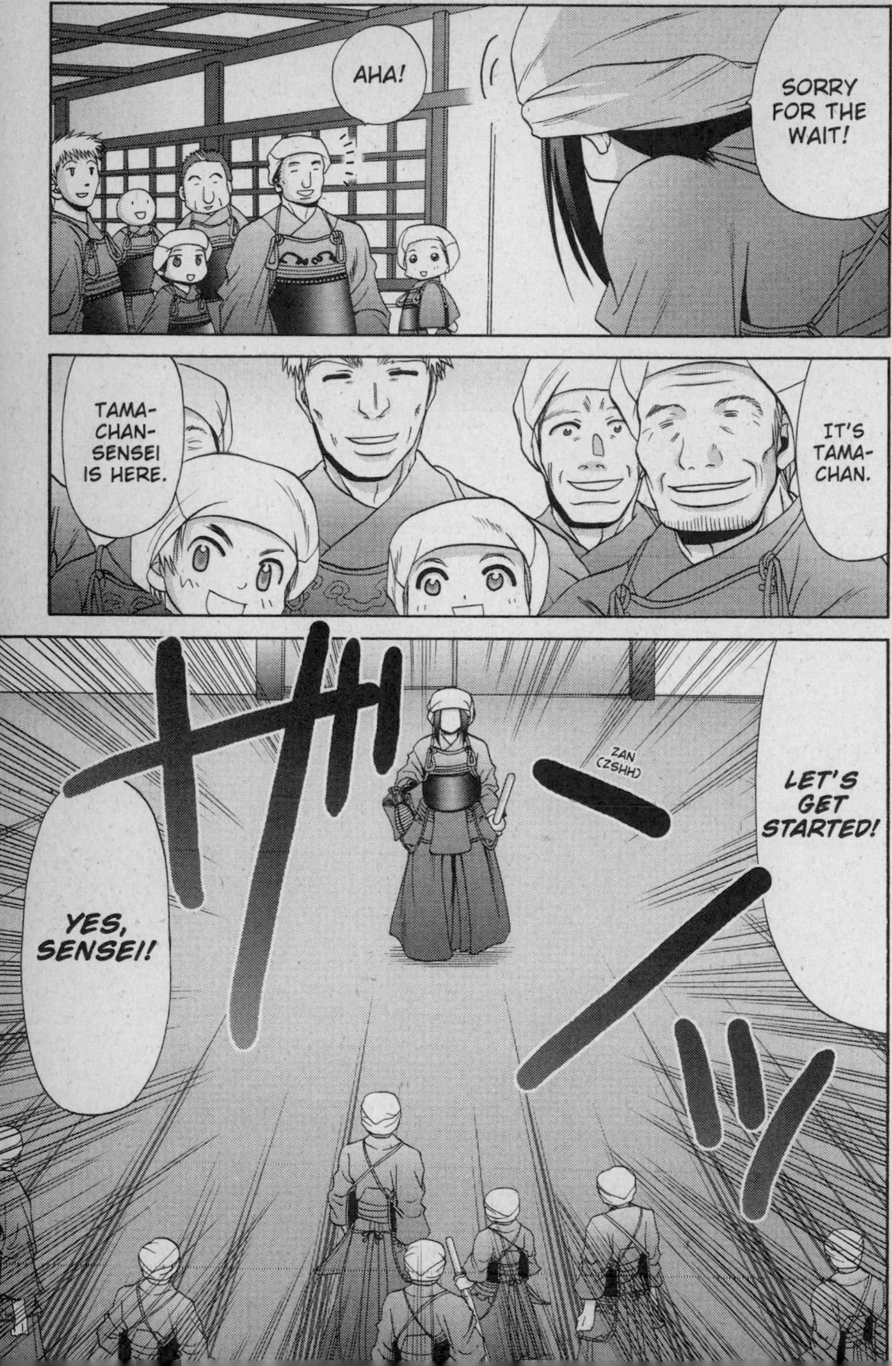
SORRY FOR THE WAIT!
AHA!
IT'S TAMA-CHAN.
TAMA-CHAN-SENSEI IS HERE.
LET'S GET STARTED!
ZAN (ZSHH)
YES, SENSEI!

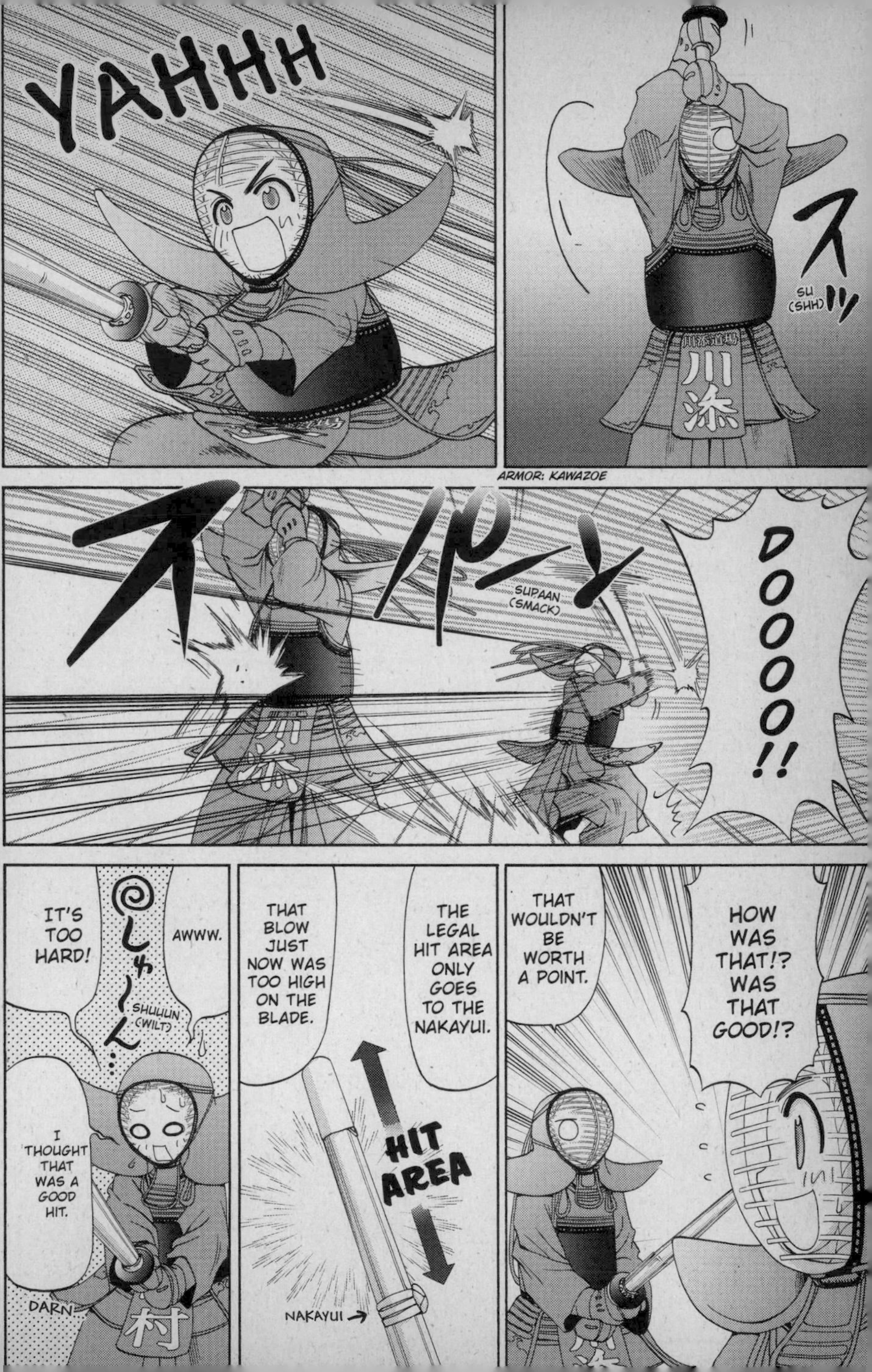

SU (SHH)
川添道場
川添
YAHHH
ARMOR: KAWAZOE
DOOOOO!!
SUPAAN (SMACK)
HOW WAS THAT!? WAS THAT GOOD!?
THAT WOULDN'T BE WORTH A POINT.
THE LEGAL HIT AREA ONLY GOES TO THE NAKAYUI.
THAT BLOW JUST NOW WAS TOO HIGH ON THE BLADE.
HIT AREA
NAKAYUI →
AWWW.
IT'S TOO HARD!
SHUUUN (WILT)
I THOUGHT THAT WAS A GOOD HIT.
DARN...
村

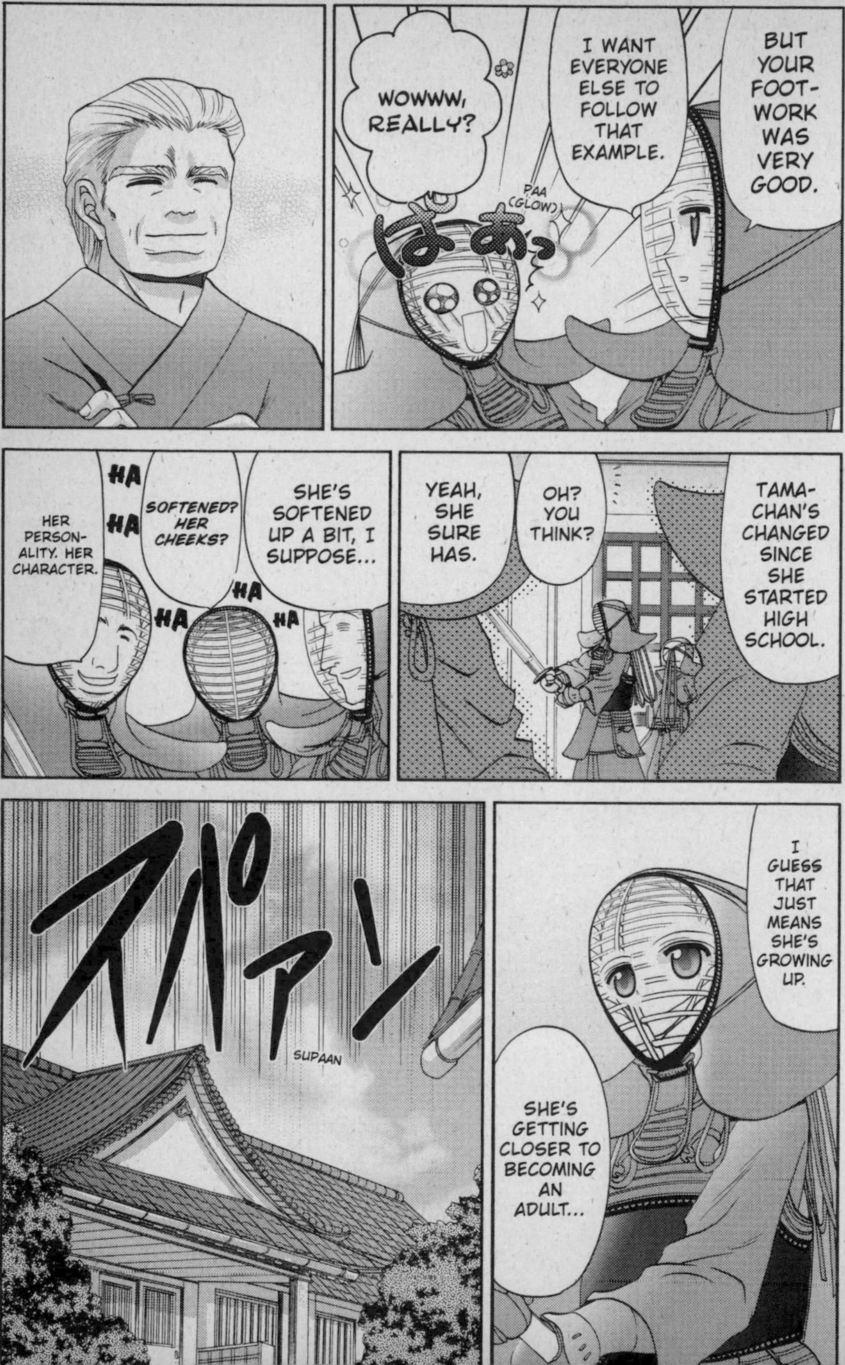
BUT YOUR FOOT-WORK WAS VERY GOOD.
I WANT EVERYONE ELSE TO FOLLOW THAT EXAMPLE.
ぱあっ
PAA (GLOW)
WOWWW, REALLY?
TAMA-CHAN'S CHANGED SINCE SHE STARTED HIGH SCHOOL.
OH? YOU THINK?
YEAH, SHE SURE HAS.
SHE'S SOFTENED UP A BIT, I SUPPOSE...
SOFTENED? HER CHEEKS?
HER PERSONALITY. HER CHARACTER.
HA HA HA HA HA HA
I GUESS THAT JUST MEANS SHE'S GROWING UP.
SHE'S GETTING CLOSER TO BECOMING AN ADULT...
スパァン
SUPAAN

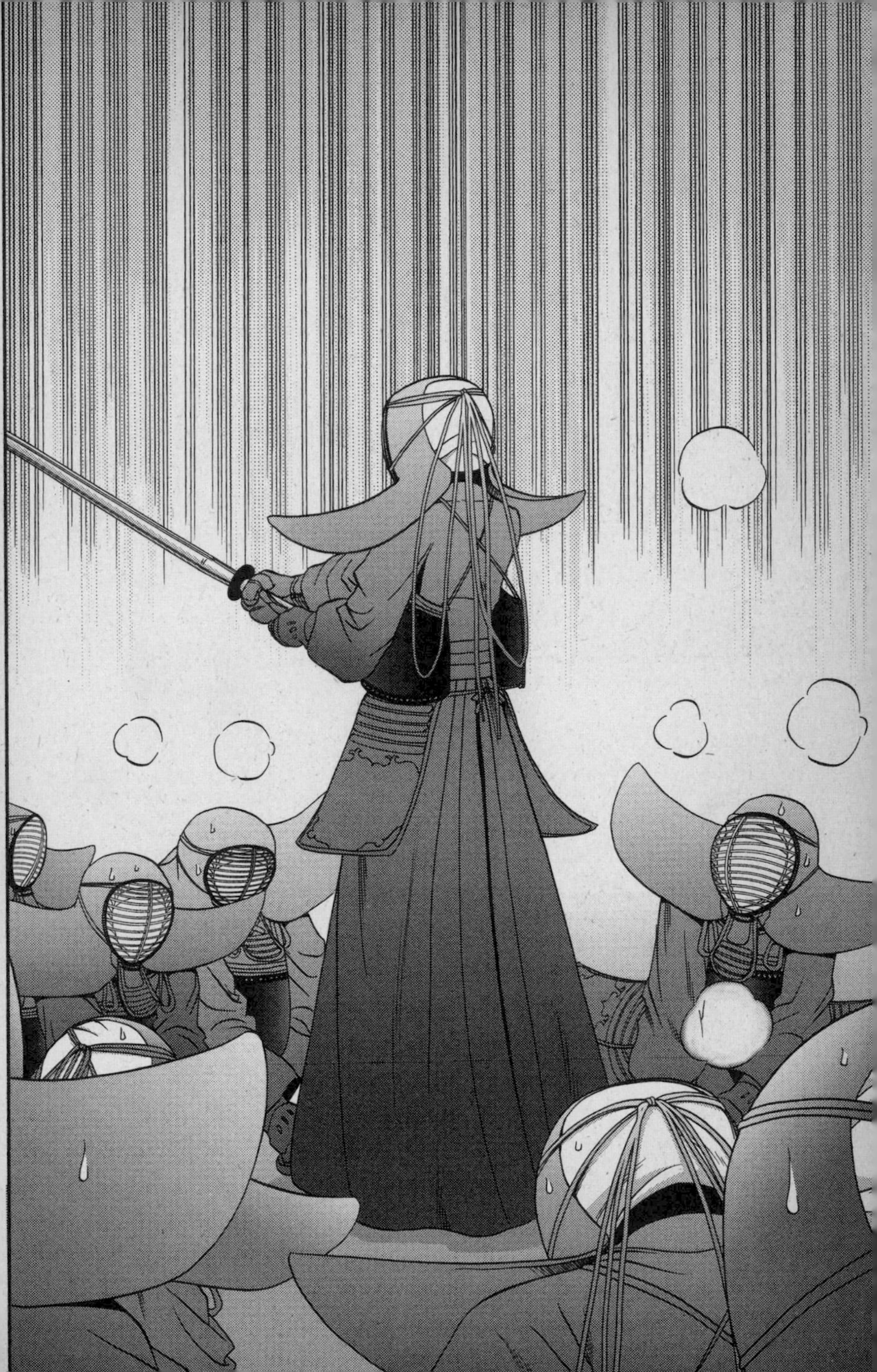

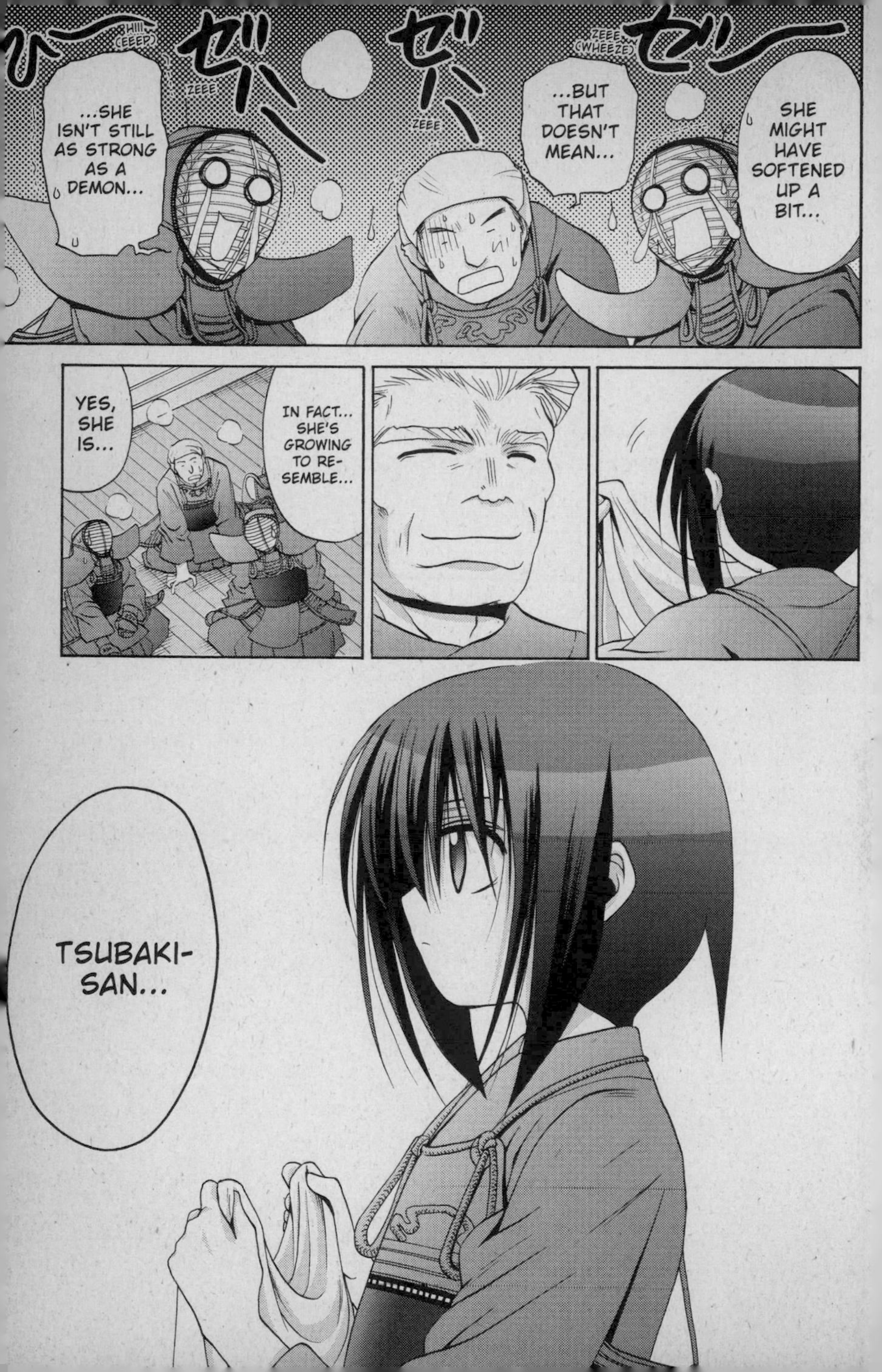
ゼー
ZEEE (WHEEZE)
SHE MIGHT HAVE SOFTENED UP A BIT...
...BUT THAT DOESN'T MEAN...
ZEEE
ゼー
ZEEE
ゼー
HIII (EEEP)
ひー
...SHE ISN'T STILL AS STRONG AS A DEMON...
IN FACT... SHE'S GROWING TO RE-SEMBLE...
YES, SHE IS...
TSUBAKI-SAN...

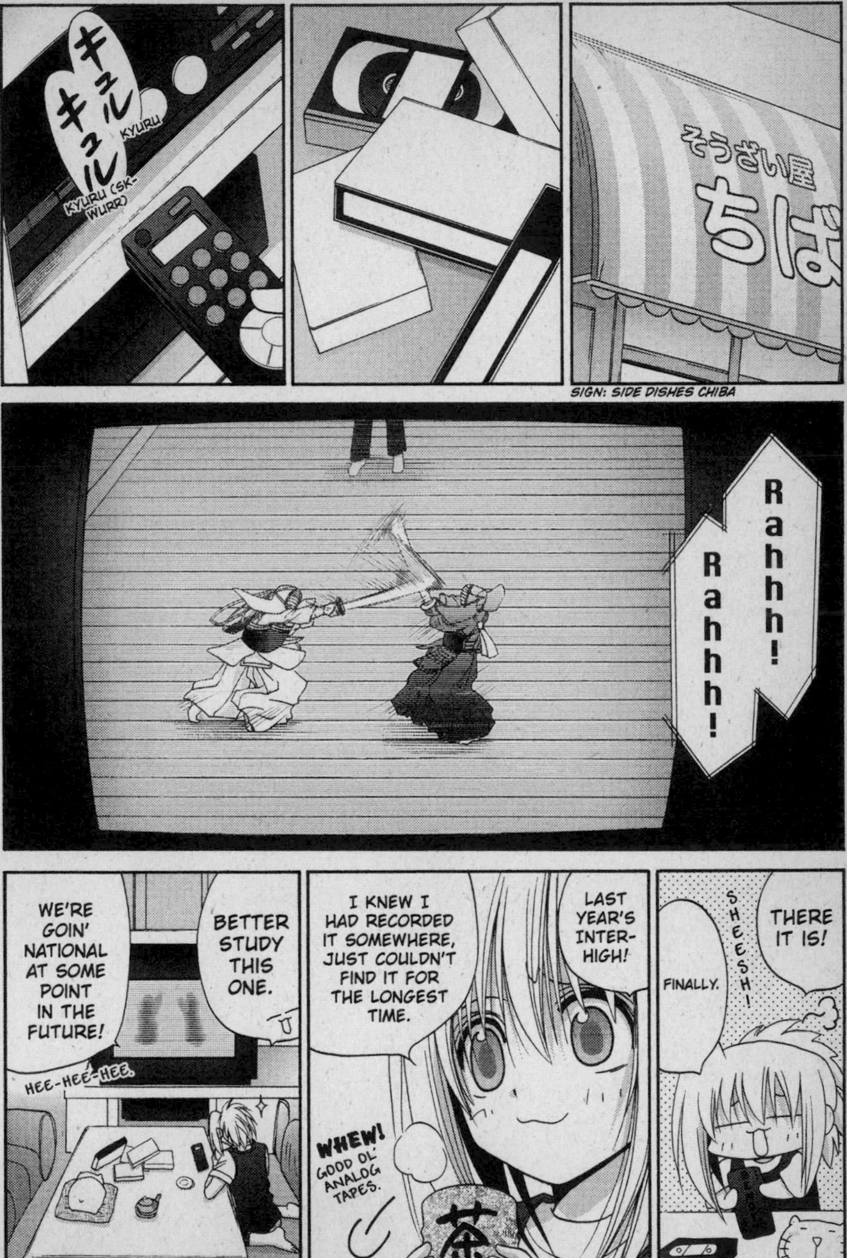

そうざい屋 ちば
SIGN: SIDE DISHES CHIBA
キュルキュル
KYURU KYURU (SK-WURR)
Rahhh!
Rahhh!
THERE IT IS!
SHEESH!
FINALLY.
LAST YEAR'S INTER-HIGH!
I KNEW I HAD RECORDED IT SOMEWHERE, JUST COULDN'T FIND IT FOR THE LONGEST TIME.
WHEW! GOOD OL' ANALOG TAPES.
茶
CUP: TEA
BETTER STUDY THIS ONE.
WE'RE GOIN' NATIONAL AT SOME POINT IN THE FUTURE!
HEE-HEE-HEE.

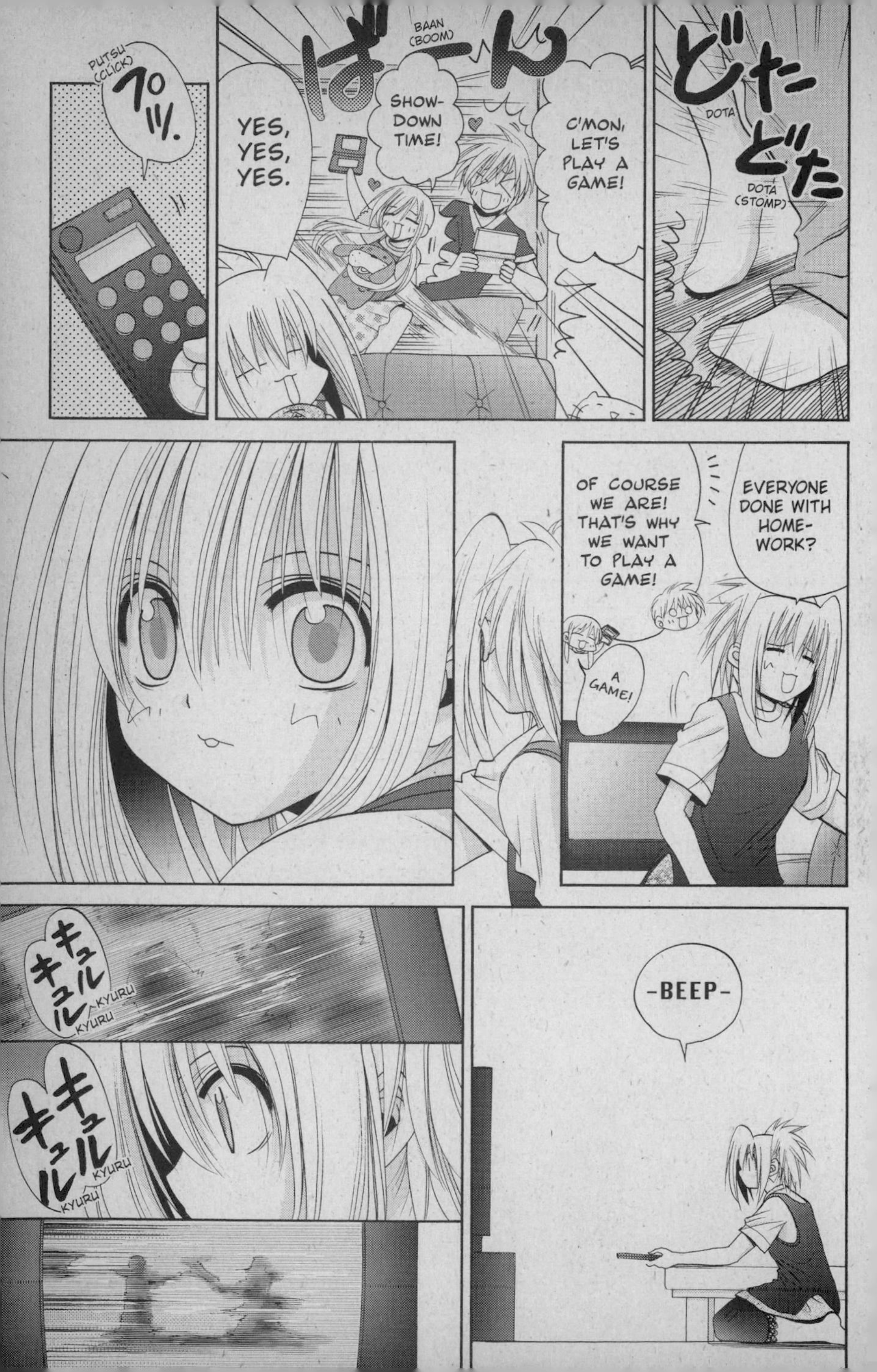
どたーどた
DOTA
DOTA (STOMP)
ばーん
BAAN (BOOM)
C'MON, LET'S PLAY A GAME!
SHOW-DOWN TIME!
YES, YES, YES.
プツ
PUTSU (CLICK)
EVERYONE DONE WITH HOME-WORK?
OF COURSE WE ARE! THAT'S WHY WE WANT TO PLAY A GAME!
A GAME!
-BEEP-
キュルキュル
KYURU KYURU
キュルキュル
KYURU KYURU

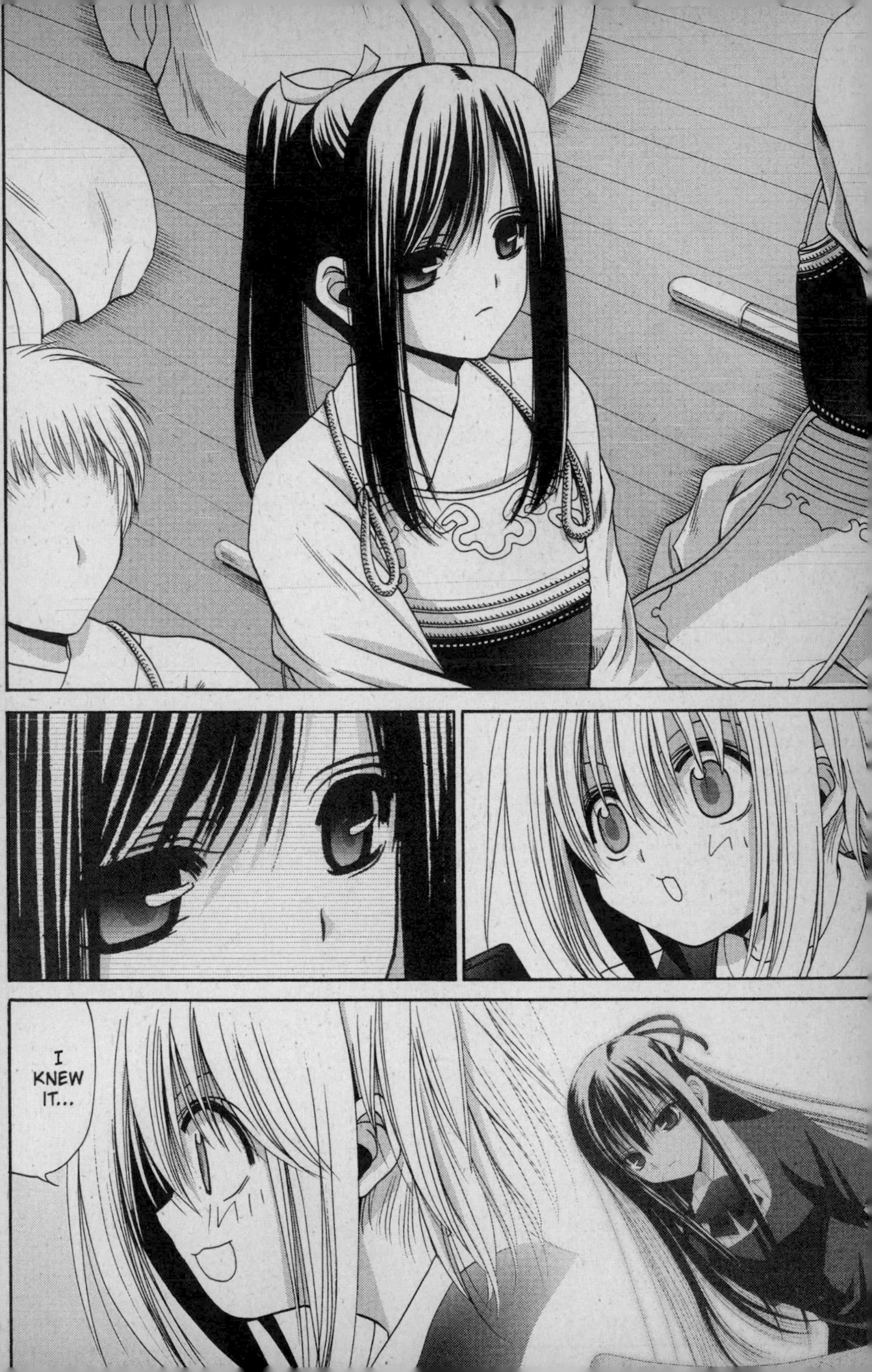
I KNEW IT...

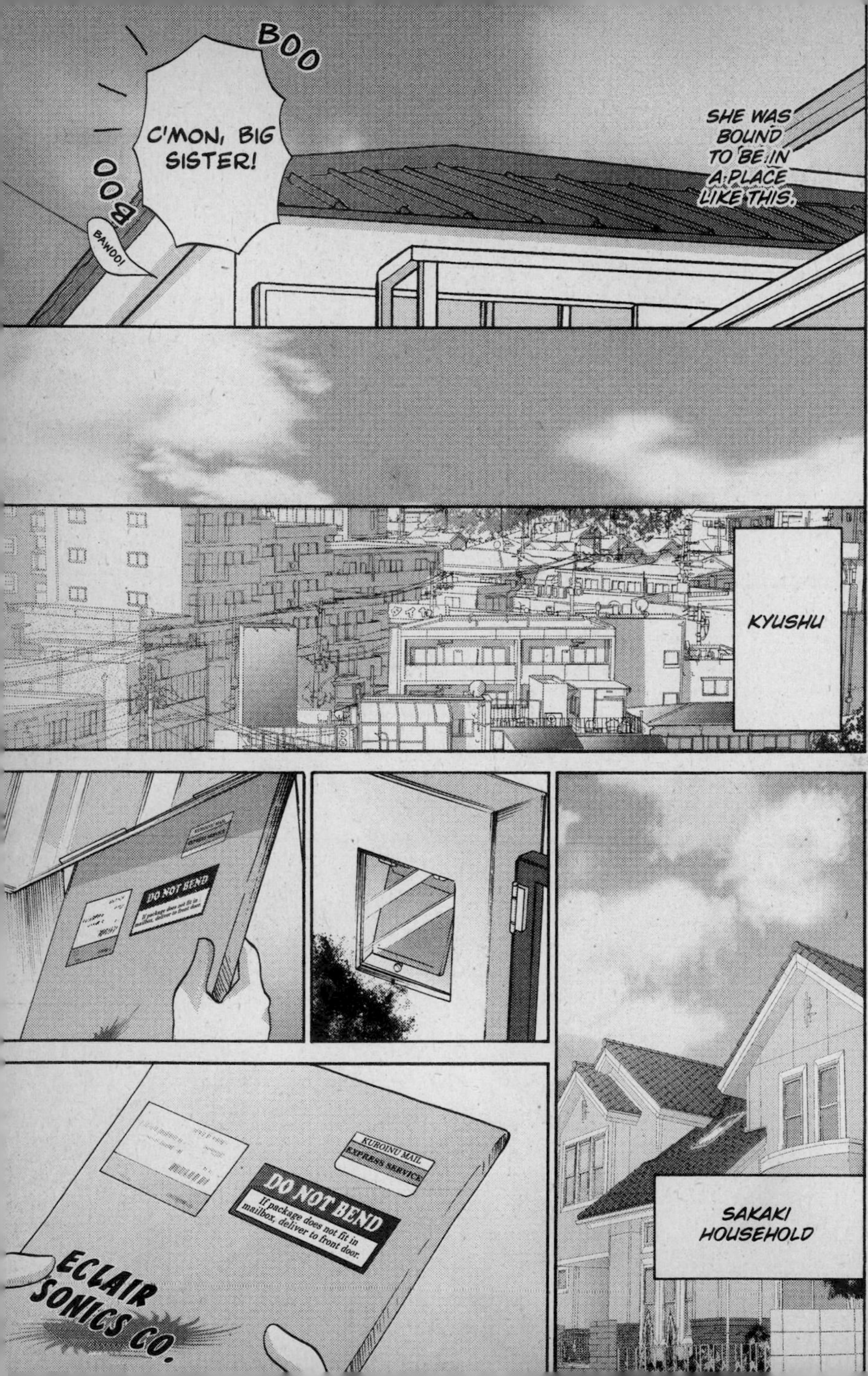
SHE WAS BOUND TO BE IN A PLACE LIKE THIS.
BOO
C'MON, BIG SISTER!
BOO
BAWOO!
KYUSHU
SAKAKI HOUSEHOLD
DO NOT BEND
KUROINU MAIL
EXPRESS SERVICE
DO NOT BEND
If package does not fit in mailbox, deliver to front door.
ECLAIR SONICS CO.

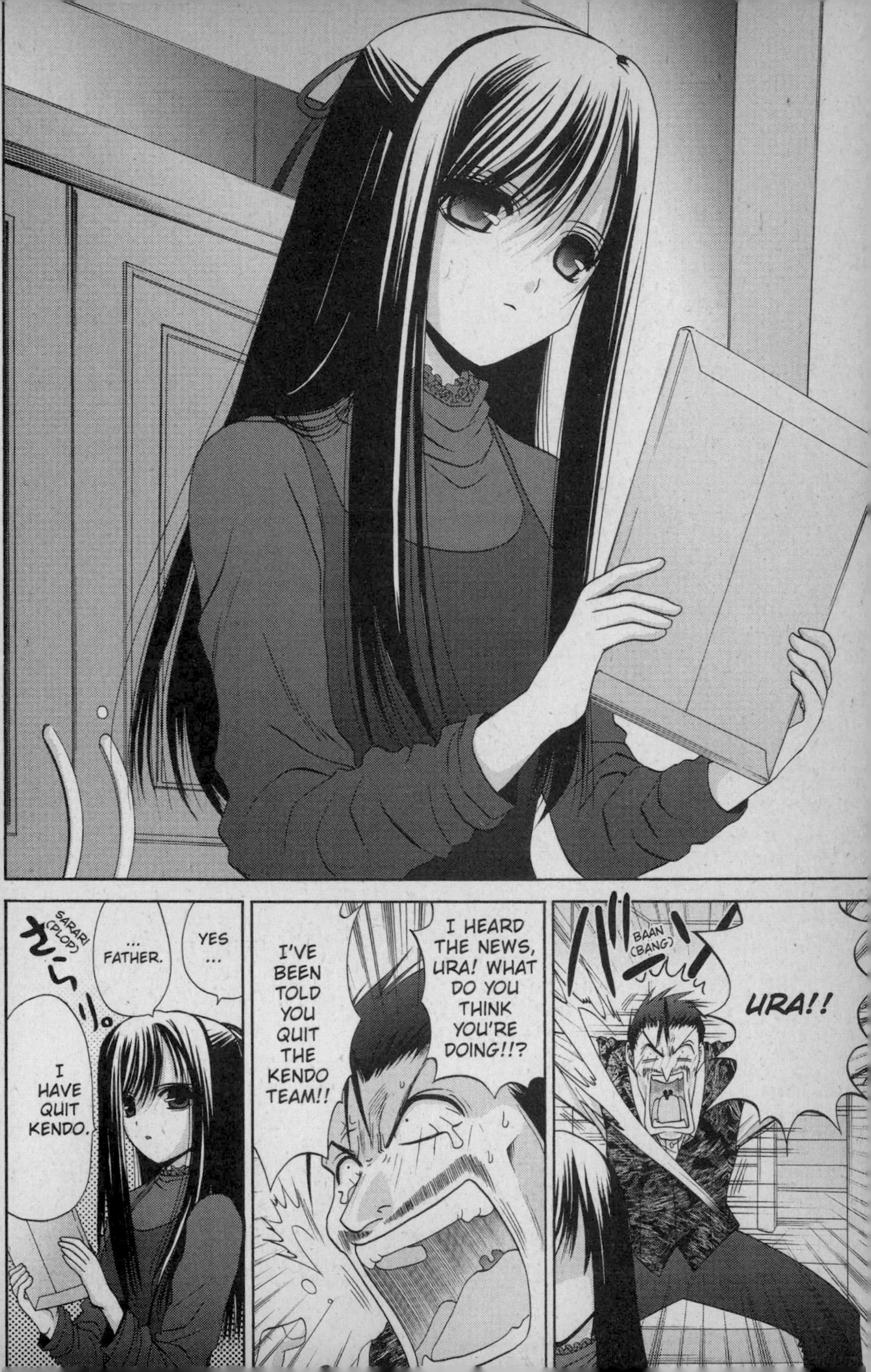
BAAN (BANG)
URA!!
I HEARD THE NEWS, URA! WHAT DO YOU THINK YOU'RE DOING!!?
I'VE BEEN TOLD YOU QUIT THE KENDO TEAM!!
YES ...
... FATHER.
SARARI (PLOP)
I HAVE QUIT KENDO.

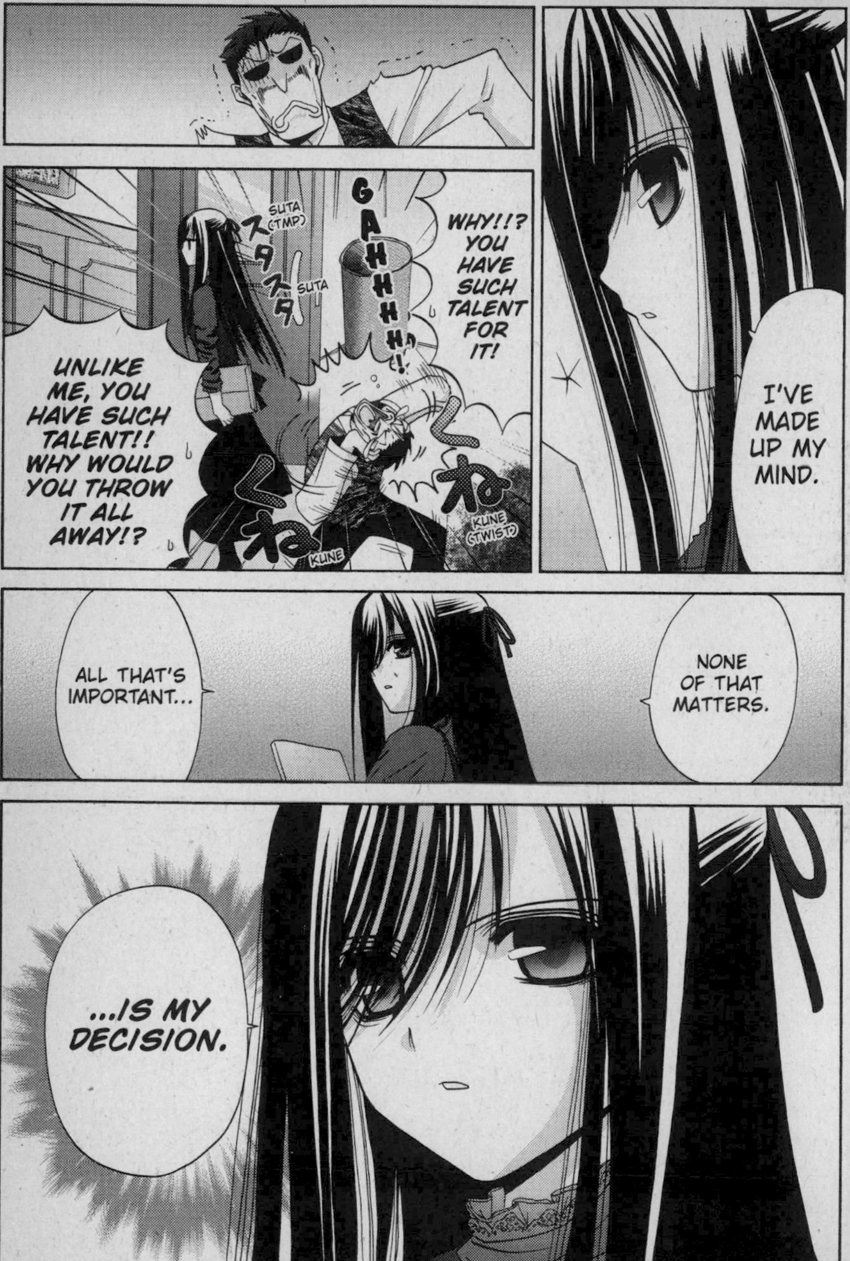
I'VE MADE UP MY MIND.
WHY!!? YOU HAVE SUCH TALENT FOR IT!
GAHHHHH!
スタスタ
SUTA (TMP)
SUTA
くねくね
KUNE (TWIST)
KUNE
UNLIKE ME, YOU HAVE SUCH TALENT!! WHY WOULD YOU THROW IT ALL AWAY!?
NONE OF THAT MATTERS.
ALL THAT'S IMPORTANT...
...IS MY DECISION.

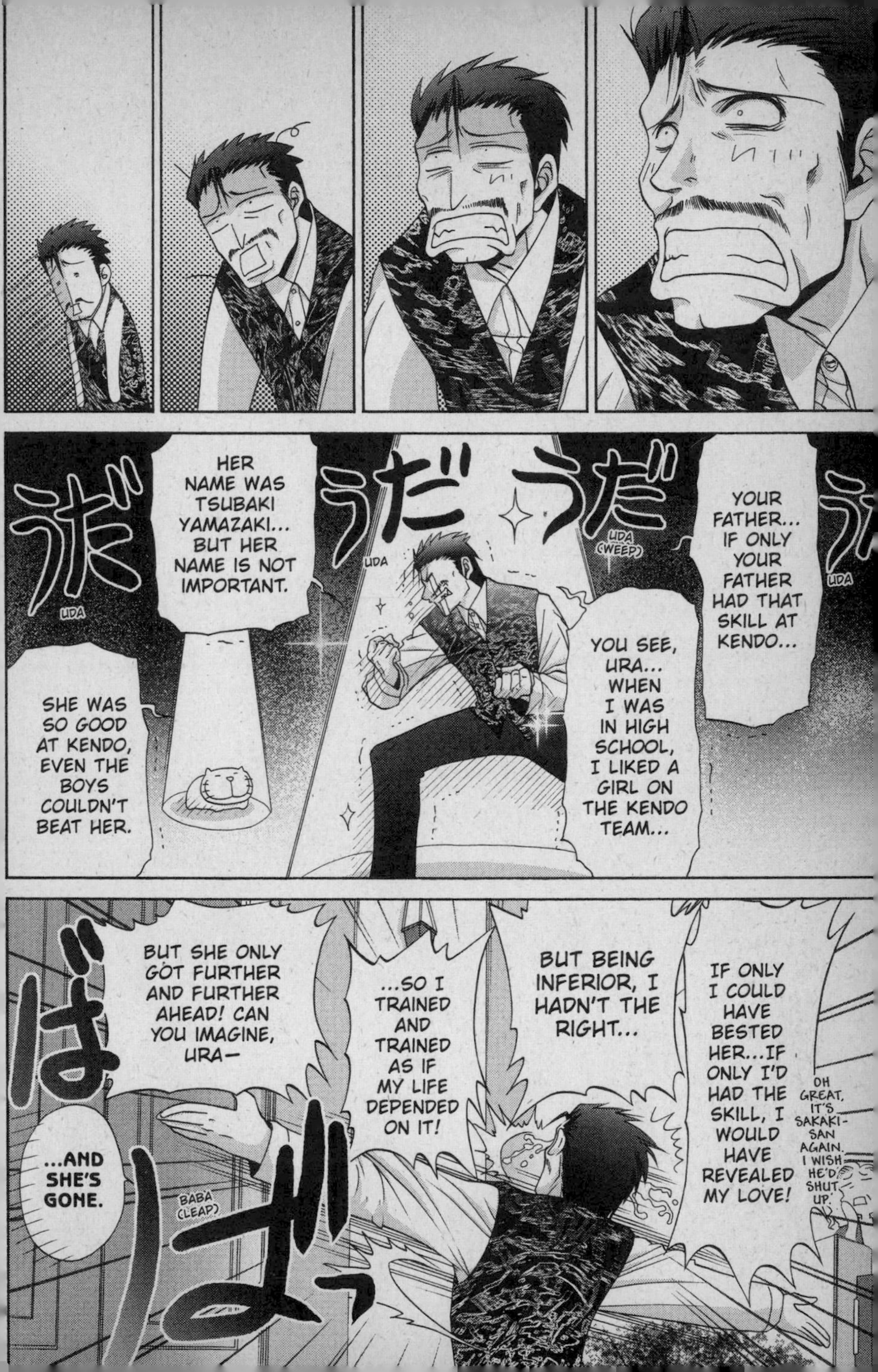
YOUR FATHER... IF ONLY YOUR FATHER HAD THAT SKILL AT KENDO...
UDA
うだ
UDA (WEEP)
YOU SEE, URA... WHEN I WAS IN HIGH SCHOOL, I LIKED A GIRL ON THE KENDO TEAM...
うだ
UDA
HER NAME WAS TSUBAKI YAMAZAKI... BUT HER NAME IS NOT IMPORTANT.
SHE WAS SO GOOD AT KENDO, EVEN THE BOYS COULDN'T BEAT HER.
うだ
UDA
OH GREAT, IT'S SAKAKI-SAN AGAIN. I WISH HE'D SHUT UP.
IF ONLY I COULD HAVE BESTED HER...IF ONLY I'D HAD THE SKILL, I WOULD HAVE REVEALED MY LOVE!
BUT BEING INFERIOR, I HADN'T THE RIGHT...
...SO I TRAINED AND TRAINED AS IF MY LIFE DEPENDED ON IT!
BUT SHE ONLY GOT FURTHER AND FURTHER AHEAD! CAN YOU IMAGINE, URA—
...AND SHE'S GONE.
ばっ
BABA (LEAP)

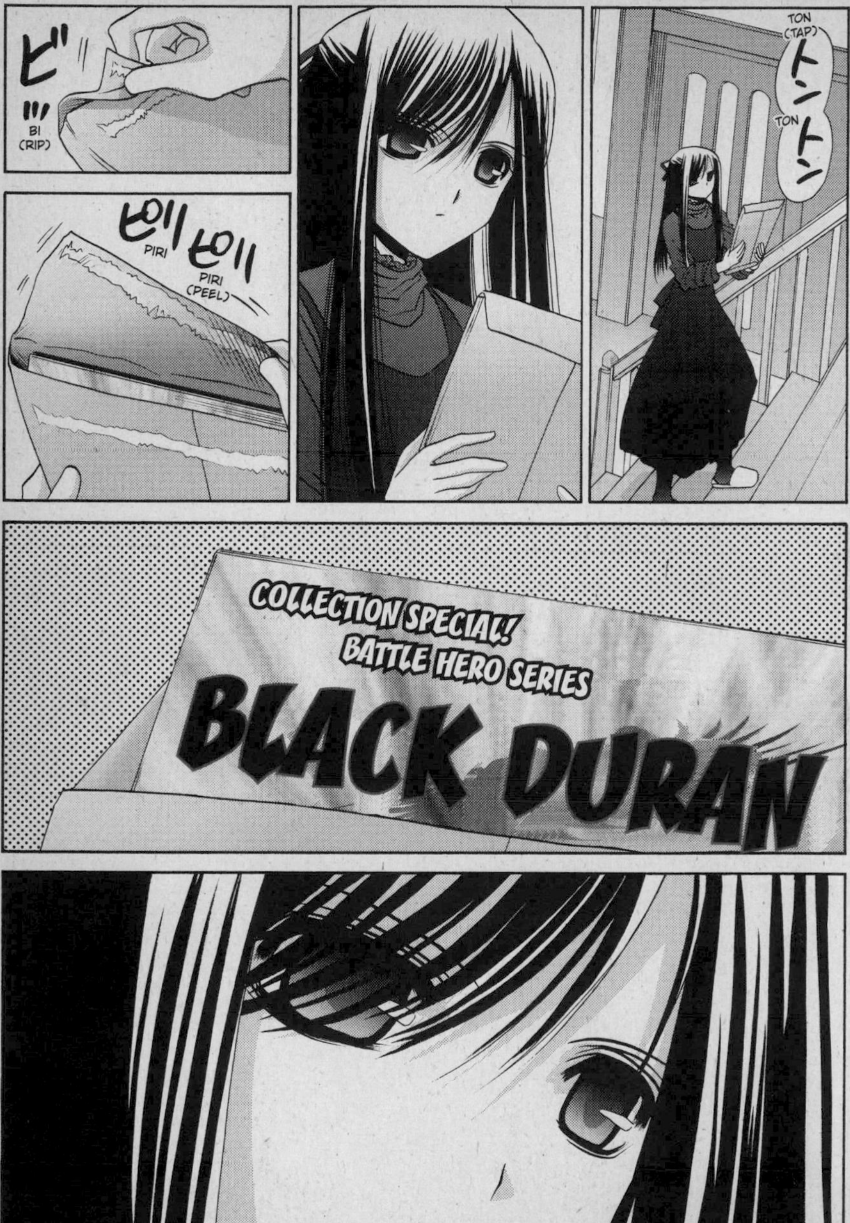
トン
TON (TAP)
トン
TON
ビッ
BI (RIP)
ピリ
PIRI
ピリ
PIRI (PEEL)
COLLECTION SPECIAL!
BATTLE HERO SERIES
BLACK DURAN

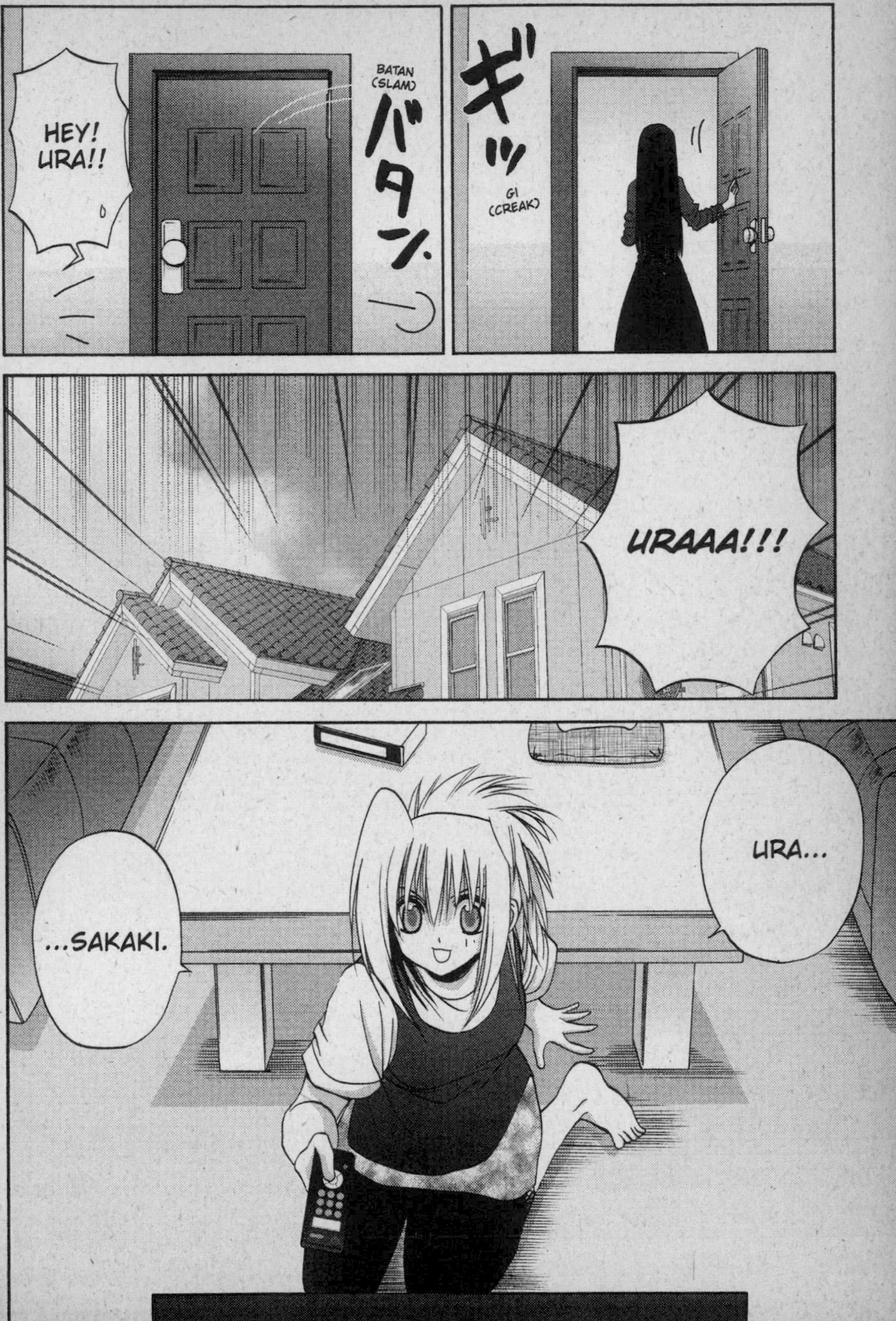
ギッ
GI (CREAK)
BATAN (SLAM)
バタン
HEY! URA!!
URAAA!!!
URA...
...SAKAKI.

BAMBOO BLADE

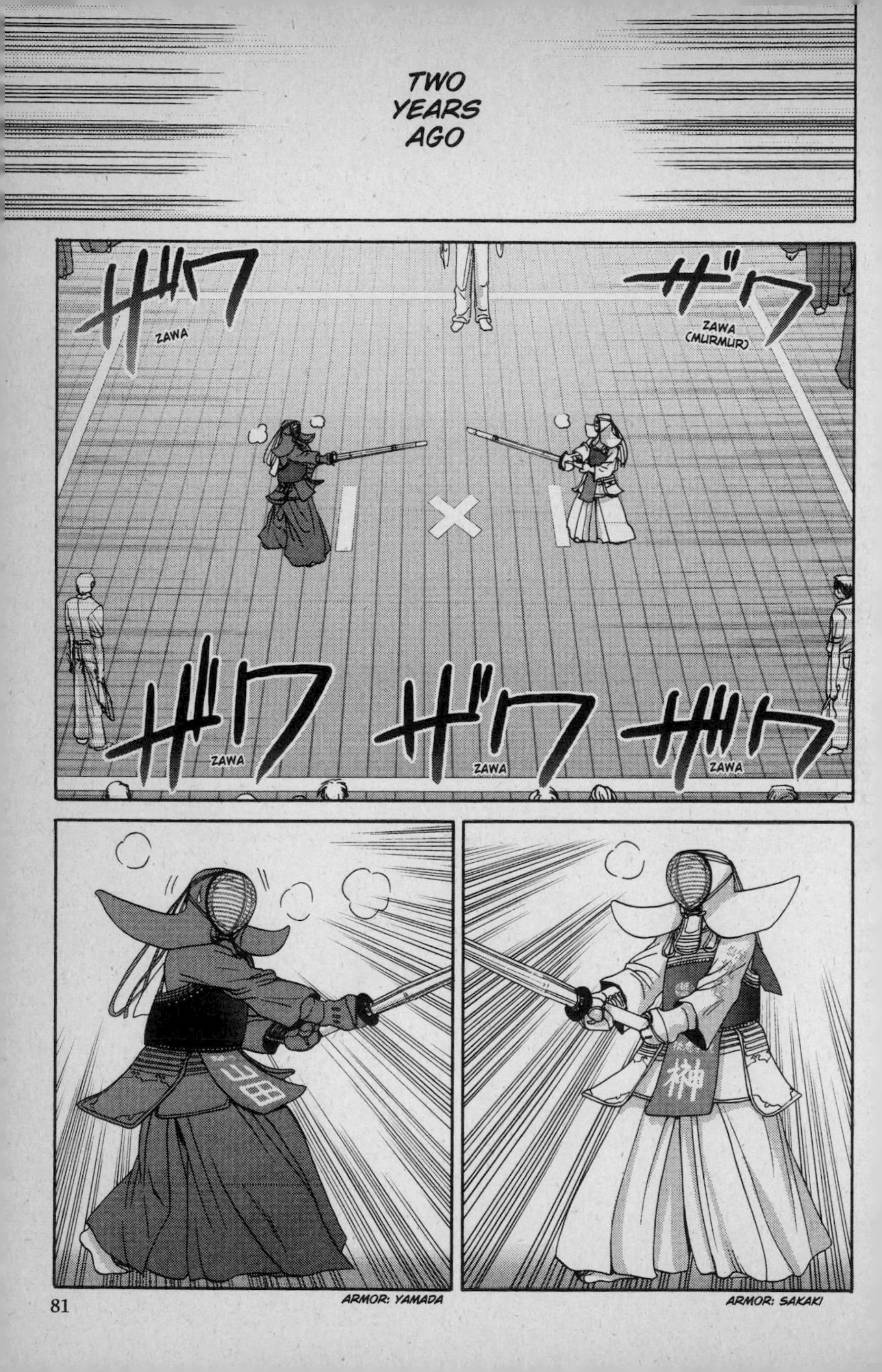
TWO YEARS AGO
ザワ
ZAWA (MURMUR)
ザワ
ZAWA
ザワ
ZAWA
ザワ
ZAWA
ザワ
ZAWA

ARMOR: SAKAKI

ARMOR: YAMADA

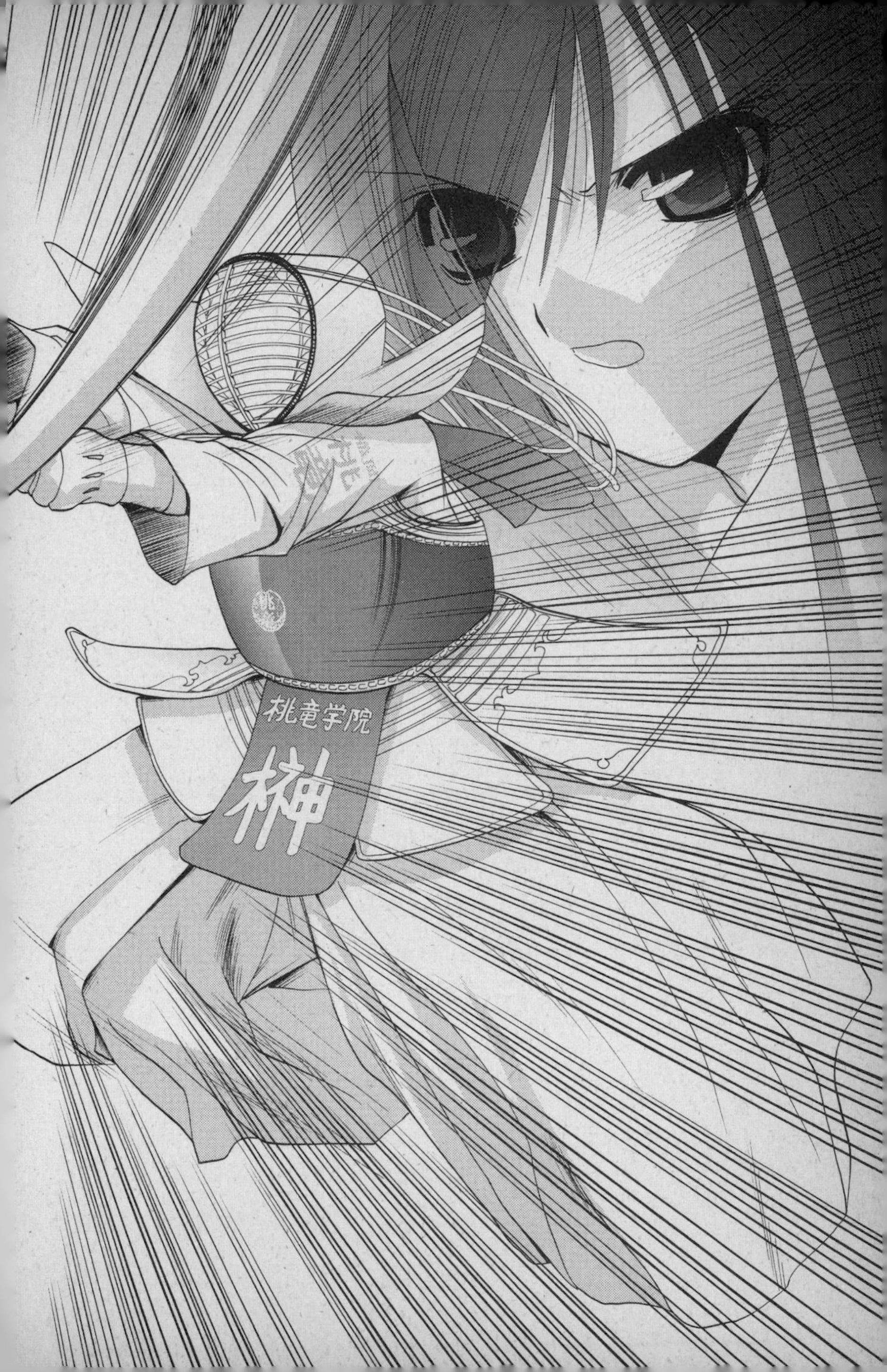
桃竜学院
榊

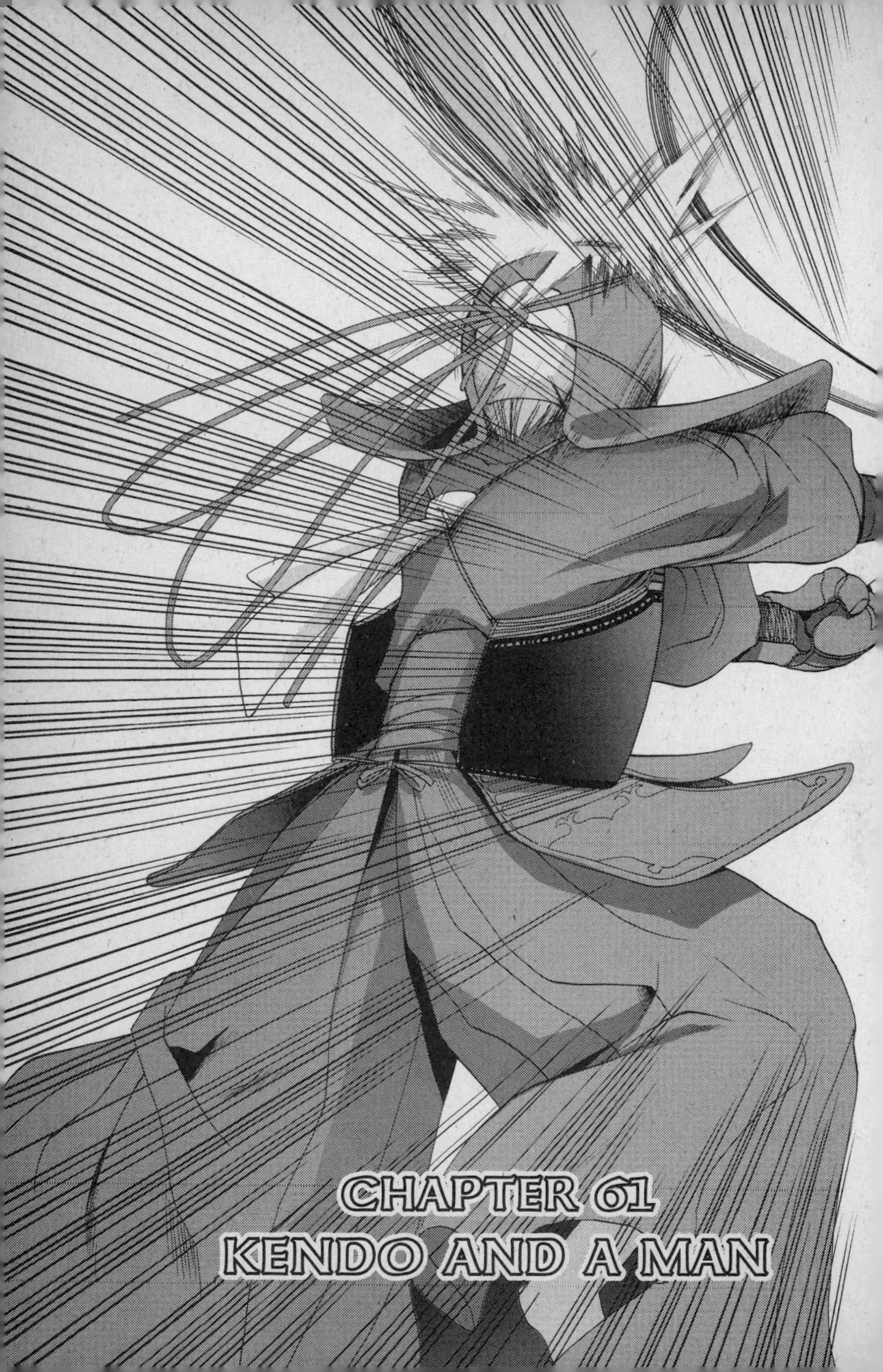
CHAPTER 61
KENDO AND A MAN

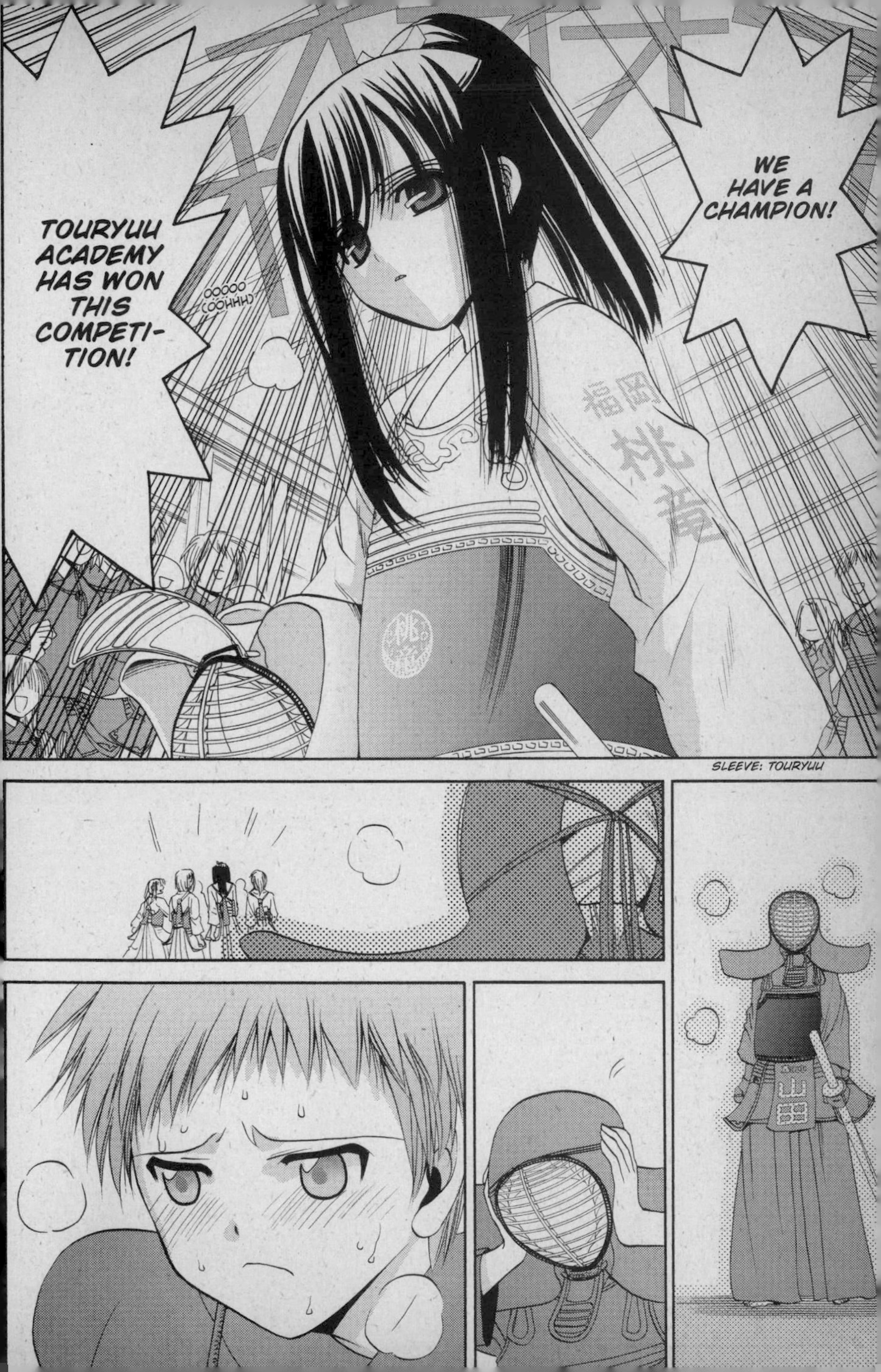
WE HAVE A CHAMPION!
TOURYUU ACADEMY HAS WON THIS COMPETI- TION!
OOOOO (OOHHH)
福岡
桃竜
山田
SLEEVE: TOURYUU

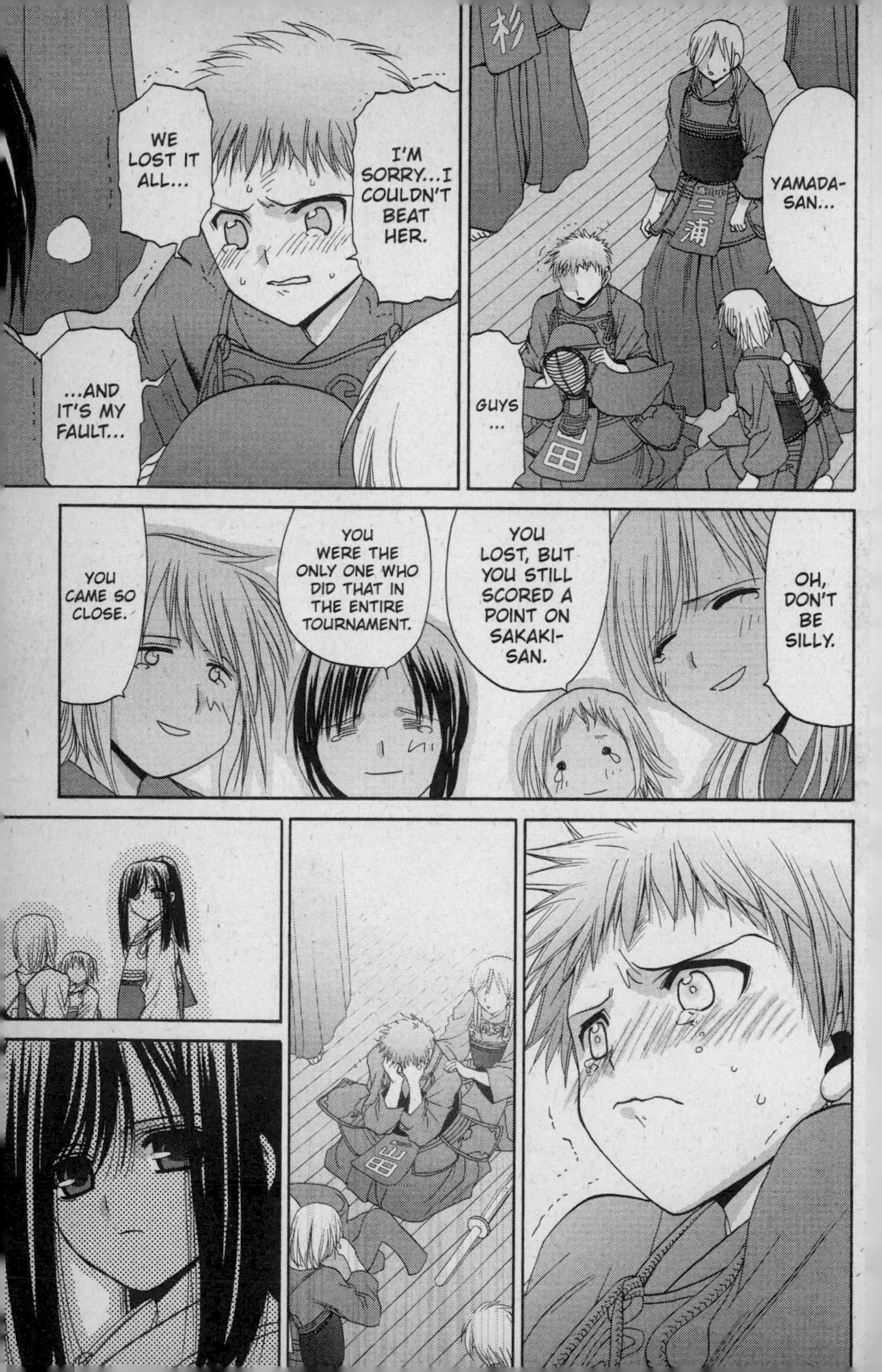
YAMADA-SAN...
GUYS ...
I'M SORRY...I COULDN'T BEAT HER.
WE LOST IT ALL...
...AND IT'S MY FAULT...
OH, DON'T BE SILLY.
YOU LOST, BUT YOU STILL SCORED A POINT ON SAKAKI-SAN.
YOU WERE THE ONLY ONE WHO DID THAT IN THE ENTIRE TOURNAMENT.
YOU CAME SO CLOSE.

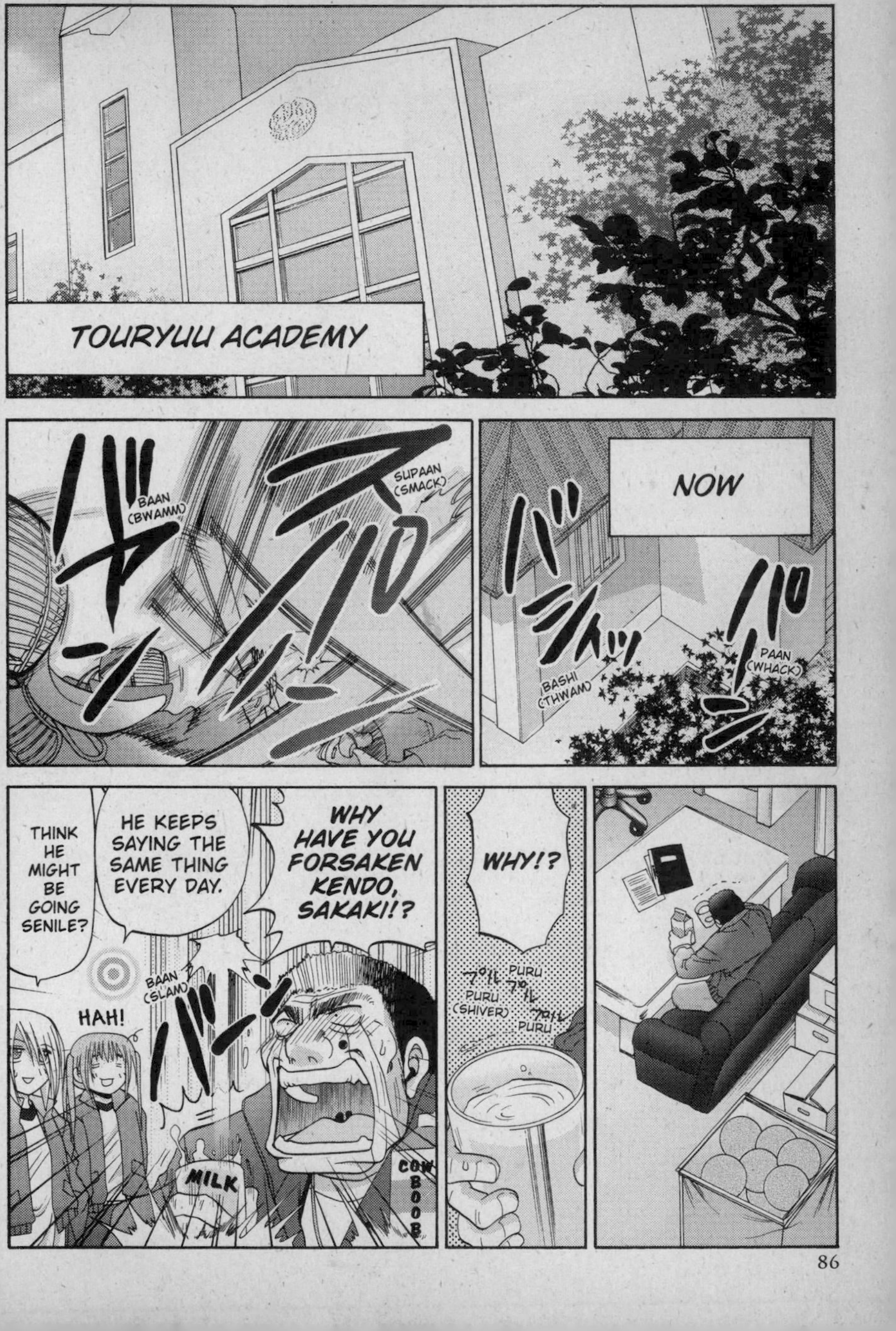
TOURYUU ACADEMY
NOW
PAAN (WHACK)
BASHI (THWAM)
SUPAAN (SMACK)
BAAN (BWAMM)
WHY!?
PURU PURU PURU (SHIVER)
WHY HAVE YOU FORSAKEN KENDO, SAKAKI!?
HE KEEPS SAYING THE SAME THING EVERY DAY.
THINK HE MIGHT BE GOING SENILE?
BAAN (SLAM)
HAH!
COW BOOB
MILK

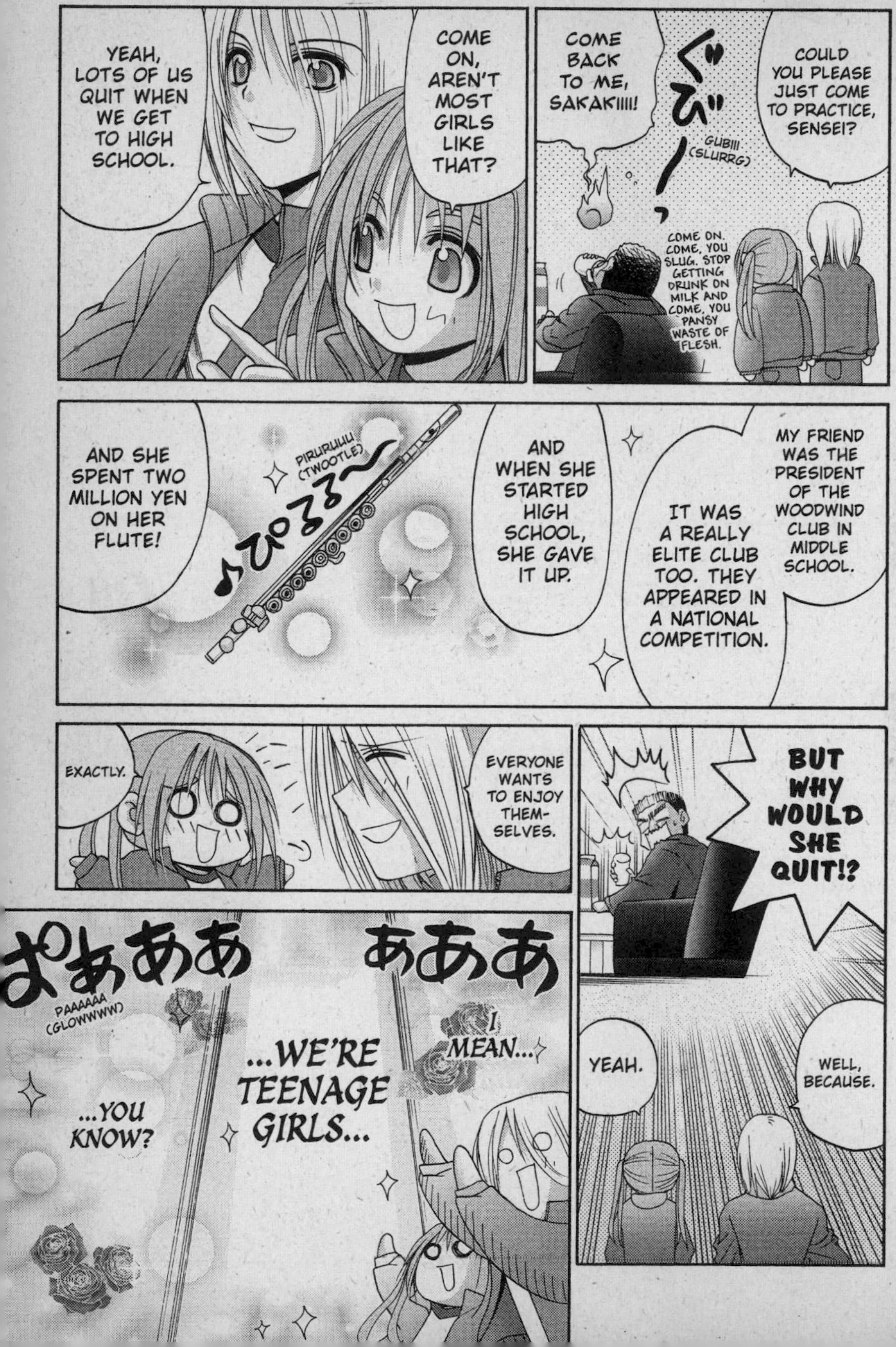
COULD YOU PLEASE JUST COME TO PRACTICE, SENSEI?
ぐびー
GUBIII (SLURRG)
COME BACK TO ME, SAKAKIIII!
COME ON. COME, YOU SLUG. STOP GETTING DRUNK ON MILK AND COME, YOU PANSY WASTE OF FLESH.
COME ON, AREN'T MOST GIRLS LIKE THAT?
YEAH, LOTS OF US QUIT WHEN WE GET TO HIGH SCHOOL.
MY FRIEND WAS THE PRESIDENT OF THE WOODWIND CLUB IN MIDDLE SCHOOL.
IT WAS A REALLY ELITE CLUB TOO. THEY APPEARED IN A NATIONAL COMPETITION.
AND WHEN SHE STARTED HIGH SCHOOL, SHE GAVE IT UP.
♪ぴるる〜
PIRURUUU (TWOOTLE)
AND SHE SPENT TWO MILLION YEN ON HER FLUTE!
BUT WHY WOULD SHE QUIT!?
WELL, BECAUSE.
YEAH.
EVERYONE WANTS TO ENJOY THEM-SELVES.
EXACTLY.
ぱあああ
あああ
PAAAAAA (GLOWWWW)
I MEAN...
...WE'RE TEENAGE GIRLS...
...YOU KNOW?

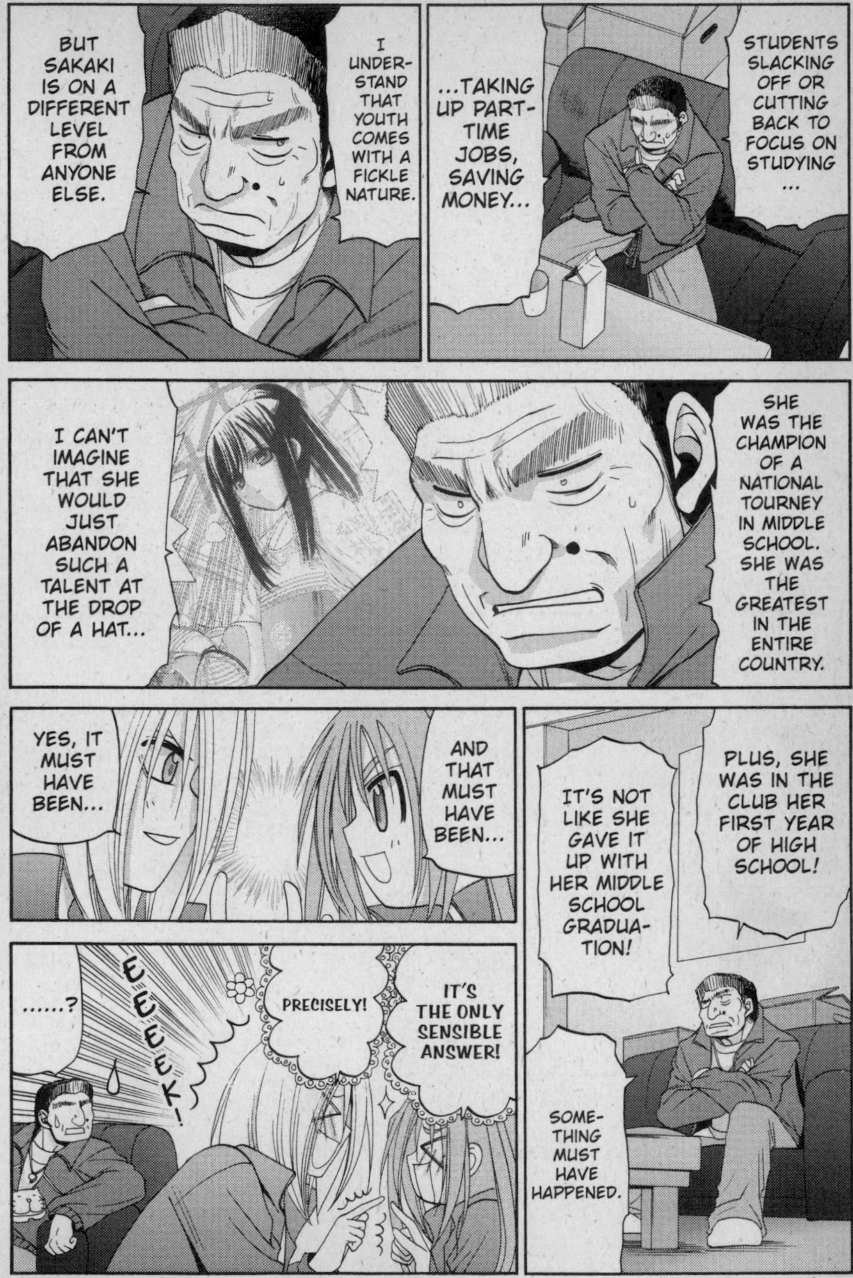
STUDENTS SLACKING OFF OR CUTTING BACK TO FOCUS ON STUDYING ...
...TAKING UP PART-TIME JOBS, SAVING MONEY...
I UNDERSTAND THAT YOUTH COMES WITH A FICKLE NATURE.
BUT SAKAKI IS ON A DIFFERENT LEVEL FROM ANYONE ELSE.
SHE WAS THE CHAMPION OF A NATIONAL TOURNEY IN MIDDLE SCHOOL. SHE WAS THE GREATEST IN THE ENTIRE COUNTRY.
I CAN'T IMAGINE THAT SHE WOULD JUST ABANDON SUCH A TALENT AT THE DROP OF A HAT...
PLUS, SHE WAS IN THE CLUB HER FIRST YEAR OF HIGH SCHOOL!
IT'S NOT LIKE SHE GAVE IT UP WITH HER MIDDLE SCHOOL GRADUATION!
SOMETHING MUST HAVE HAPPENED.
AND THAT MUST HAVE BEEN...
YES, IT MUST HAVE BEEN...
IT'S THE ONLY SENSIBLE ANSWER!
PRECISELY!
EEEEK!
......?

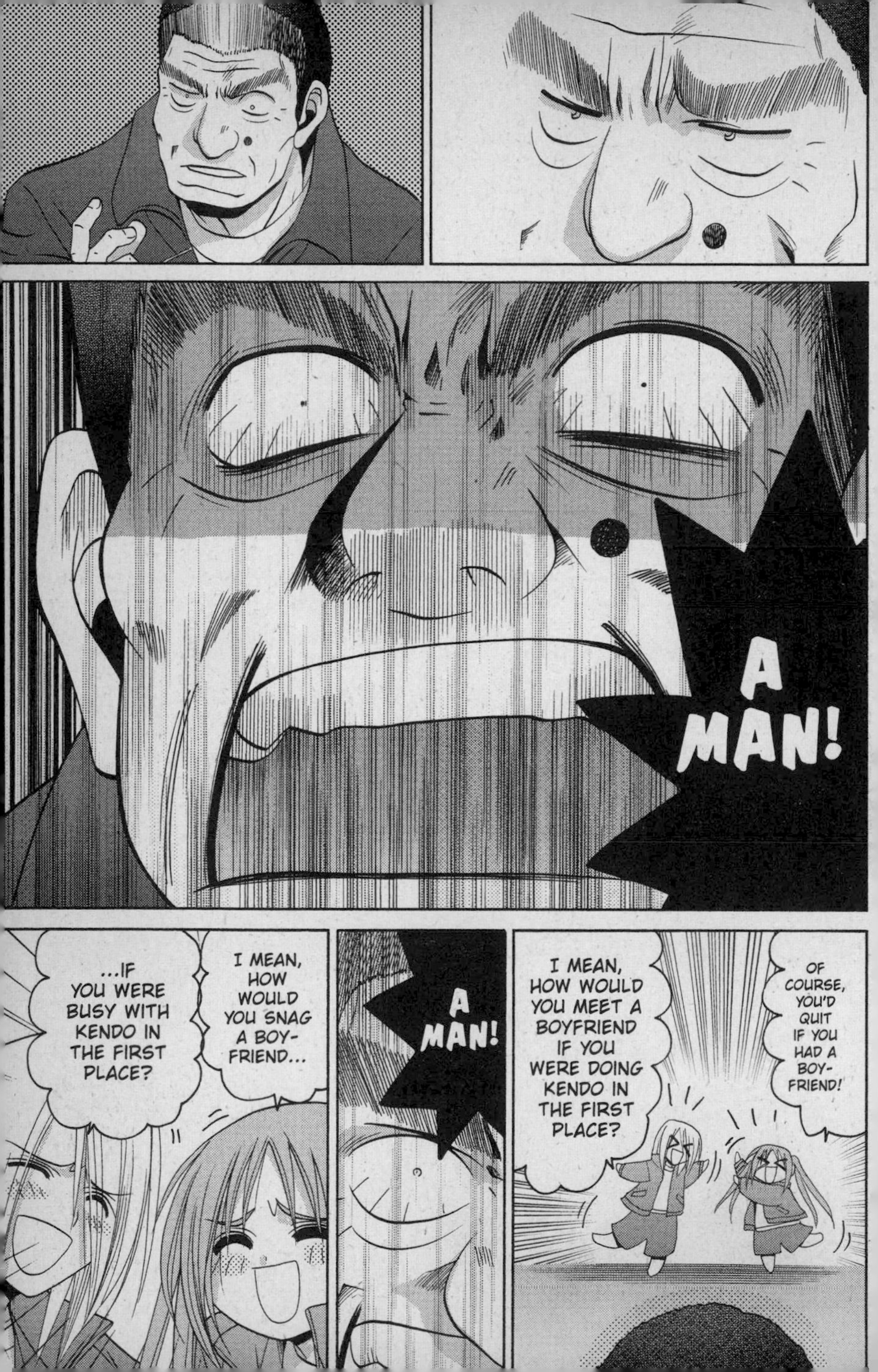
A MAN!
OF COURSE, YOU'D QUIT IF YOU HAD A BOY-FRIEND!
I MEAN, HOW WOULD YOU MEET A BOYFRIEND IF YOU WERE DOING KENDO IN THE FIRST PLACE?
A MAN!
I MEAN, HOW WOULD YOU SNAG A BOY-FRIEND...
...IF YOU WERE BUSY WITH KENDO IN THE FIRST PLACE?

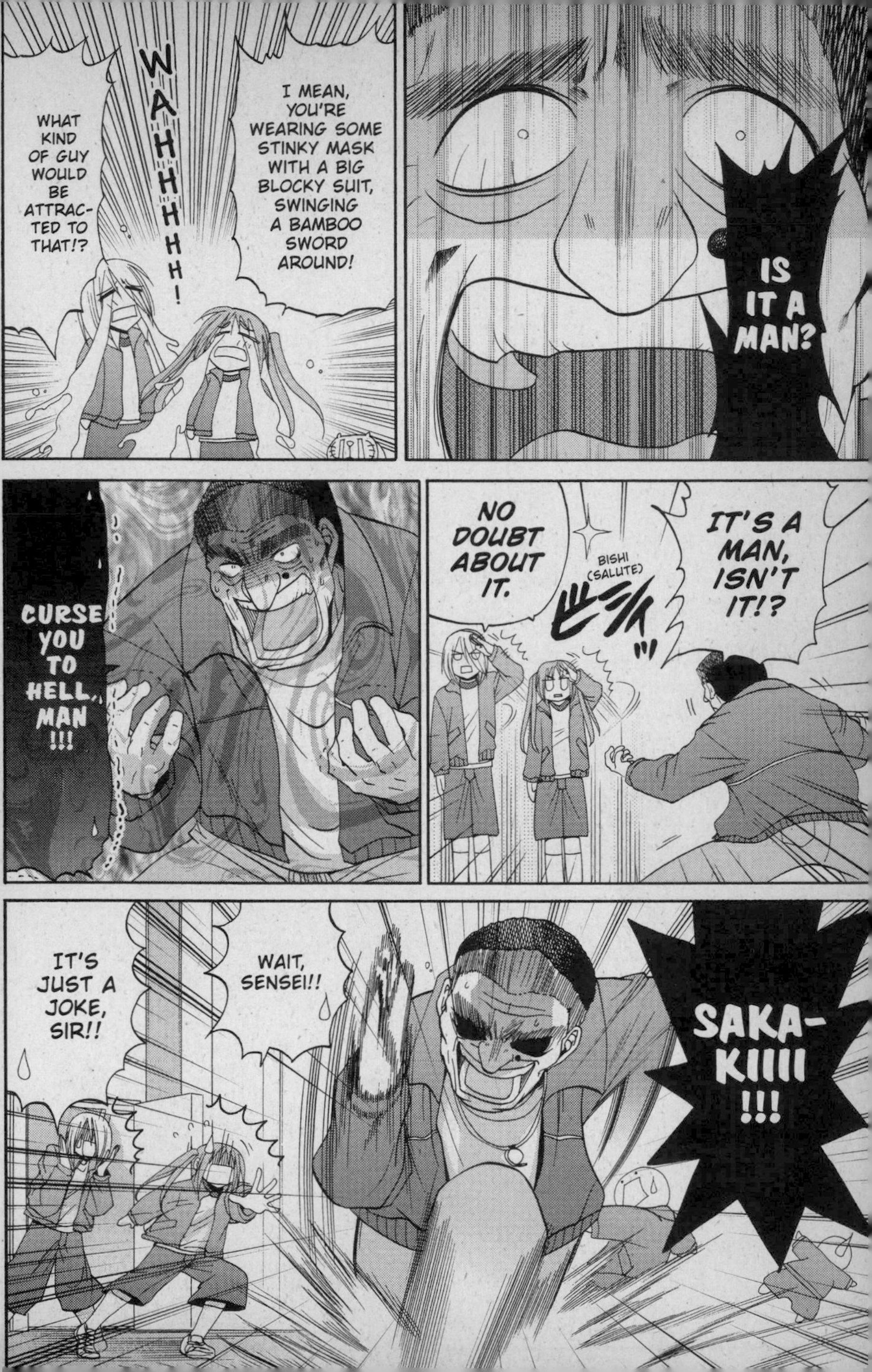
IS IT A MAN?
I MEAN, YOU'RE WEARING SOME STINKY MASK WITH A BIG BLOCKY SUIT, SWINGING A BAMBOO SWORD AROUND!
WAHHHHHHH!
WHAT KIND OF GUY WOULD BE ATTRAC-TED TO THAT!?
IT'S A MAN, ISN'T IT!?
NO DOUBT ABOUT IT.
BISHI (SALUTE)
CURSE YOU TO HELL, MAN!!!
SAKA-KIIII!!!
WAIT, SENSEI!!
IT'S JUST A JOKE, SIR!!

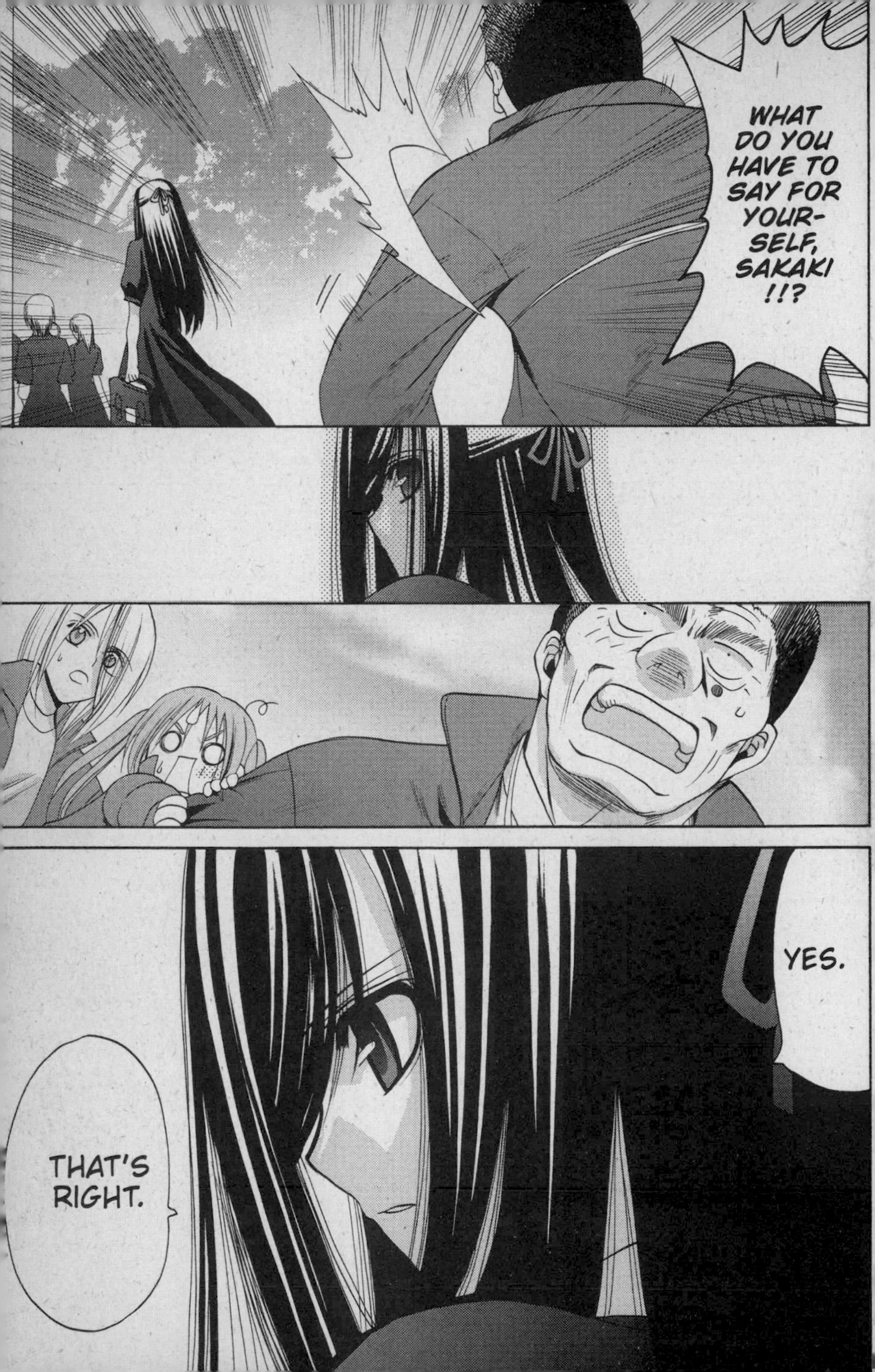
WHAT DO YOU HAVE TO SAY FOR YOURSELF, SAKAKI!!?
YES.
THAT'S RIGHT.

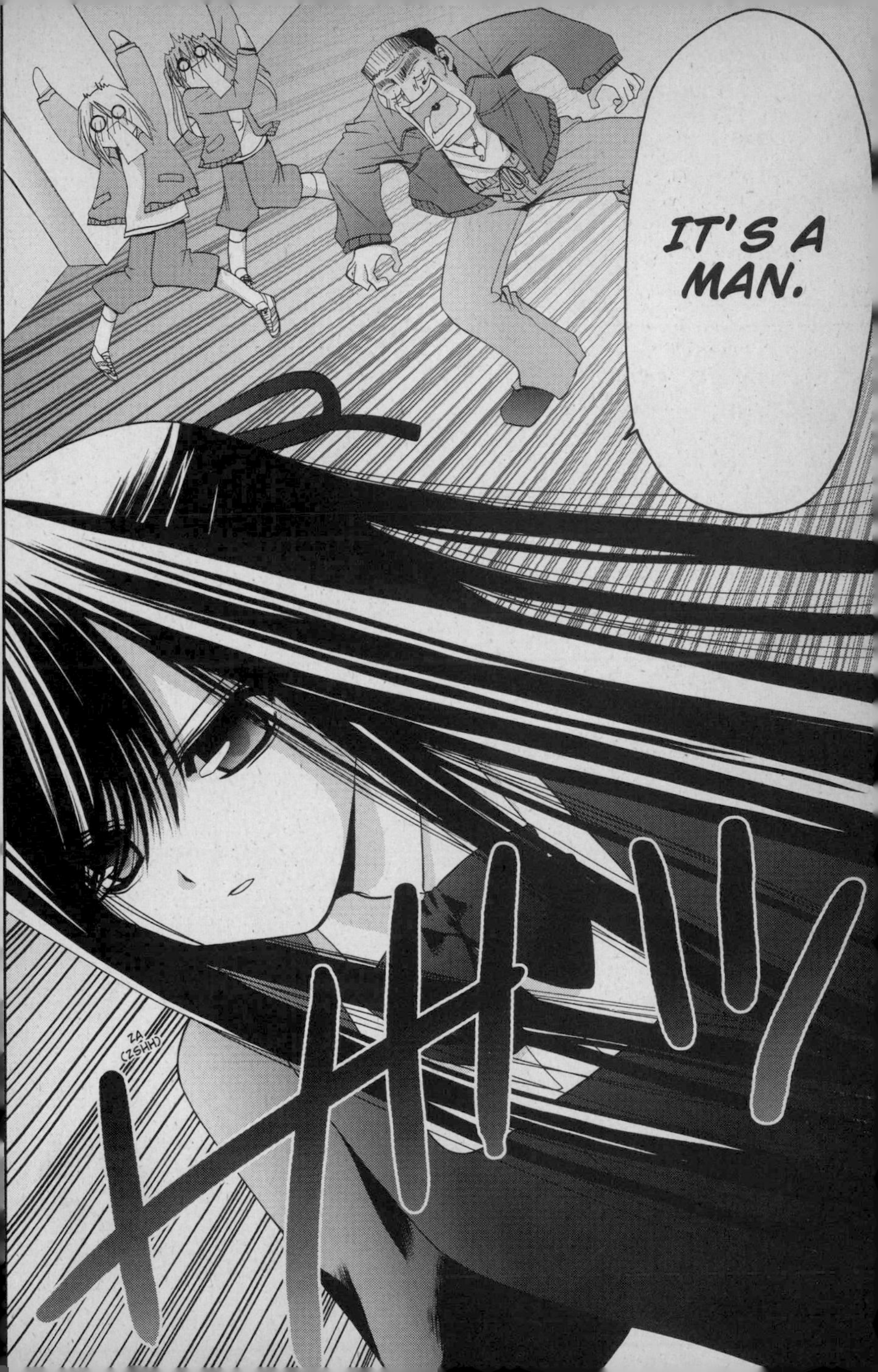
IT'S A MAN.
ZA (ZSHH)

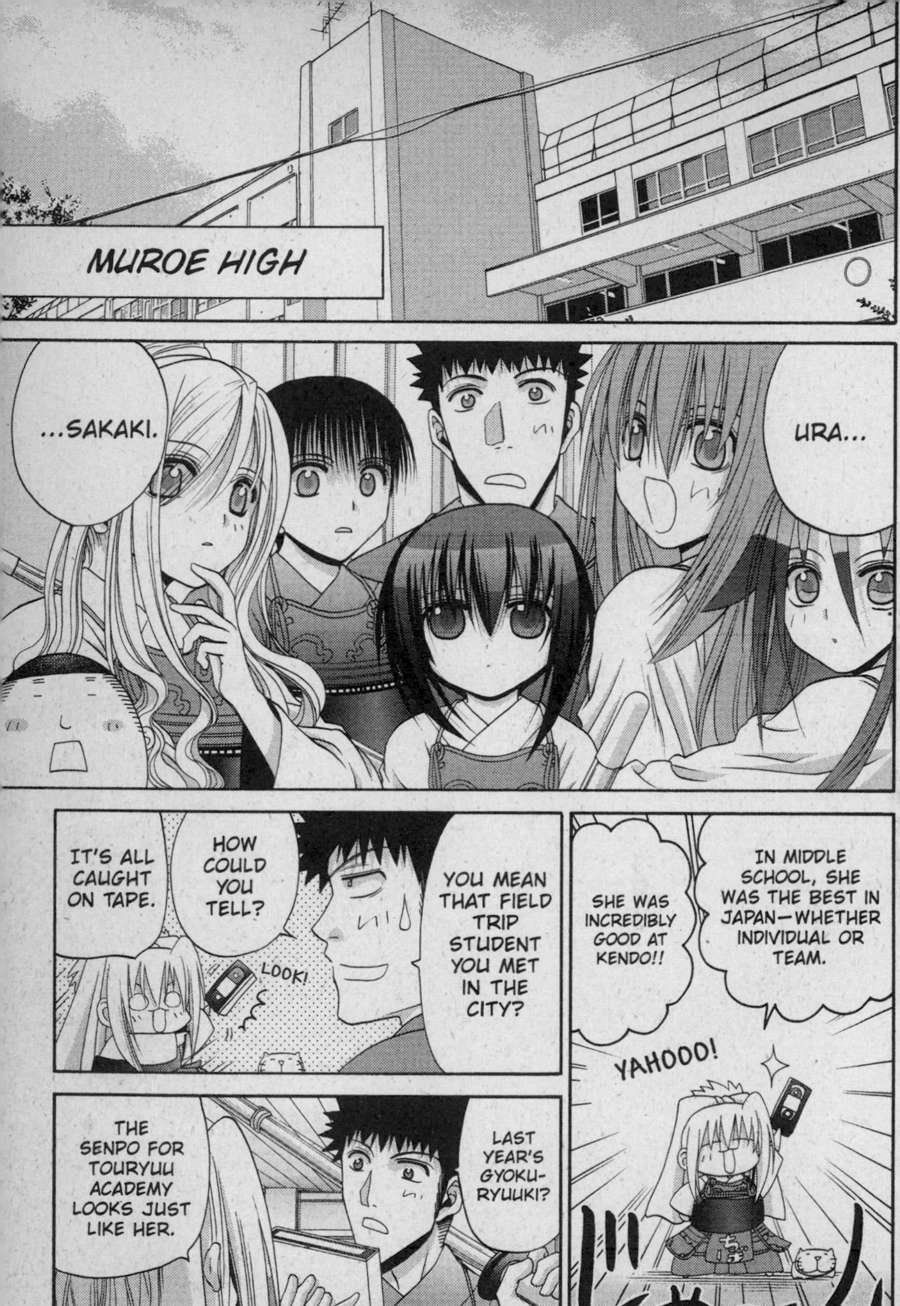
MUROE HIGH
URA...
...SAKAKI.
IN MIDDLE SCHOOL, SHE WAS THE BEST IN JAPAN—WHETHER INDIVIDUAL OR TEAM.
SHE WAS INCREDIBLY GOOD AT KENDO!!
YAHOOO!
じゃーん
JAAAAN (TA-DAA)
YOU MEAN THAT FIELD TRIP STUDENT YOU MET IN THE CITY?
HOW COULD YOU TELL?
IT'S ALL CAUGHT ON TAPE.
LOOK!
LAST YEAR'S GYOKU-RYUUKI?
THE SENPO FOR TOURYUU ACADEMY LOOKS JUST LIKE HER.

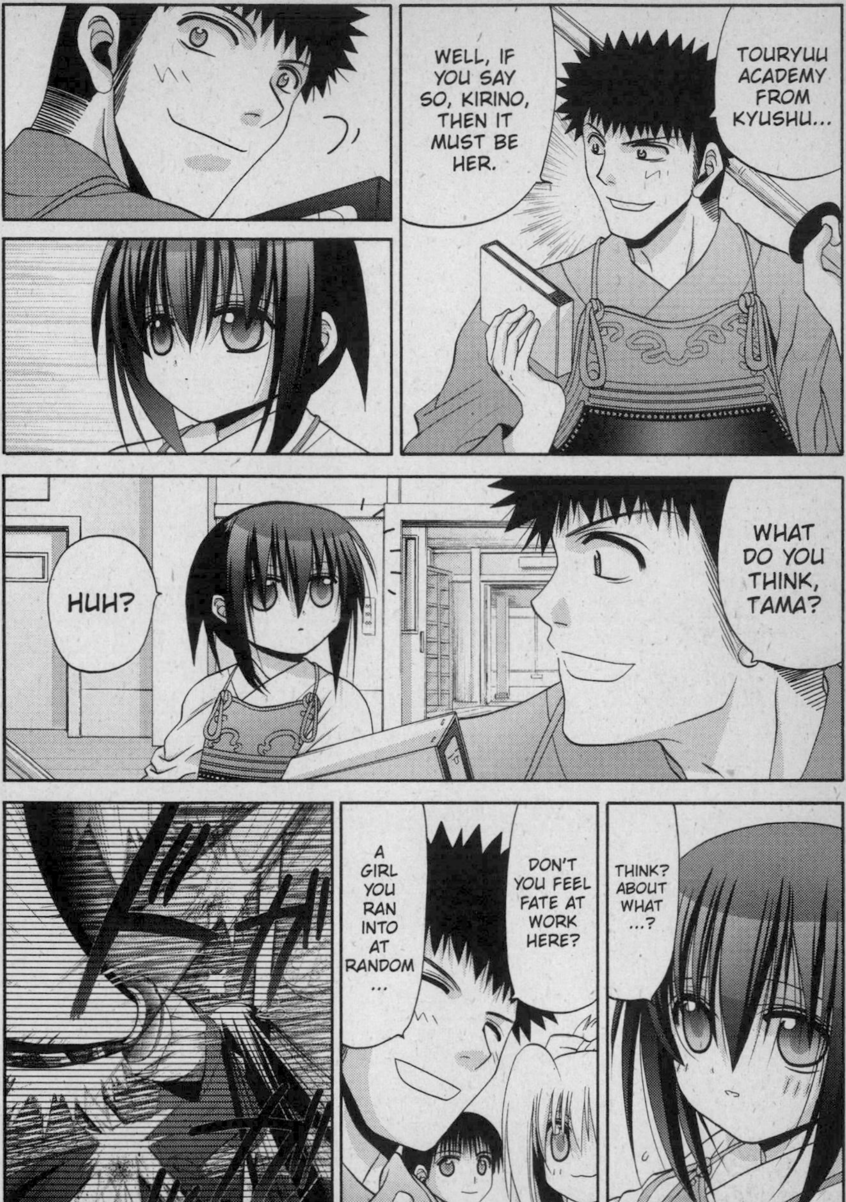
TOURYUU ACADEMY FROM KYUSHU...
WELL, IF YOU SAY SO, KIRINO, THEN IT MUST BE HER.
WHAT DO YOU THINK, TAMA?
HUH?
THINK? ABOUT WHAT ...?
DON'T YOU FEEL FATE AT WORK HERE?
A GIRL YOU RAN INTO AT RANDOM ...
DOGAGA (KAKANG)

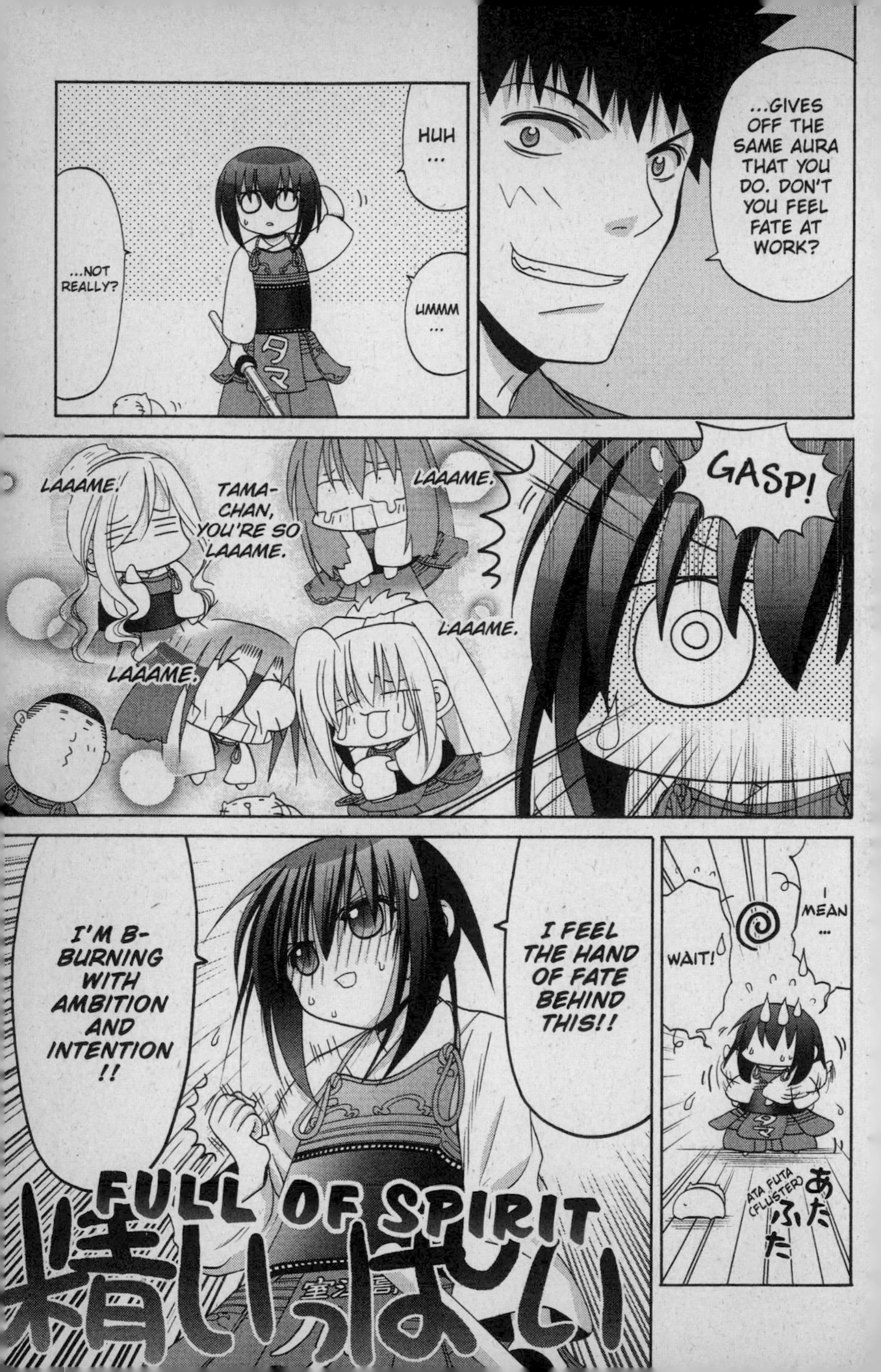
...GIVES OFF THE SAME AURA THAT YOU DO. DON'T YOU FEEL FATE AT WORK?
HUH ...
UMMM ...
...NOT REALLY?
GASP!
LAAAME.
TAMA-CHAN, YOU'RE SO LAAAME.
LAAAME.
LAAAME.
LAAAME.
I MEAN ...
WAIT!
ATA FUTA (FLUSTER)
あたふた
I FEEL THE HAND OF FATE BEHIND THIS!!
I'M B-BURNING WITH AMBITION AND INTENTION!!
FULL OF SPIRIT
精いっぱい

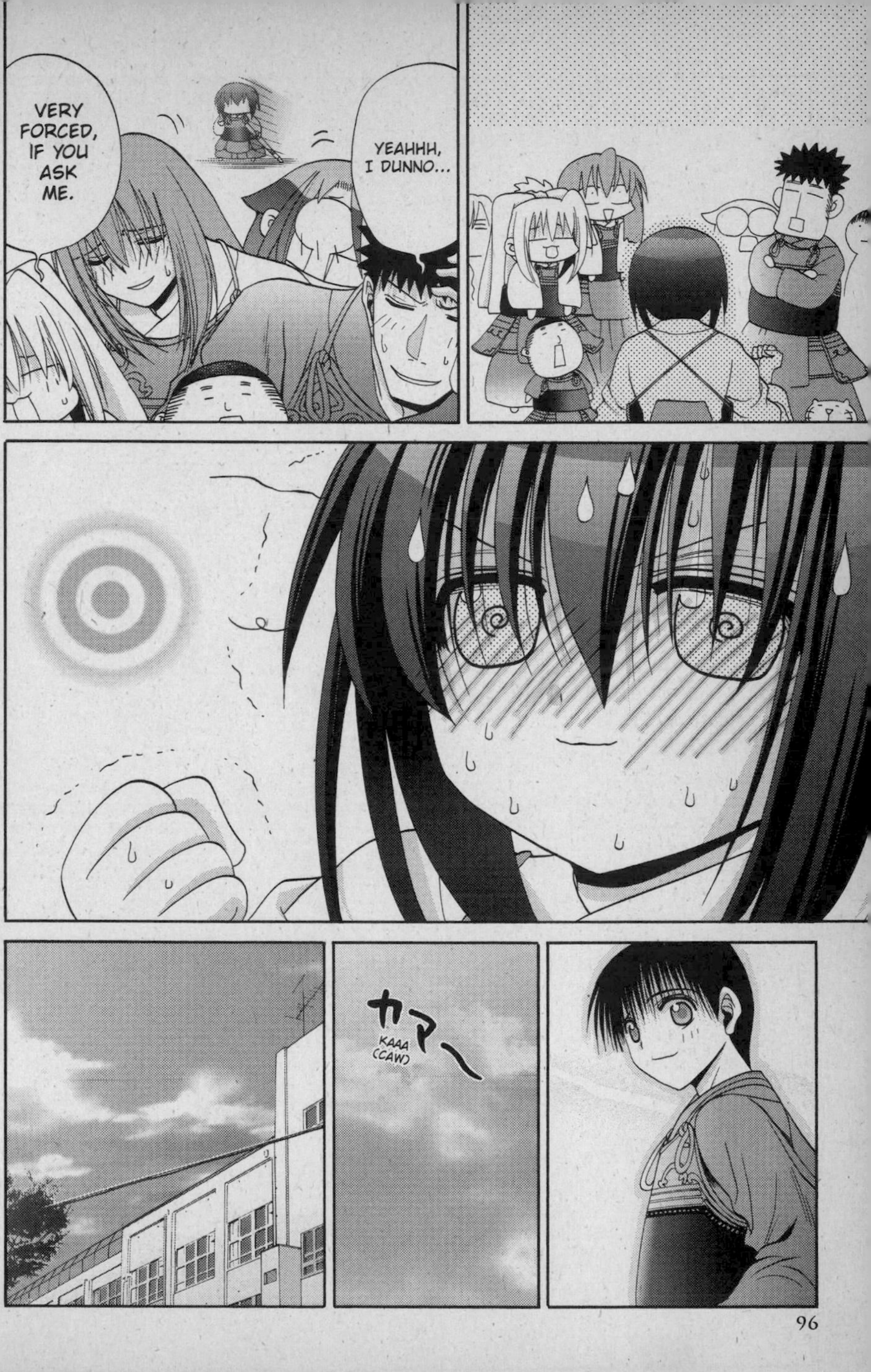
YEAHHH, I DUNNO...
VERY FORCED, IF YOU ASK ME.
カァ〜
KAAA (CAW)

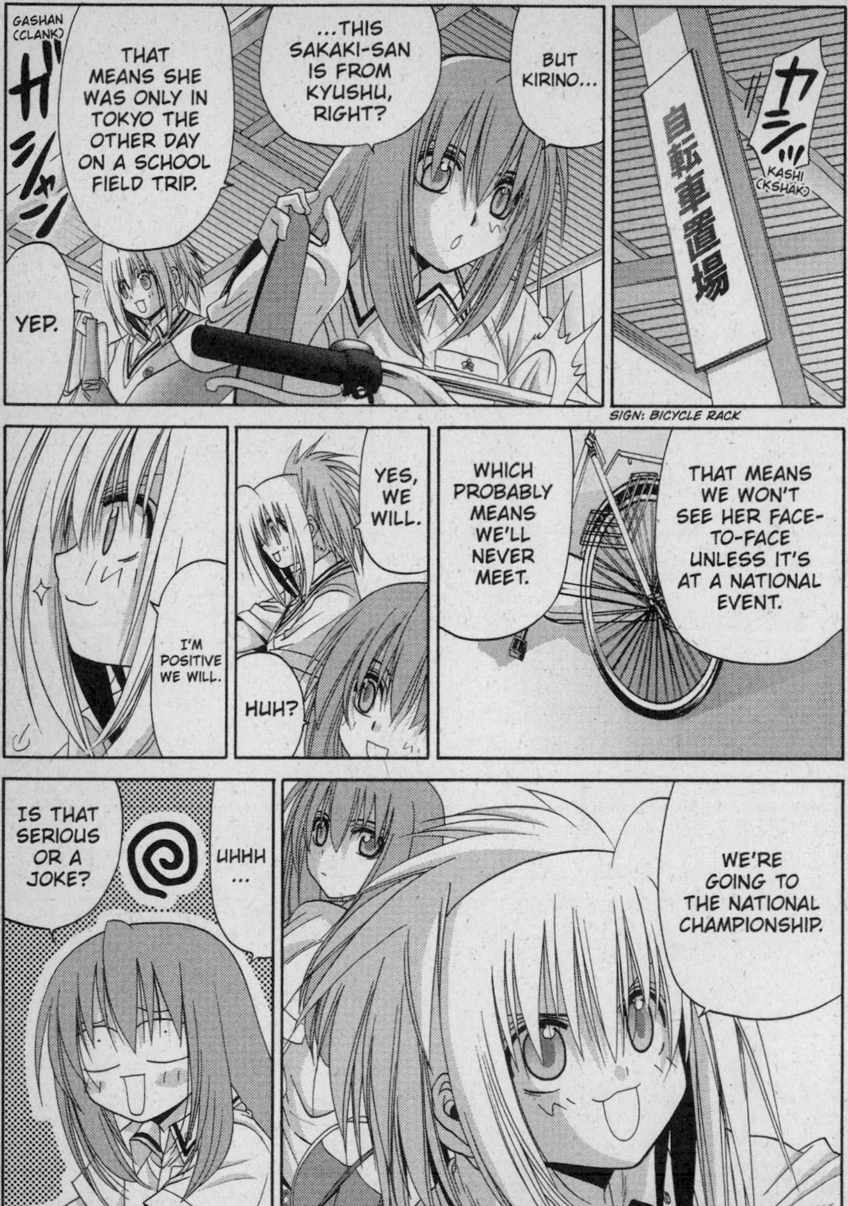
カシッ
KASHI (KSHAK)
自転車置場
SIGN: BICYCLE RACK
BUT KIRINO...
...THIS SAKAKI-SAN IS FROM KYUSHU, RIGHT?
THAT MEANS SHE WAS ONLY IN TOKYO THE OTHER DAY ON A SCHOOL FIELD TRIP.
ガシャン
GASHAN (CLANK)
YEP.
THAT MEANS WE WON'T SEE HER FACE-TO-FACE UNLESS IT'S AT A NATIONAL EVENT.
WHICH PROBABLY MEANS WE'LL NEVER MEET.
YES, WE WILL.
HUH?
I'M POSITIVE WE WILL.
WE'RE GOING TO THE NATIONAL CHAMPIONSHIP.
UHHH ...
IS THAT SERIOUS OR A JOKE?

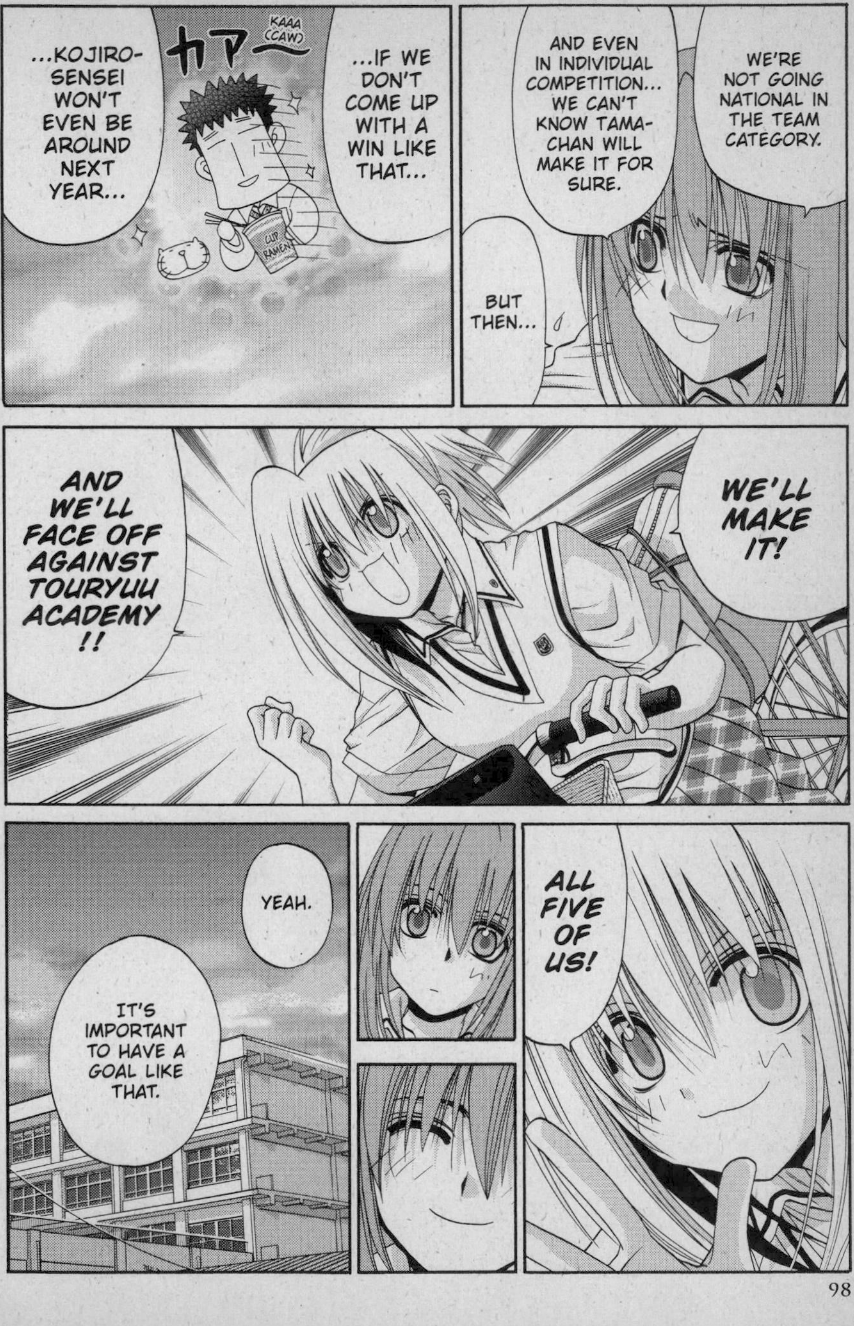
WE'RE NOT GOING NATIONAL IN THE TEAM CATEGORY.
AND EVEN IN INDIVIDUAL COMPETITION... WE CAN'T KNOW TAMA-CHAN WILL MAKE IT FOR SURE.
BUT THEN...
...IF WE DON'T COME UP WITH A WIN LIKE THAT...
カアー
KAAA (CAW)
CUP RAMEN
...KOJIRO-SENSEI WON'T EVEN BE AROUND NEXT YEAR...
WE'LL MAKE IT!
AND WE'LL FACE OFF AGAINST TOURYUU ACADEMY!!
ALL FIVE OF US!
YEAH.
IT'S IMPORTANT TO HAVE A GOAL LIKE THAT.

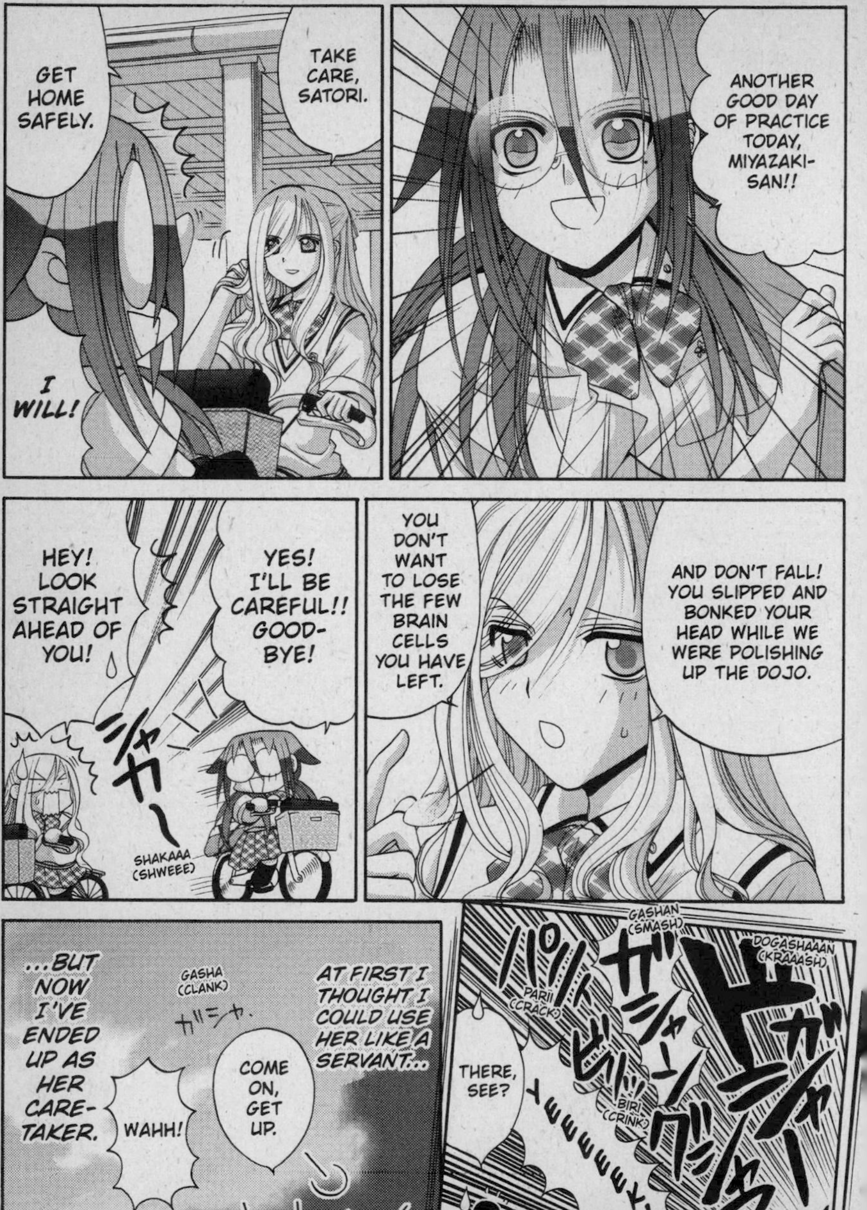
ANOTHER GOOD DAY OF PRACTICE TODAY, MIYAZAKI-SAN!!
TAKE CARE, SATORI.
GET HOME SAFELY.
I WILL!
AND DON'T FALL! YOU SLIPPED AND BONKED YOUR HEAD WHILE WE WERE POLISHING UP THE DOJO.
YOU DON'T WANT TO LOSE THE FEW BRAIN CELLS YOU HAVE LEFT.
YES! I'LL BE CAREFUL!! GOOD-BYE!
HEY! LOOK STRAIGHT AHEAD OF YOU!
SHAKAAA (SHWEEE)
GASHAN (SMASH)
DOGASHAAAN (KRAAASH)
PARII (CRACK)
BIRI (CRINK)
THERE, SEE?
GUSHAAN (SPLAT)
AT FIRST I THOUGHT I COULD USE HER LIKE A SERVANT...
GASHA (CLANK)
ガシャ.
COME ON, GET UP.
...BUT NOW I'VE ENDED UP AS HER CARE-TAKER.
WAHH!

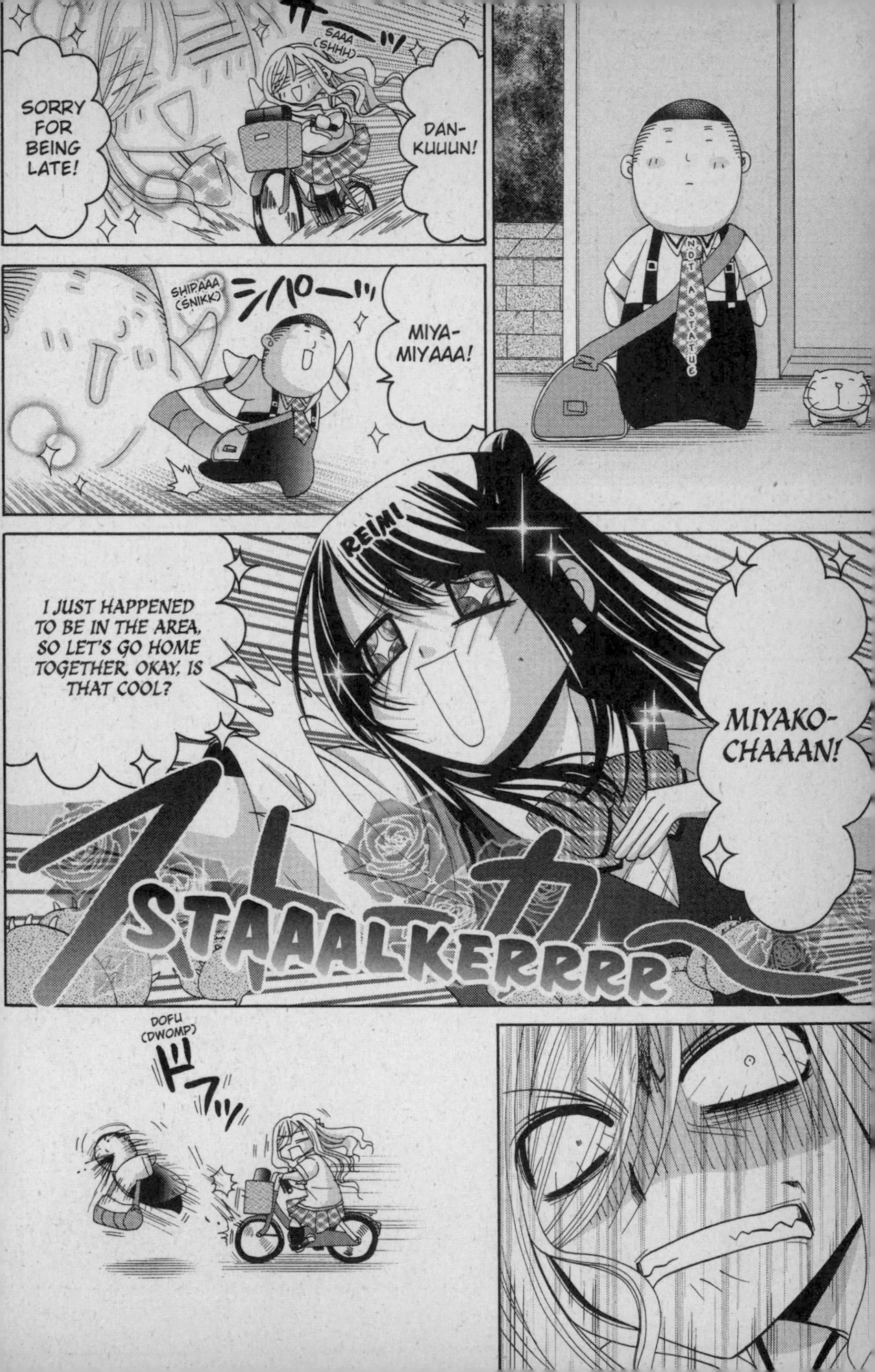
NOT A STATUE
SAAA (SHHH)
DAN-KUUUN!
SORRY FOR BEING LATE!
SHIPAAA (SNIKK)
MIYA-MIYAAA!
REIMI
MIYAKO-CHAAAN!
I JUST HAPPENED TO BE IN THE AREA, SO LET'S GO HOME TOGETHER, OKAY, IS THAT COOL?
STAAALKERRRR
DOFU (DWOMP)

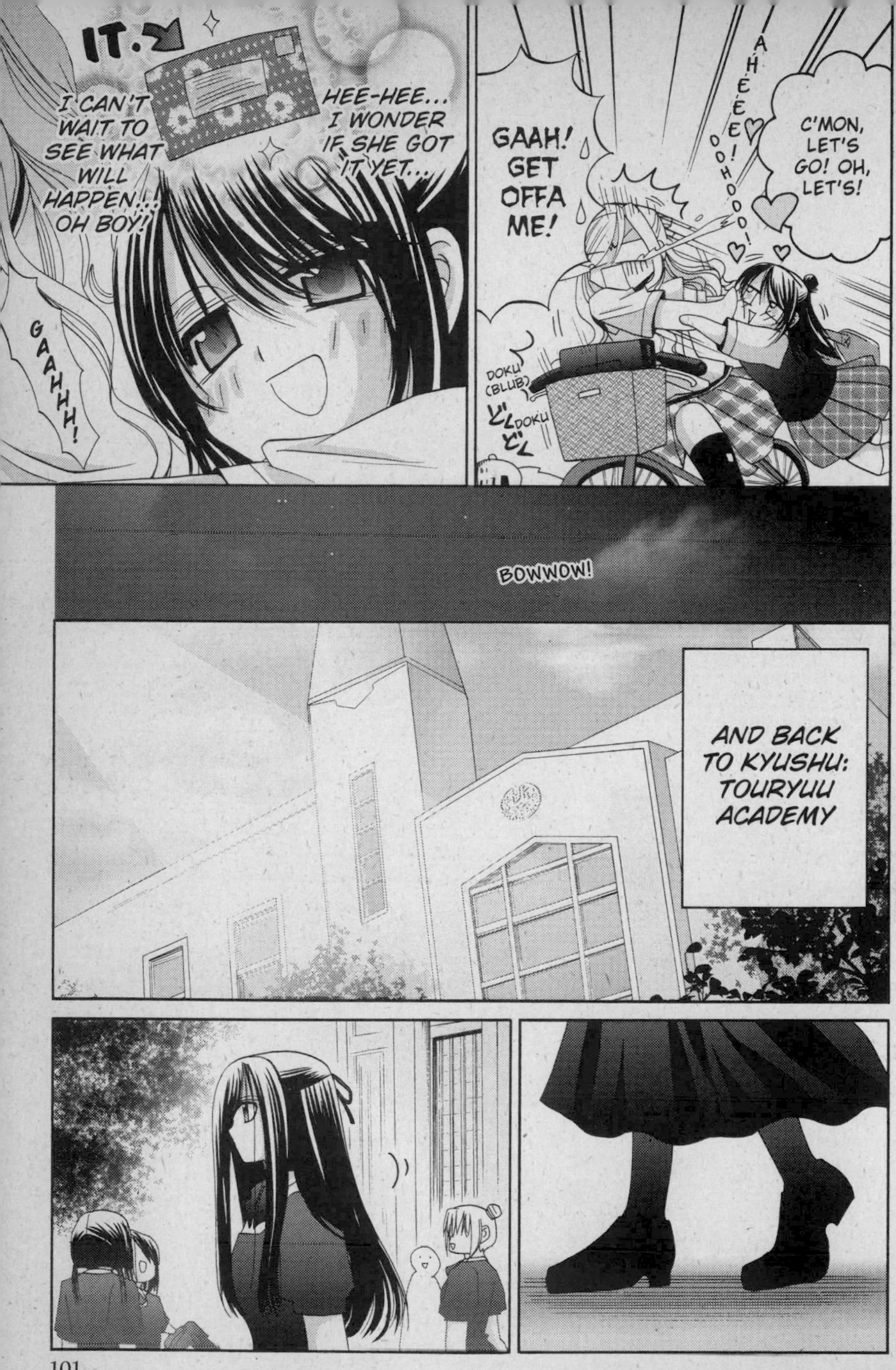
C'MON, LET'S GO! OH, LET'S!
AHEEE!
OOHOOOO!
GAAH! GET OFFA ME!
DOKU (BLUB)
どくどく
DOKU
IT.
HEE-HEE... I WONDER IF SHE GOT IT YET...
I CAN'T WAIT TO SEE WHAT WILL HAPPEN... OH BOY!
GAAHHH!
BOWWOW!
AND BACK TO KYUSHU: TOURYUU ACADEMY

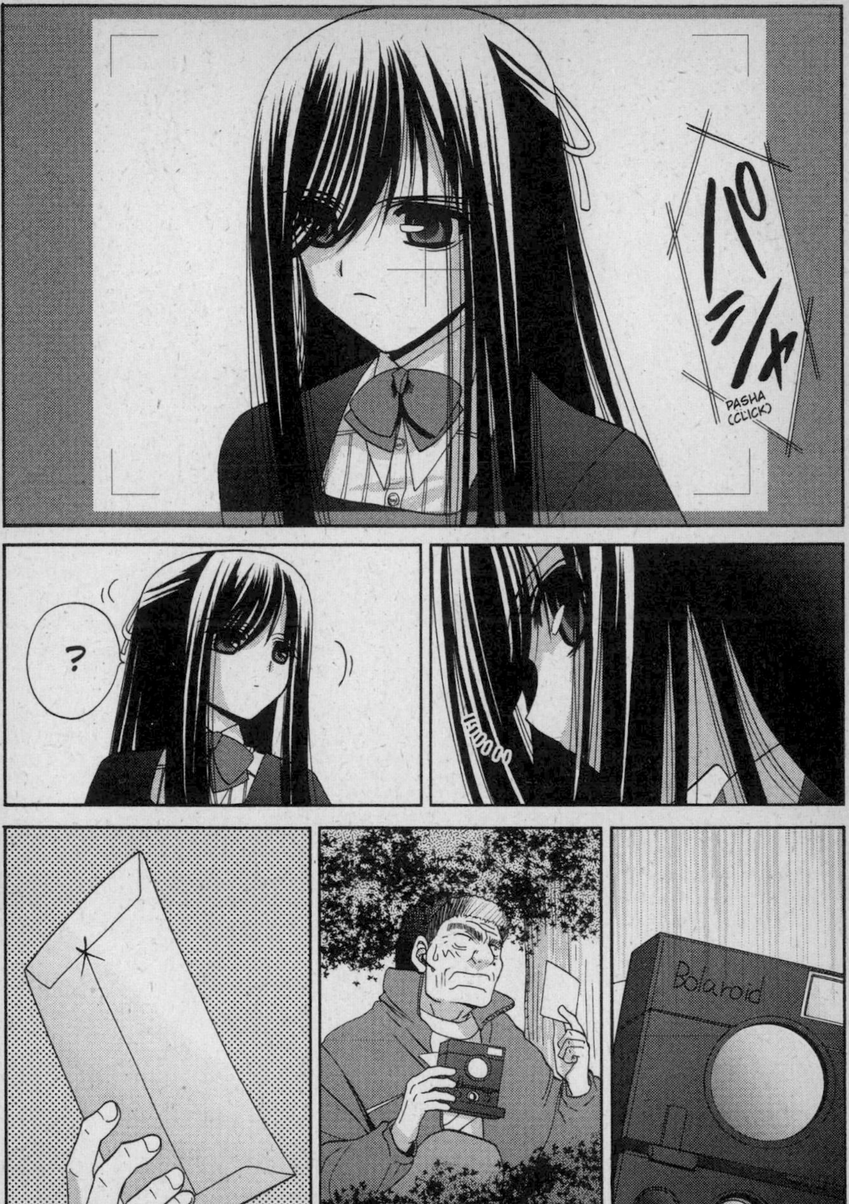
パシャ
PASHA (CLICK)
?
Bolaroid

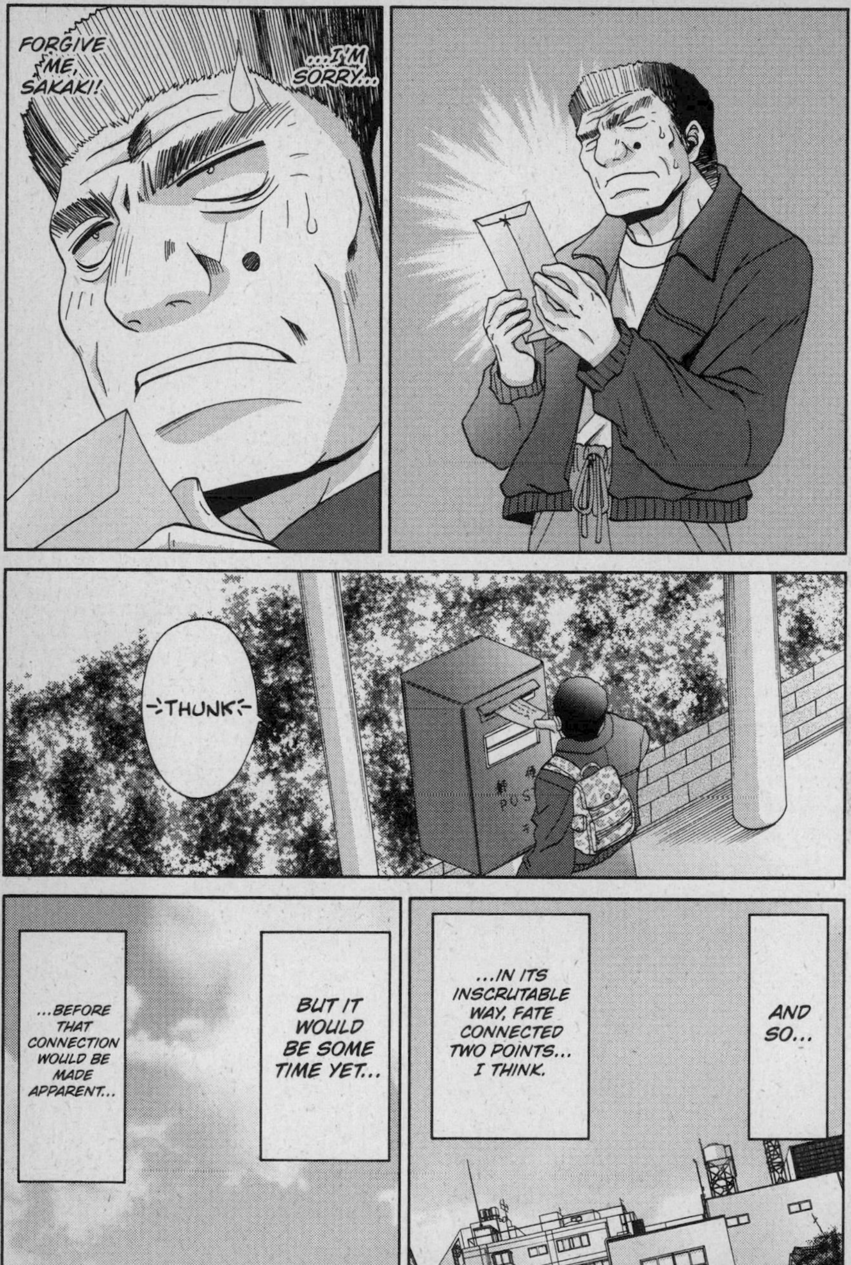
...I'M SORRY...
FORGIVE ME, SAKAKI!
-THUNK-
AND SO...
...IN ITS INSCRUTABLE WAY, FATE CONNECTED TWO POINTS... I THINK.
BUT IT WOULD BE SOME TIME YET...
...BEFORE THAT CONNECTION WOULD BE MADE APPARENT...

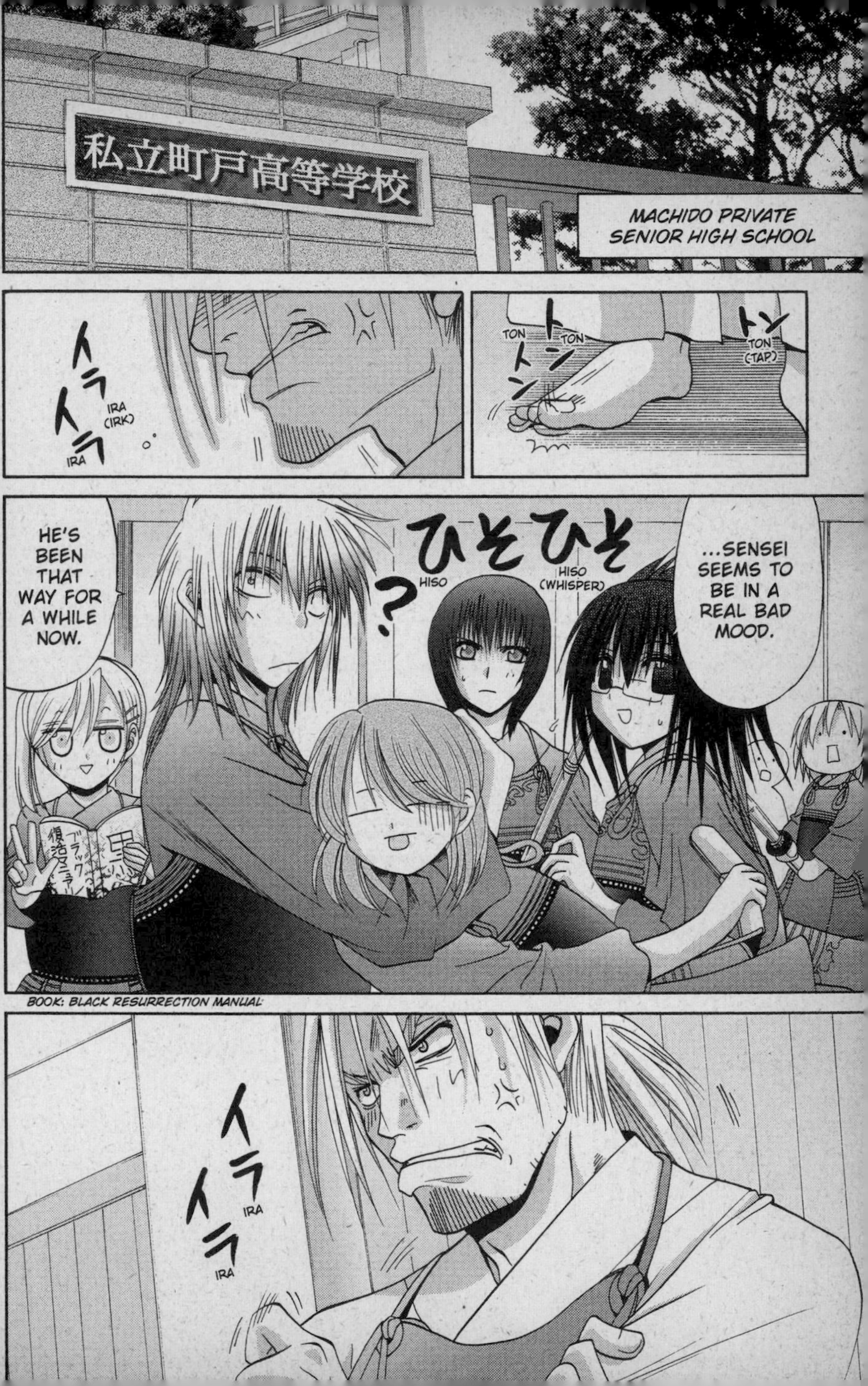
私立町戸高等学校
MACHIDO PRIVATE SENIOR HIGH SCHOOL
トントン
TON TON
トン
TON (TAP)
イライラ
IRA (IRK)
IRA
...SENSEI SEEMS TO BE IN A REAL BAD MOOD.
ひそひそ
HISO HISO (WHISPER)
?
HE'S BEEN THAT WAY FOR A WHILE NOW.
BOOK: BLACK RESURRECTION MANUAL
イライラ
IRA
IRA

BAMBOO BLADE

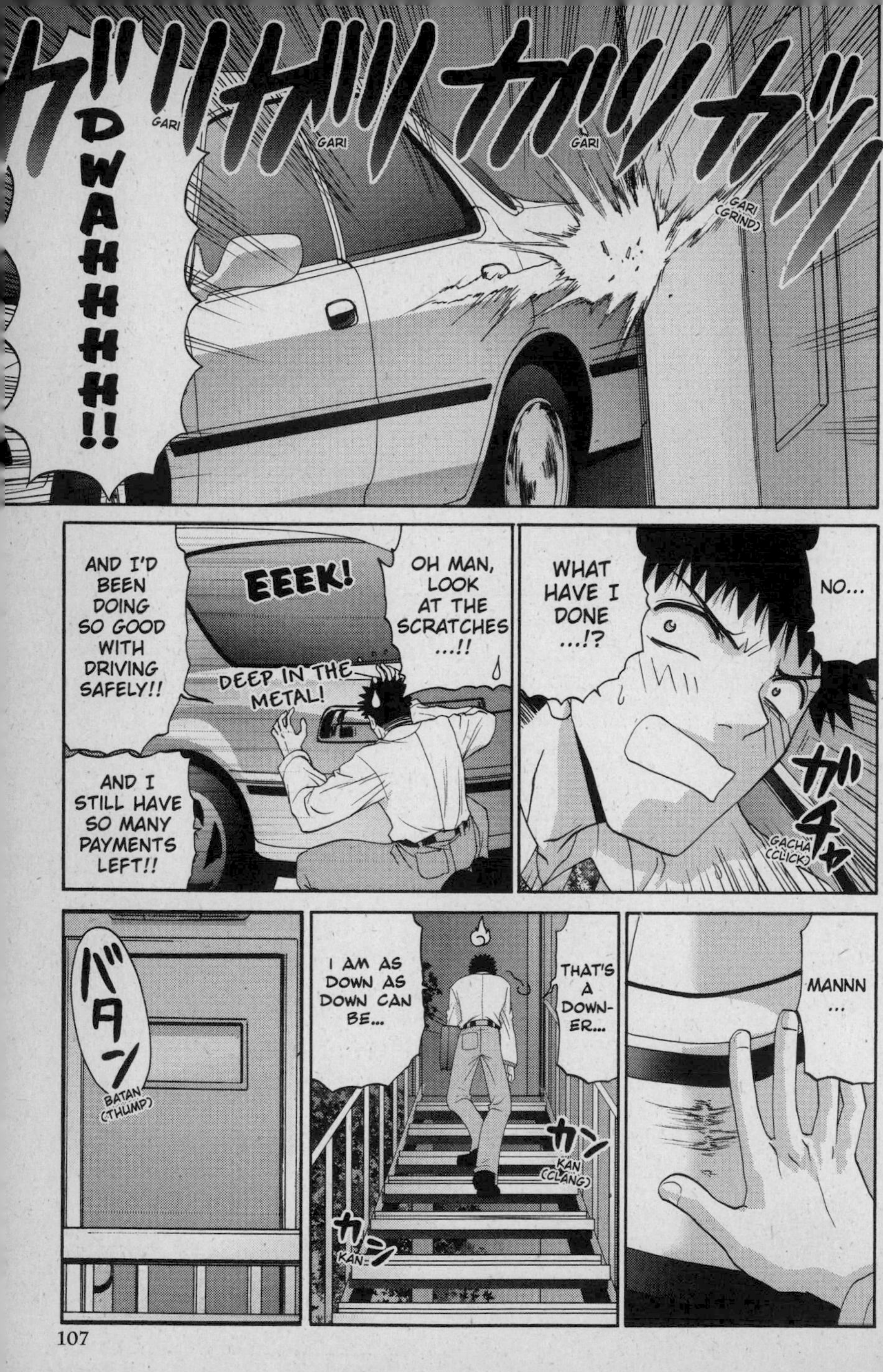
GARI (GRIND)
GARI
GARI
GARI
DWAHHHH!!
NO...
WHAT HAVE I DONE ...!?
GACHA (CLICK)
OH MAN, LOOK AT THE SCRATCHES ...!!
EEEK!
DEEP IN THE METAL!
AND I'D BEEN DOING SO GOOD WITH DRIVING SAFELY!!
AND I STILL HAVE SO MANY PAYMENTS LEFT!!
MANNN ...
THAT'S A DOWN-ER...
I AM AS DOWN AS DOWN CAN BE...
KAN (CLANG)
KAN
BATAN (THUMP)

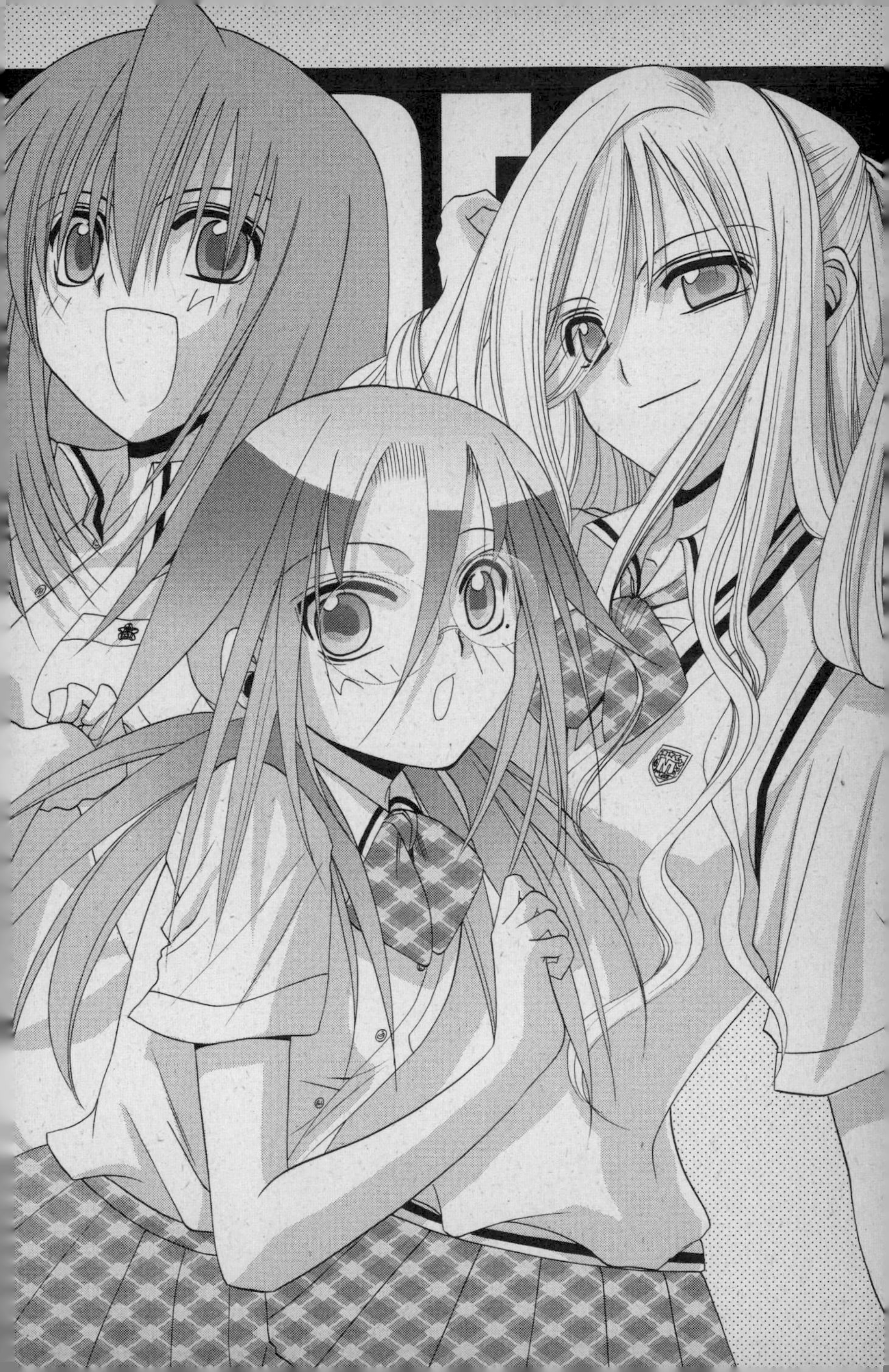

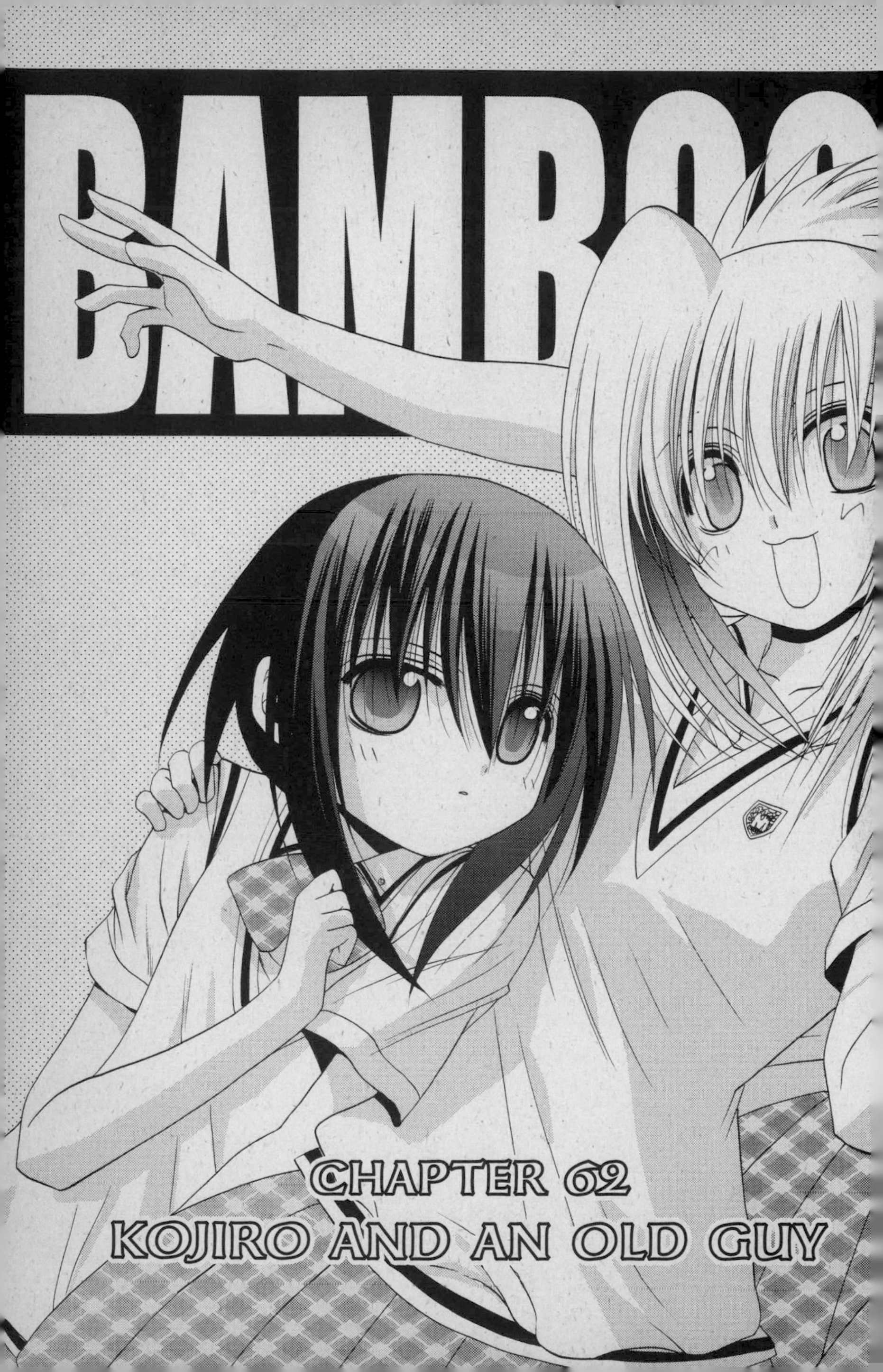
CHAPTER 62
KOJIRO AND AN OLD GUY

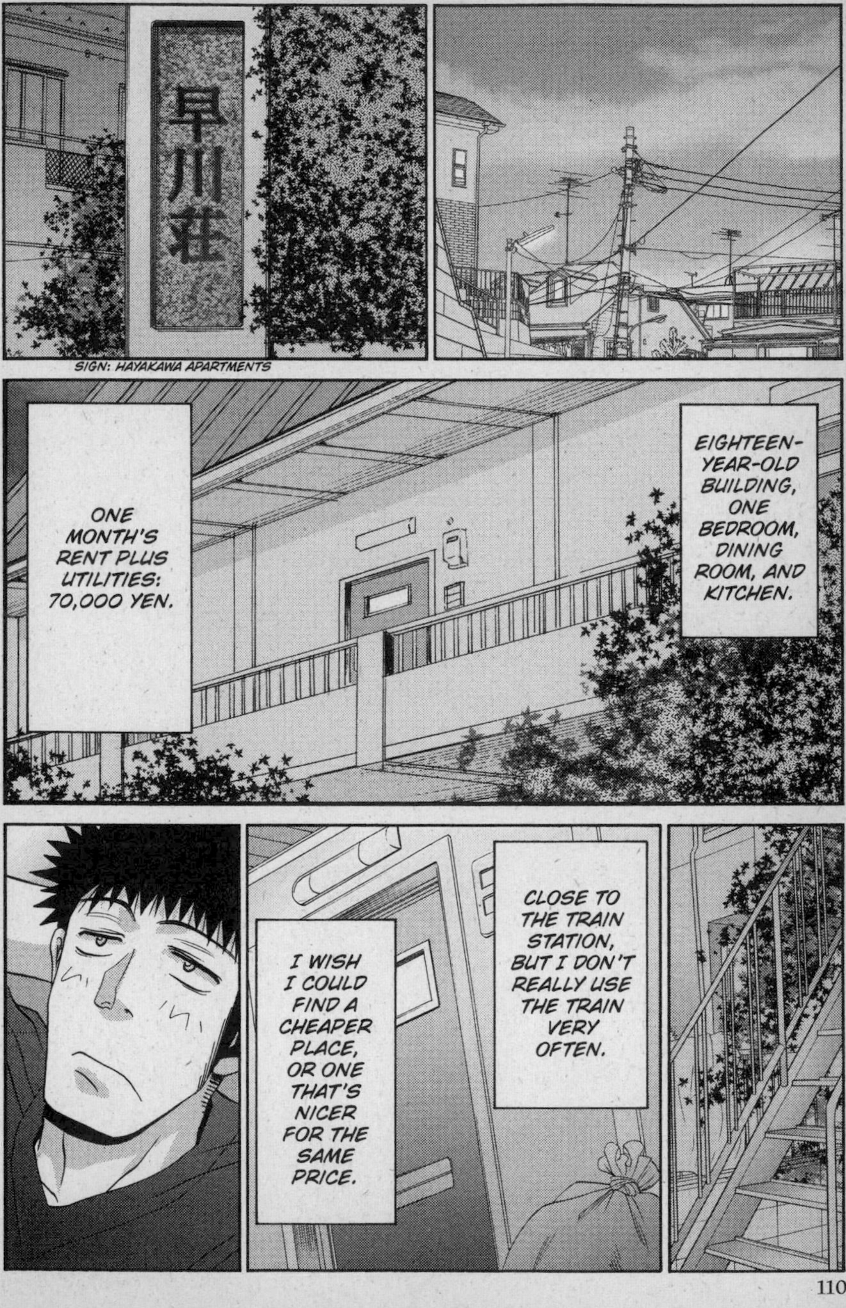
早川荘
SIGN: HAYAKAWA APARTMENTS
EIGHTEEN-YEAR-OLD BUILDING, ONE BEDROOM, DINING ROOM, AND KITCHEN.
ONE MONTH'S RENT PLUS UTILITIES: 70,000 YEN.
CLOSE TO THE TRAIN STATION, BUT I DON'T REALLY USE THE TRAIN VERY OFTEN.
I WISH I COULD FIND A CHEAPER PLACE, OR ONE THAT'S NICER FOR THE SAME PRICE.

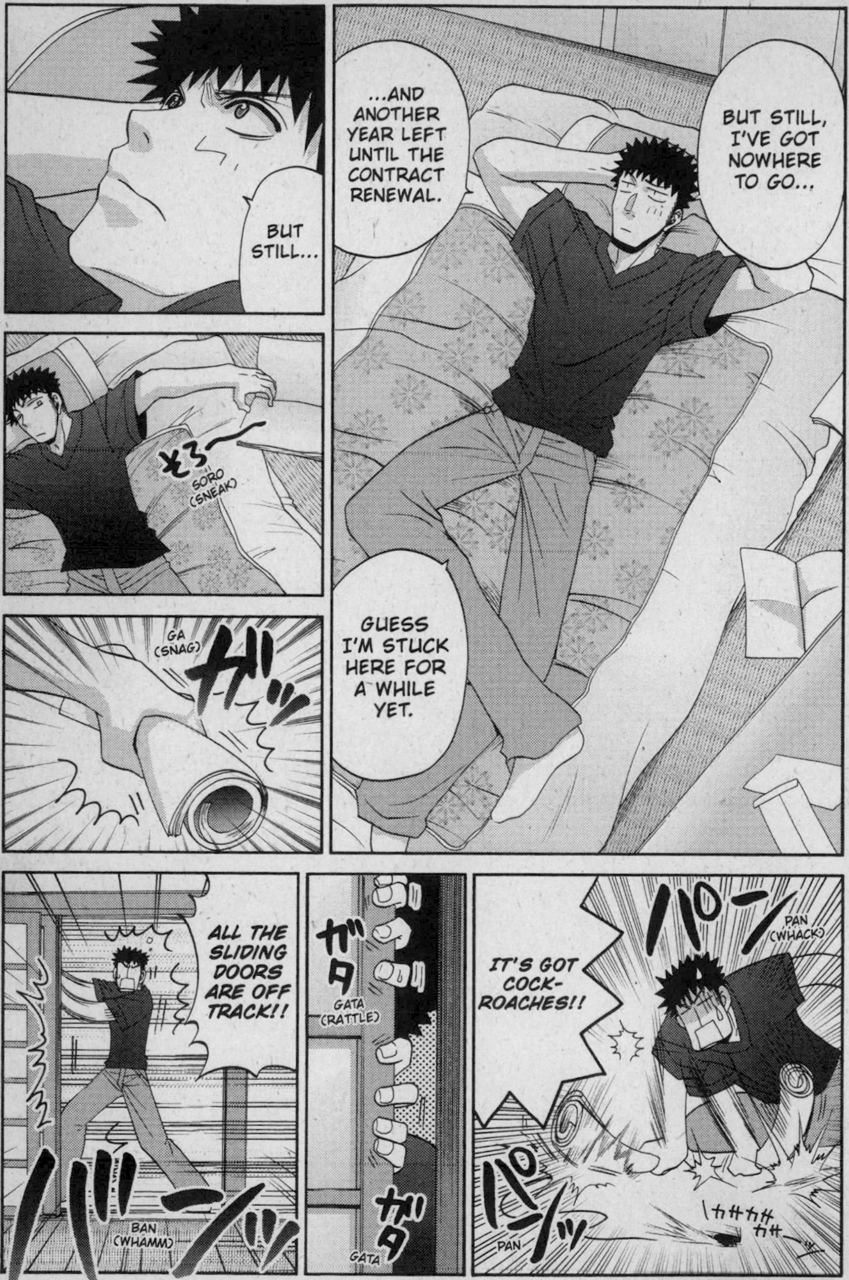
BUT STILL, I'VE GOT NOWHERE TO GO...
...AND ANOTHER YEAR LEFT UNTIL THE CONTRACT RENEWAL.
GUESS I'M STUCK HERE FOR A WHILE YET.
BUT STILL...
そろ〜
SORO (SNEAK)
GA (SNAG)
ガッ
パー
PAN (WHACK)
IT'S GOT COCK-ROACHES!!
パンッ
PAN
ガタ
GATA (RATTLE)
ガタ
GATA
ALL THE SLIDING DOORS ARE OFF TRACK!!
BAN (WHAMM)

SFX: KASAKASAKASA (SCUTTLE)

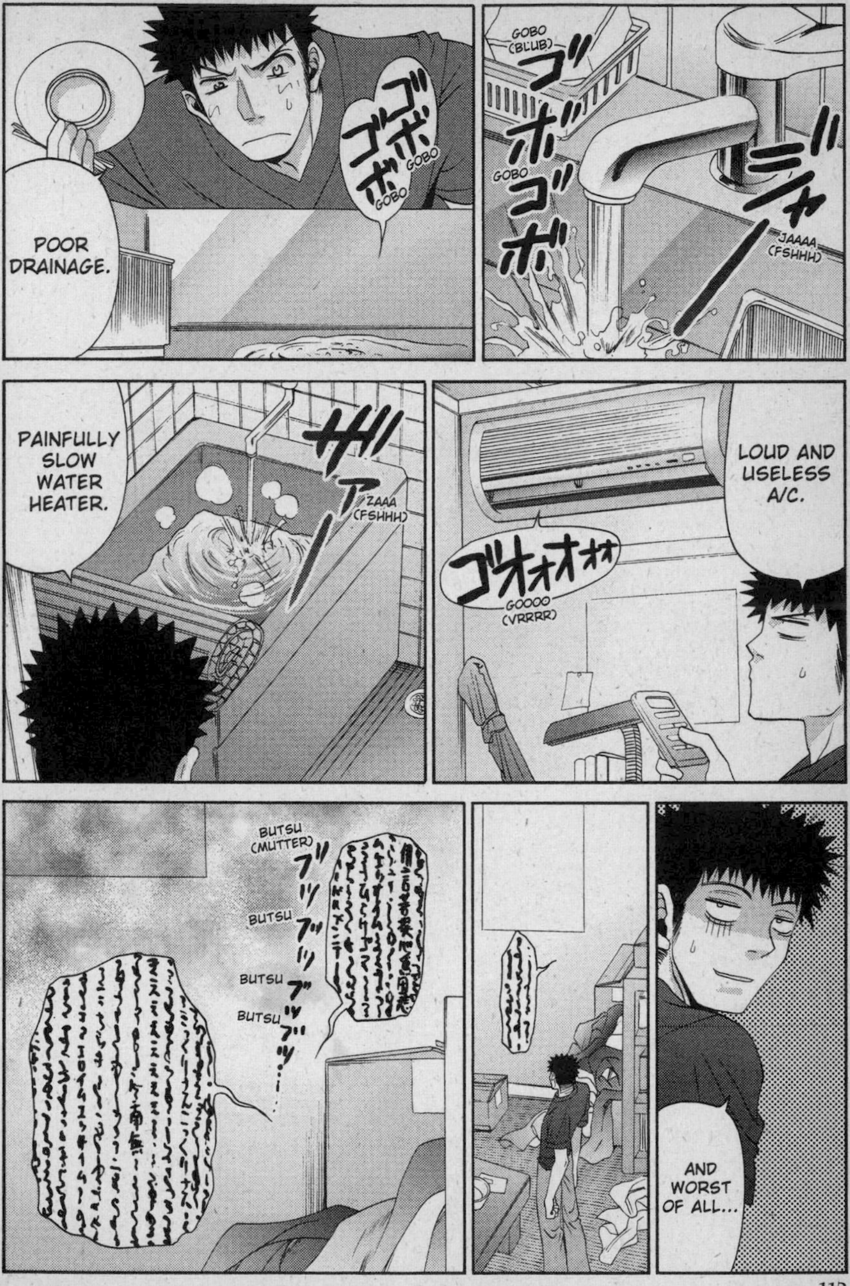
GOBO (BLUB)
ゴボゴボ
GOBO
ジャー
JAAAA (FSHHH)
ゴボゴボ
GOBO
GOBO
POOR DRAINAGE.
LOUD AND USELESS A/C.
ゴオオオオオ
GOOOO (VRRRR)
PAINFULLY SLOW WATER HEATER.
ザァー
ZAAA (FSHHH)
AND WORST OF ALL...
BUTSU (MUTTER)
ブツ
BUTSU
ブツ
BUTSU
ブツ
BUTSU
ブツ

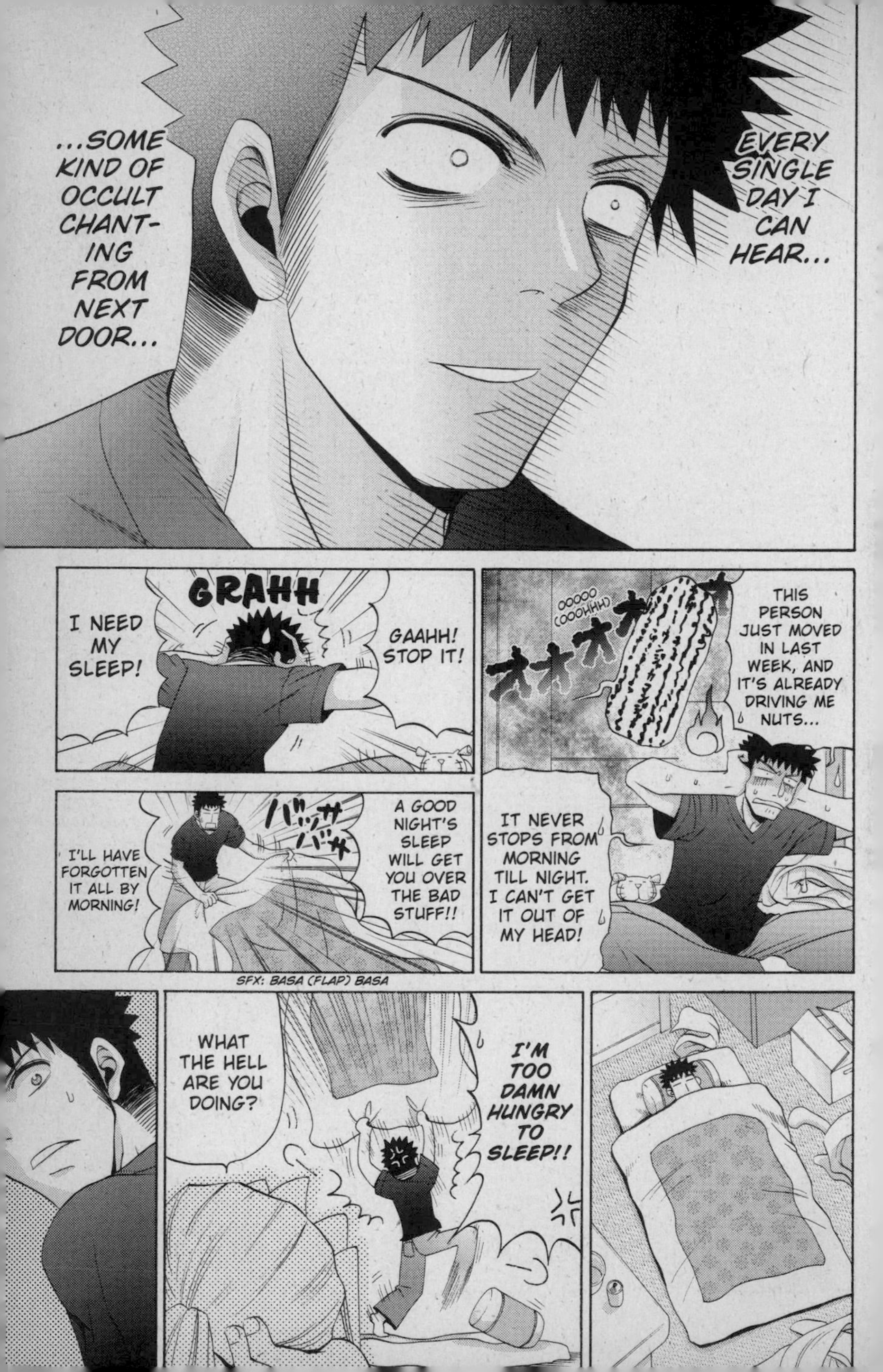
EVERY SINGLE DAY I CAN HEAR...
...SOME KIND OF OCCULT CHANT-ING FROM NEXT DOOR...
OOOOO (OOOHHH)
THIS PERSON JUST MOVED IN LAST WEEK, AND IT'S ALREADY DRIVING ME NUTS...
IT NEVER STOPS FROM MORNING TILL NIGHT. I CAN'T GET IT OUT OF MY HEAD!
GAAHH! STOP IT!
GRAHH
I NEED MY SLEEP!
A GOOD NIGHT'S SLEEP WILL GET YOU OVER THE BAD STUFF!!
I'LL HAVE FORGOTTEN IT ALL BY MORNING!
SFX: BASA (FLAP) BASA
I'M TOO DAMN HUNGRY TO SLEEP!!
WHAT THE HELL ARE YOU DOING?

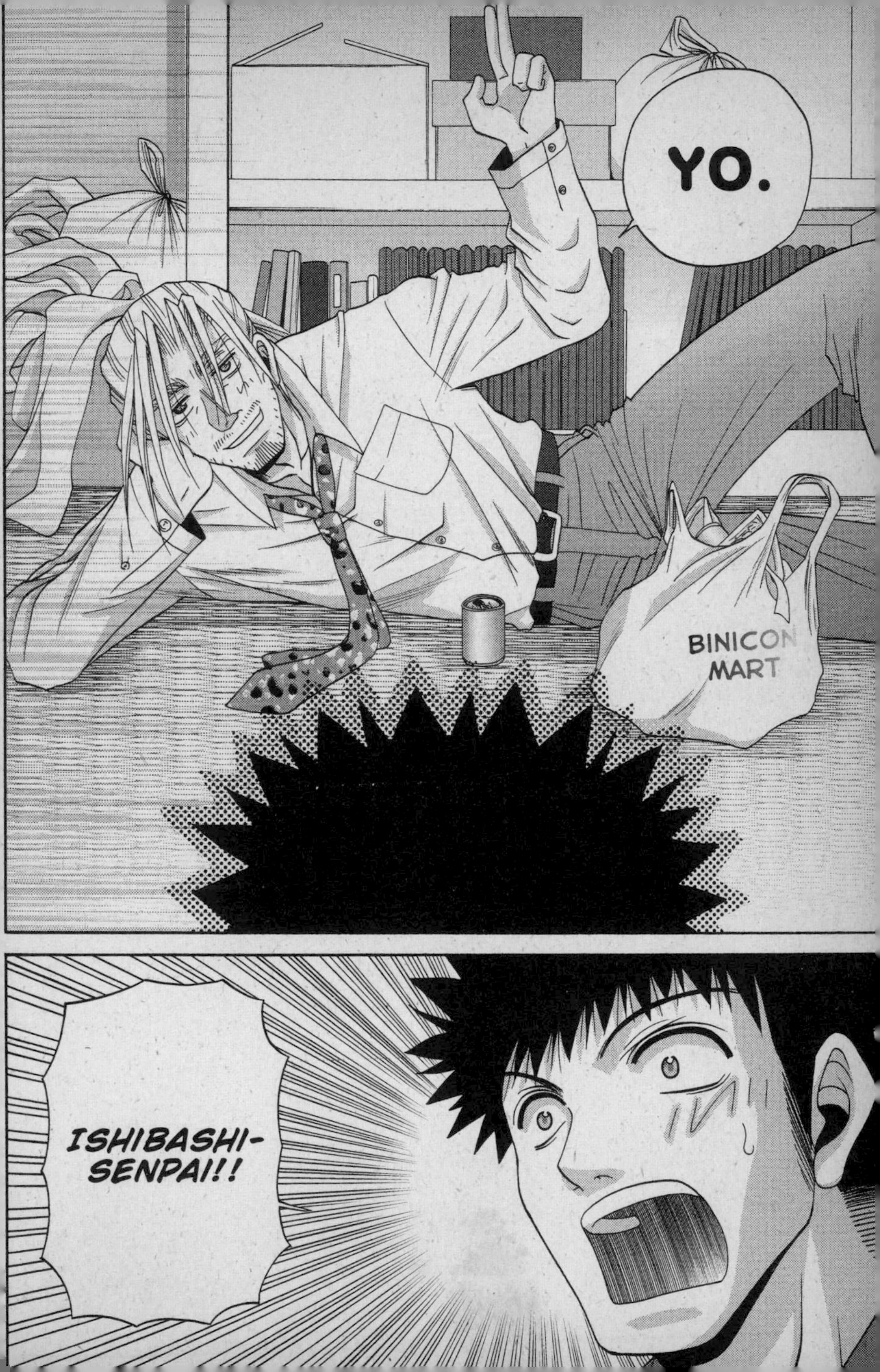
YO.
BINICON MART
ISHIBASHI-SENPAI!!

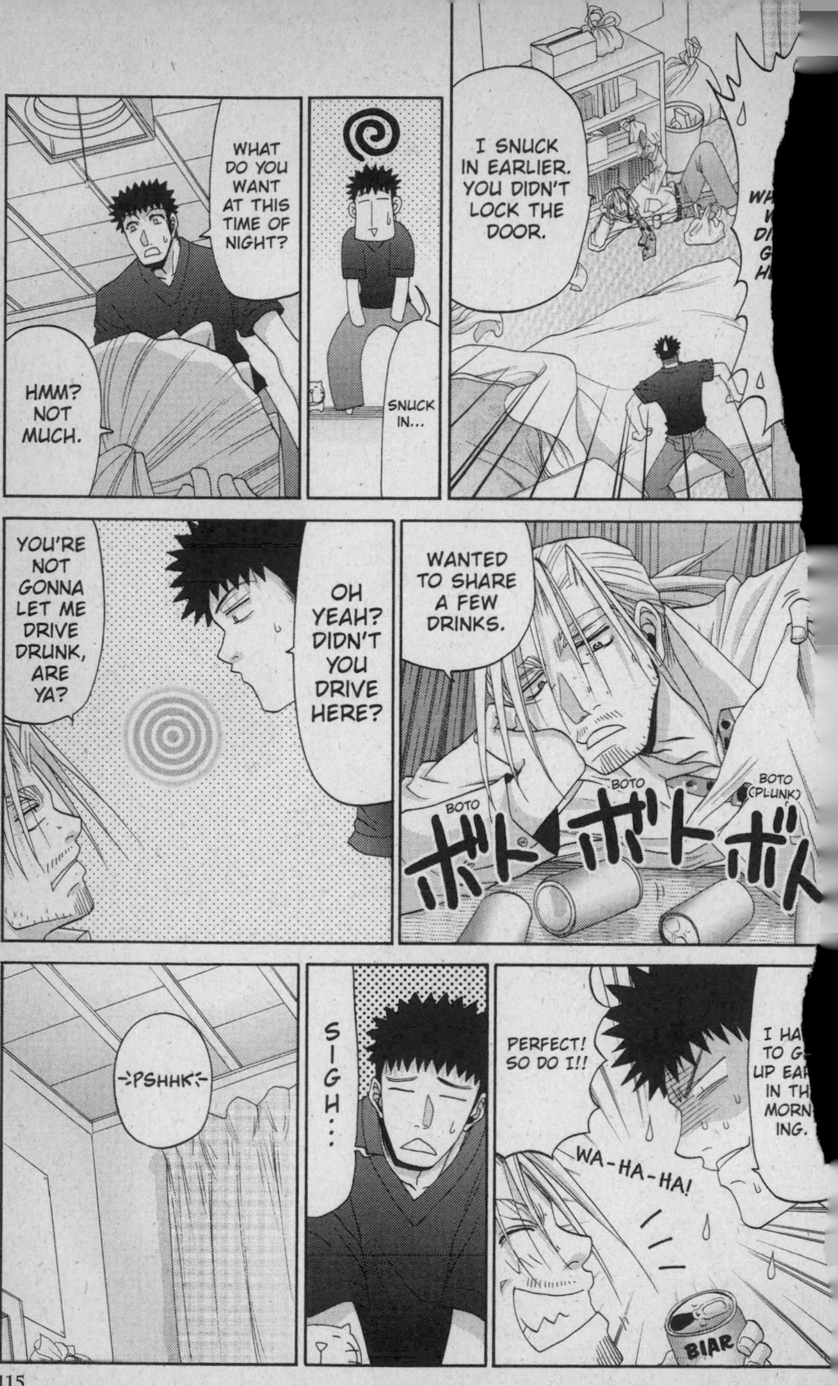
I SNUCK IN EARLIER. YOU DIDN'T LOCK THE DOOR.
SNUCK IN...
WHAT DO YOU WANT AT THIS TIME OF NIGHT?
HMM? NOT MUCH.
WANTED TO SHARE A FEW DRINKS.
BOTO
BOTO (PLUNK)
BOTO
ボトボトボ
OH YEAH? DIDN'T YOU DRIVE HERE?
YOU'RE NOT GONNA LET ME DRIVE DRUNK, ARE YA?
PERFECT! SO DO I!!
WA-HA-HA!
BIAR
SIGH...
PSHHK

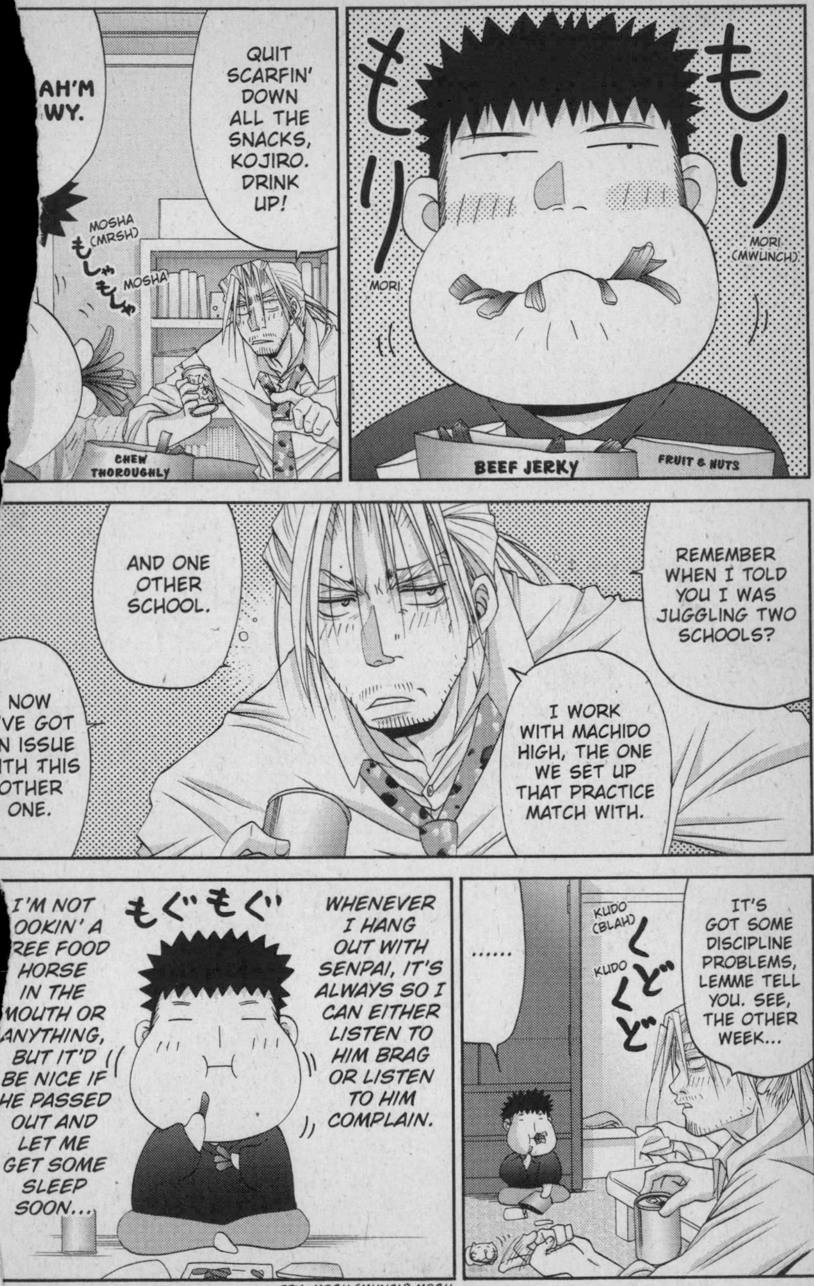
もり もり
MORI (MWUNCH) MORI
BEEF JERKY
FRUIT & NUTS
QUIT SCARFIN' DOWN ALL THE SNACKS, KOJIRO. DRINK UP!
AH'M WY.
MOSHA (MRSH) もしゃもしゃ MOSHA
CHEW THOROUGHLY
REMEMBER WHEN I TOLD YOU I WAS JUGGLING TWO SCHOOLS?
I WORK WITH MACHIDO HIGH, THE ONE WE SET UP THAT PRACTICE MATCH WITH.
AND ONE OTHER SCHOOL.
NOW 'VE GOT N ISSUE ITH THIS OTHER ONE.
IT'S GOT SOME DISCIPLINE PROBLEMS, LEMME TELL YOU. SEE, THE OTHER WEEK...
KUDO (BLAH) くどくど KUDO
......
WHENEVER I HANG OUT WITH SENPAI, IT'S ALWAYS SO I CAN EITHER LISTEN TO HIM BRAG OR LISTEN TO HIM COMPLAIN.
I'M NOT OOKIN' A REE FOOD HORSE IN THE MOUTH OR ANYTHING, BUT IT'D BE NICE IF HE PASSED OUT AND LET ME GET SOME SLEEP SOON...
もぐもぐ

SFX: MOGU (MUNCH) MOGU

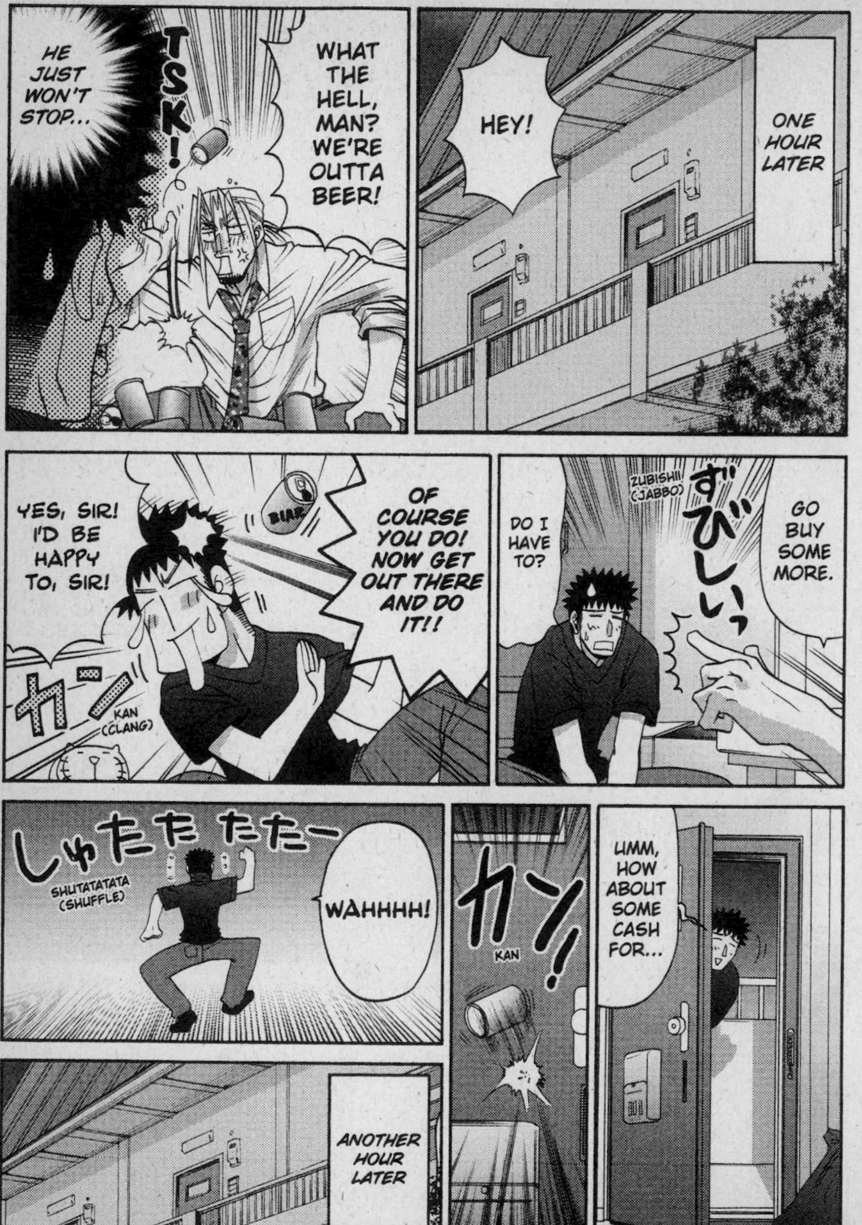

HEY!
ONE HOUR LATER
WHAT THE HELL, MAN? WE'RE OUTTA BEER!
TSK!
HE JUST WON'T STOP...
GO BUY SOME MORE.
ずびしぃっ
ZUBISHI! (JABBO)
DO I HAVE TO?
OF COURSE YOU DO! NOW GET OUT THERE AND DO IT!!
BIAR
YES, SIR! I'D BE HAPPY TO, SIR!
カン
KAN (CLANG)
UMM, HOW ABOUT SOME CASH FOR...
カン!
KAN
WAHHHH!
しゅたた たたー
SHUTATATATA (SHUFFLE)
ANOTHER HOUR LATER

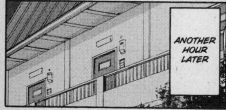

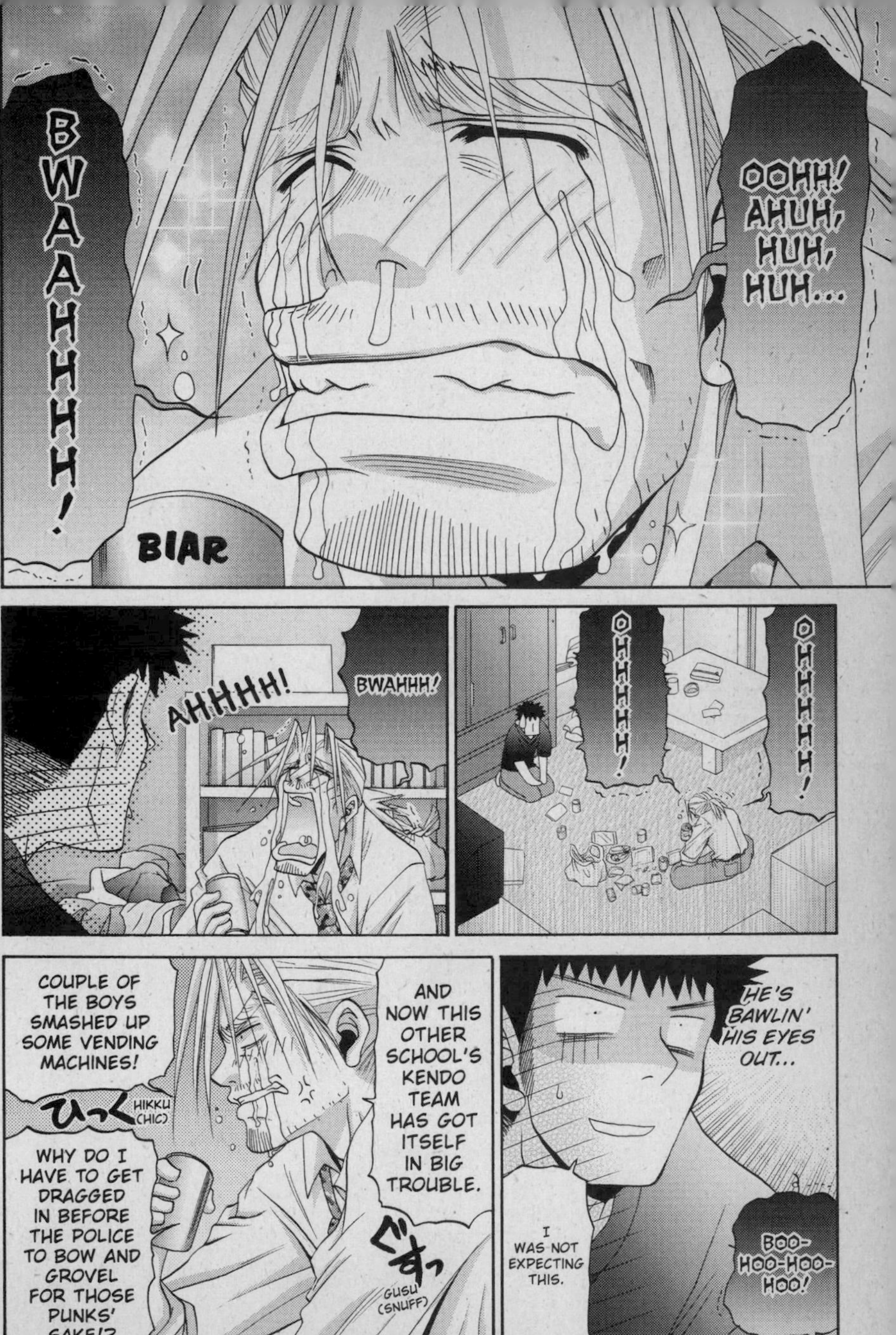
OOHH! AHUH, HUH, HUH...
BWAAHHHHH!
BIAR
OHHHHHH!
OHHHHHH!
BWAHHH!
AHHHHH!
HE'S BAWLIN' HIS EYES OUT...
BOO-HOO-HOO-HOO!
I WAS NOT EXPECTING THIS.
AND NOW THIS OTHER SCHOOL'S KENDO TEAM HAS GOT ITSELF IN BIG TROUBLE.
COUPLE OF THE BOYS SMASHED UP SOME VENDING MACHINES!
ひっく HIKKU (HIC)
WHY DO I HAVE TO GET DRAGGED IN BEFORE THE POLICE TO BOW AND GROVEL FOR THOSE PUNKS' SAKE!?
ぐすっ GUSU (SNUFF)

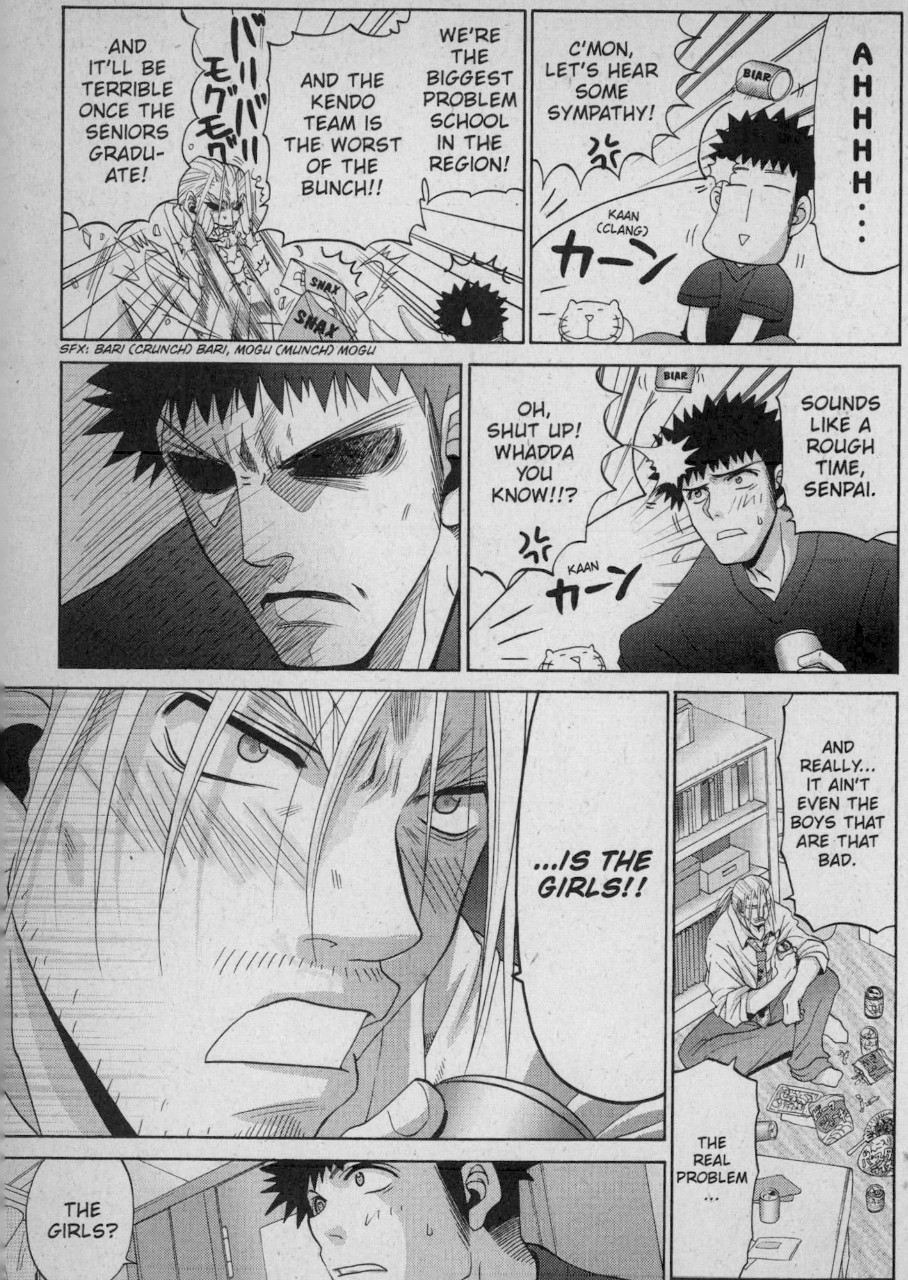
AHHHH...
C'MON, LET'S HEAR SOME SYMPATHY!
KAAN (CLANG)
カーン
WE'RE THE BIGGEST PROBLEM SCHOOL IN THE REGION!
AND THE KENDO TEAM IS THE WORST OF THE BUNCH!!
AND IT'LL BE TERRIBLE ONCE THE SENIORS GRADU-ATE!
SNAX
SNAX
SFX: BARI (CRUNCH) BARI, MOGU (MUNCH) MOGU
SOUNDS LIKE A ROUGH TIME, SENPAI.
OH, SHUT UP! WHADDA YOU KNOW!!?
KAAN
カーン
AND REALLY... IT AIN'T EVEN THE BOYS THAT ARE THAT BAD.
THE REAL PROBLEM ...
...IS THE GIRLS!!
THE GIRLS?

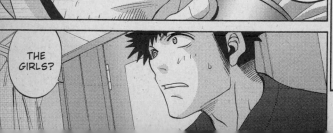

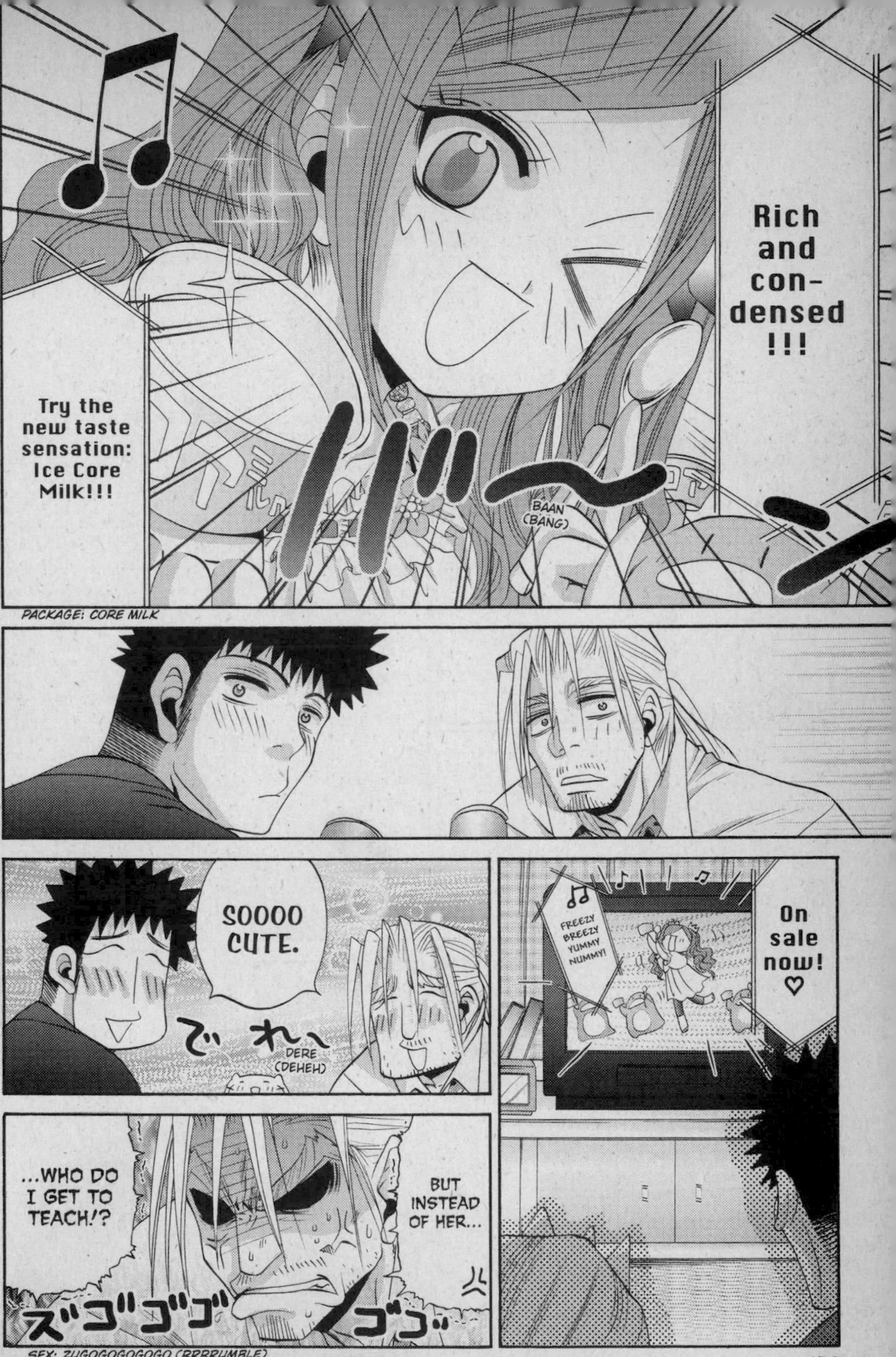
Rich and con-densed!!!
Try the new taste sensation: Ice Core Milk!!!
BAAN (BANG)
PACKAGE: CORE MILK
On sale now! ♡
FREEZY BREEZY YUMMY NUMMY!
SOOOO CUTE.
DERE (DEHEH)
BUT INSTEAD OF HER...
...WHO DO I GET TO TEACH!?
SFX: ZUGOGOGOGOGO (RRRRUMBLE)

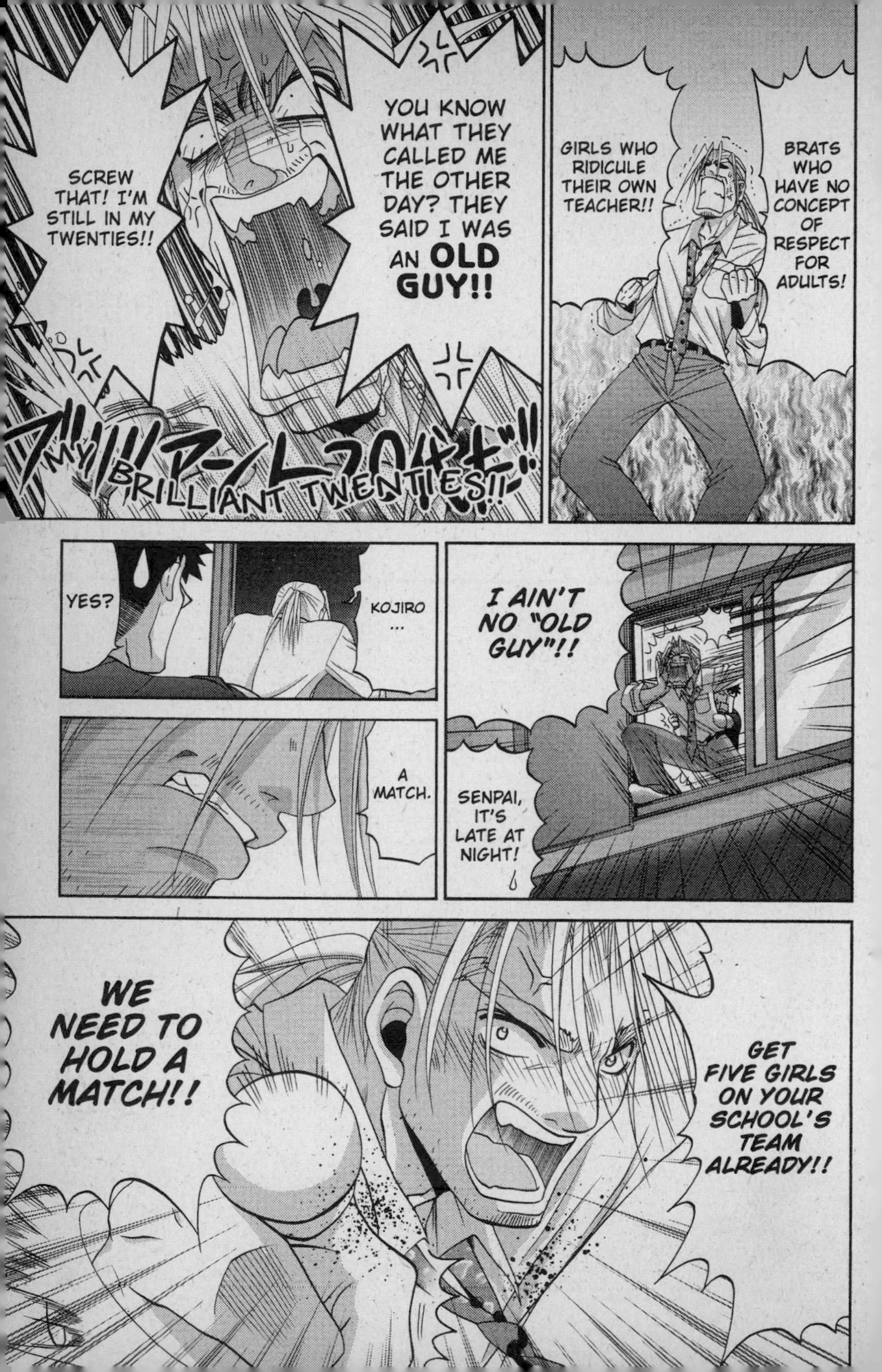
BRATS WHO HAVE NO CONCEPT OF RESPECT FOR ADULTS!
GIRLS WHO RIDICULE THEIR OWN TEACHER!!
YOU KNOW WHAT THEY CALLED ME THE OTHER DAY? THEY SAID I WAS AN **OLD GUY!!**
SCREW THAT! I'M STILL IN MY TWENTIES!!
MY BRILLIANT TWENTIES!!
I AIN'T NO "OLD GUY"!!
SENPAI, IT'S LATE AT NIGHT!
KOJIRO ...
YES?
A MATCH.
GET FIVE GIRLS ON YOUR SCHOOL'S TEAM ALREADY!!
WE NEED TO HOLD A MATCH!!

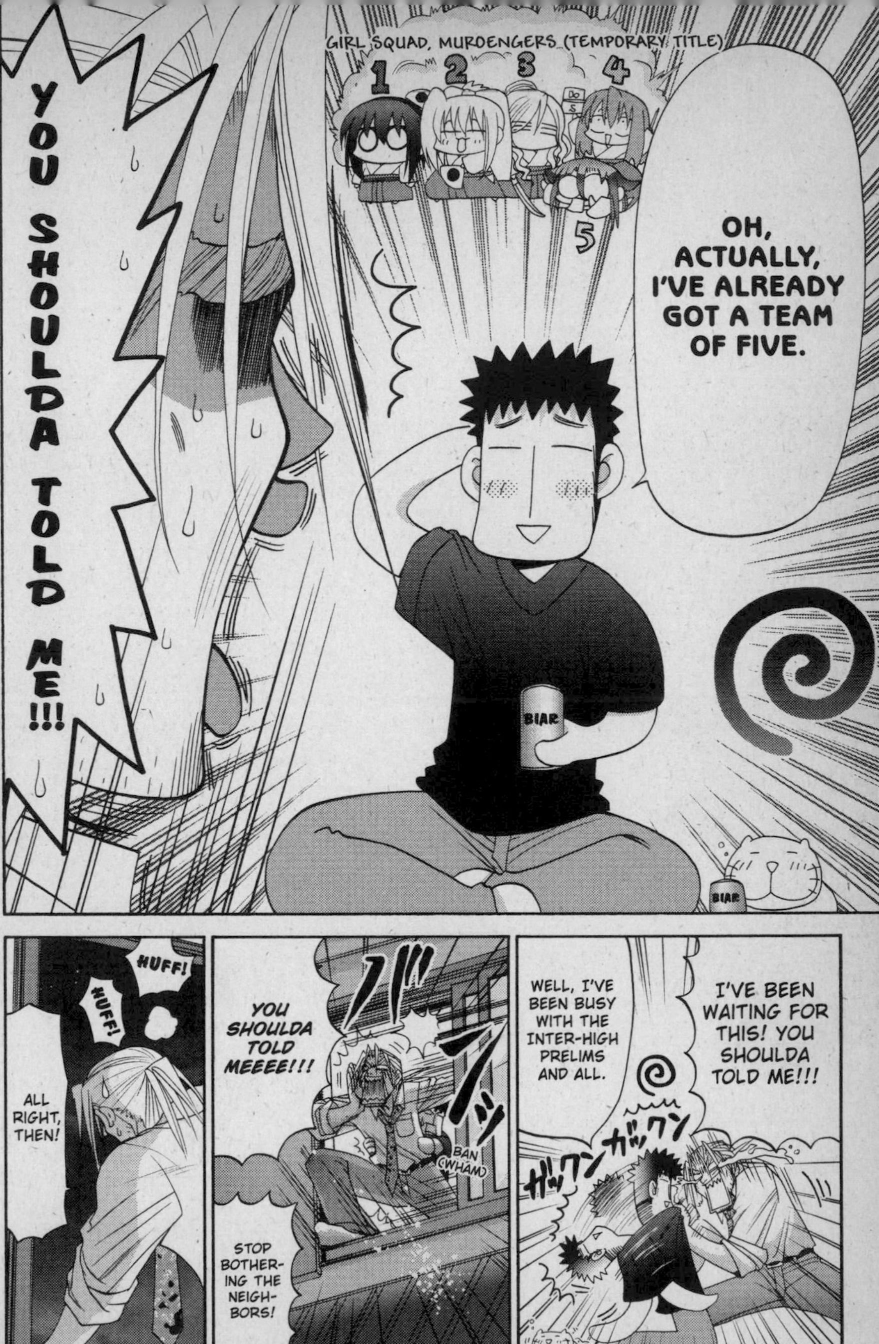
GIRL SQUAD, MURDENGERS (TEMPORARY TITLE)
1 2 3 4 5
OH, ACTUALLY, I'VE ALREADY GOT A TEAM OF FIVE.
YOU SHOULDA TOLD ME!!!
BIAR
BIAR
I'VE BEEN WAITING FOR THIS! YOU SHOULDA TOLD ME!!!
WELL, I'VE BEEN BUSY WITH THE INTER-HIGH PRELIMS AND ALL.
ガックン ガックン
YOU SHOULDA TOLD MEEEE!!!
BAN (WHAM)
STOP BOTHER-ING THE NEIGH-BORS!
HUFF!
HUFF!
ALL RIGHT, THEN!

SFX: GAKKUN (THUNK) GAKKUN

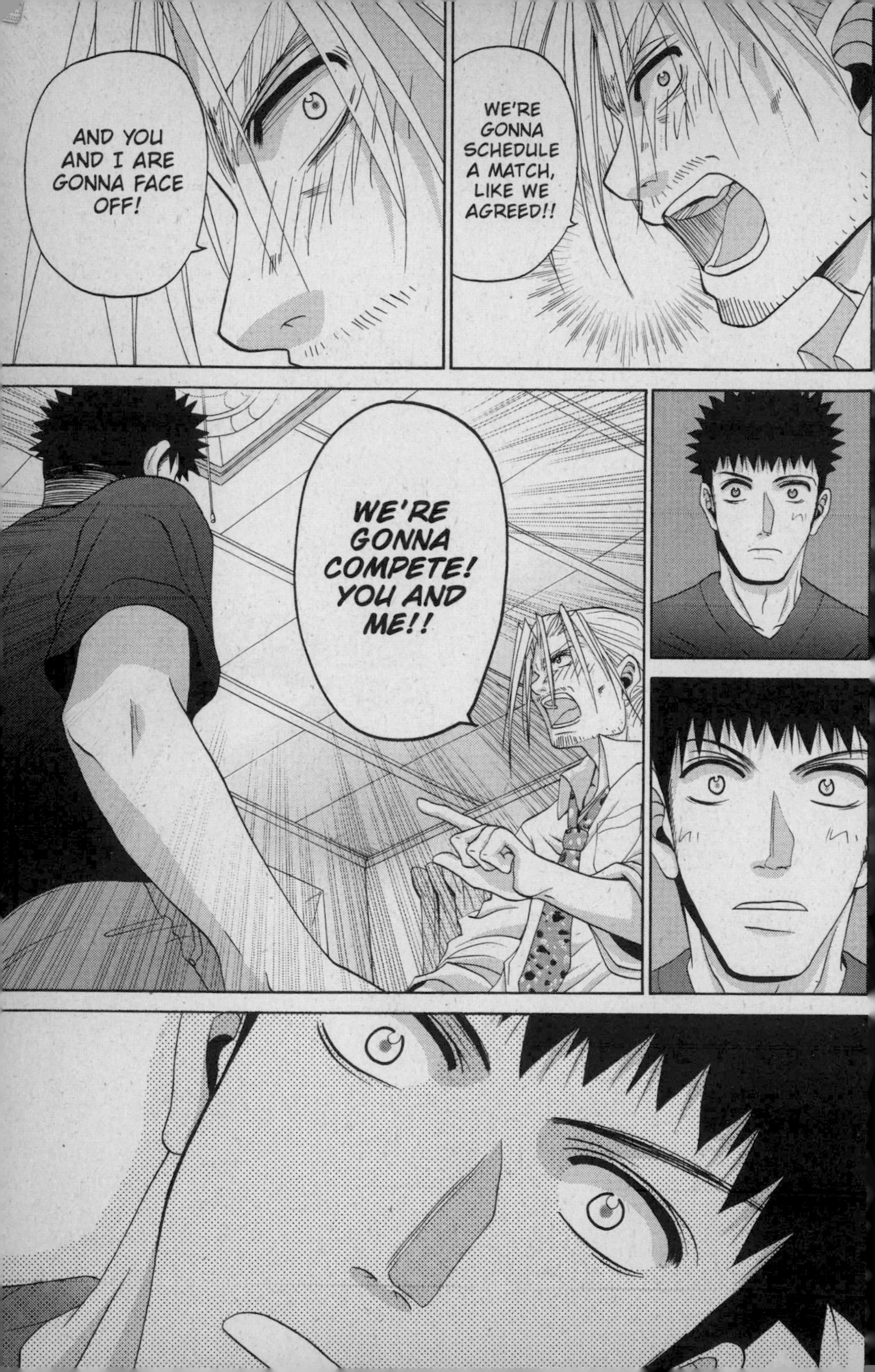
WE'RE GONNA SCHEDULE A MATCH, LIKE WE AGREED!!
AND YOU AND I ARE GONNA FACE OFF!
WE'RE GONNA COMPETE! YOU AND ME!!

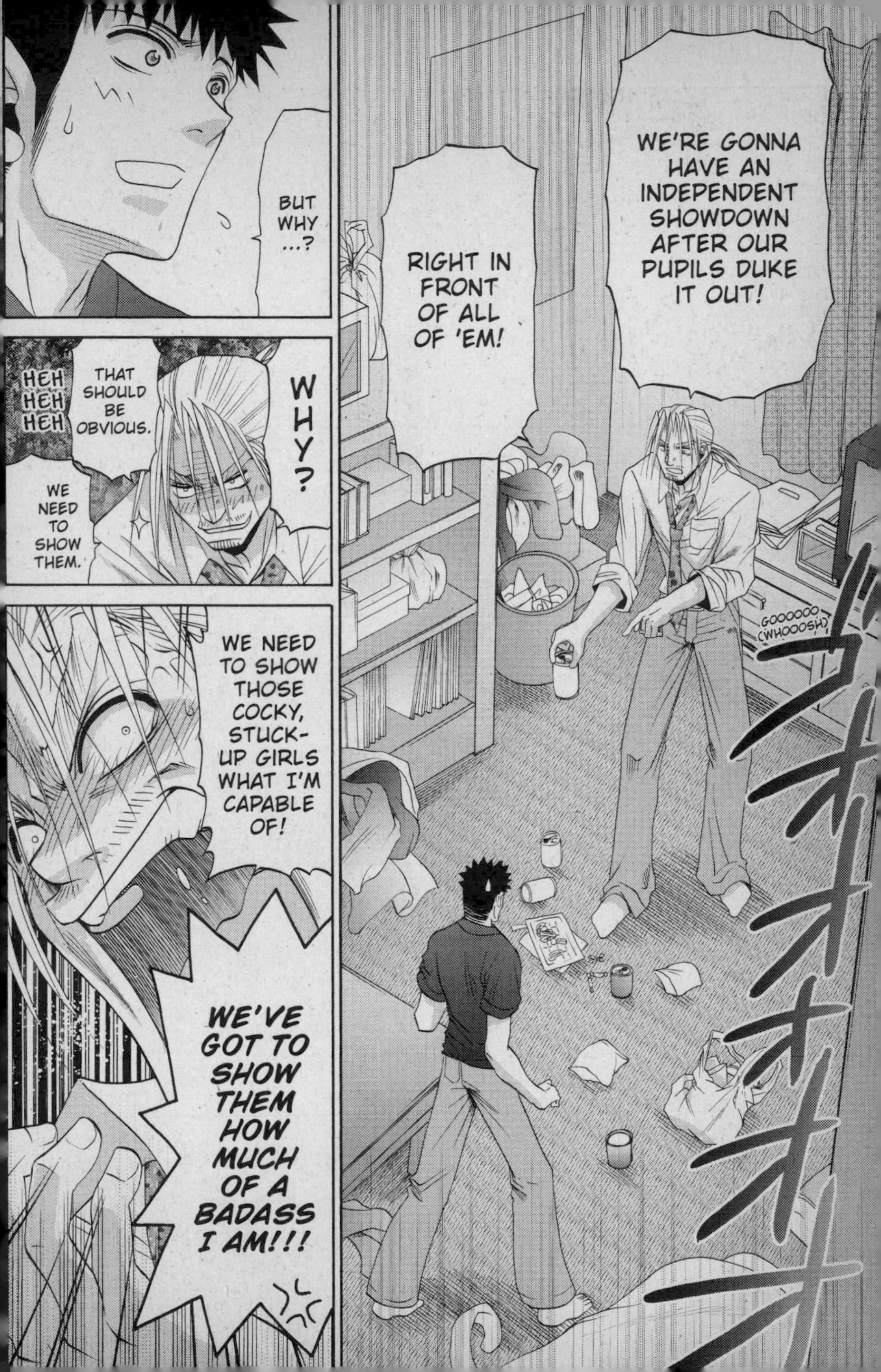
WE'RE GONNA HAVE AN INDEPENDENT SHOWDOWN AFTER OUR PUPILS DUKE IT OUT!
RIGHT IN FRONT OF ALL OF 'EM!
GOOOOOO (WHOOOSH)
BUT WHY ...?
WHY?
THAT SHOULD BE OBVIOUS.
HEH HEH HEH
WE NEED TO SHOW THEM.
WE NEED TO SHOW THOSE COCKY, STUCK-UP GIRLS WHAT I'M CAPABLE OF!
WE'VE GOT TO SHOW THEM HOW MUCH OF A BADASS I AM!!!

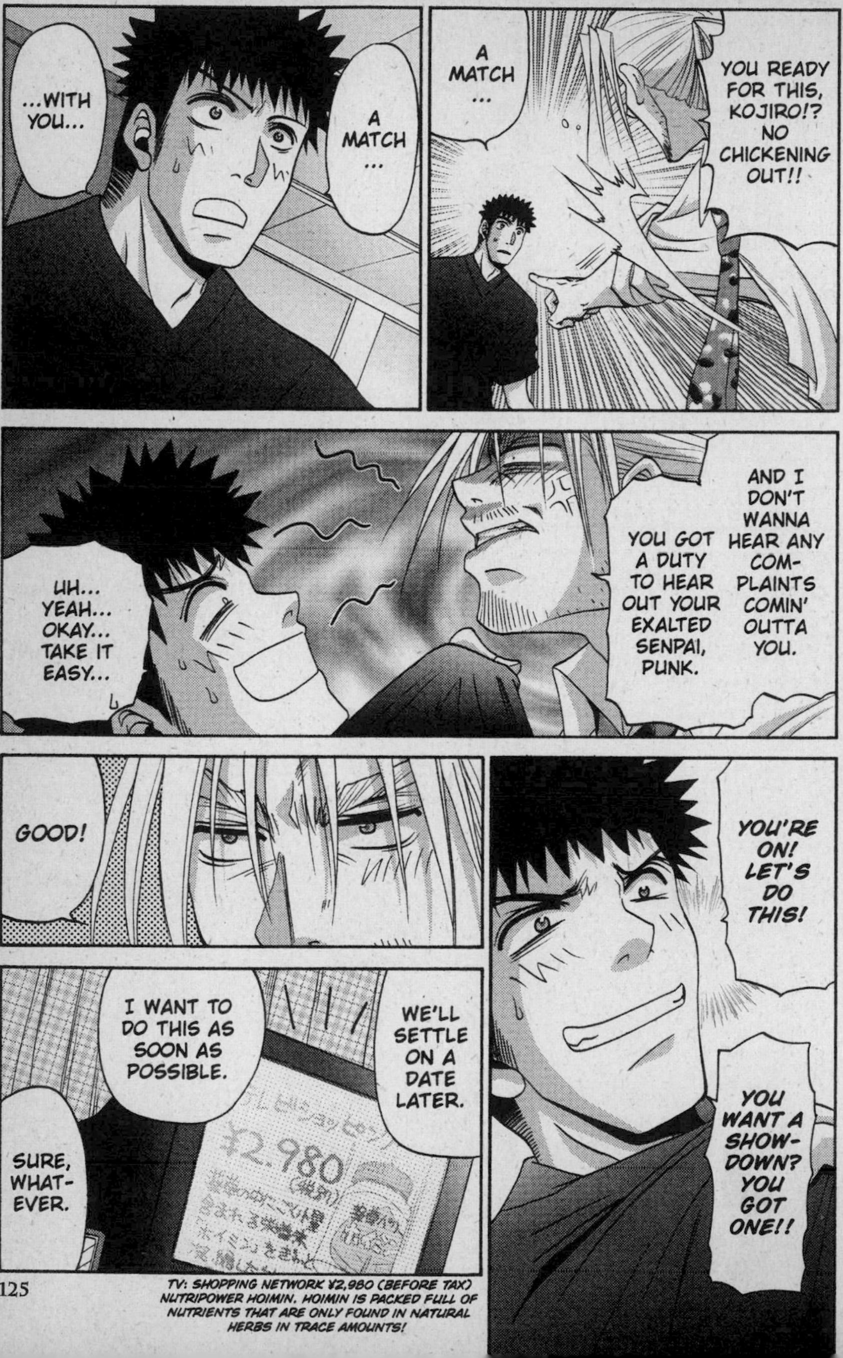
YOU READY FOR THIS, KOJIRO!? NO CHICKENING OUT!!
A MATCH ...
A MATCH ...
...WITH YOU...
AND I DON'T WANNA HEAR ANY COM- PLAINTS COMIN' OUTTA YOU.
YOU GOT A DUTY TO HEAR OUT YOUR EXALTED SENPAI, PUNK.
UH... YEAH... OKAY... TAKE IT EASY...
YOU'RE ON! LET'S DO THIS!
YOU WANT A SHOW- DOWN? YOU GOT ONE!!
GOOD!
WE'LL SETTLE ON A DATE LATER.
I WANT TO DO THIS AS SOON AS POSSIBLE.
SURE, WHAT- EVER.
¥2,980

TV: SHOPPING NETWORK ¥2,980 (BEFORE TAX) NUTRIPOWER HOIMIN. HOIMIN IS PACKED FULL OF NUTRIENTS THAT ARE ONLY FOUND IN NATURAL HERBS IN TRACE AMOUNTS!

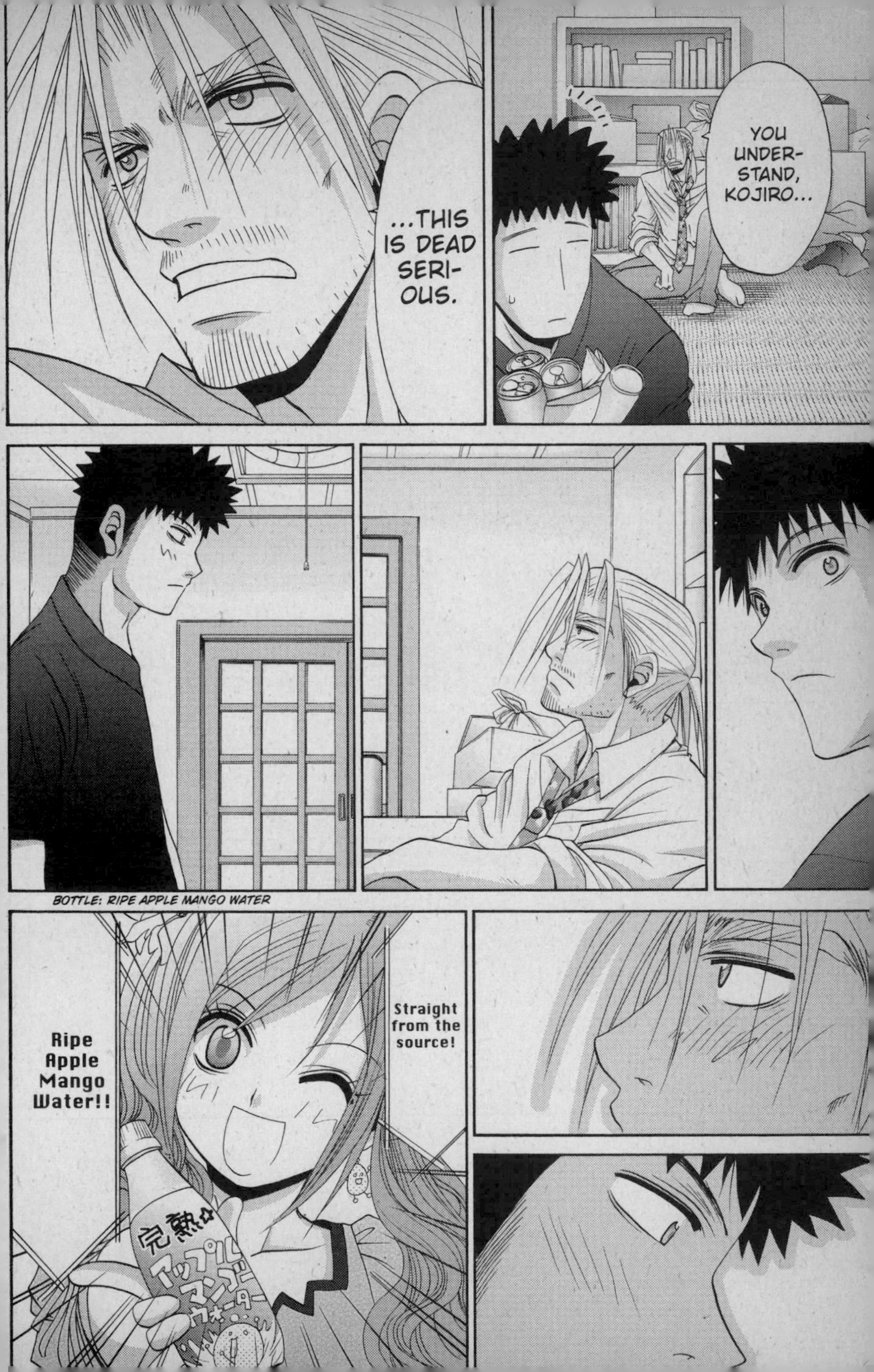
YOU UNDER-STAND, KOJIRO...
...THIS IS DEAD SERI-OUS.
BOTTLE: RIPE APPLE MANGO WATER
Straight from the source!
Ripe Apple Mango Water!!
完熟☆

HERA
(FLIMP)

SOOOO
CUTE.

On sale now!

(GUB!!!
GLUGG)

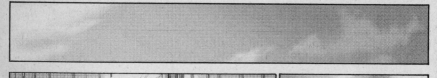

MM...

127

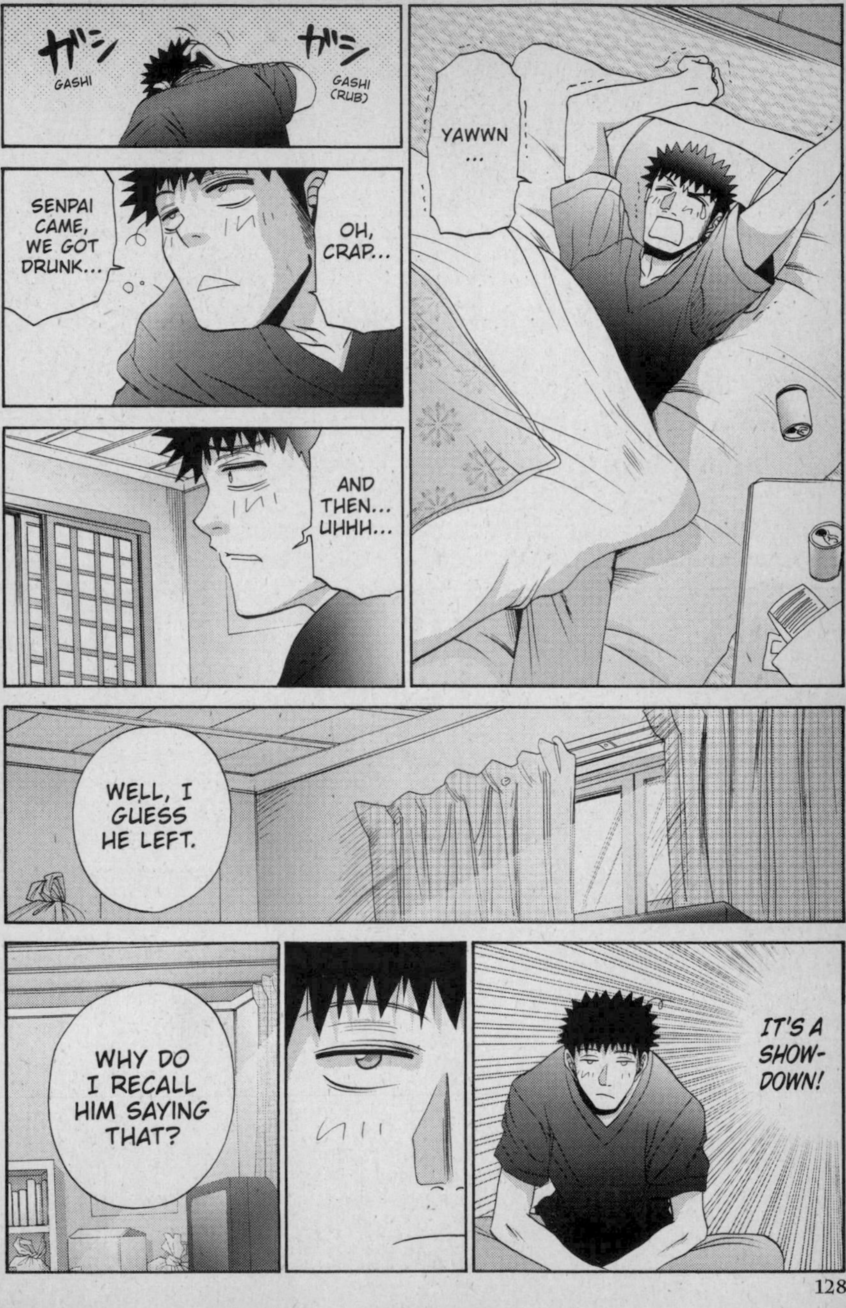
YAWWN ...
GASHI (RUB)
GASHI
OH, CRAP...
SENPAI CAME, WE GOT DRUNK...
AND THEN... UHHH...
WELL, I GUESS HE LEFT.
IT'S A SHOW-DOWN!
WHY DO I RECALL HIM SAYING THAT?

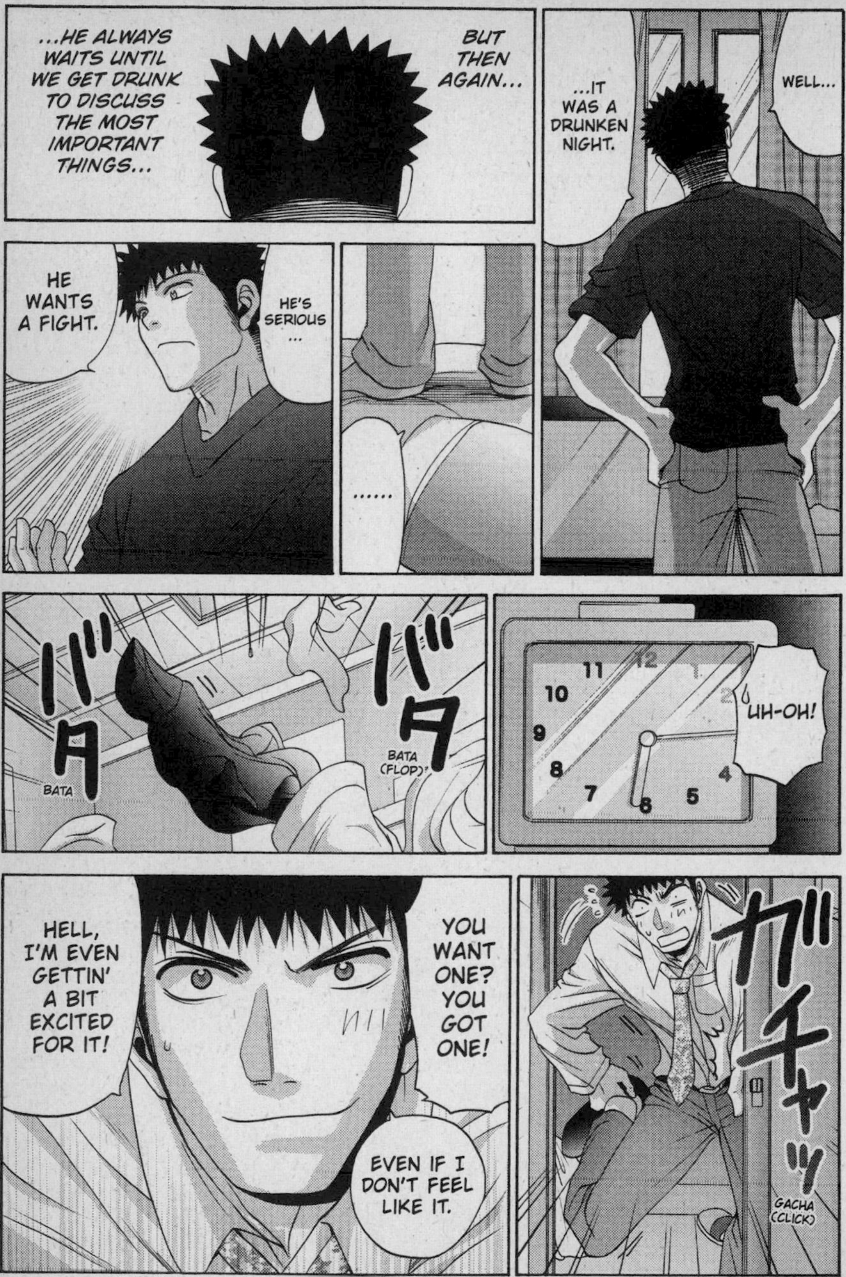
WELL...
...IT WAS A DRUNKEN NIGHT.
BUT THEN AGAIN...
...HE ALWAYS WAITS UNTIL WE GET DRUNK TO DISCUSS THE MOST IMPORTANT THINGS...
......
HE'S SERIOUS...
HE WANTS A FIGHT.
UH-OH!
バタ
BATA (FLOP)
バタ
BATA
ガチャッ
GACHA (CLICK)
YOU WANT ONE? YOU GOT ONE!
EVEN IF I DON'T FEEL LIKE IT.
HELL, I'M EVEN GETTIN' A BIT EXCITED FOR IT!

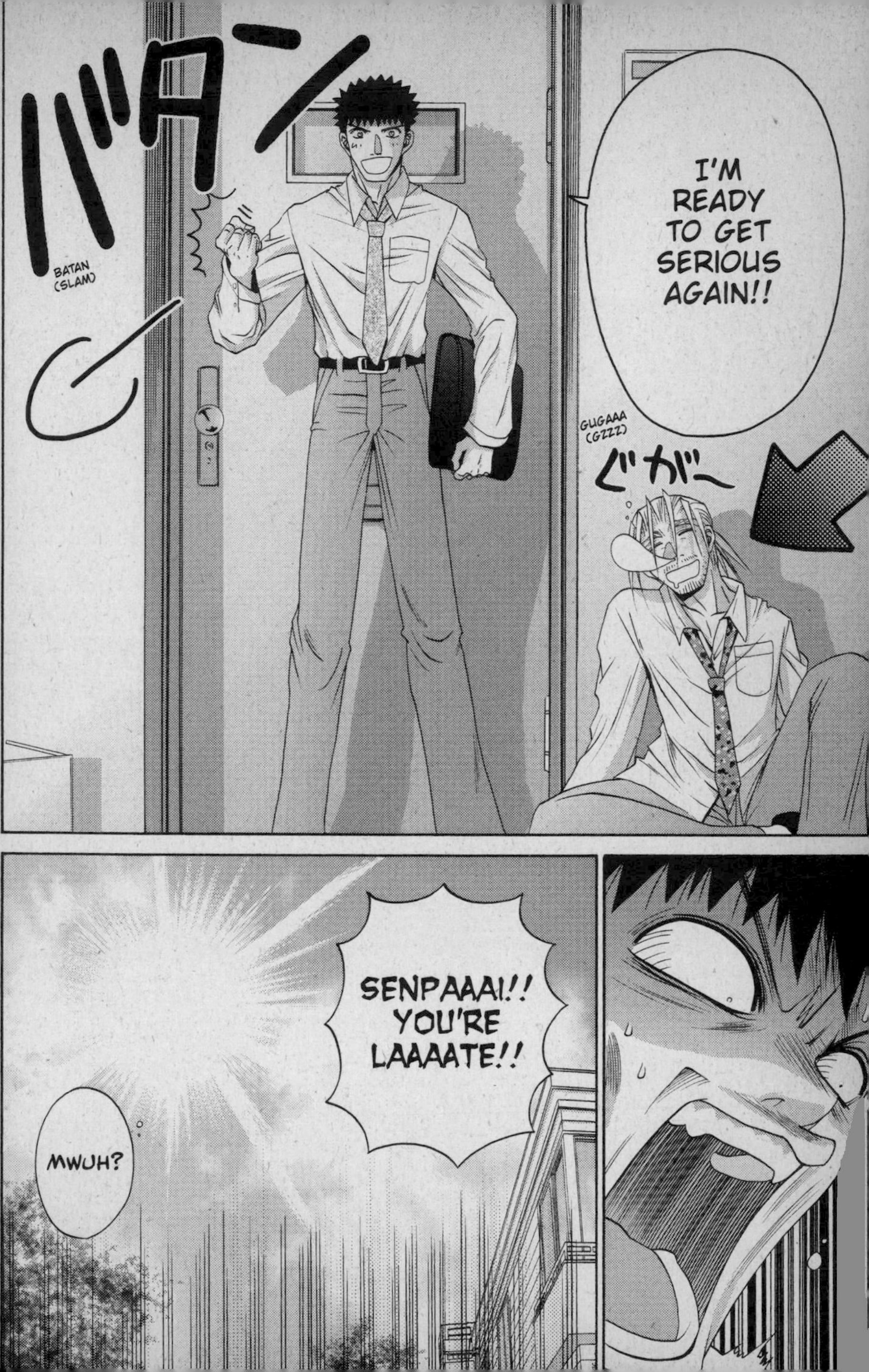
I'M READY TO GET SERIOUS AGAIN!!
バタン
BATAN (SLAM)
ぐがー
GUGAAA (GZZZ)
SENPAAAI!! YOU'RE LAAAATE!!
MWUH?

BAMBOO BLADE

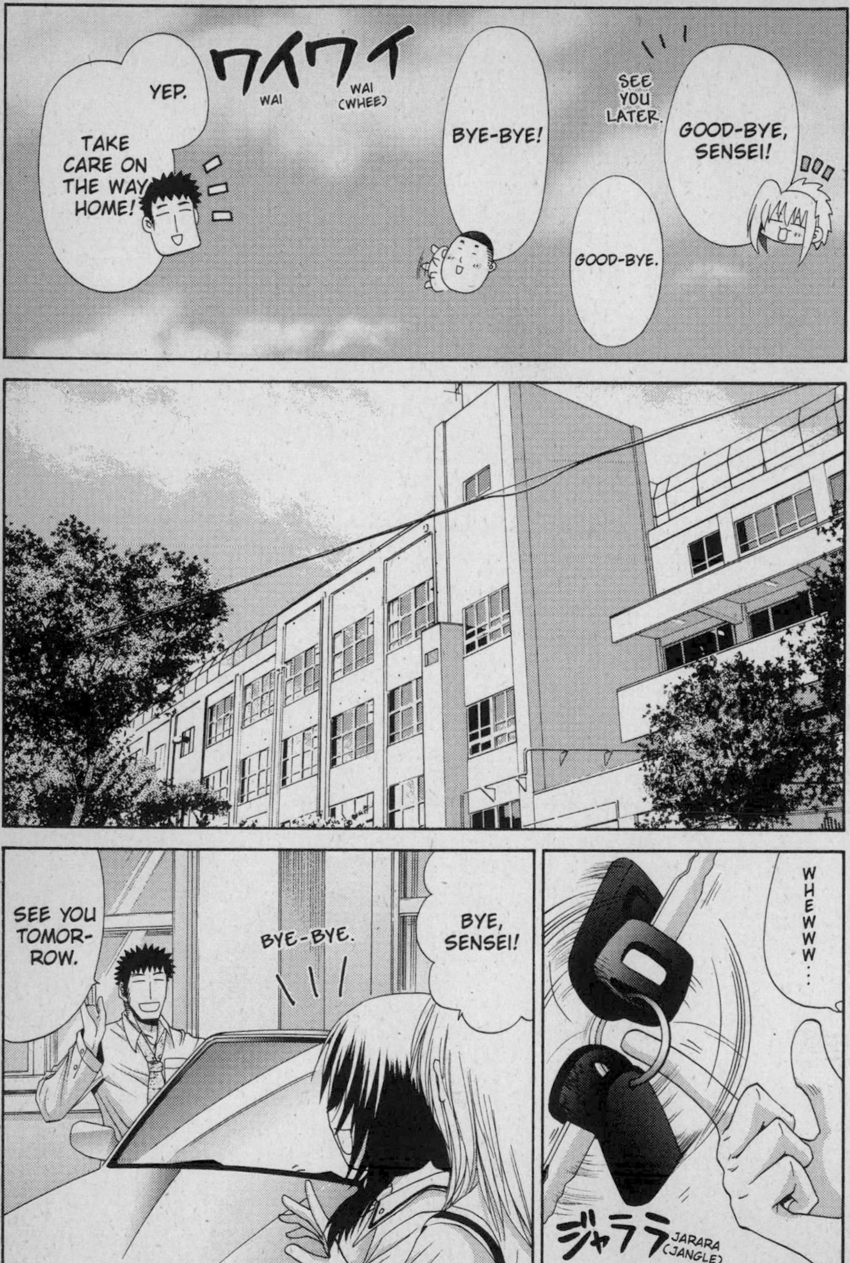
GOOD-BYE, SENSEI!
SEE YOU LATER.
GOOD-BYE.
BYE-BYE!
ワイワイ WAI WAI (WHEE)
YEP.
TAKE CARE ON THE WAY HOME!
WHEWWW...
ジャララ JARARA (JANGLE)
BYE, SENSEI!
BYE-BYE.
SEE YOU TOMOR-ROW.

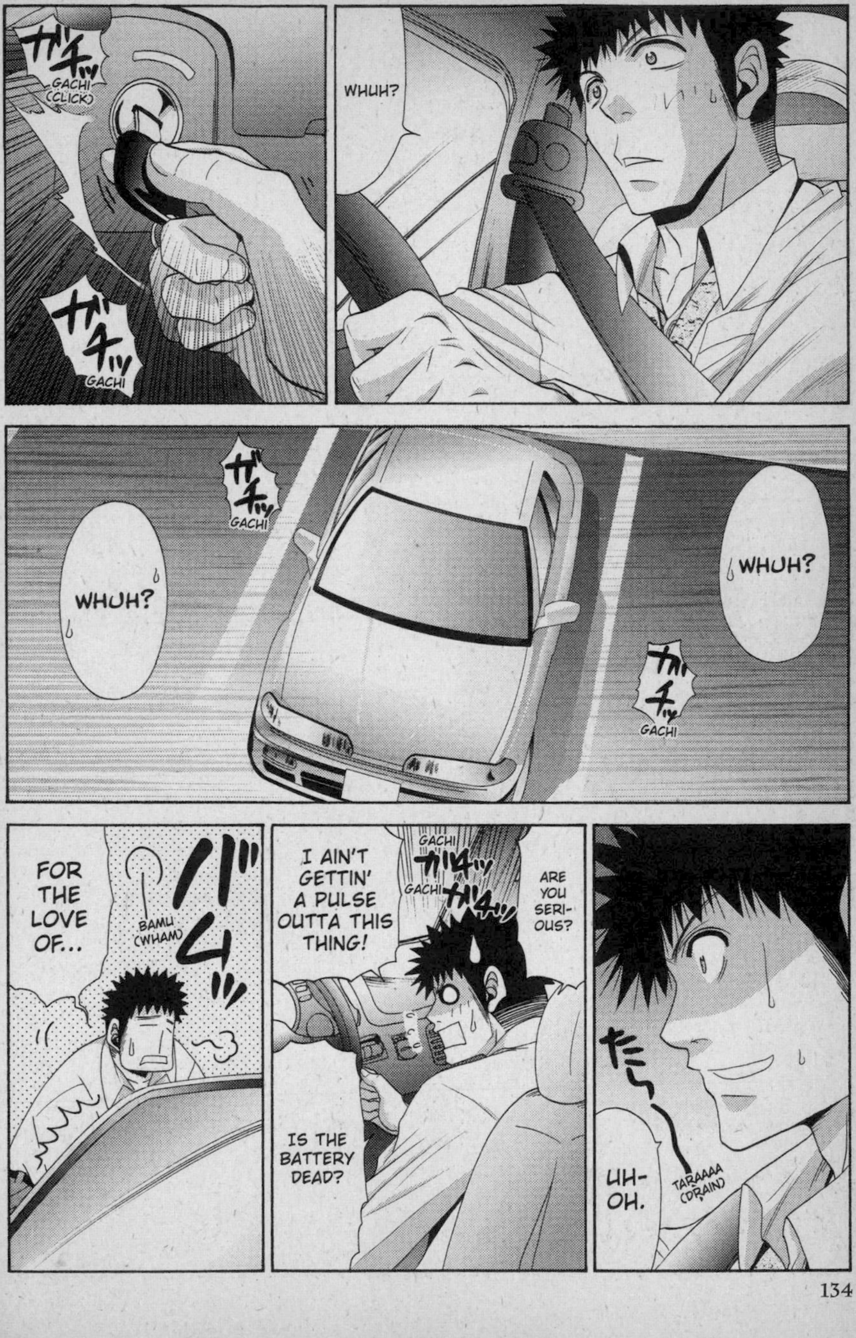
WHUH?
GACHI (CLICK)
GACHI
WHUH?
GACHI
GACHI
WHUH?
UH-OH.
TARAAAA (DRAIN)
ARE YOU SERIOUS?
GACHI
GACHI
I AIN'T GETTIN' A PULSE OUTTA THIS THING!
IS THE BATTERY DEAD?
BAMU (WHAM)
FOR THE LOVE OF...

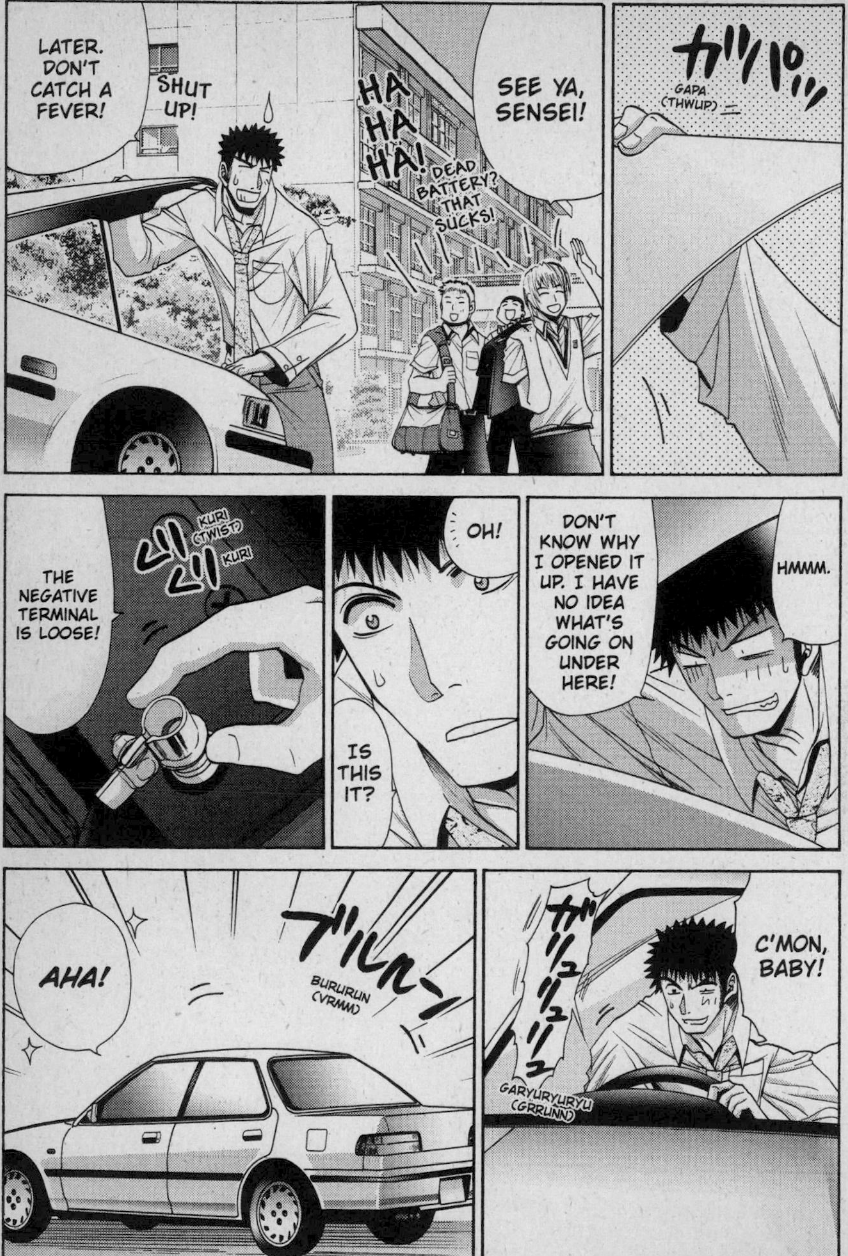
GAPA (THWUP)
SEE YA, SENSEI!
DEAD BATTERY? THAT SUCKS!
HA HA HA!
SHUT UP!
LATER. DON'T CATCH A FEVER!
HMMM.
DON'T KNOW WHY I OPENED IT UP. I HAVE NO IDEA WHAT'S GOING ON UNDER HERE!
OH!
IS THIS IT?
KURI (TWIST) KURI
THE NEGATIVE TERMINAL IS LOOSE!
C'MON, BABY!
GARYURYURYU (GRRUNN)
BURURUN (VRMM)
AHA!

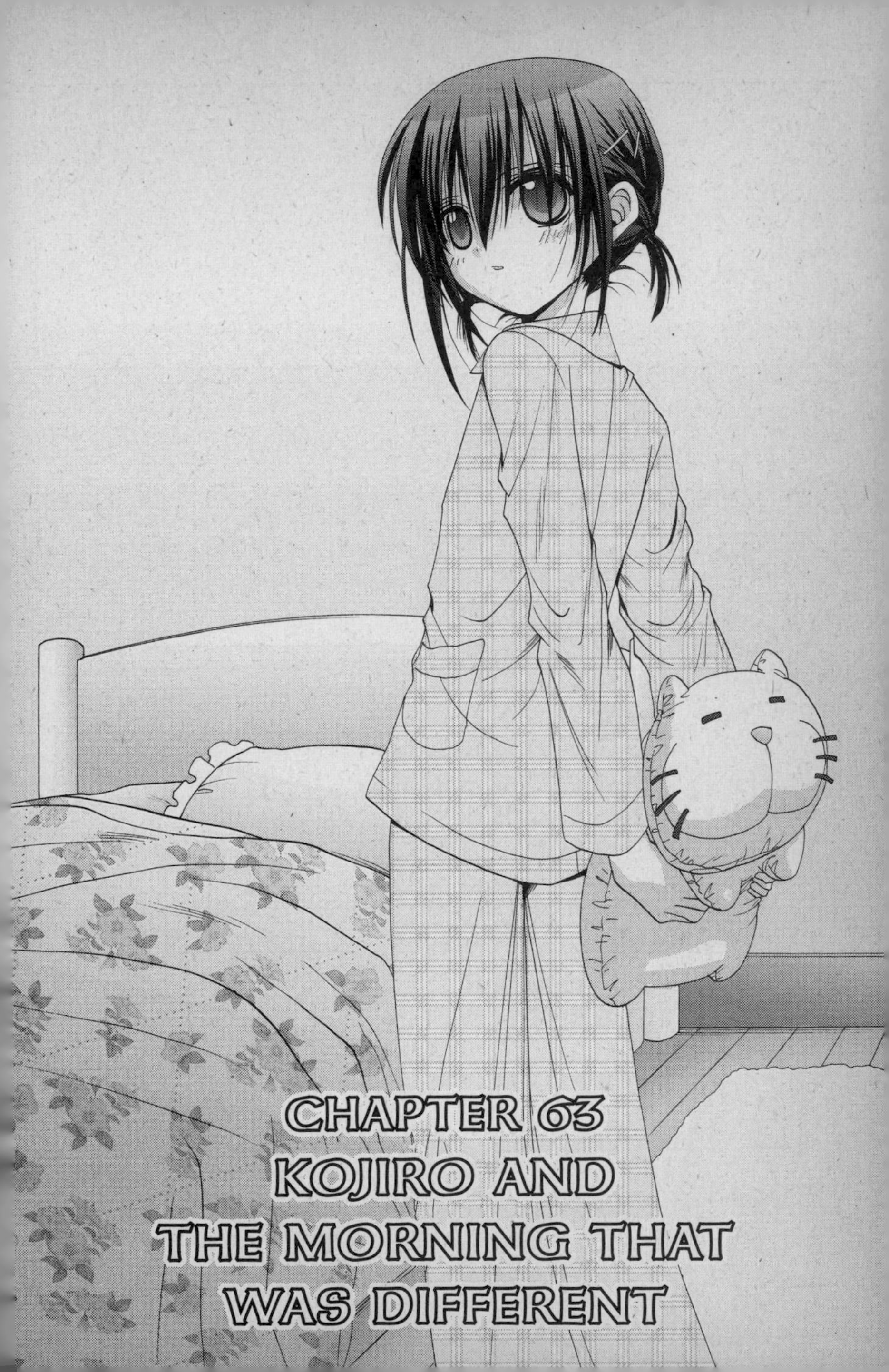
CHAPTER 63
KOJIRO AND
THE MORNING THAT
WAS DIFFERENT

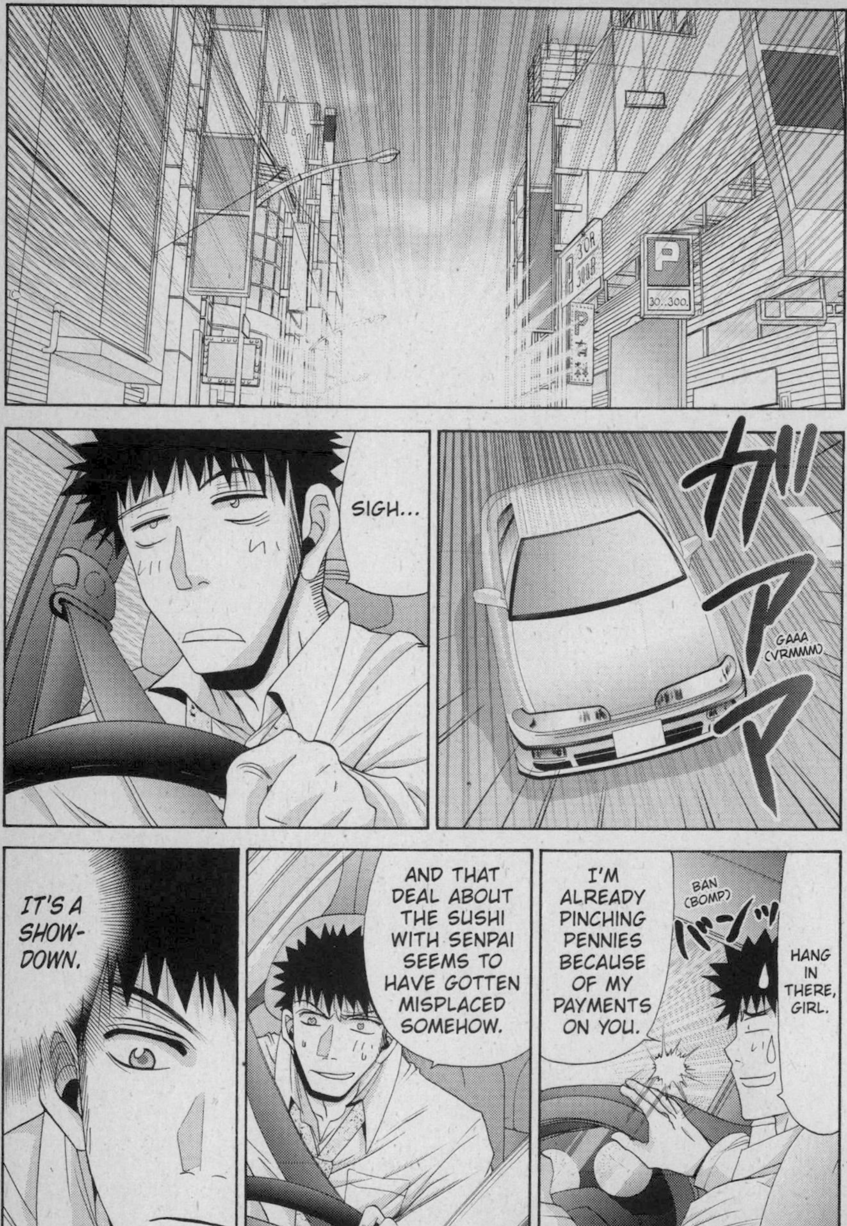
ガアア
GAAA (VRMMM)
SIGH...
BAN (BOMP)
バーンッ
HANG IN THERE, GIRL.
I'M ALREADY PINCHING PENNIES BECAUSE OF MY PAYMENTS ON YOU.
AND THAT DEAL ABOUT THE SUSHI WITH SENPAI SEEMS TO HAVE GOTTEN MISPLACED SOMEHOW.
IT'S A SHOW-DOWN.

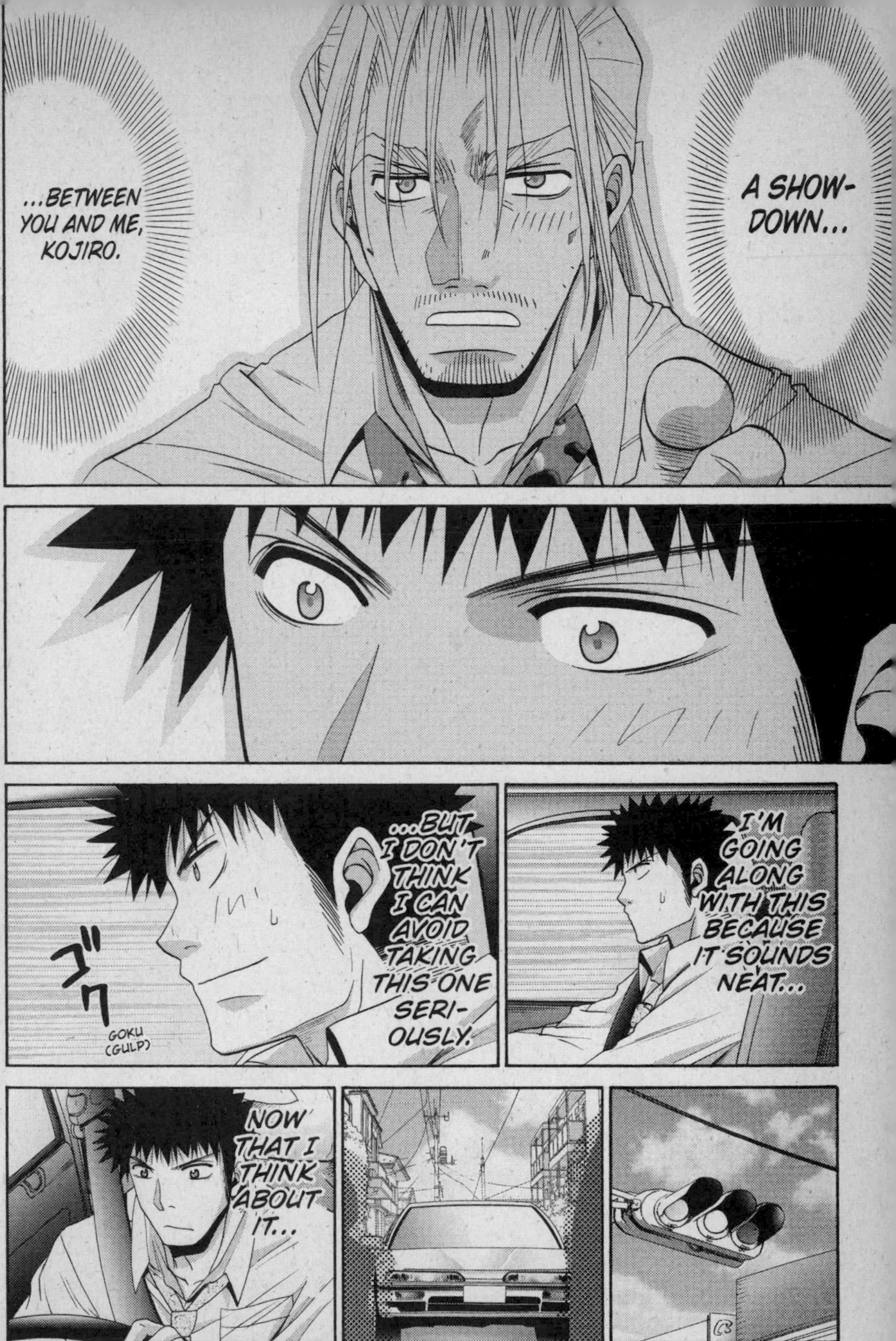
A SHOW-DOWN...
...BETWEEN YOU AND ME, KOJIRO.
I'M GOING ALONG WITH THIS BECAUSE IT SOUNDS NEAT...
...BUT I DON'T THINK I CAN AVOID TAKING THIS ONE SERIOUSLY.
ゴク
GOKU (GULP)
NOW THAT I THINK ABOUT IT...

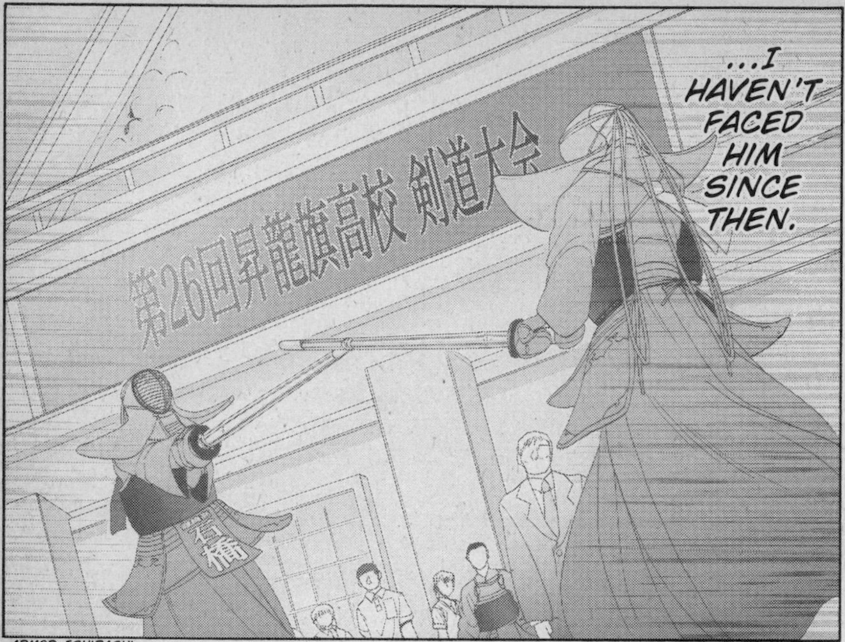
...I HAVEN'T FACED HIM SINCE THEN.
第26回昇龍旗高校 剣道大会
石橋

SIGN: 26TH SHOURYUUKI HIGH SCHOOL KENDO CHAMPIONSHIP

ARMOR: ISHIBASHI

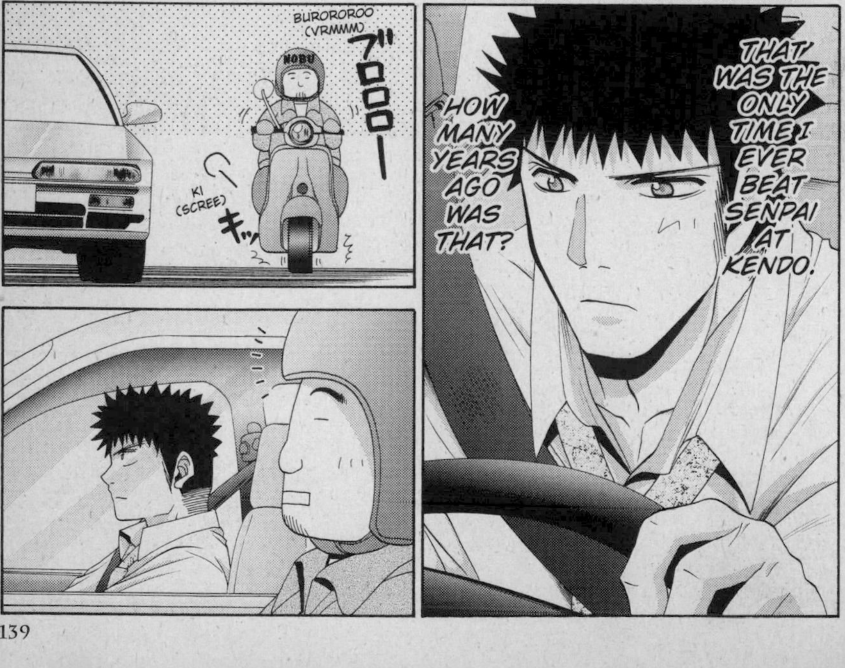
THAT WAS THE ONLY TIME I EVER BEAT SENPAI AT KENDO.
HOW MANY YEARS AGO WAS THAT?
BUROROROO (VRMMM)
ブロロロー
NOBU
KI (SCREE)
キッ

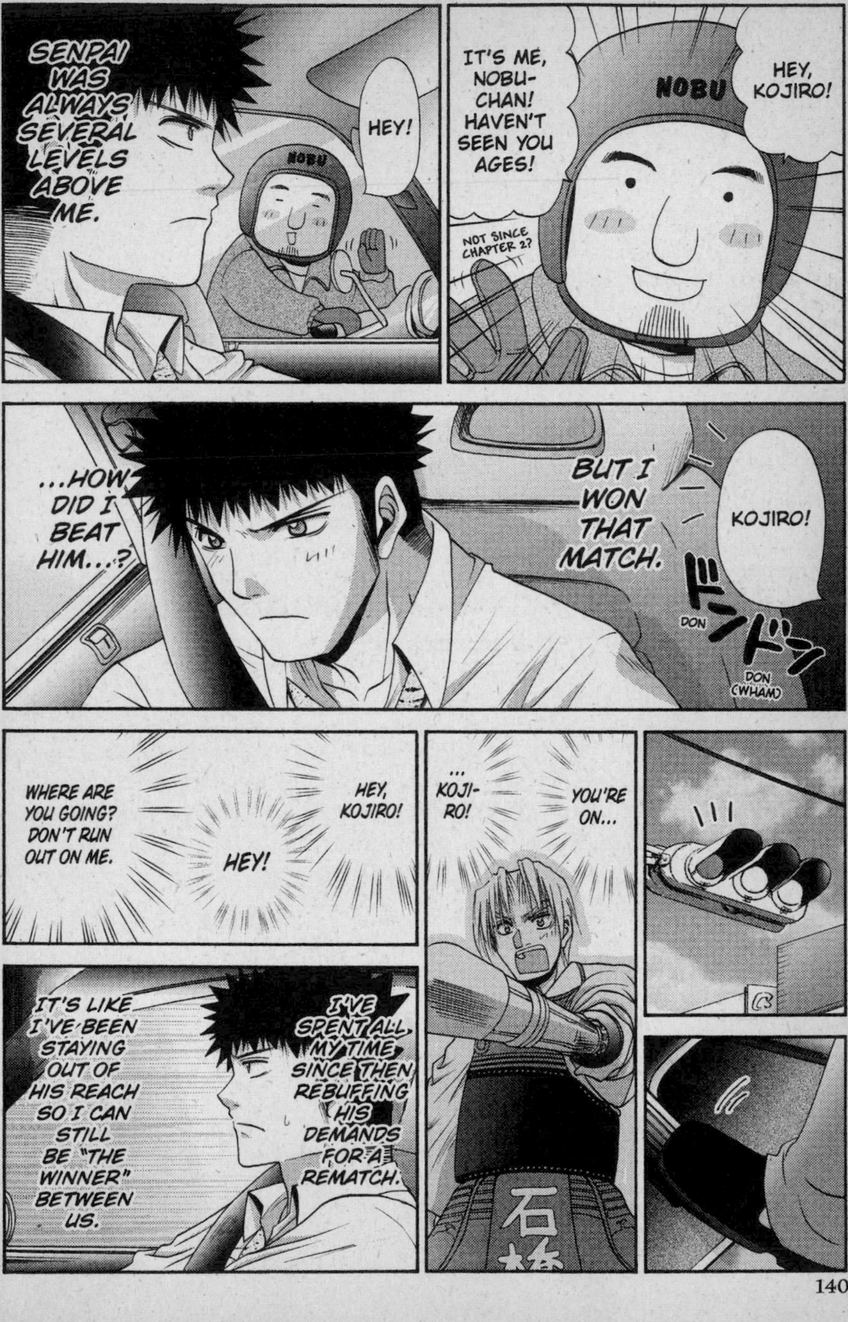
HEY, KOJIRO!
NOBU
IT'S ME, NOBU-CHAN! HAVEN'T SEEN YOU AGES!
NOT SINCE CHAPTER 2?
HEY!
NOBU
SENPAI WAS ALWAYS SEVERAL LEVELS ABOVE ME.
KOJIRO!
BUT I WON THAT MATCH.
ドンドン
DON DON (WHAM)
...HOW DID I BEAT HIM...?
YOU'RE ON...
...KOJIRO!
石
HEY, KOJIRO!
HEY!
WHERE ARE YOU GOING? DON'T RUN OUT ON ME.
I'VE SPENT ALL MY TIME SINCE THEN REBUFFING HIS DEMANDS FOR A REMATCH.
IT'S LIKE I'VE BEEN STAYING OUT OF HIS REACH SO I CAN STILL BE "THE WINNER" BETWEEN US.

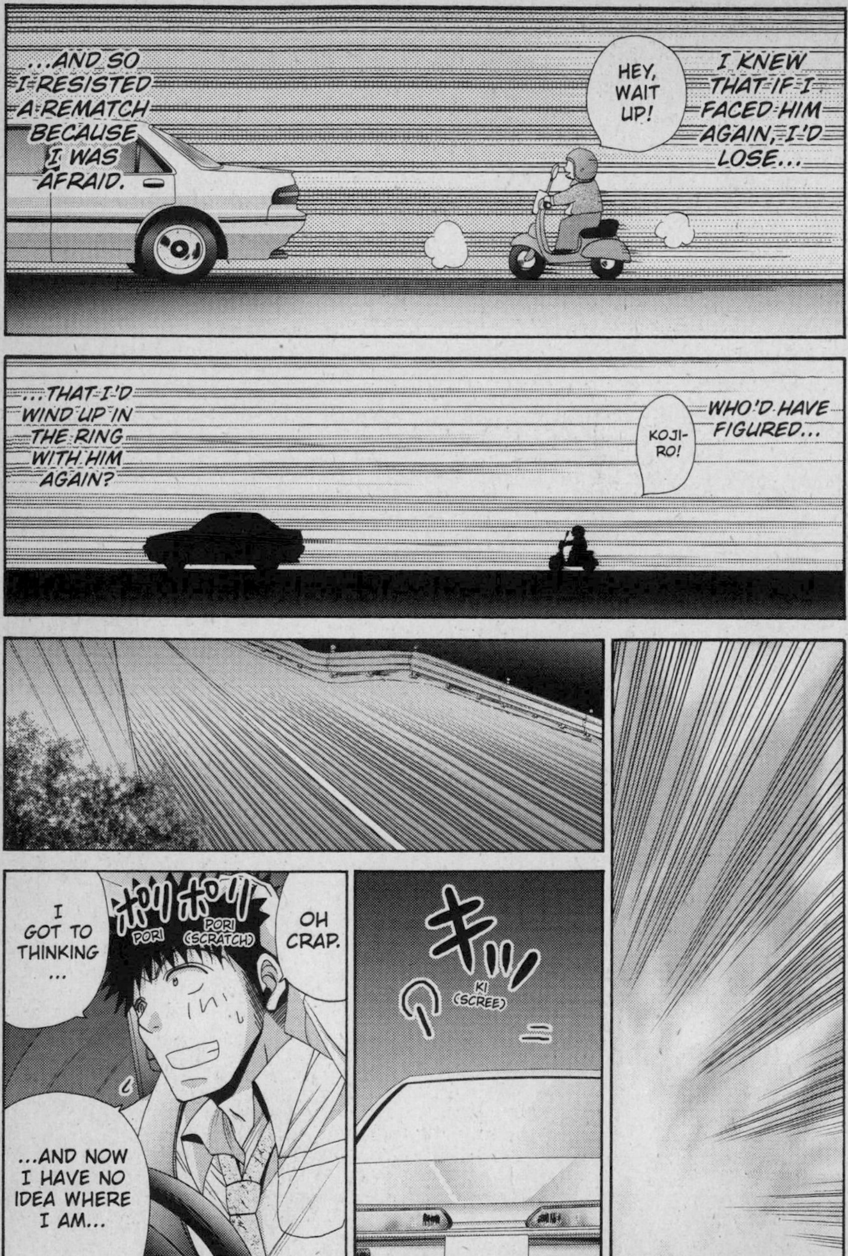
I KNEW THAT IF I FACED HIM AGAIN, I'D LOSE...
HEY, WAIT UP!
...AND SO I RESISTED A REMATCH BECAUSE I WAS AFRAID.
WHO'D HAVE FIGURED...
KOJI-RO!
...THAT I'D WIND UP IN THE RING WITH HIM AGAIN?
キッ
KI (SCREE)
OH CRAP.
ポリポリ
PORI PORI (SCRATCH)
I GOT TO THINKING...
...AND NOW I HAVE NO IDEA WHERE I AM...

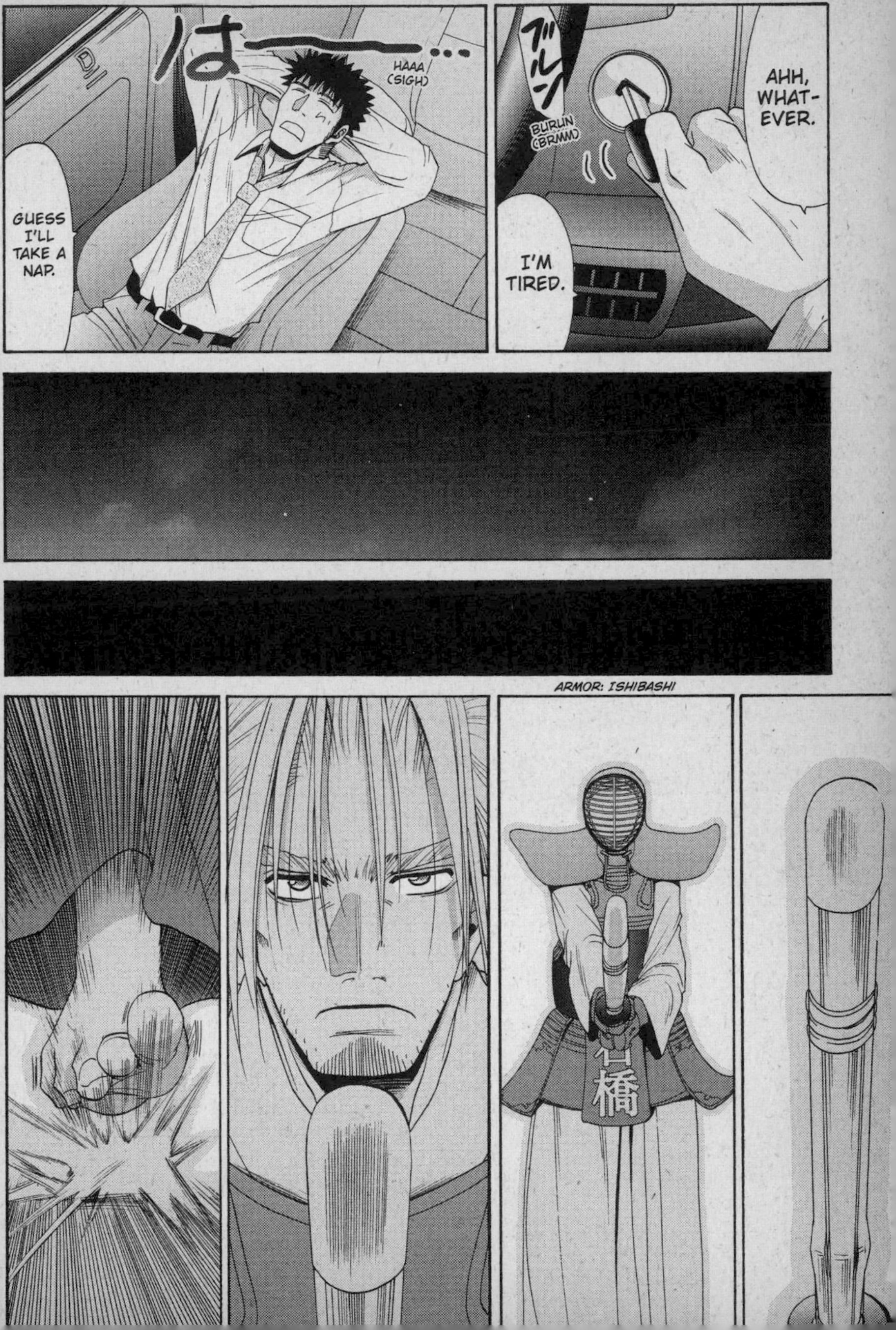
AHH, WHAT-EVER.
ブルン
BURUN (BRMM)
I'M TIRED.
は———...
HAAA (SIGH)
GUESS I'LL TAKE A NAP.
ARMOR: ISHIBASHI
石橋

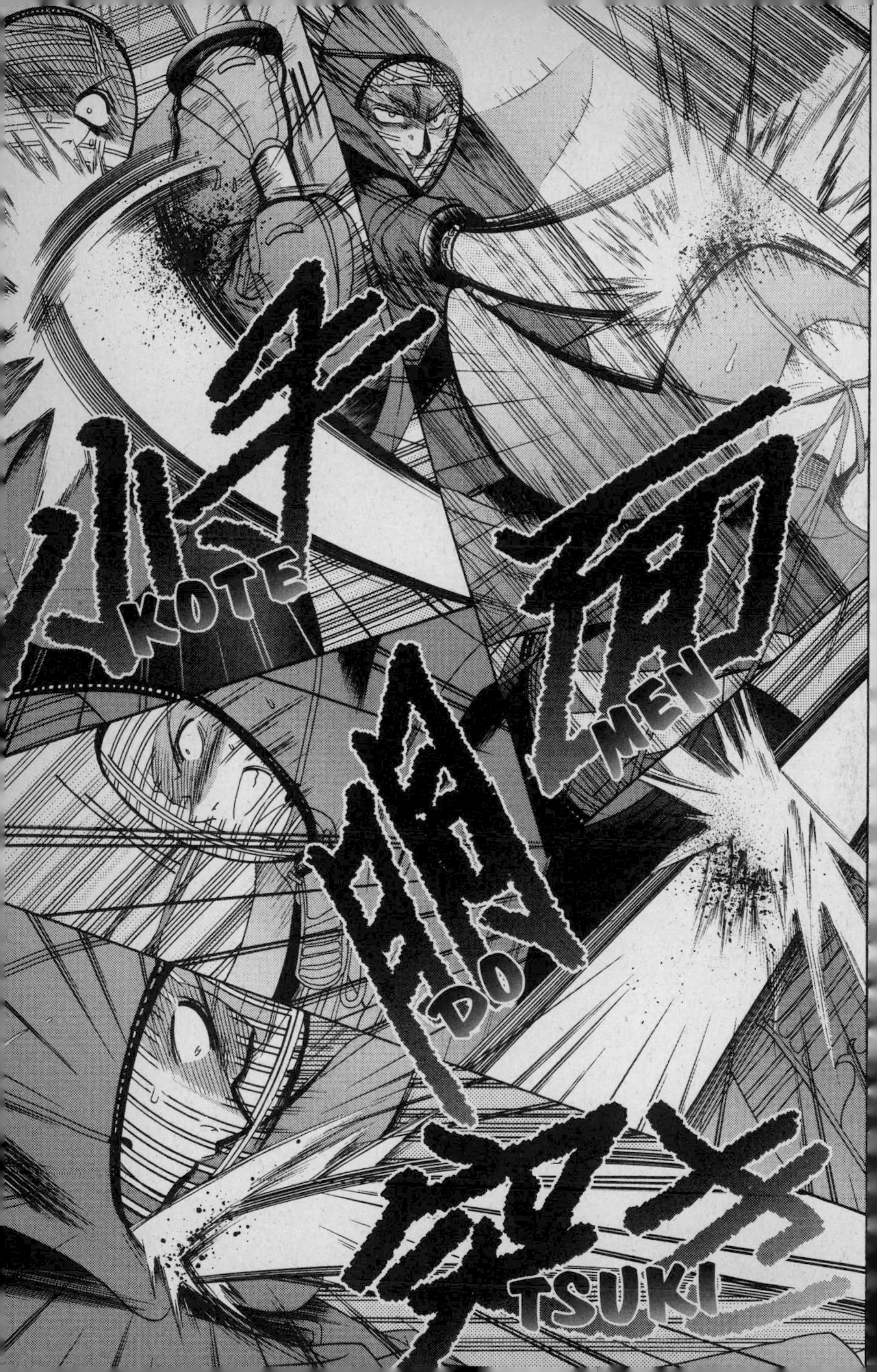
KOTE
MEN
DO
TSUKI

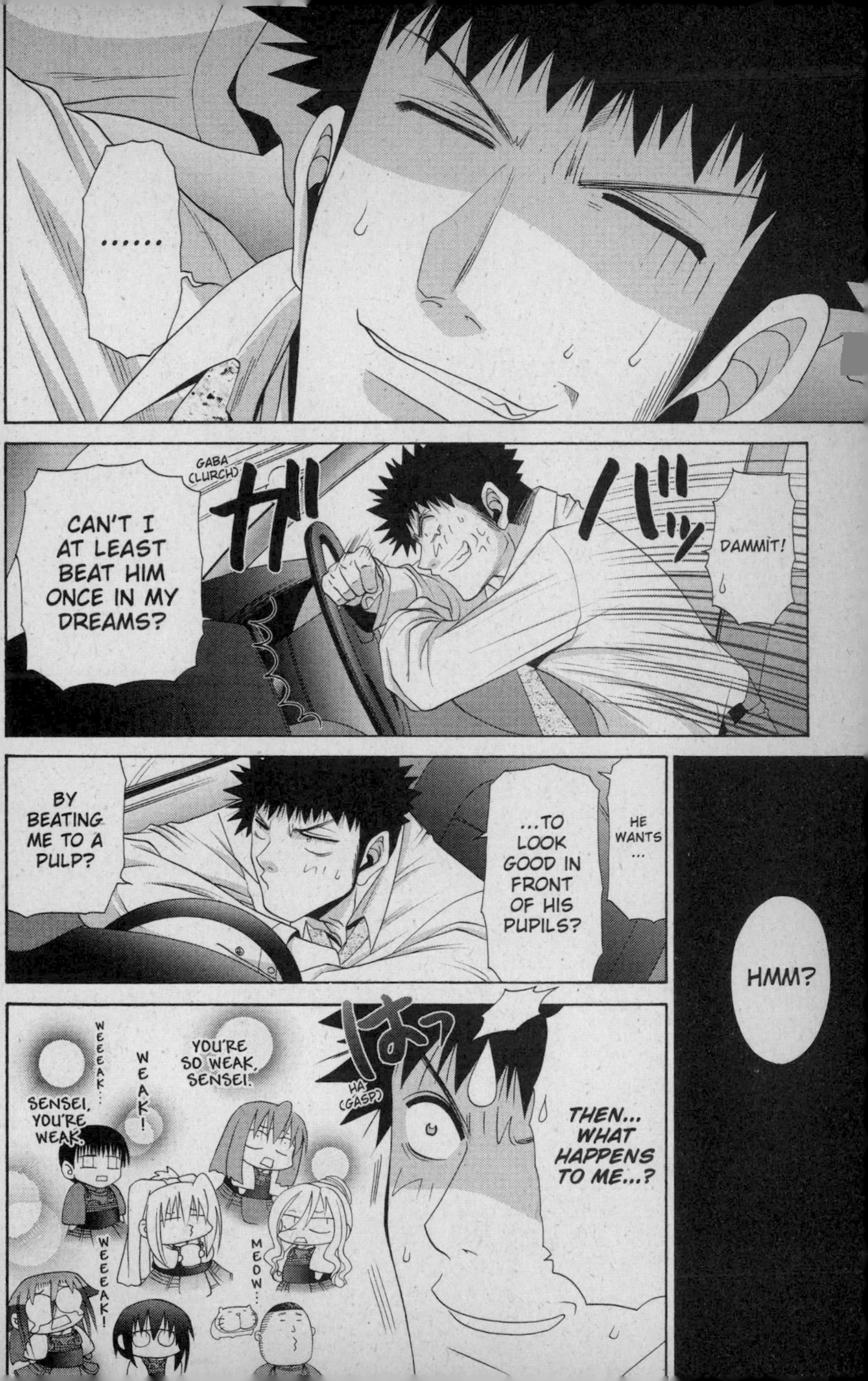
......
DAMMIT!
GABA (LURCH)
CAN'T I AT LEAST BEAT HIM ONCE IN MY DREAMS?
HMM?
HE WANTS ...
...TO LOOK GOOD IN FRONT OF HIS PUPILS?
BY BEATING ME TO A PULP?
HA (GASP)
THEN... WHAT HAPPENS TO ME...?
YOU'RE SO WEAK, SENSEI.
WEAK!
WEEEEAK...
SENSEI, YOU'RE WEAK.
MEOW...
WEEEEAK!

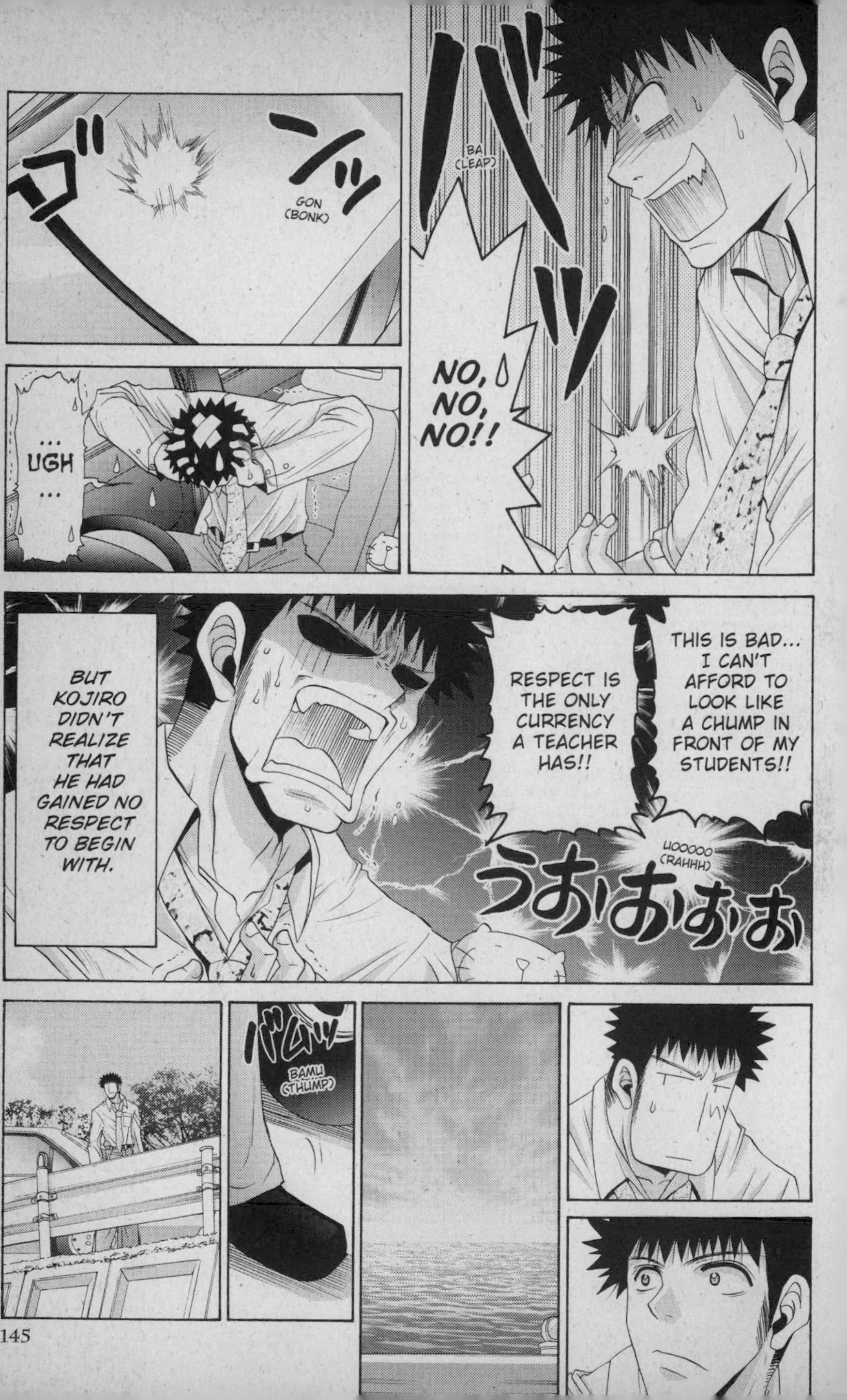
バッ
BA (LEAP)
NO, NO, NO!!
ゴンッ
GON (BONK)
... UGH ...
THIS IS BAD... I CAN'T AFFORD TO LOOK LIKE A CHUMP IN FRONT OF MY STUDENTS!!
RESPECT IS THE ONLY CURRENCY A TEACHER HAS!!
うおおおお
UOOOOO (RAHHH)
BUT KOJIRO DIDN'T REALIZE THAT HE HAD GAINED NO RESPECT TO BEGIN WITH.
バムッ
BAMU (THUMP)

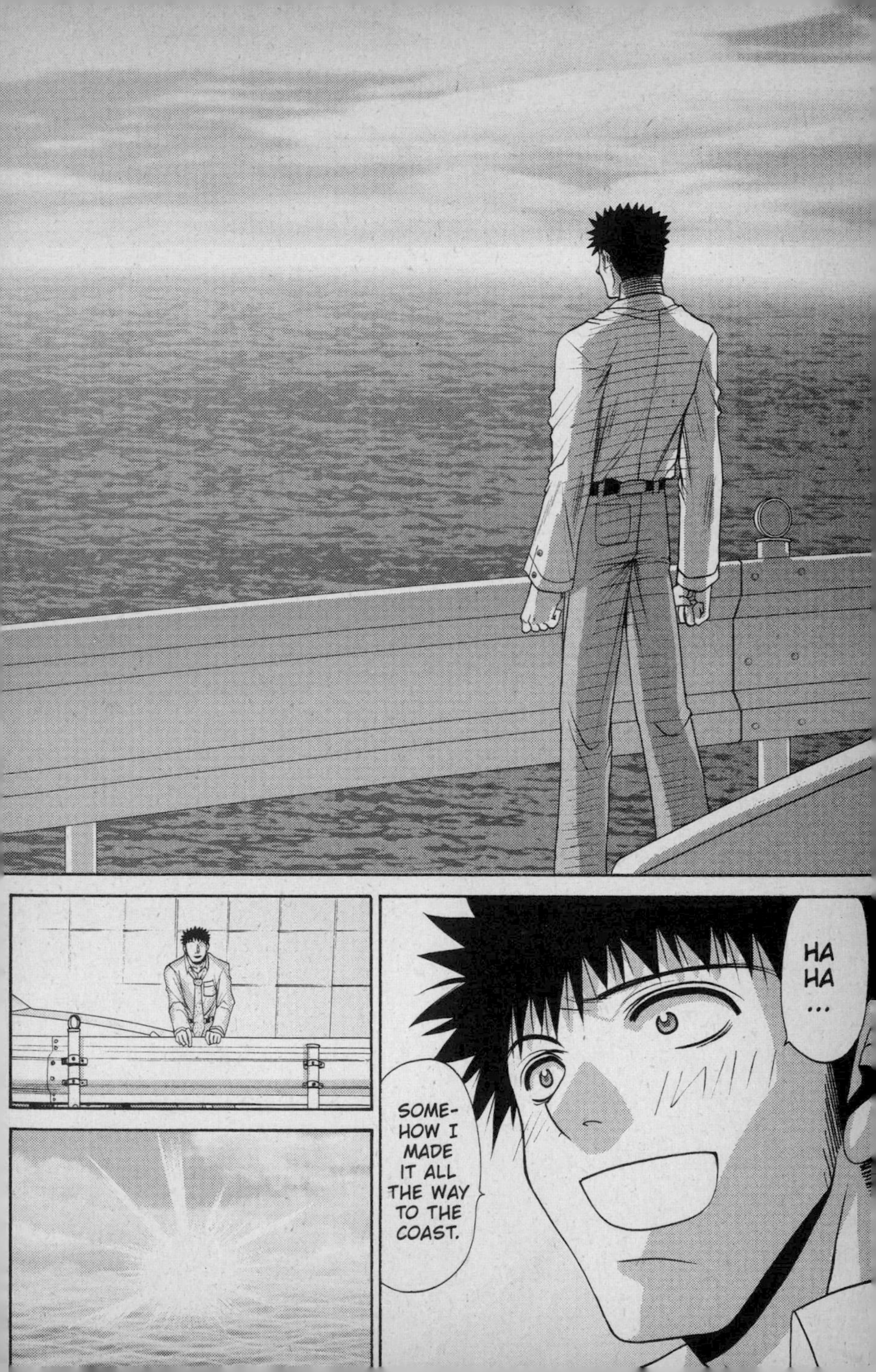
HA HA ...
SOME-HOW I MADE IT ALL THE WAY TO THE COAST.

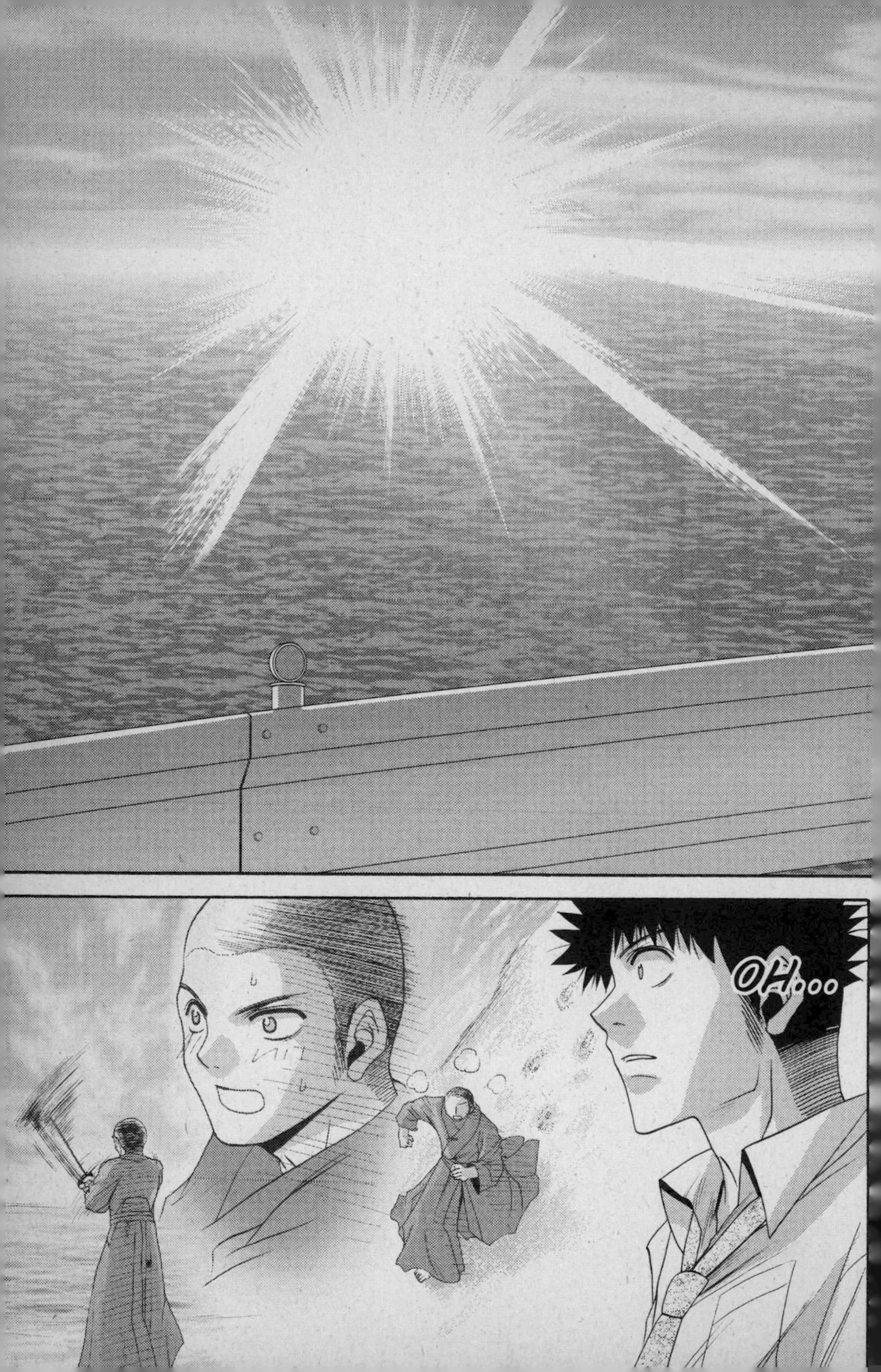
OH...

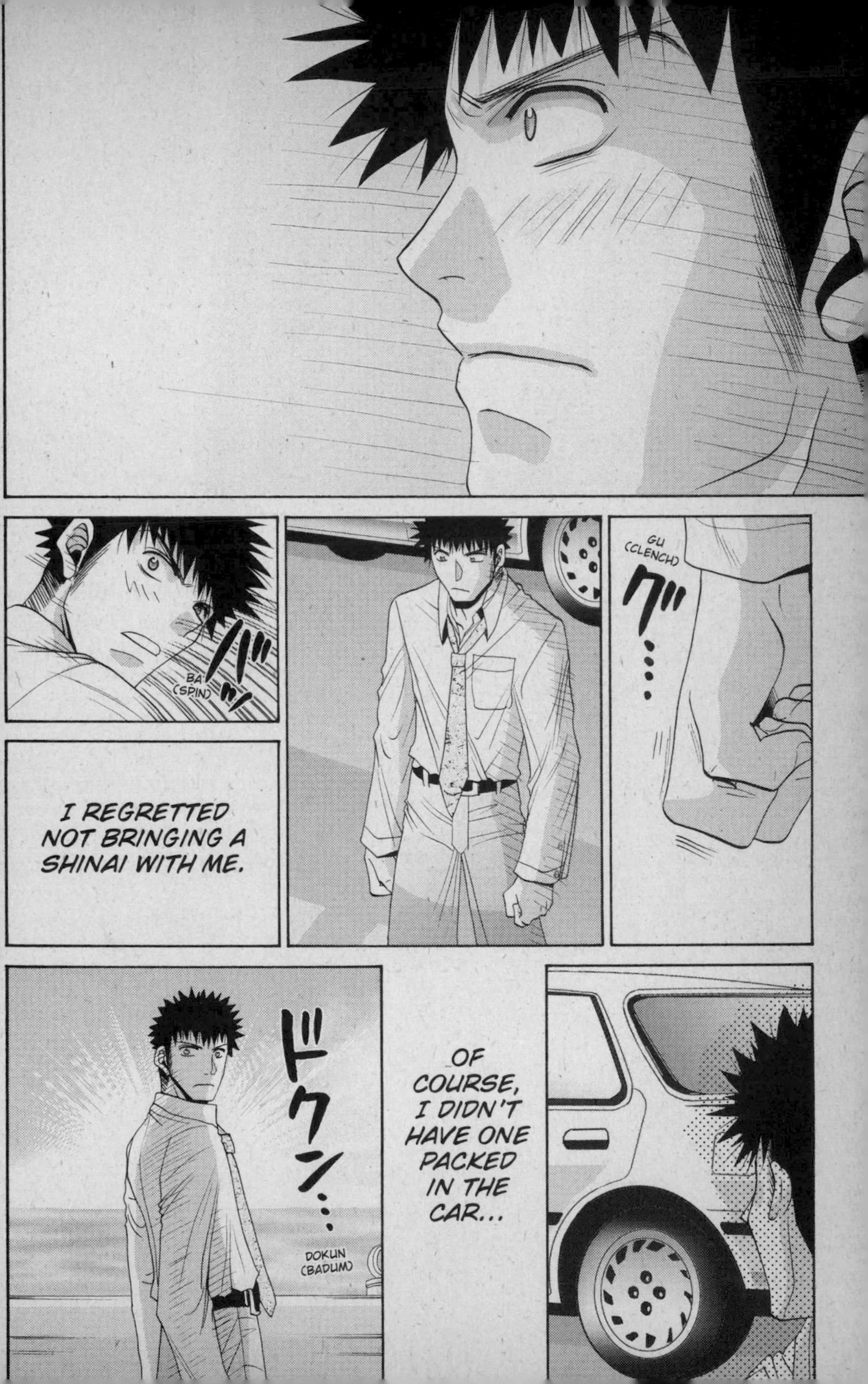
グ…
GU (CLENCH)
バッ
BA (SPIN)
I REGRETTED NOT BRINGING A SHINAI WITH ME.
OF COURSE, I DIDN'T HAVE ONE PACKED IN THE CAR...
ドクン…
DOKUN (BADUM)

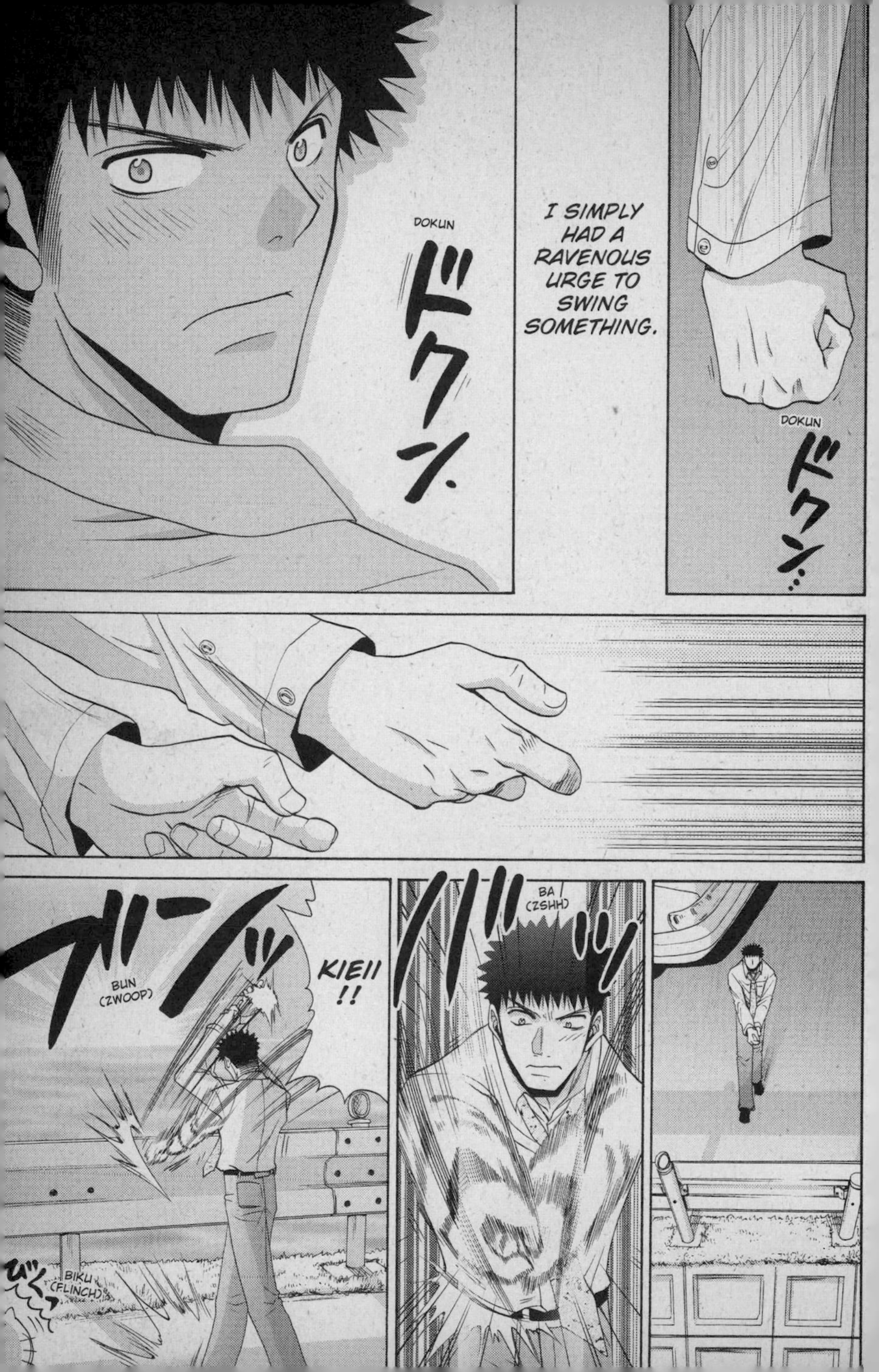

DOKUN
ドクン…
I SIMPLY HAD A RAVENOUS URGE TO SWING SOMETHING.
DOKUN
ドクン
BA (ZSHH)
バッ
KIEII !!
BUN (ZWOOP)
ブーンッ
BIKU (FLINCH)
びくっ

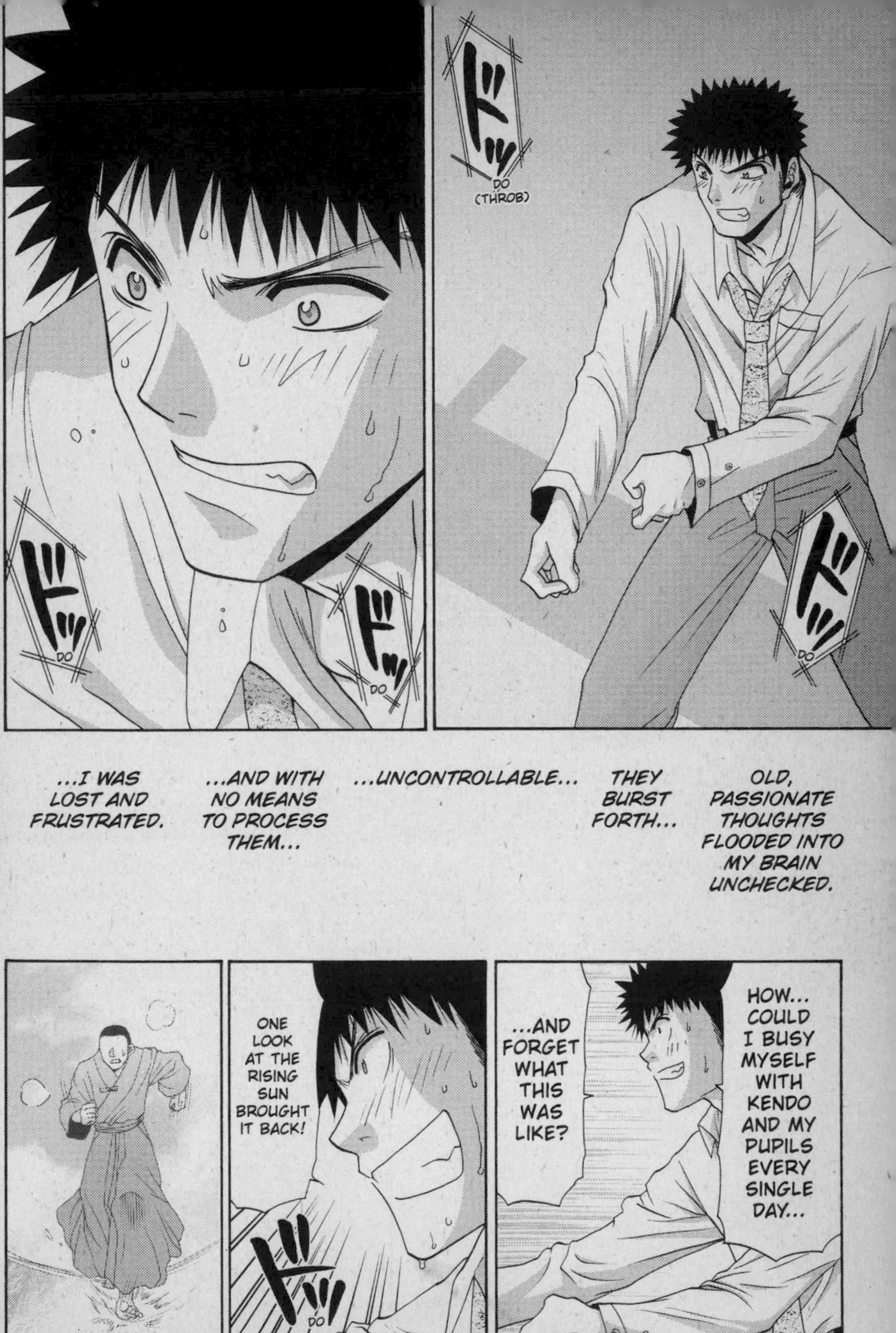
DO (THROB)
DO
DO
DO
OLD, PASSIONATE THOUGHTS FLOODED INTO MY BRAIN UNCHECKED.
THEY BURST FORTH...
...UNCONTROLLABLE...
...AND WITH NO MEANS TO PROCESS THEM...
...I WAS LOST AND FRUSTRATED.
HOW... COULD I BUSY MYSELF WITH KENDO AND MY PUPILS EVERY SINGLE DAY...
...AND FORGET WHAT THIS WAS LIKE?
ONE LOOK AT THE RISING SUN BROUGHT IT BACK!
DO

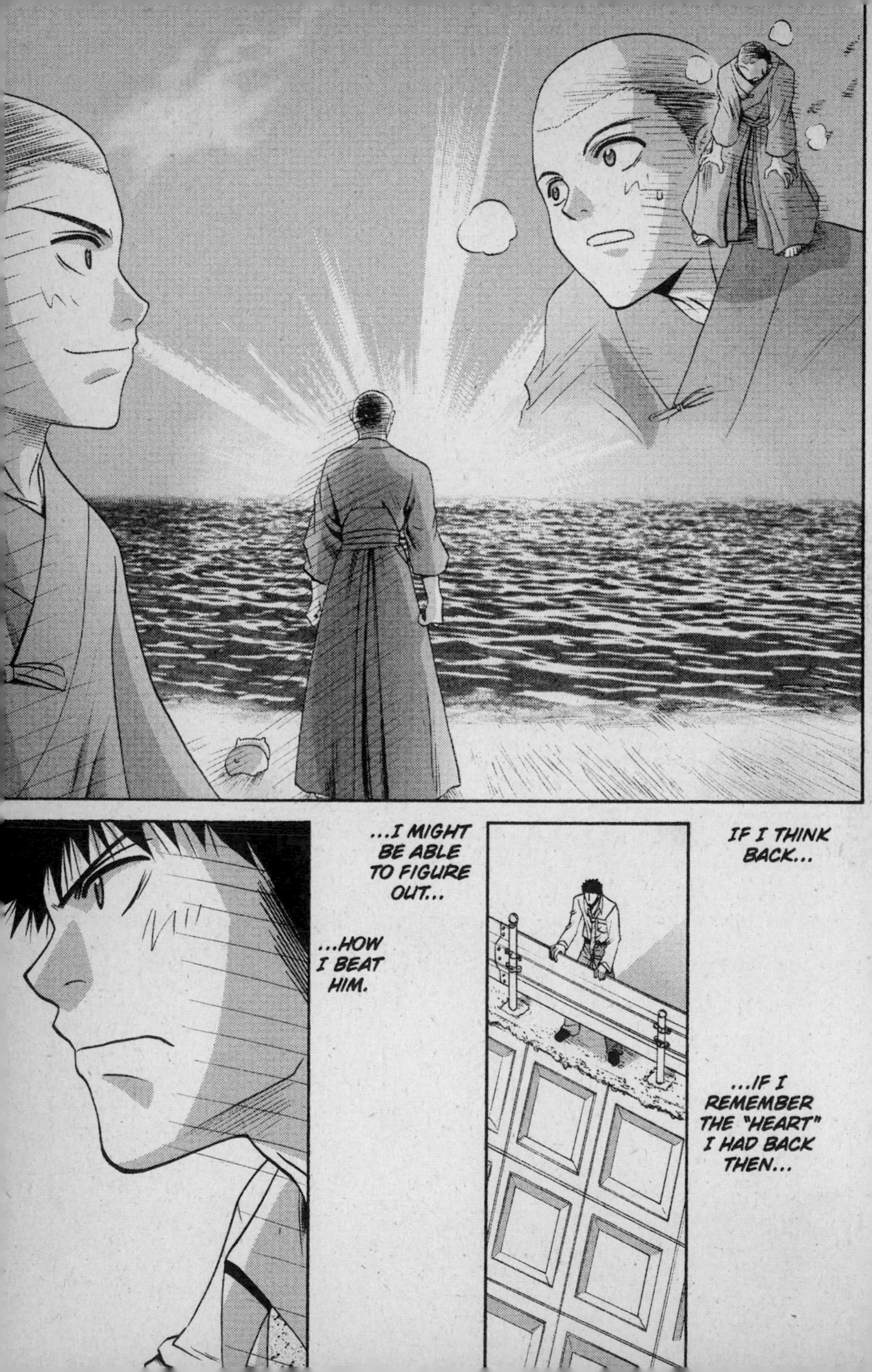
IF I THINK BACK...
...IF I REMEMBER THE "HEART" I HAD BACK THEN...
...I MIGHT BE ABLE TO FIGURE OUT...
...HOW I BEAT HIM.

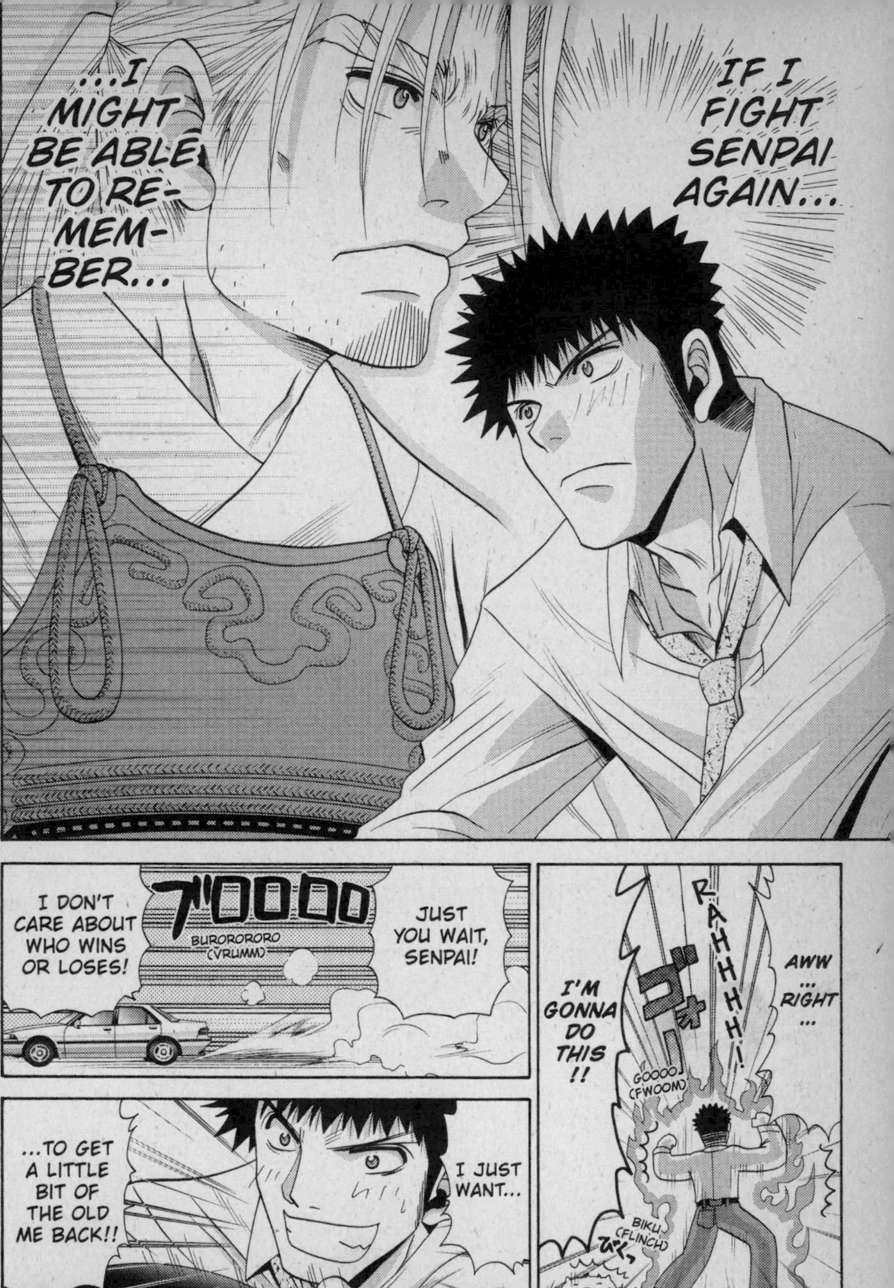
IF I FIGHT SENPAI AGAIN...
...I MIGHT BE ABLE TO RE-MEMBER...
AWW ... RIGHT ...
RAHHHH!
I'M GONNA DO THIS !!
GOOOO (FWOOM)
BIKU (FLINCH)
JUST YOU WAIT, SENPAI!
BUROROROR0 (VRUMM)
I DON'T CARE ABOUT WHO WINS OR LOSES!
I JUST WANT...
...TO GET A LITTLE BIT OF THE OLD ME BACK!!

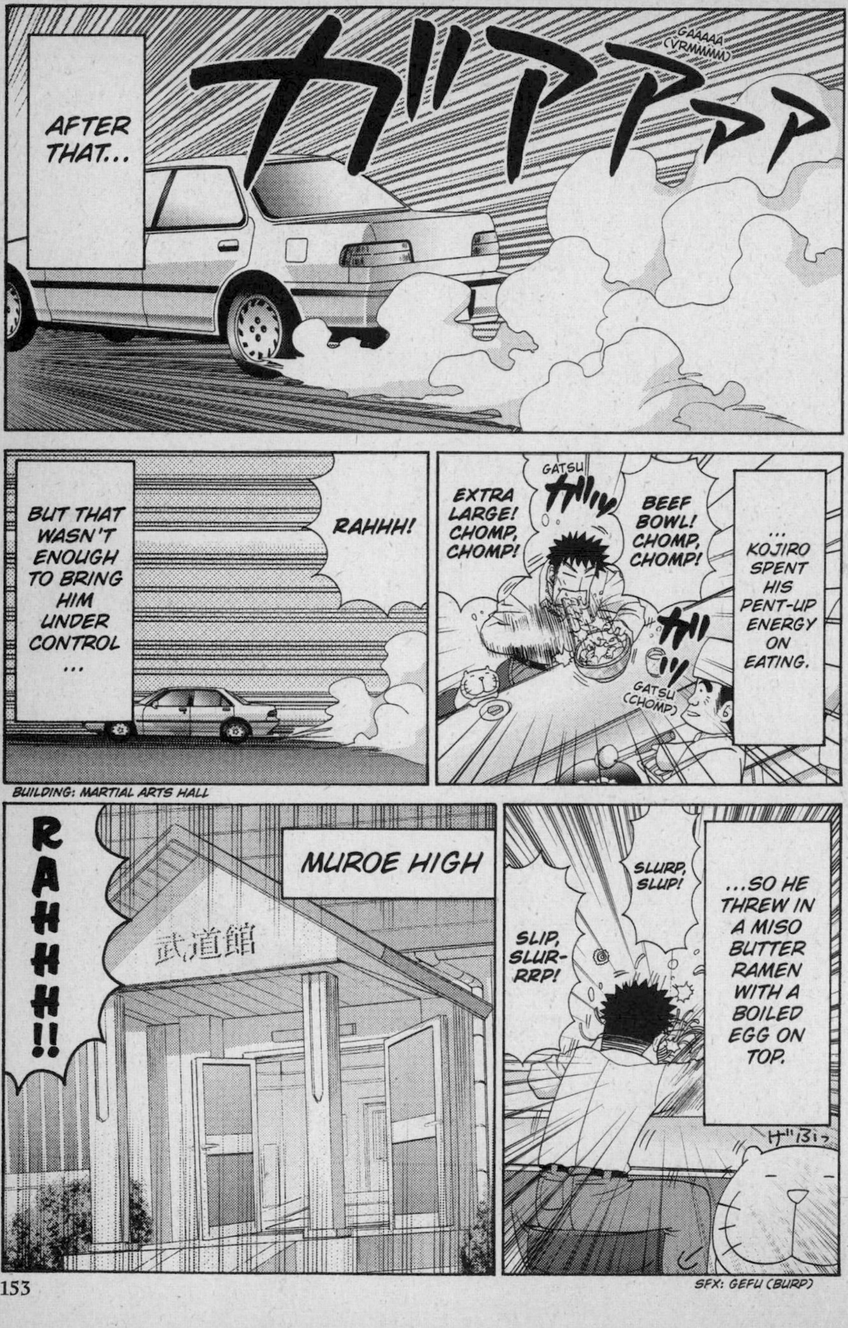
GAAAAA (VRMMMMM)
AFTER THAT...
...KOJIRO SPENT HIS PENT-UP ENERGY ON EATING.
BEEF BOWL! CHOMP, CHOMP!
GATSU
EXTRA LARGE! CHOMP, CHOMP!
GATSU (CHOMP)
RAHHH!
BUT THAT WASN'T ENOUGH TO BRING HIM UNDER CONTROL...
...SO HE THREW IN A MISO BUTTER RAMEN WITH A BOILED EGG ON TOP.
SLURP, SLUP!
SLIP, SLURRP!
MUROE HIGH
武道館
RAHHHH!!
BUILDING: MARTIAL ARTS HALL
SFX: GEFU (BURP)

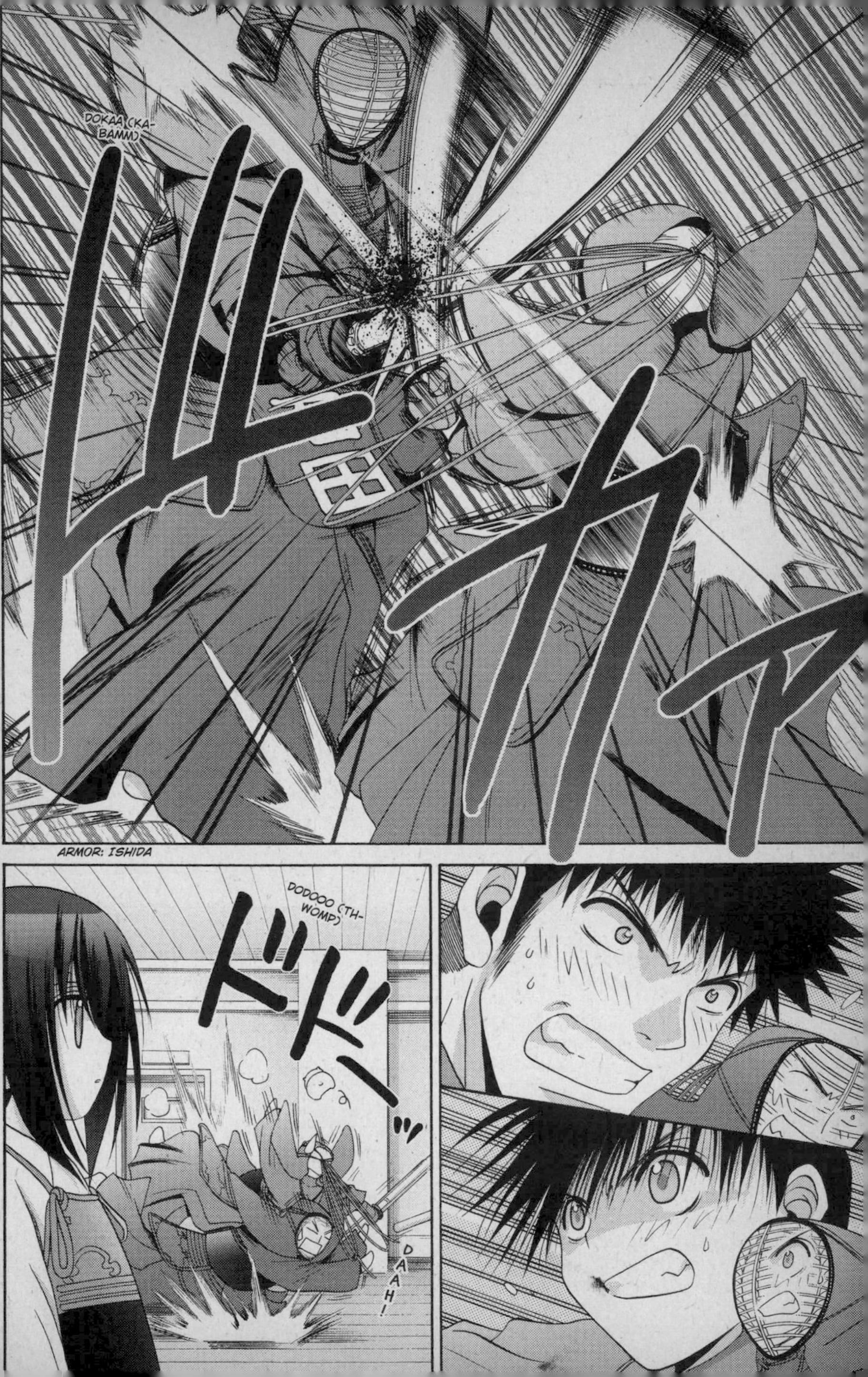
DOKAA (KA-BAMM)
ARMOR: ISHIDA
DODOOO (TH-WOMP)
DAAH!

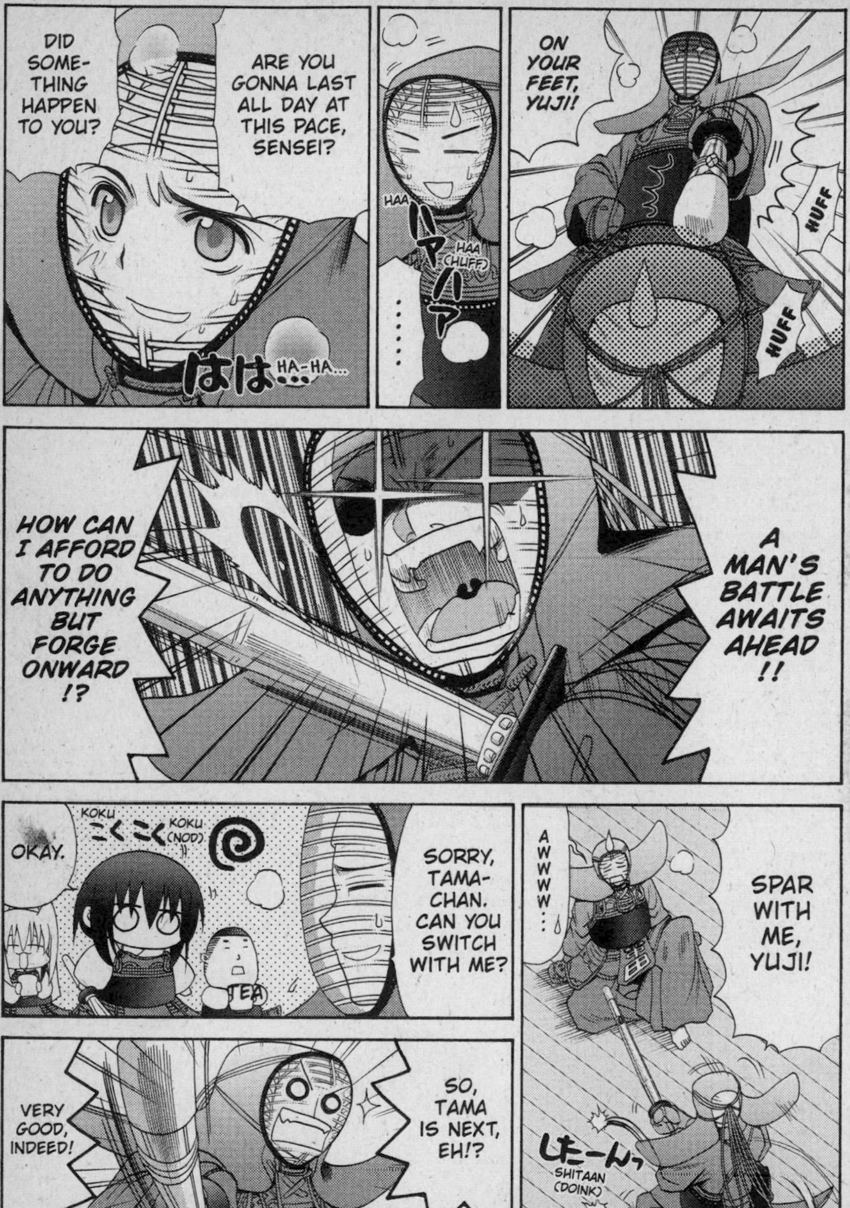
ON YOUR FEET, YUJI!
HUFF
HUFF
HAA
ハア
HAA (HUFF)
ハア
......
ARE YOU GONNA LAST ALL DAY AT THIS PACE, SENSEI?
DID SOMETHING HAPPEN TO YOU?
はは…
HA-HA...
A MAN'S BATTLE AWAITS AHEAD!!
HOW CAN I AFFORD TO DO ANYTHING BUT FORGE ONWARD!?
SPAR WITH ME, YUJI!
AWWWW...
したーんっ
SHITAAN (DOINK)
したーんっ
SHITAAN
SORRY, TAMA-CHAN. CAN YOU SWITCH WITH ME?
こくこく
KOKU KOKU (NOD)
OKAY.
TEA
SO, TAMA IS NEXT, EH!?
VERY GOOD, INDEED!

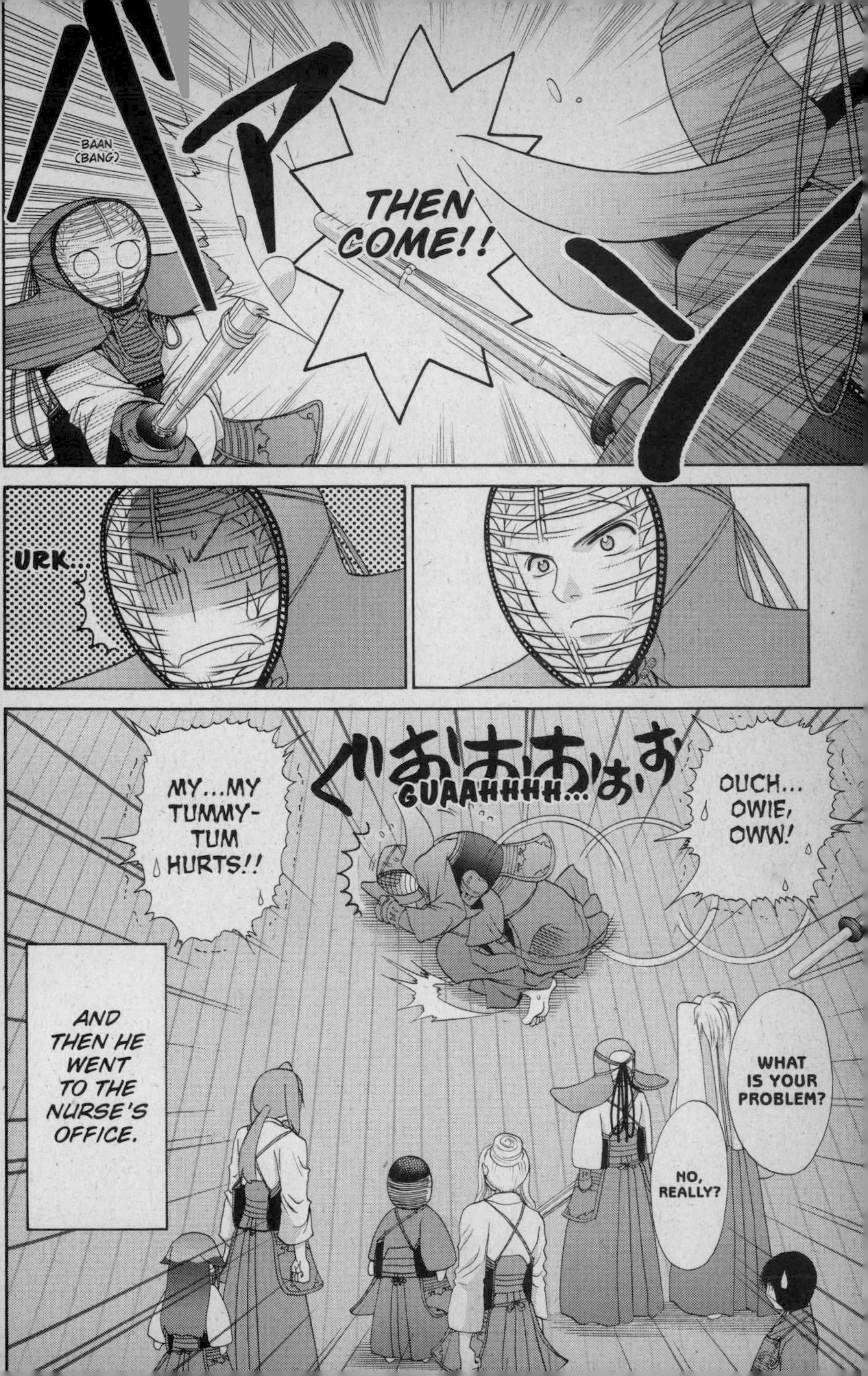

BAAN (BANG)
THEN COME!!
URK...
OUCH... OWIE, OWW!
GUAAHHHH...
MY...MY TUMMY-TUM HURTS!!
WHAT IS YOUR PROBLEM?
NO, REALLY?
AND THEN HE WENT TO THE NURSE'S OFFICE.

BAMBOO BLADE

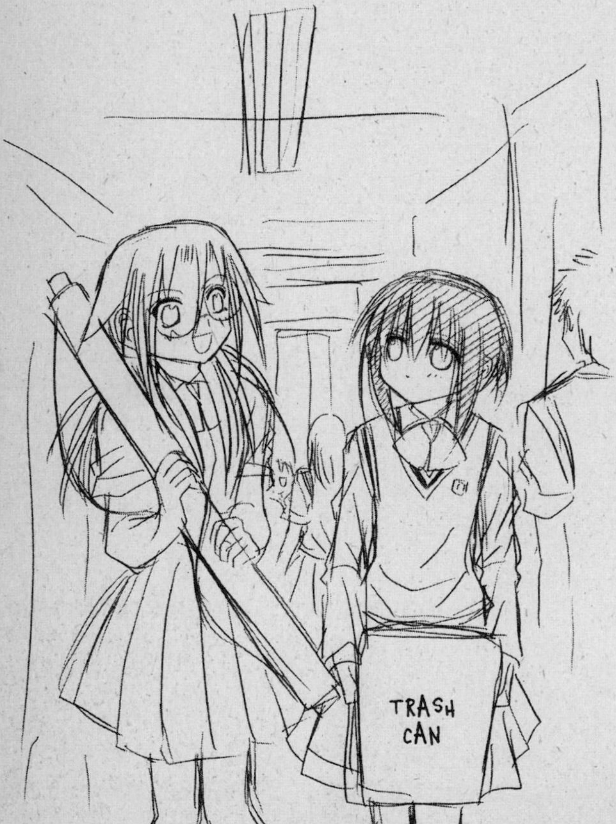
TRASH
CAN

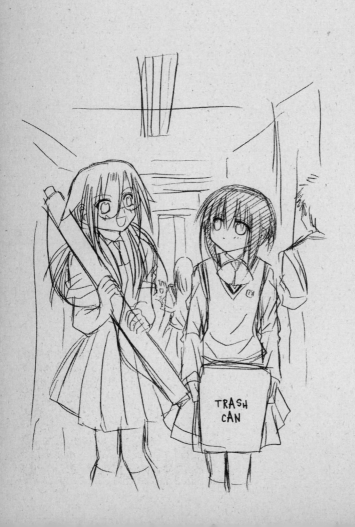

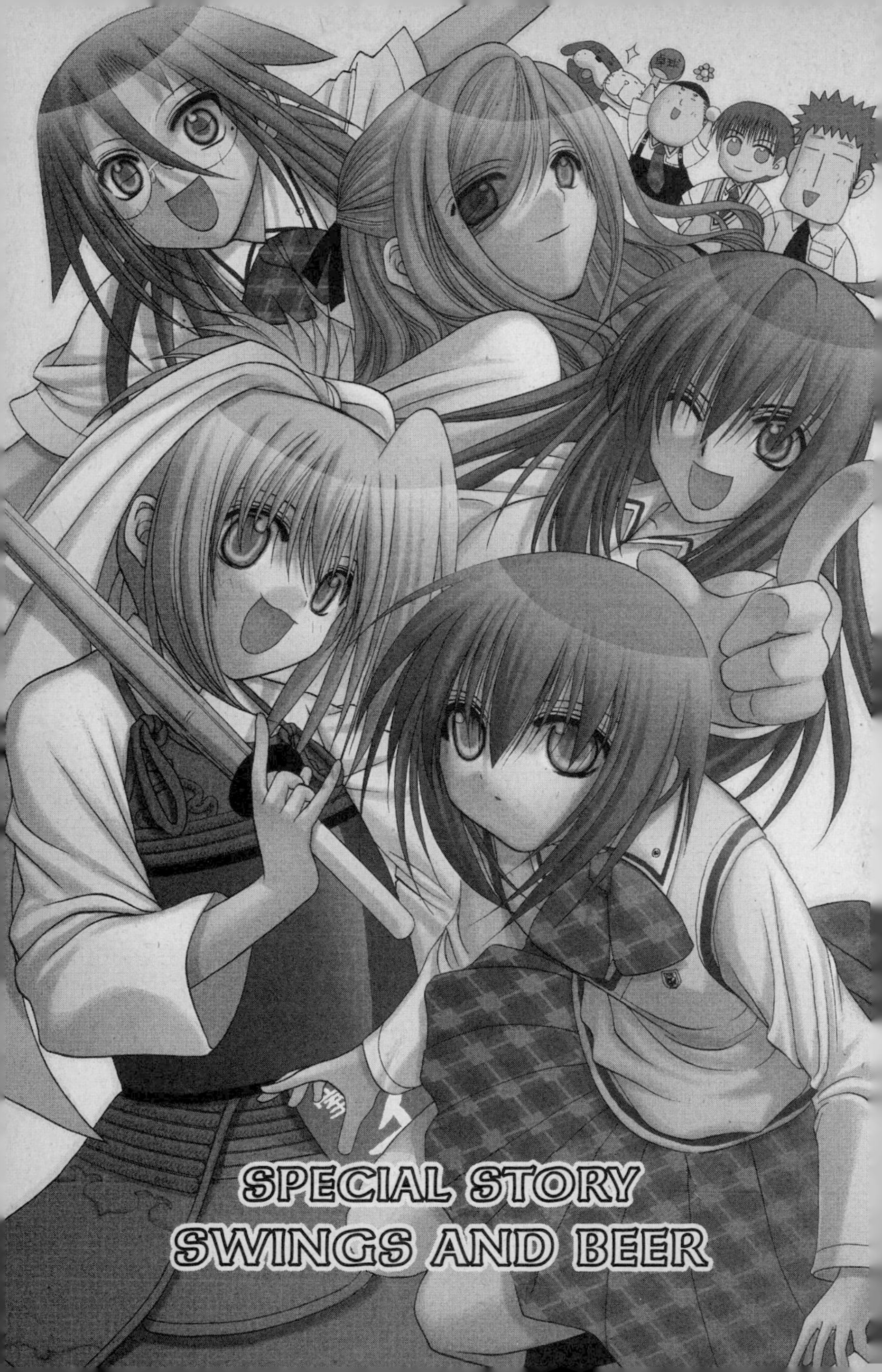
SPECIAL STORY
SWINGS AND BEER

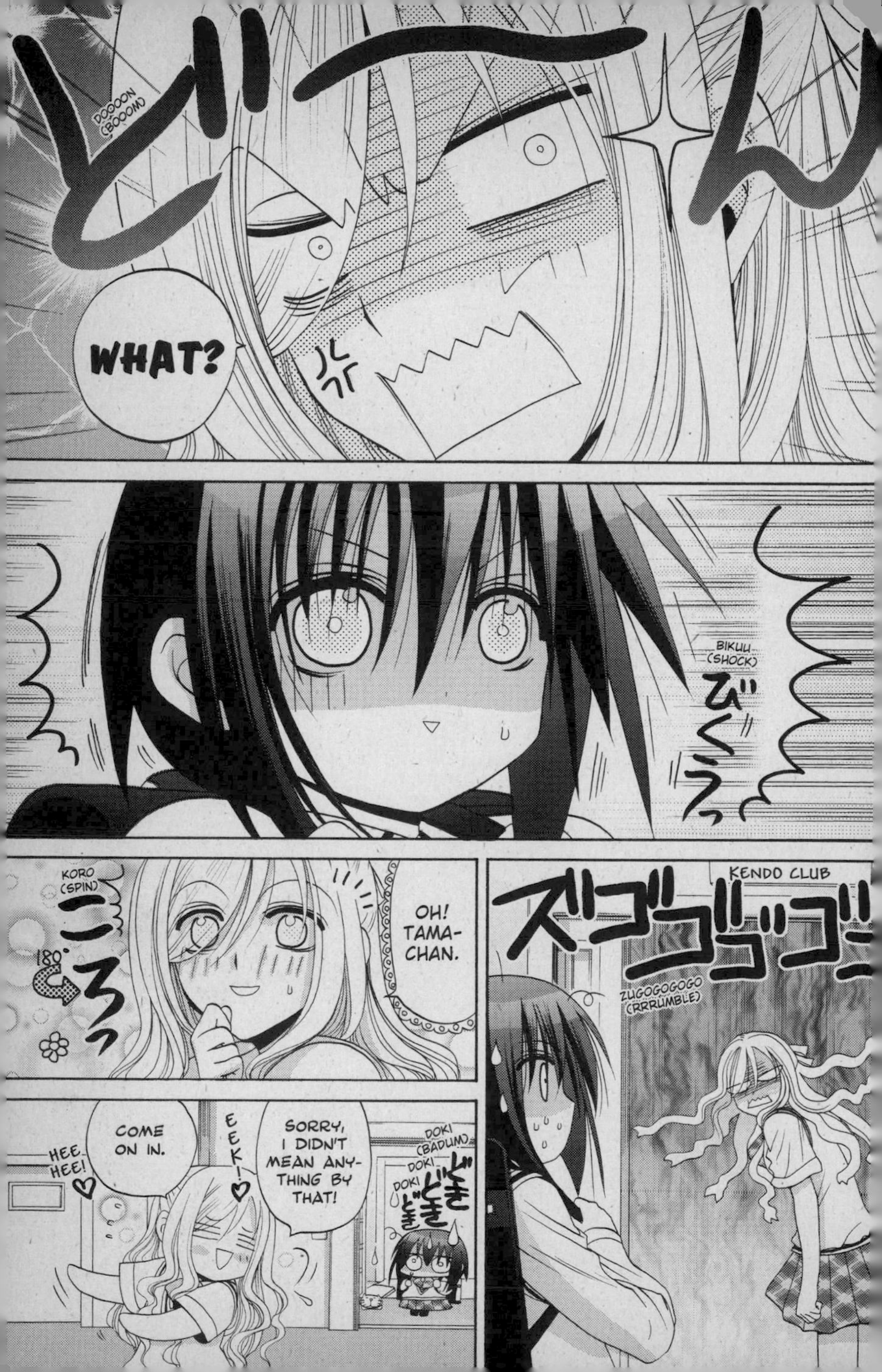
DOOOON (BOOOM)
WHAT?
BIKUU (SHOCK)
KENDO CLUB
ZUGOGOGOGO (RRRUMBLE)
KORO (SPIN)
180°
OH! TAMA-CHAN.
DOKI (BADUM) DOKI DOKI
SORRY, I DIDN'T MEAN ANYTHING BY THAT!
EEK!
COME ON IN.
HEE HEE!

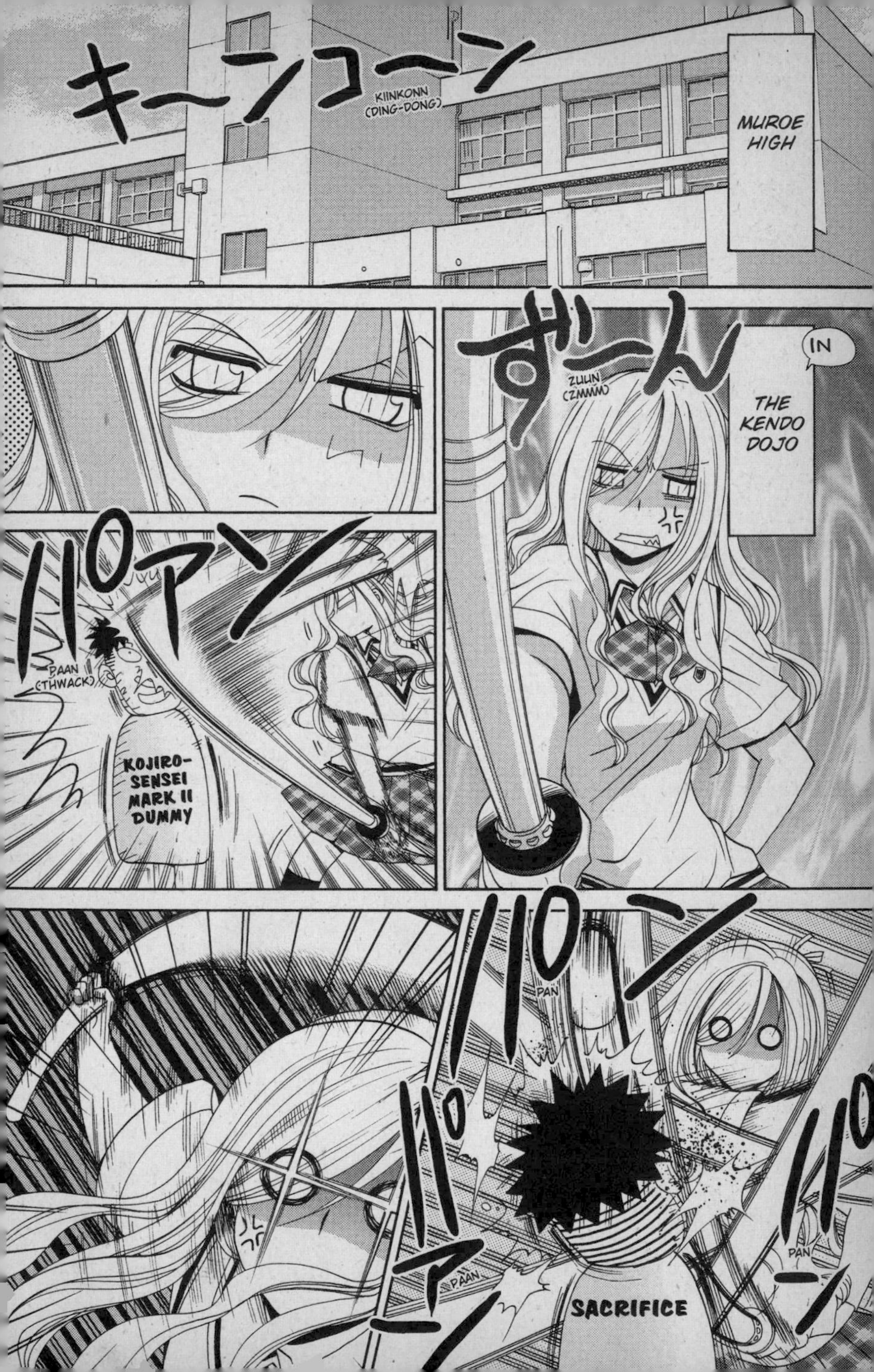

MUROE HIGH
キ～ンコ～ン
KIINKONN (DING-DONG)
IN
THE KENDO DOJO
ず～ん
ZUUN (ZMMM)
パアン
PAAN (THWACK)
KOJIRO-SENSEI MARK II DUMMY
パアン
PAN
PAN
PAAN
SACRIFICE

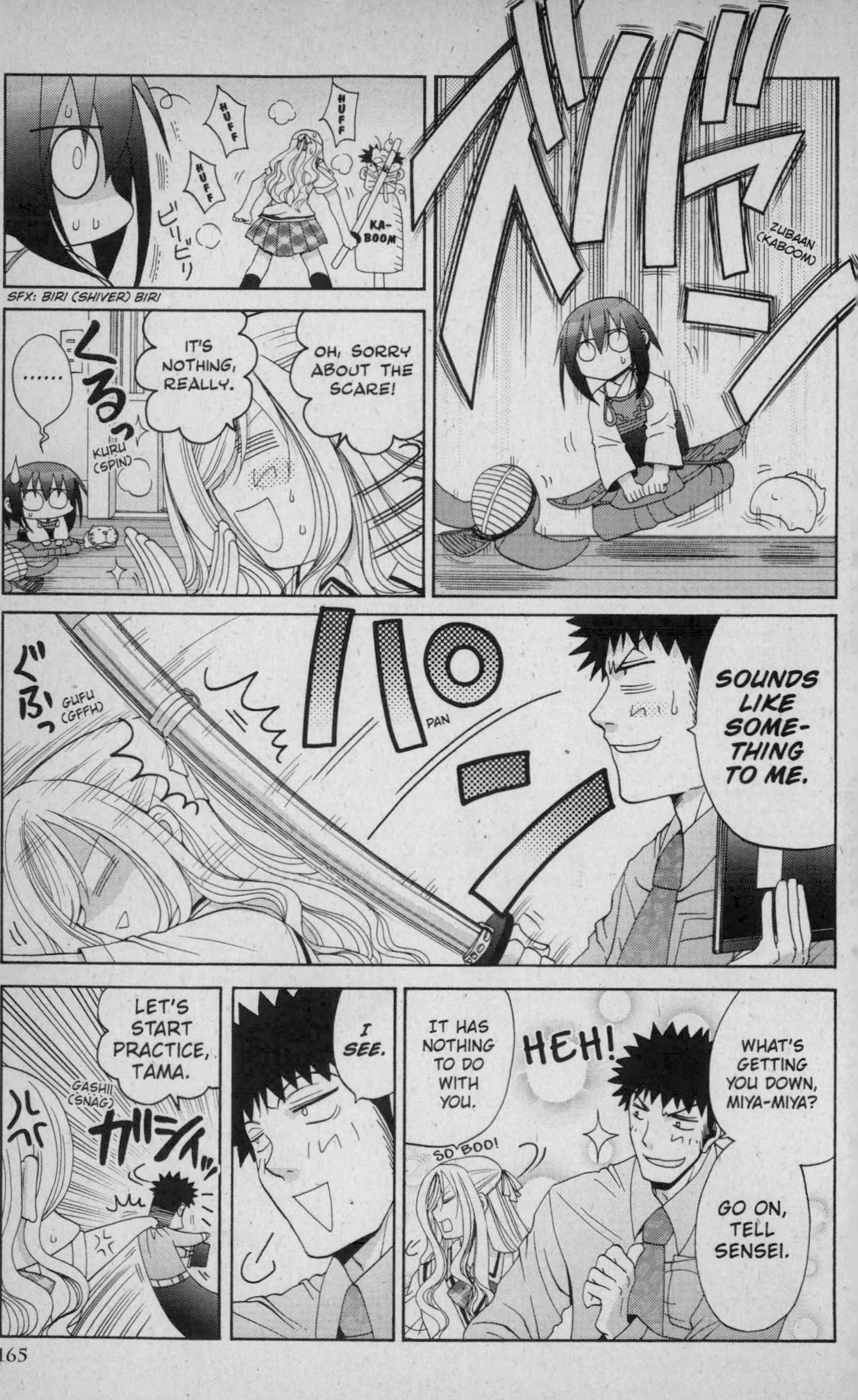
ZUBAAN (KABOOM)
HUFF
HUFF
HUFF
ビリビリ
KA-BOOM
SFX: BIRI (SHIVER) BIRI
OH, SORRY ABOUT THE SCARE!
IT'S NOTHING, REALLY.
......
くるっ
KURU (SPIN)
SOUNDS LIKE SOME-THING TO ME.
PAN
ぐふっ
GUFU (GFFH)
WHAT'S GETTING YOU DOWN, MIYA-MIYA?
GO ON, TELL SENSEI.
HEH!
IT HAS NOTHING TO DO WITH YOU.
SO BOO!
I SEE.
LET'S START PRACTICE, TAMA.
ガシィッ
GASHII (SNAG)

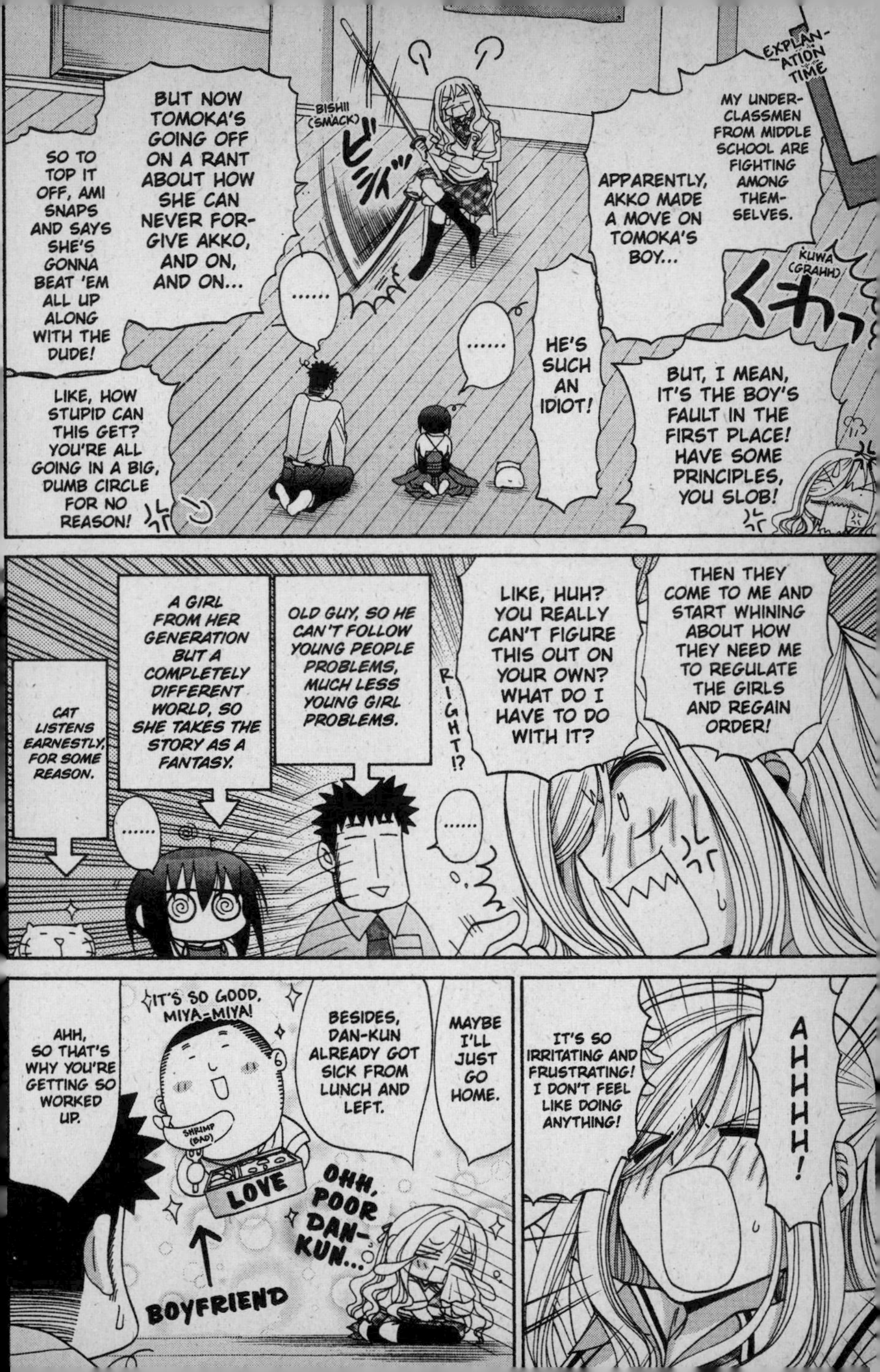
EXPLANATION TIME
MY UNDERCLASSMEN FROM MIDDLE SCHOOL ARE FIGHTING AMONG THEMSELVES.
KUWA (GRAHH)
APPARENTLY, AKKO MADE A MOVE ON TOMOKA'S BOY...
BUT, I MEAN, IT'S THE BOY'S FAULT IN THE FIRST PLACE! HAVE SOME PRINCIPLES, YOU SLOB!
HE'S SUCH AN IDIOT!
......
BISHI! (SMACK)
BUT NOW TOMOKA'S GOING OFF ON A RANT ABOUT HOW SHE CAN NEVER FORGIVE AKKO, AND ON, AND ON...
......
SO TO TOP IT OFF, AMI SNAPS AND SAYS SHE'S GONNA BEAT 'EM ALL UP ALONG WITH THE DUDE!
LIKE, HOW STUPID CAN THIS GET? YOU'RE ALL GOING IN A BIG, DUMB CIRCLE FOR NO REASON!
THEN THEY COME TO ME AND START WHINING ABOUT HOW THEY NEED ME TO REGULATE THE GIRLS AND REGAIN ORDER!
LIKE, HUH? YOU REALLY CAN'T FIGURE THIS OUT ON YOUR OWN? WHAT DO I HAVE TO DO WITH IT?
RIGHT!?
......
OLD GUY, SO HE CAN'T FOLLOW YOUNG PEOPLE PROBLEMS, MUCH LESS YOUNG GIRL PROBLEMS.
A GIRL FROM HER GENERATION BUT A COMPLETELY DIFFERENT WORLD, SO SHE TAKES THE STORY AS A FANTASY.
......
CAT LISTENS EARNESTLY, FOR SOME REASON.
AHHHH!
IT'S SO IRRITATING AND FRUSTRATING! I DON'T FEEL LIKE DOING ANYTHING!
MAYBE I'LL JUST GO HOME.
BESIDES, DAN-KUN ALREADY GOT SICK FROM LUNCH AND LEFT.
IT'S SO GOOD, MIYA-MIYA!
AHH, SO THAT'S WHY YOU'RE GETTING SO WORKED UP.
SHRIMP (BAD)
LOVE
OHH, POOR DAN-KUN...
BOYFRIEND

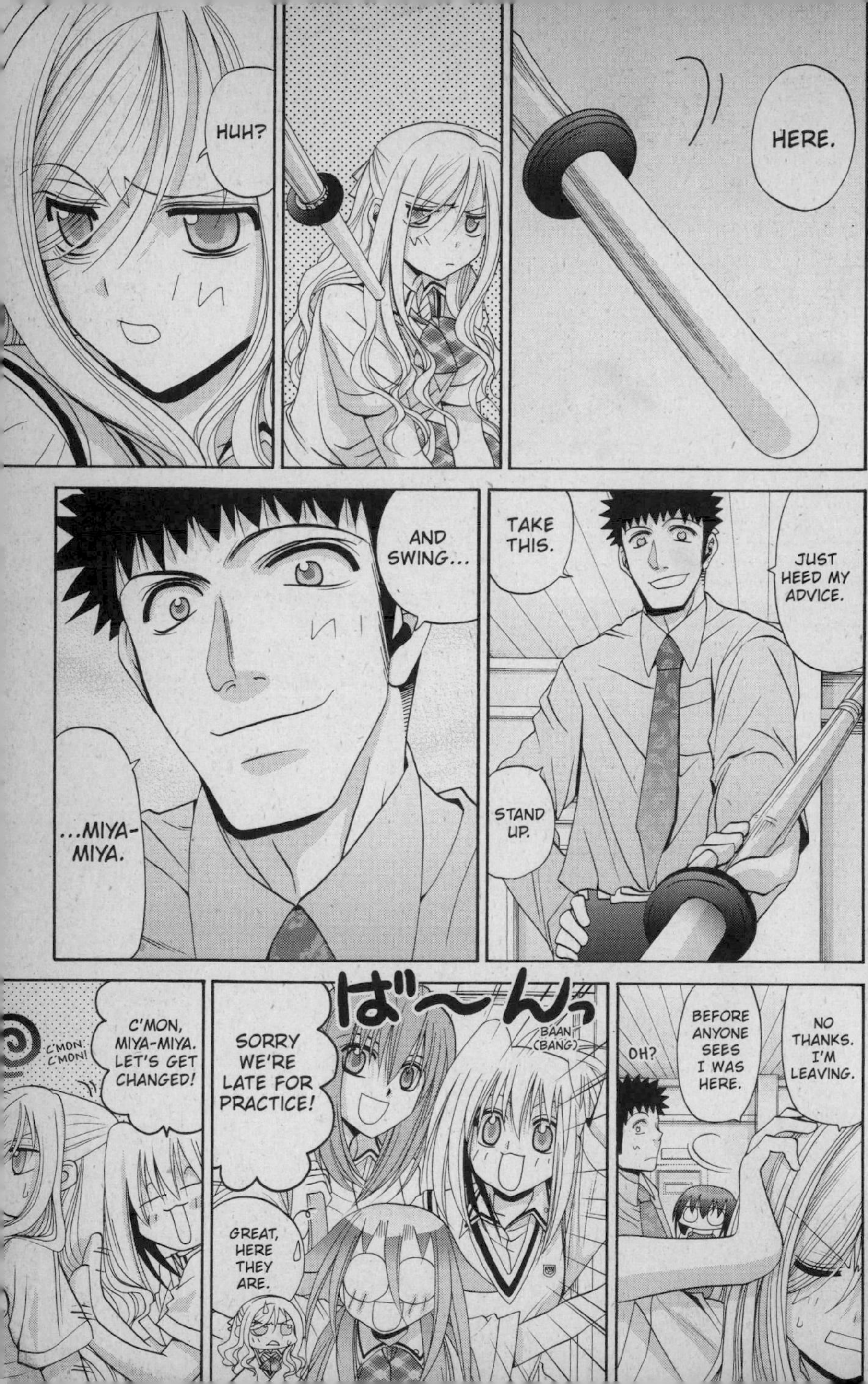
HERE.
HUH?
JUST HEED MY ADVICE.
TAKE THIS.
STAND UP.
AND SWING...
...MIYA-MIYA.
NO THANKS. I'M LEAVING.
BEFORE ANYONE SEES I WAS HERE.
OH?
ば~んっ
BAAN (BANG)
SORRY WE'RE LATE FOR PRACTICE!
GREAT, HERE THEY ARE.
C'MON, MIYA-MIYA. LET'S GET CHANGED!
C'MON C'MON!

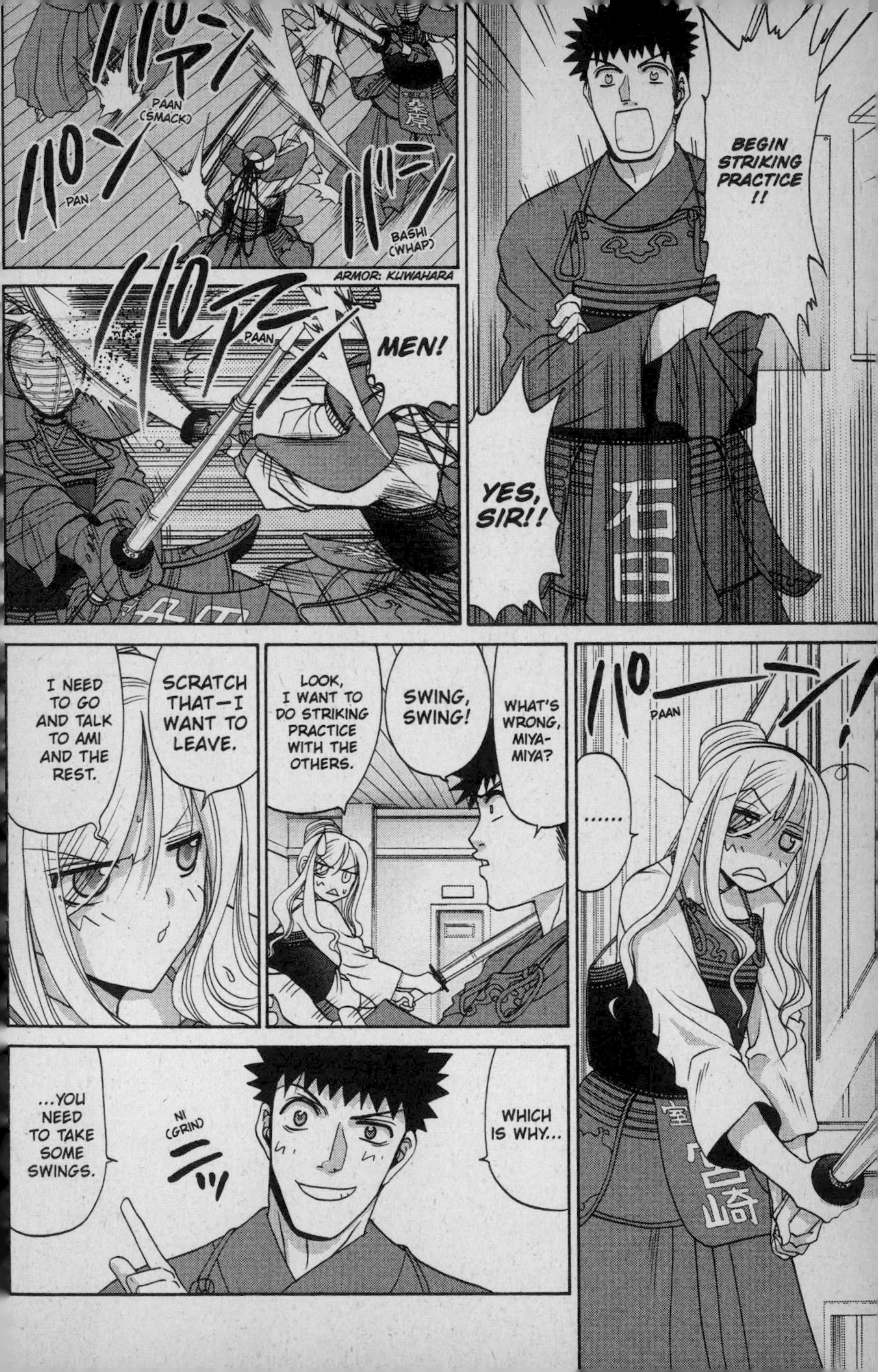
BEGIN STRIKING PRACTICE!!
YES, SIR!!
PAAN (SMACK)
PAN
BASHI (WHAP)
ARMOR: KUWAHARA
PAAN
MEN!
PAAN
......
WHAT'S WRONG, MIYA-MIYA?
SWING, SWING!
LOOK, I WANT TO DO STRIKING PRACTICE WITH THE OTHERS.
SCRATCH THAT—I WANT TO LEAVE.
I NEED TO GO AND TALK TO AMI AND THE REST.
WHICH IS WHY...
NI (GRIND)
...YOU NEED TO TAKE SOME SWINGS.

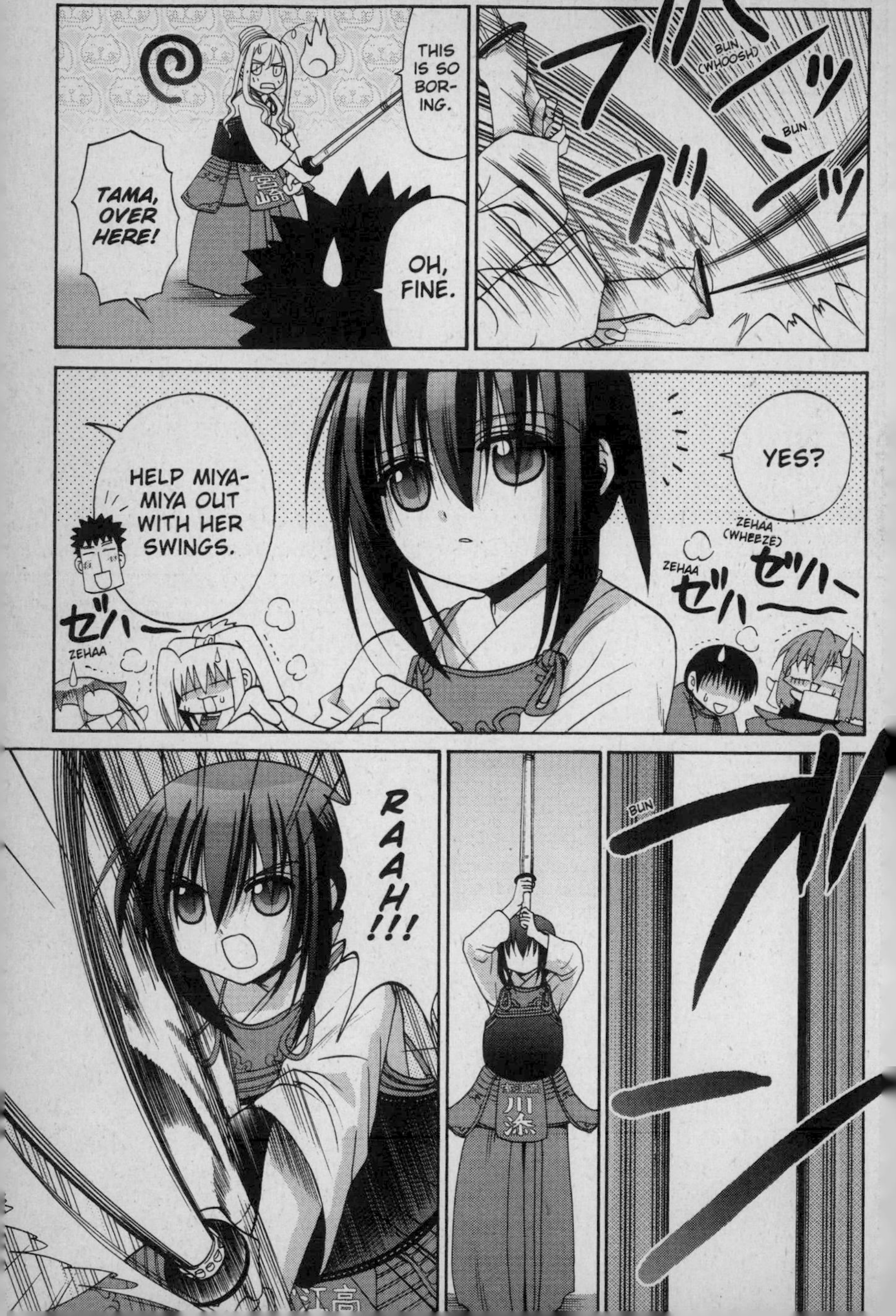
BUN (WHOOSH)
BUN
THIS IS SO BOR-ING.
OH, FINE.
TAMA, OVER HERE!
YES?
ZEHAA (WHEEZE)
ZEHAA
HELP MIYA-MIYA OUT WITH HER SWINGS.
ZEHAA
BUN
RAAAH!!!

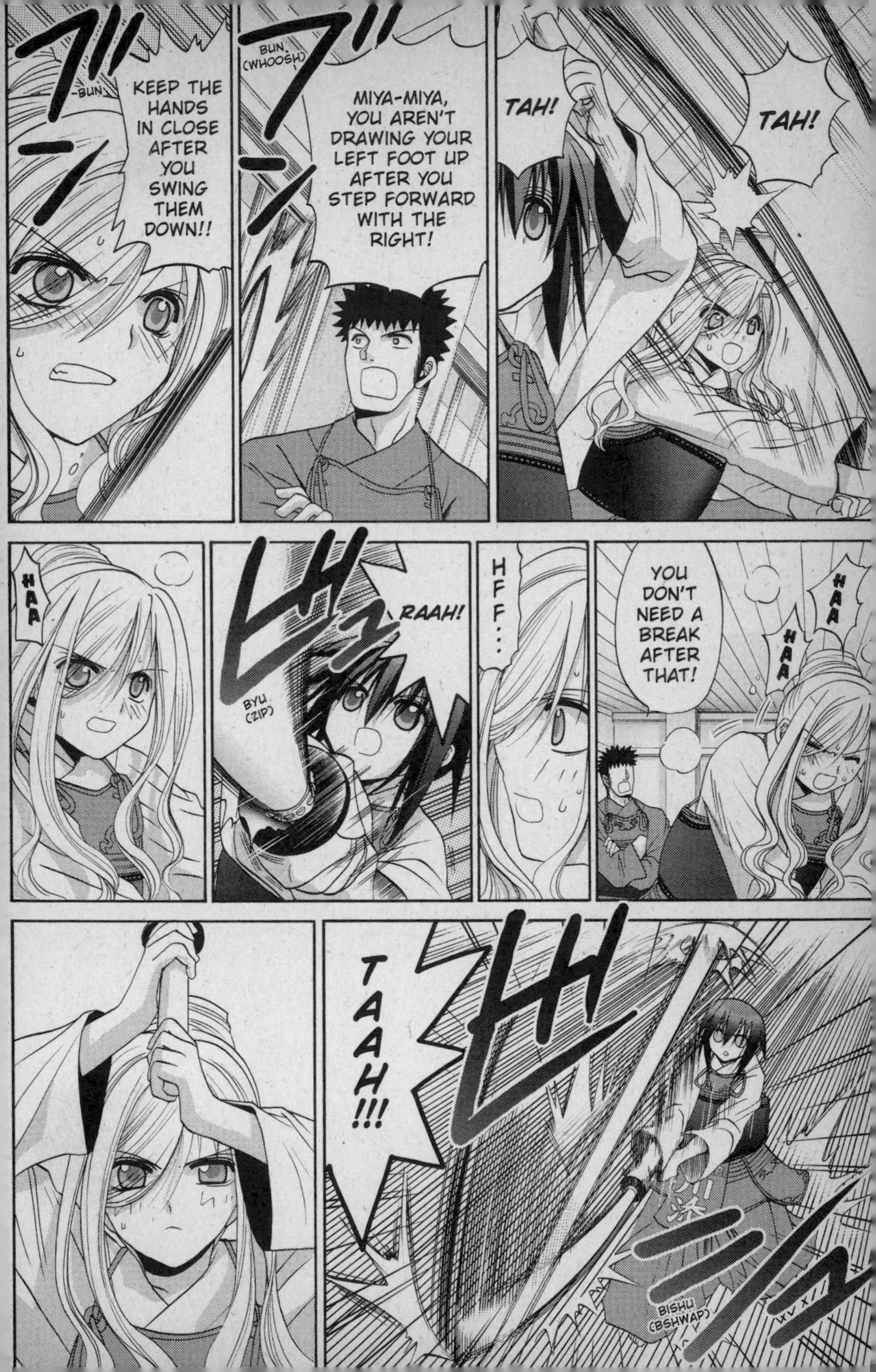
TAH!
TAH!
BUN (WHOOSH)
MIYA-MIYA, YOU AREN'T DRAWING YOUR LEFT FOOT UP AFTER YOU STEP FORWARD WITH THE RIGHT!
BUN
KEEP THE HANDS IN CLOSE AFTER YOU SWING THEM DOWN!!
HAA
HAA
YOU DON'T NEED A BREAK AFTER THAT!
HFF...
RAAH!
BYU (ZIP)
HAA
TAAH!!!
BISHU (BSHWAP)

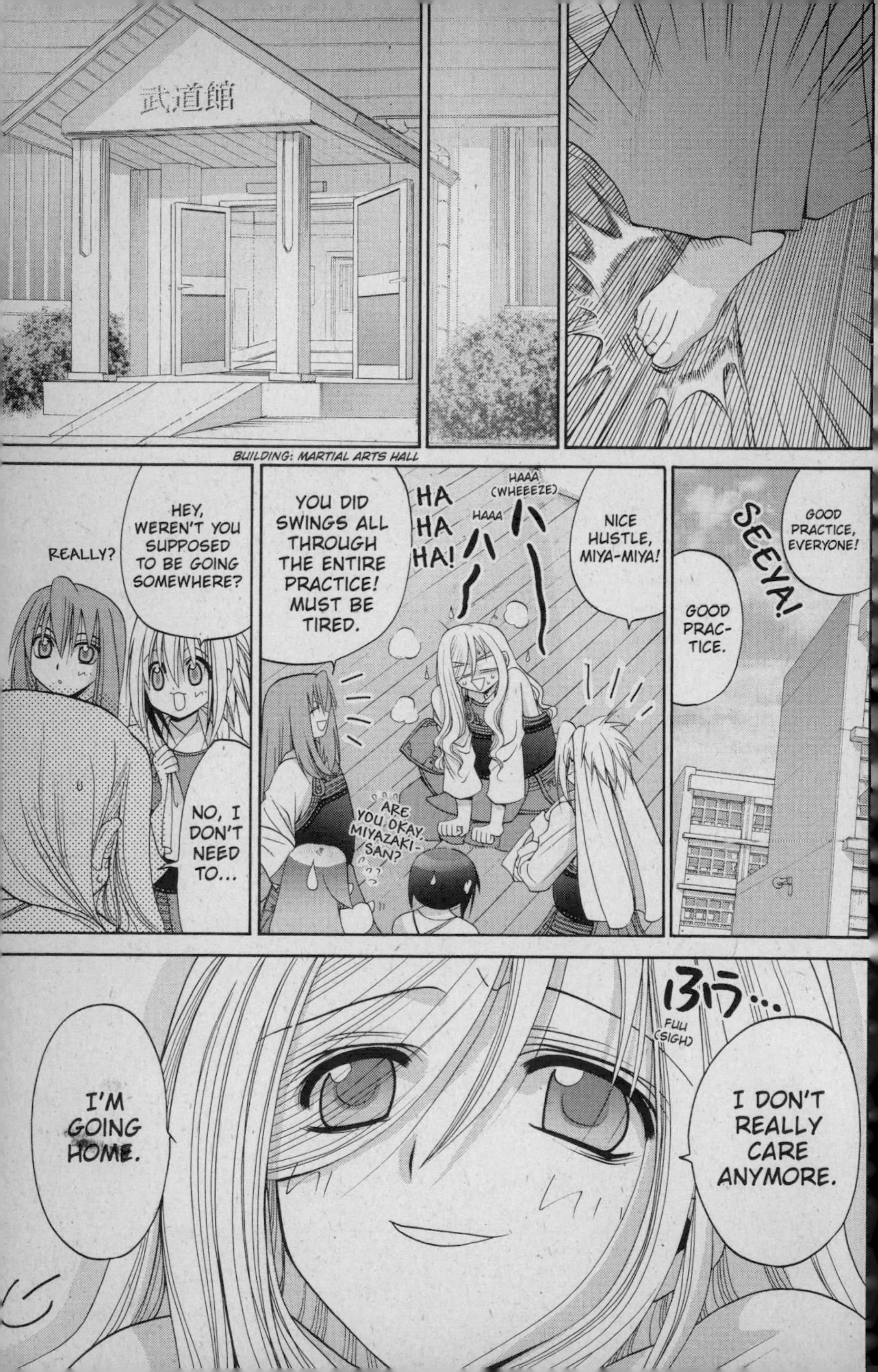
武道館
BUILDING: MARTIAL ARTS HALL
GOOD PRACTICE, EVERYONE!
SEEYA!
GOOD PRAC-TICE.
NICE HUSTLE, MIYA-MIYA!
HAAA (WHEEEZE)
HAAA
HA HA HA!
YOU DID SWINGS ALL THROUGH THE ENTIRE PRACTICE! MUST BE TIRED.
ARE YOU OKAY, MIYAZAKI-SAN?
HEY, WEREN'T YOU SUPPOSED TO BE GOING SOMEWHERE?
REALLY?
NO, I DON'T NEED TO...
ふう...
FUU (SIGH)
I DON'T REALLY CARE ANYMORE.
I'M GOING HOME.

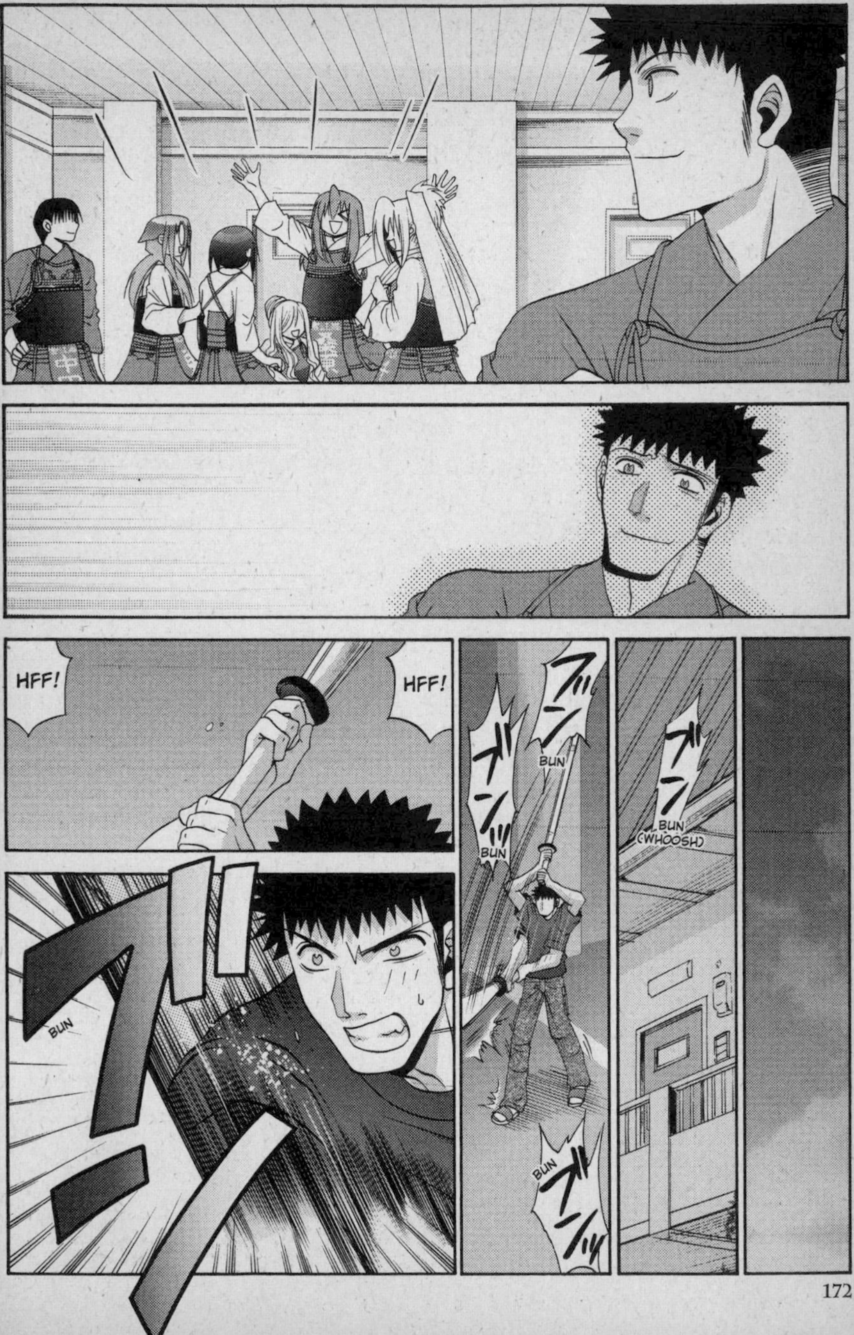
BUN
(WHOOSH)
BUN
BUN
BUN
HFF!
HFF!
BUN

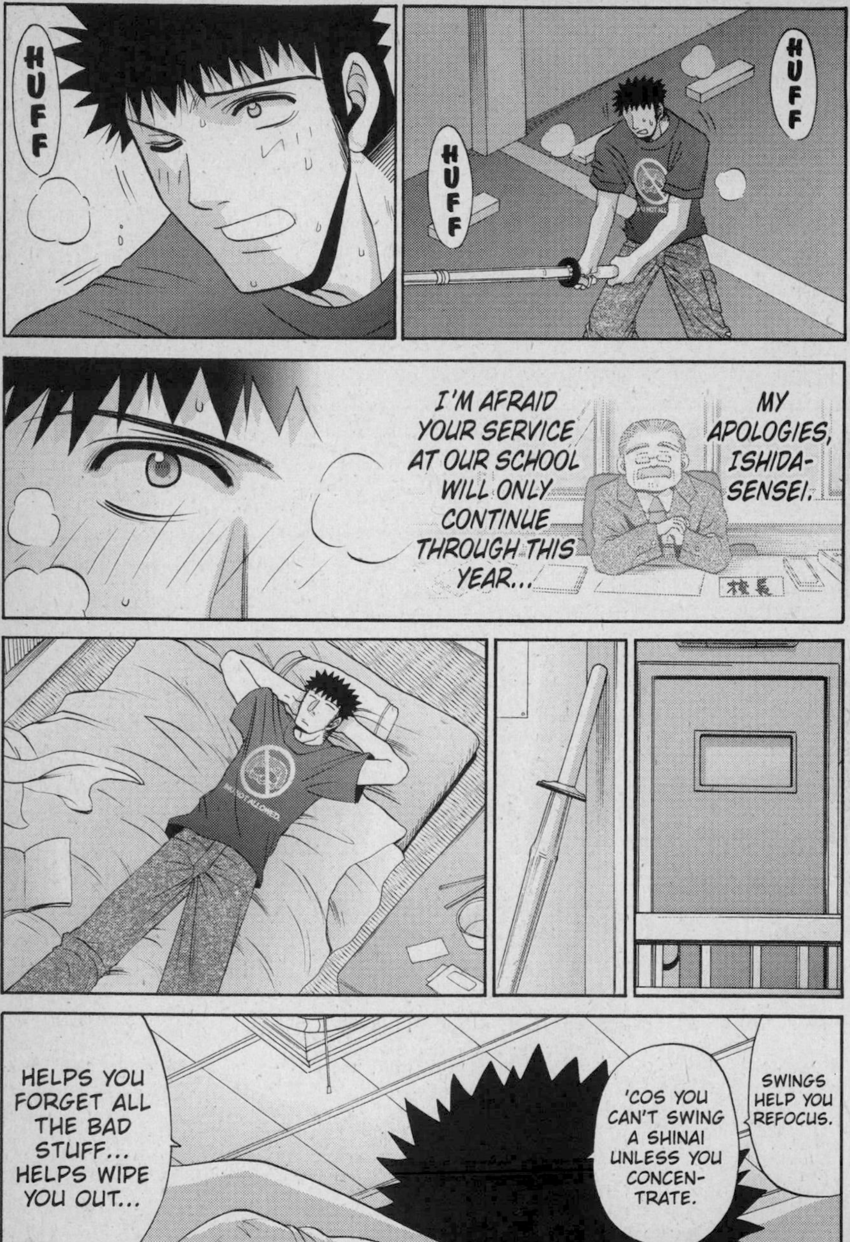
HUFF
HUFF
HUFF
MY APOLOGIES, ISHIDA-SENSEI.
I'M AFRAID YOUR SERVICE AT OUR SCHOOL WILL ONLY CONTINUE THROUGH THIS YEAR...
SWINGS HELP YOU REFOCUS.
'COS YOU CAN'T SWING A SHINAI UNLESS YOU CONCEN-TRATE.
HELPS YOU FORGET ALL THE BAD STUFF... HELPS WIPE YOU OUT...

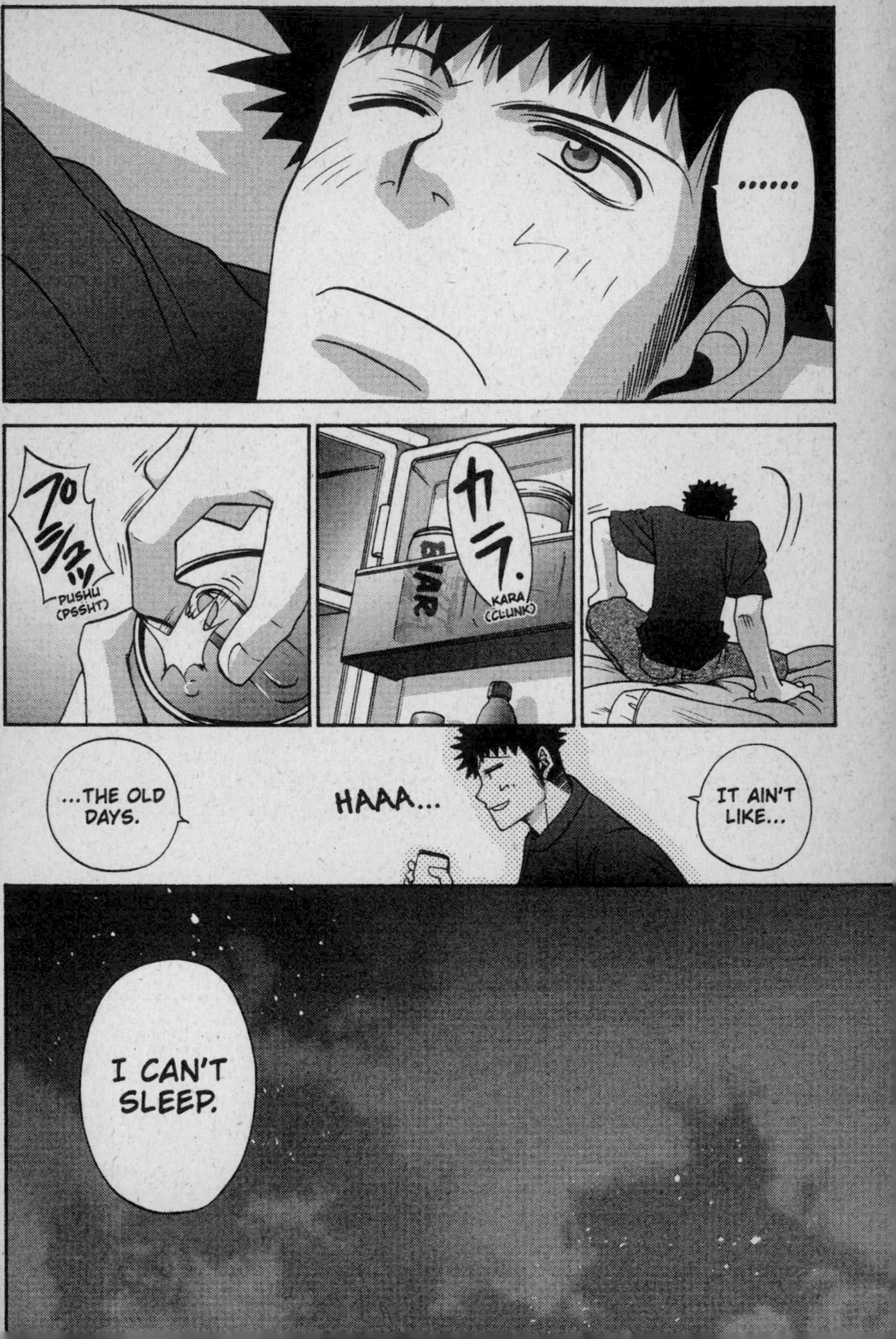
......
カラ.
KARA (CLUNK)
プシュッ
PUSHU (PSSHT)
IT AIN'T LIKE...
HAAA...
...THE OLD DAYS.
I CAN'T SLEEP.

BAMBOO BLADE

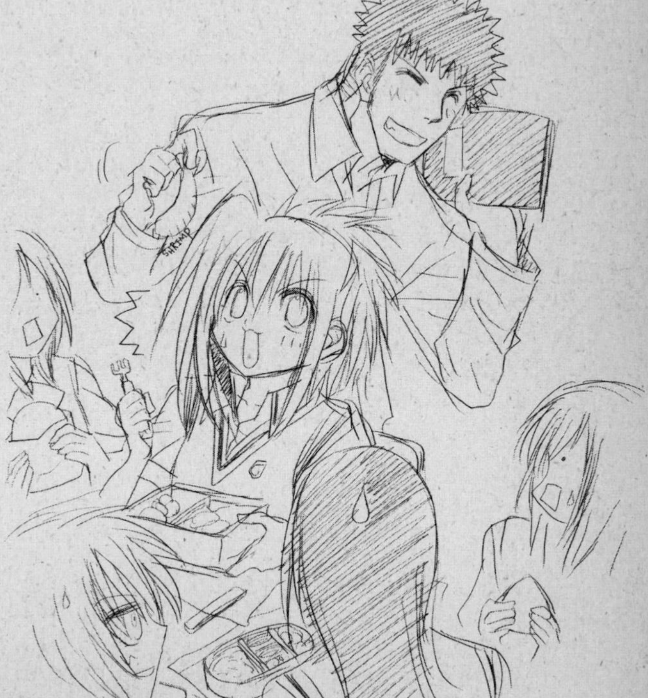
SHRIMP

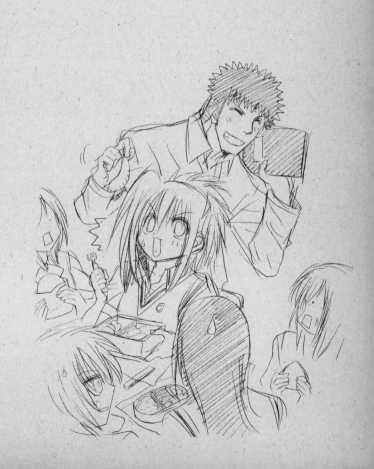

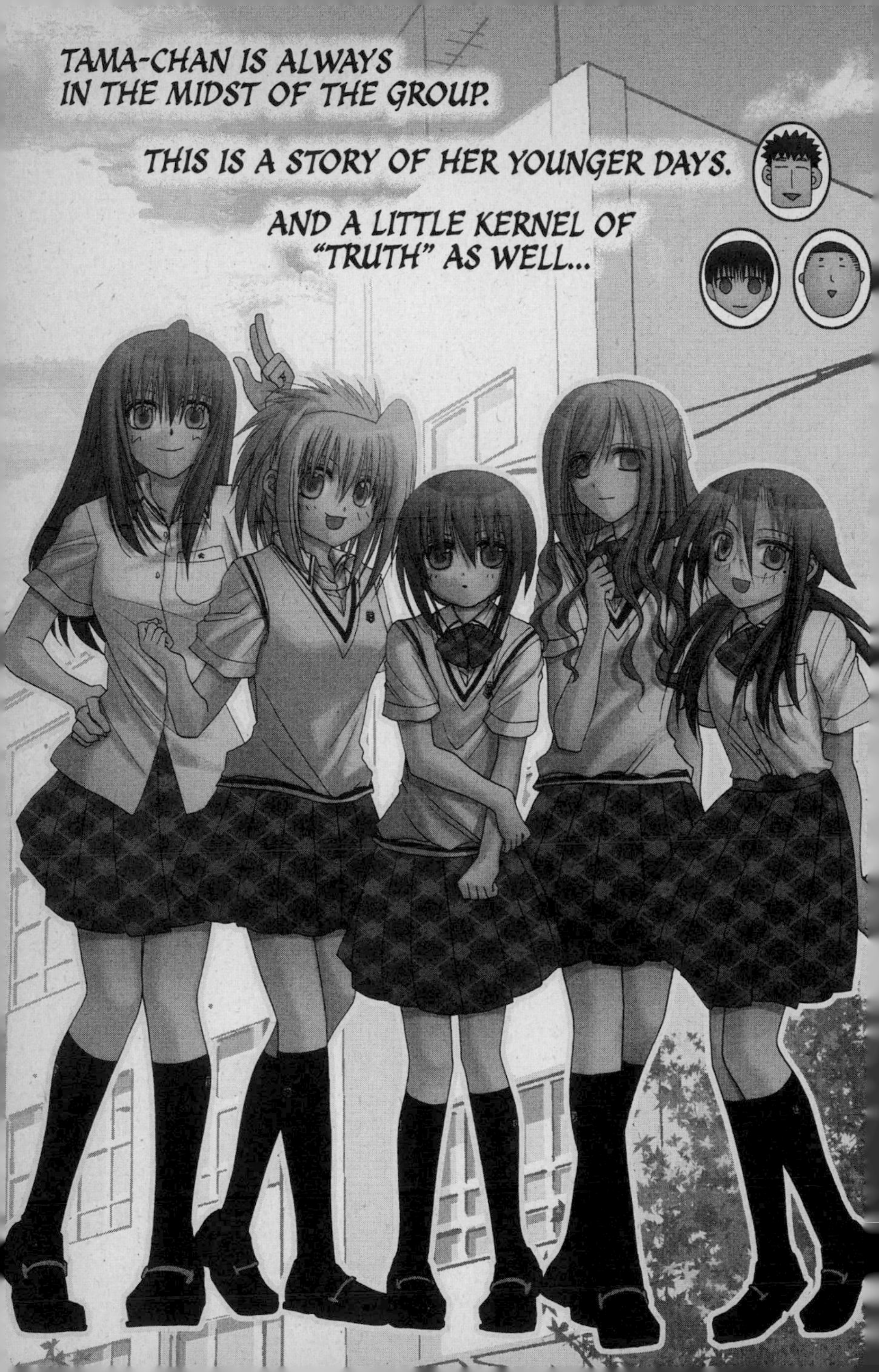
TAMA-CHAN IS ALWAYS IN THE MIDST OF THE GROUP.
THIS IS A STORY OF HER YOUNGER DAYS.
AND A LITTLE KERNEL OF "TRUTH" AS WELL...

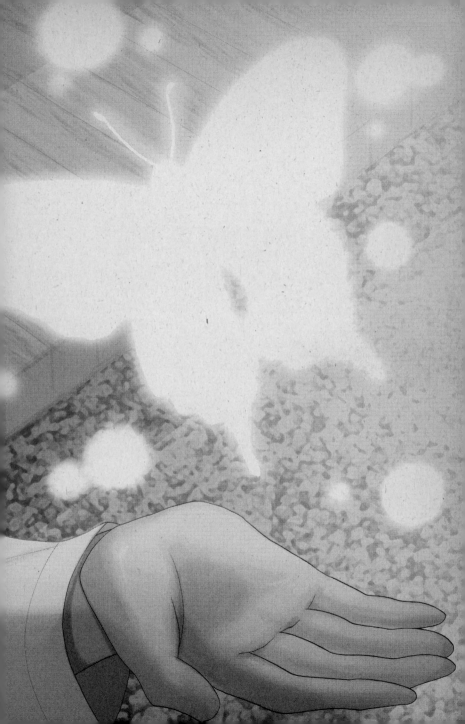

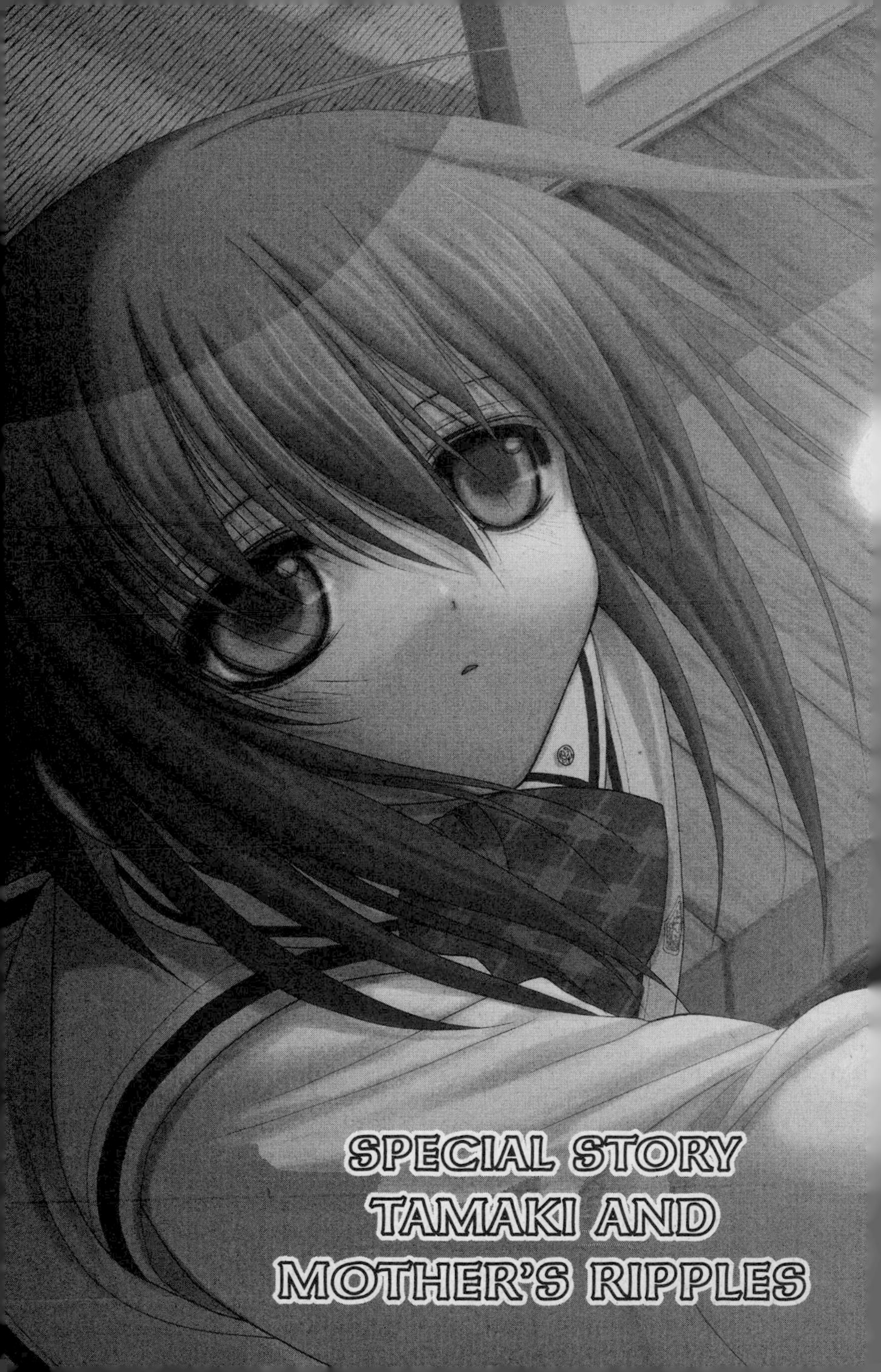
SPECIAL STORY
TAMAKI AND
MOTHER'S RIPPLES

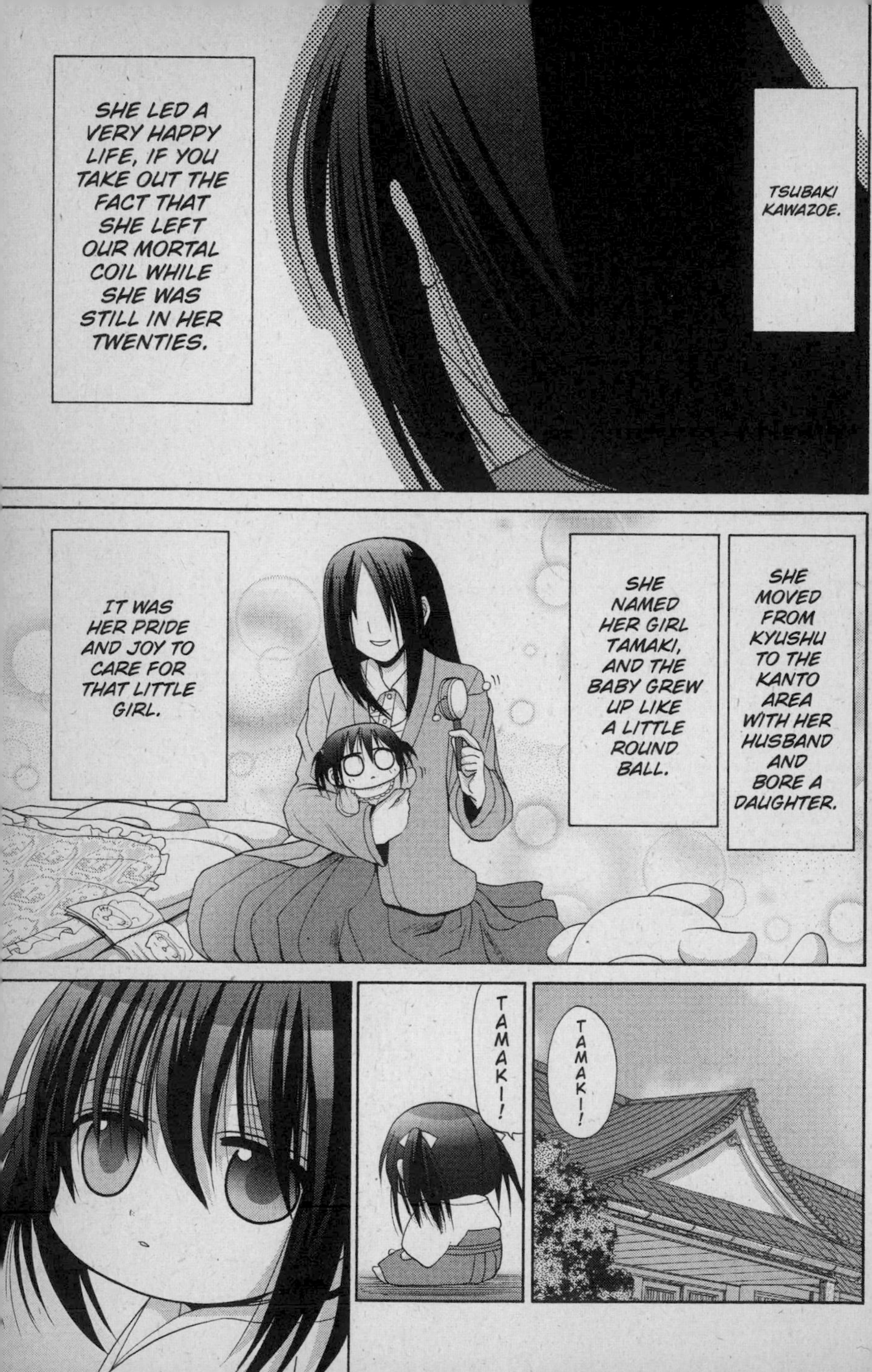
TSUBAKI KAWAZOE.
SHE LED A VERY HAPPY LIFE, IF YOU TAKE OUT THE FACT THAT SHE LEFT OUR MORTAL COIL WHILE SHE WAS STILL IN HER TWENTIES.
SHE MOVED FROM KYUSHU TO THE KANTO AREA WITH HER HUSBAND AND BORE A DAUGHTER.
SHE NAMED HER GIRL TAMAKI, AND THE BABY GREW UP LIKE A LITTLE ROUND BALL.
IT WAS HER PRIDE AND JOY TO CARE FOR THAT LITTLE GIRL.
TAMAKI!
TAMAKI!

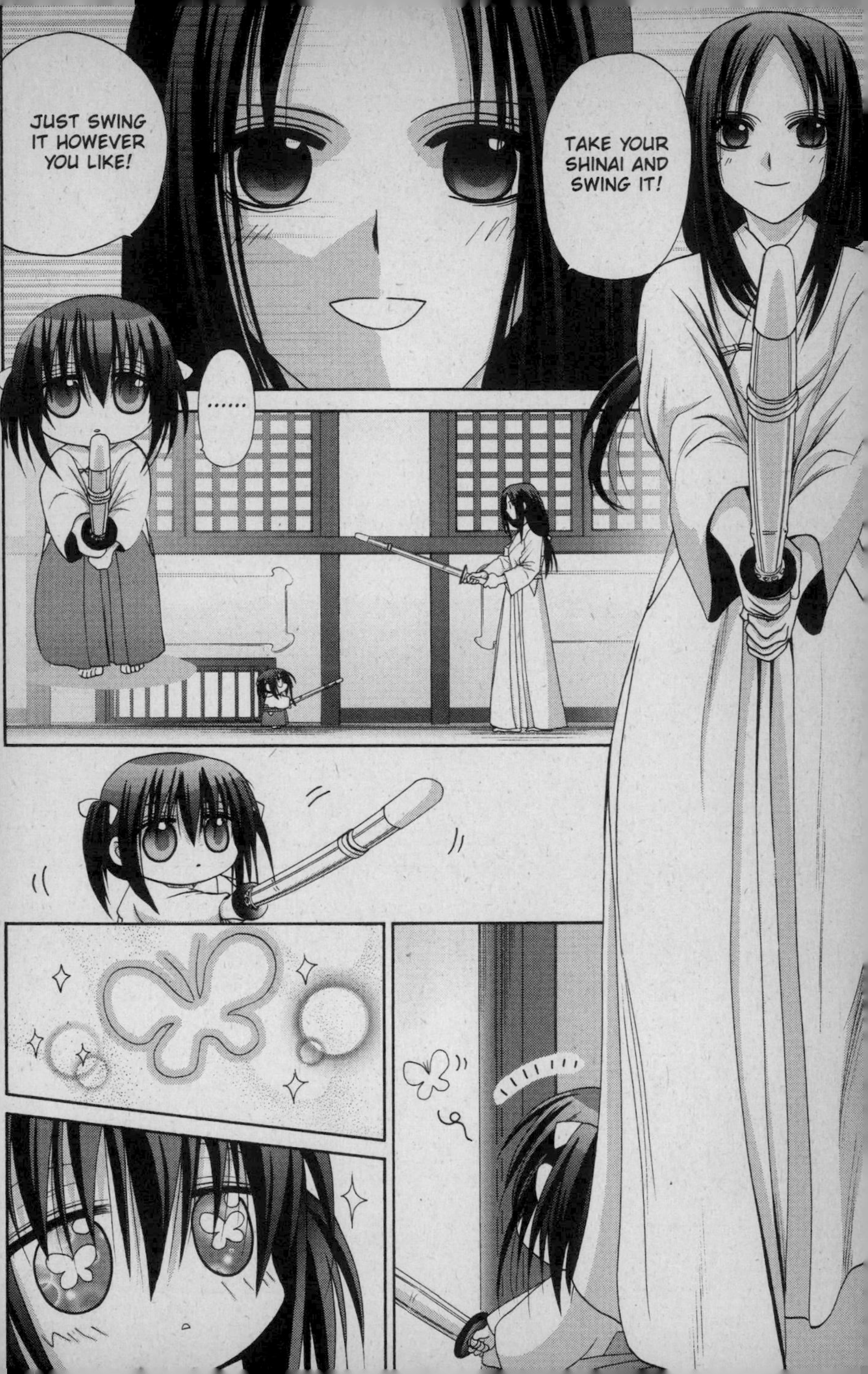
TAKE YOUR SHINAI AND SWING IT!
JUST SWING IT HOWEVER YOU LIKE!
......

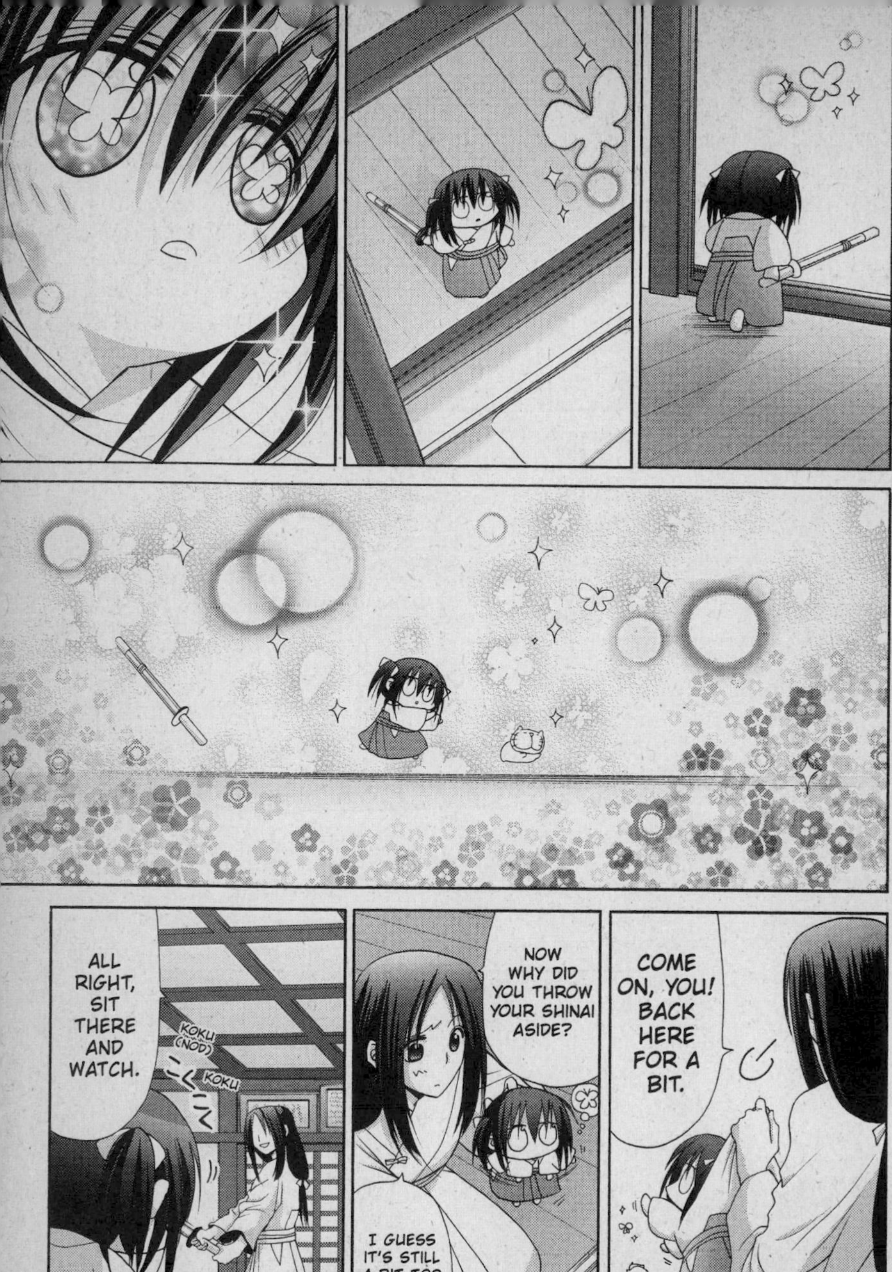
COME ON, YOU! BACK HERE FOR A BIT.
NOW WHY DID YOU THROW YOUR SHINAI ASIDE?
I GUESS IT'S STILL A BIT TOO EARLY FOR YOU.
ALL RIGHT, SIT THERE AND WATCH.
KOKU (NOD)
KOKU

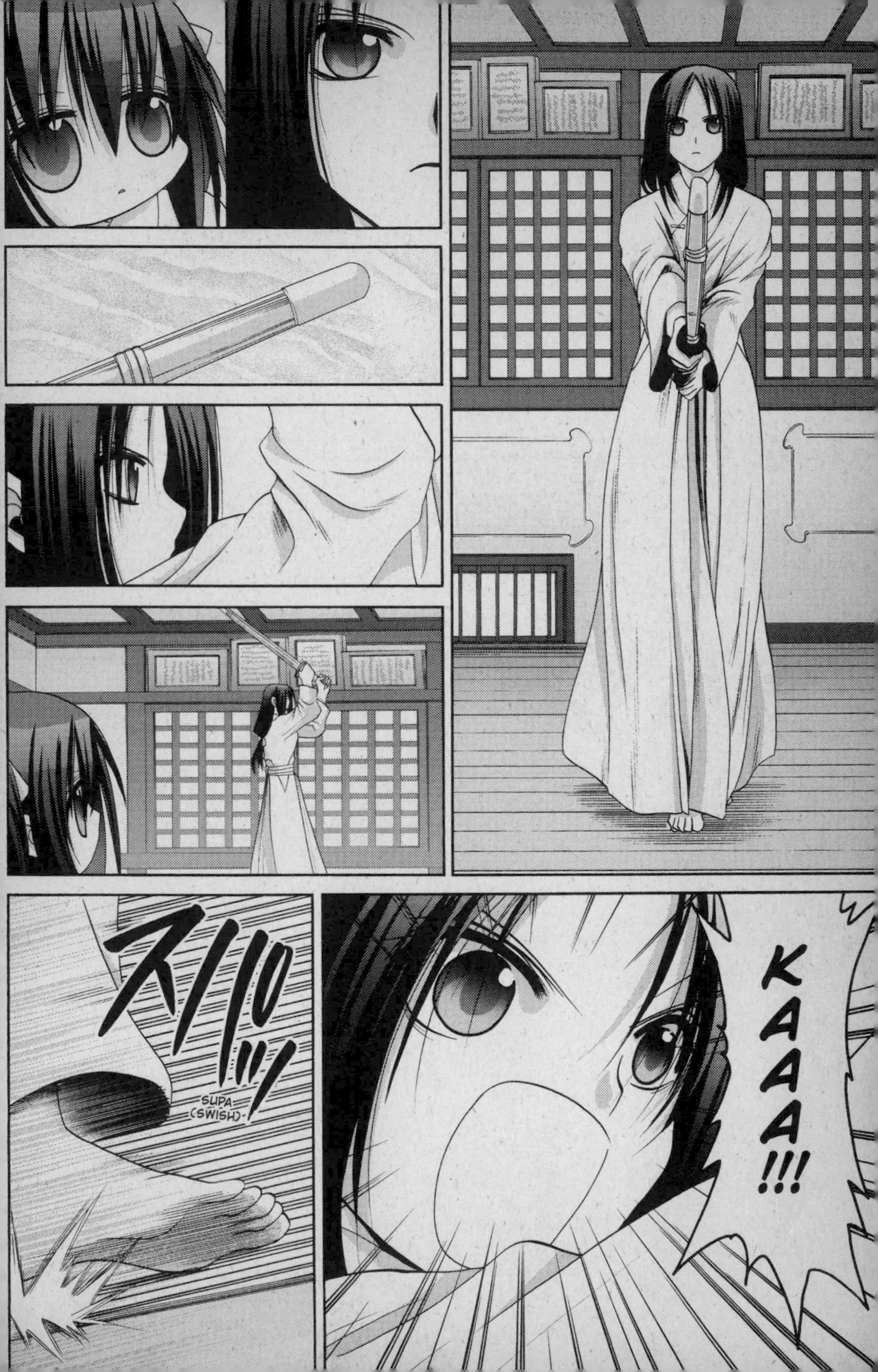
KAAAA!!!
スパッ
SUPA (SWISH)

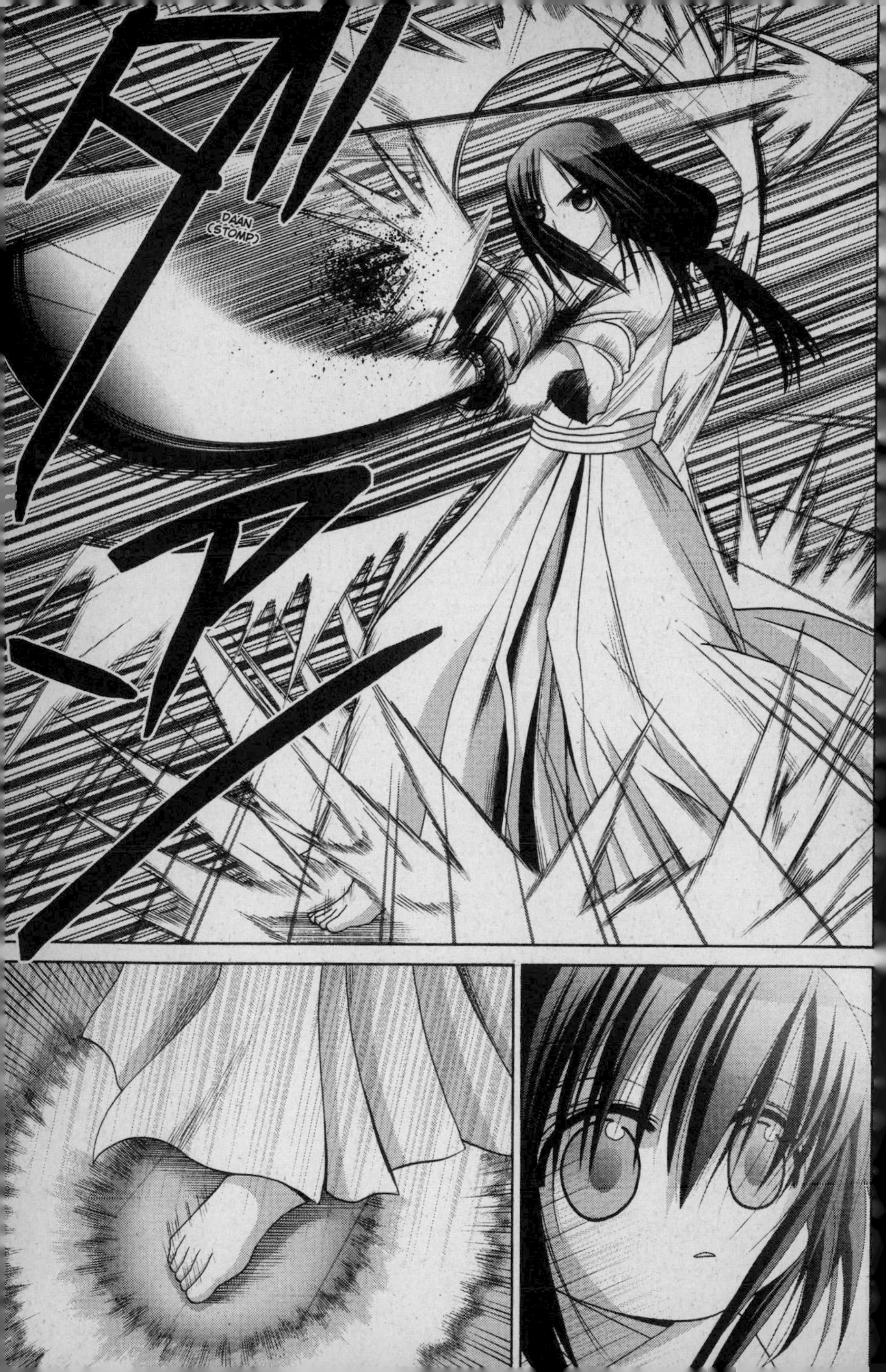
DAAN
(STOMP)

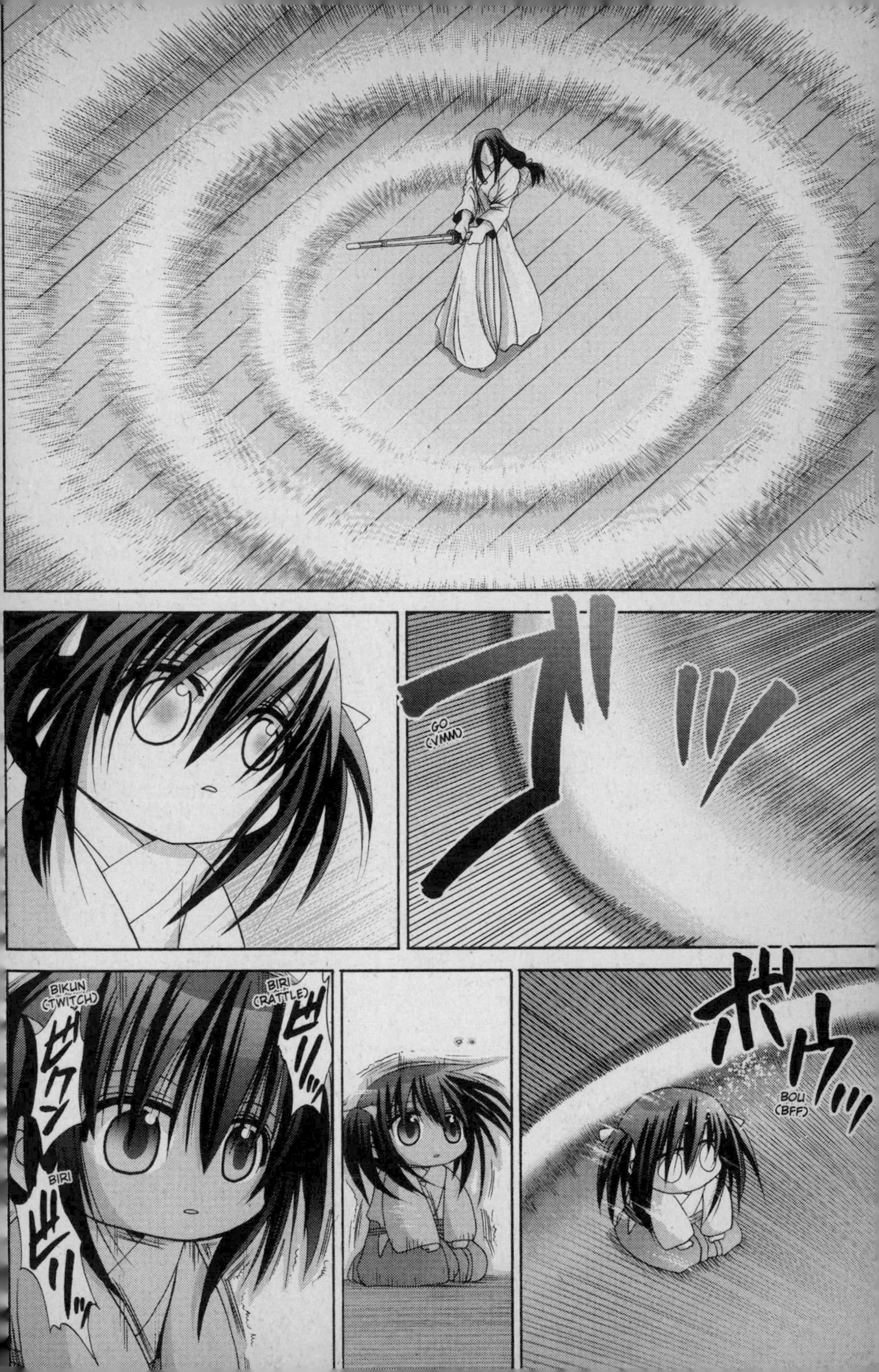
GO (VMMM)
BOU (BFF)
BIRI (RATTLE)
BIKUN (TWITCH)
BIRI

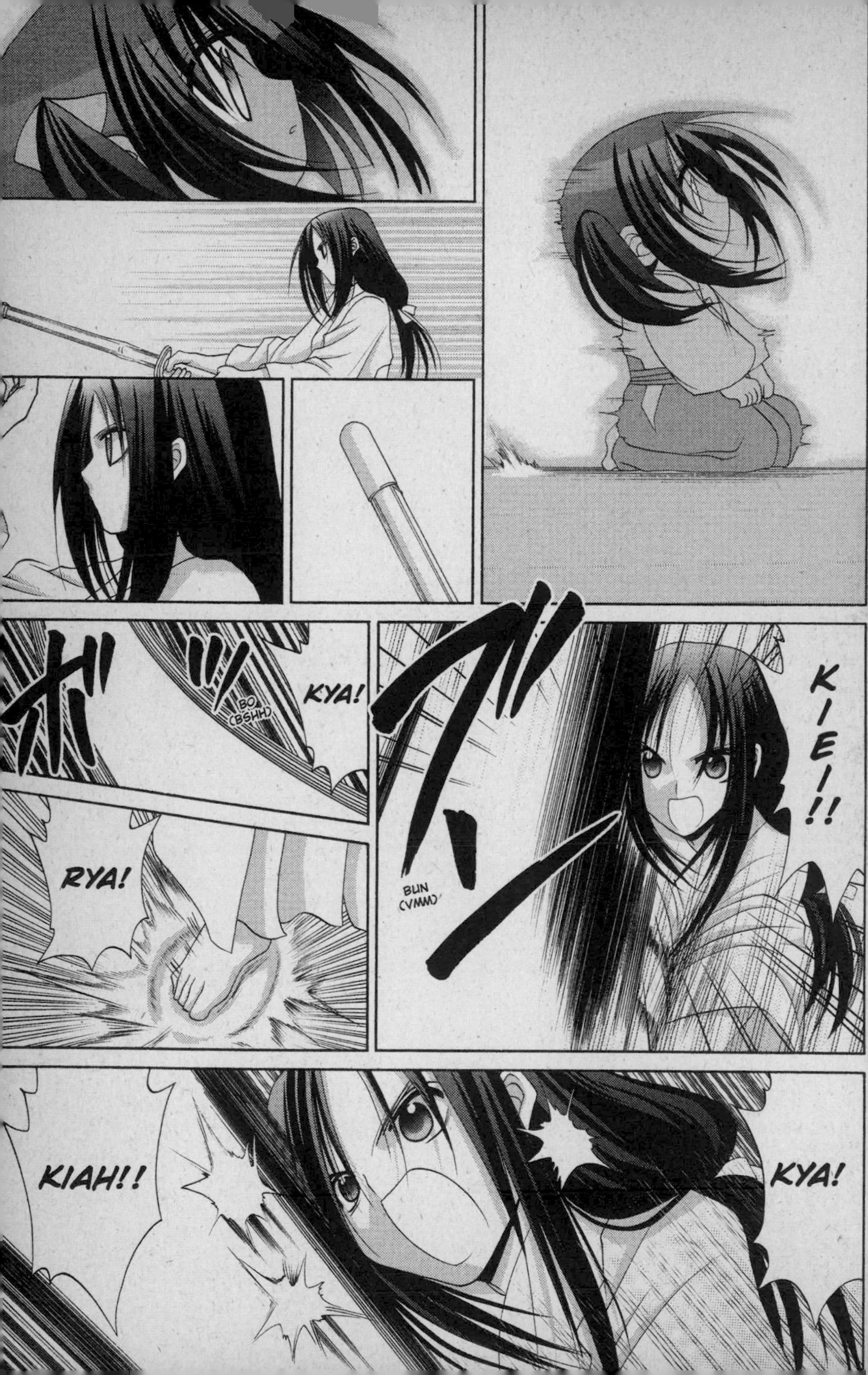
KIEI!!
BUN (VMM)
KYA!
BO (BSHH)
RYA!
KYA!
KIAH!!

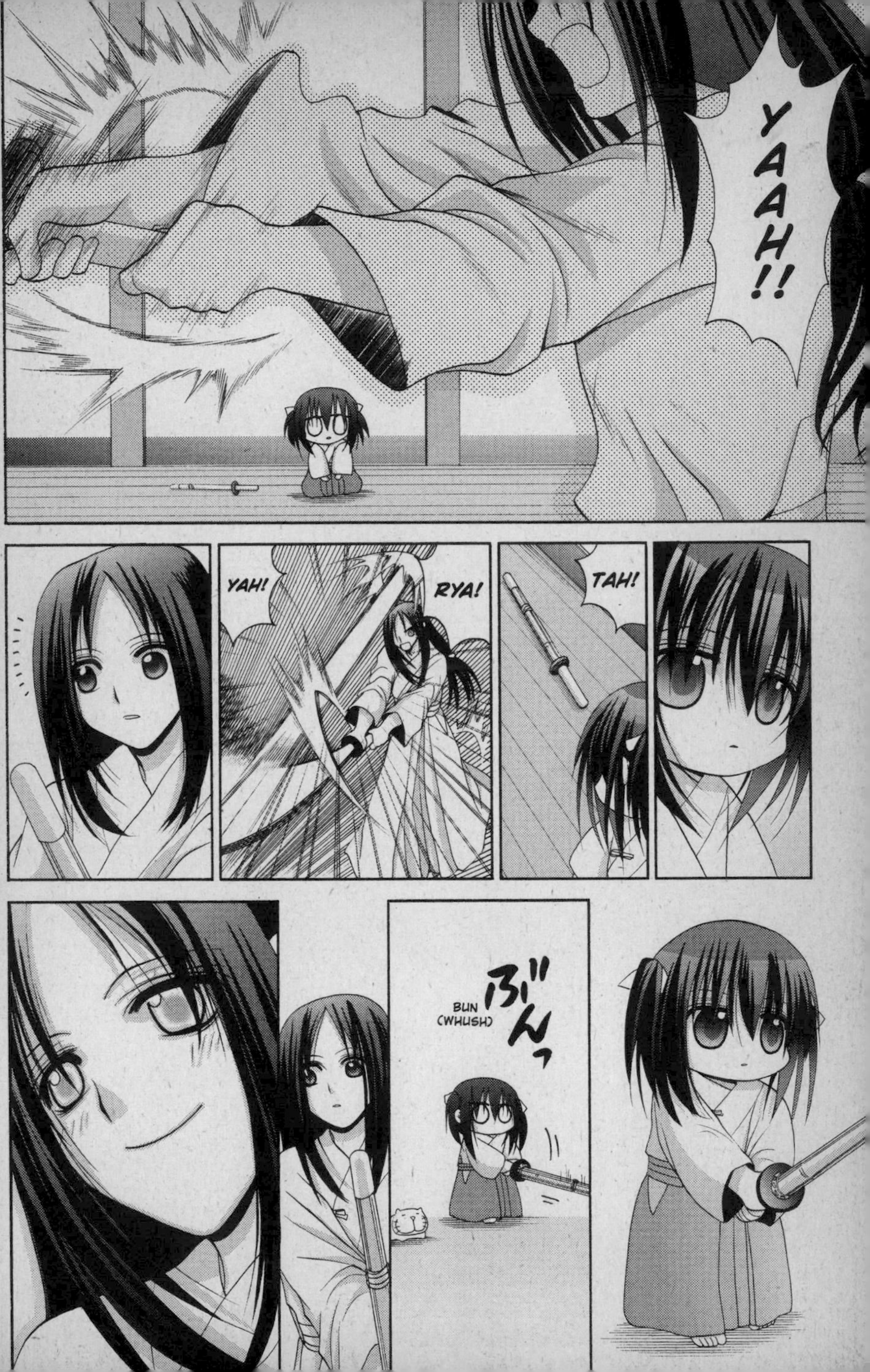
YAAH!!
TAH!
RYA!
YAH!
ぶん
BUN (WHUSH)

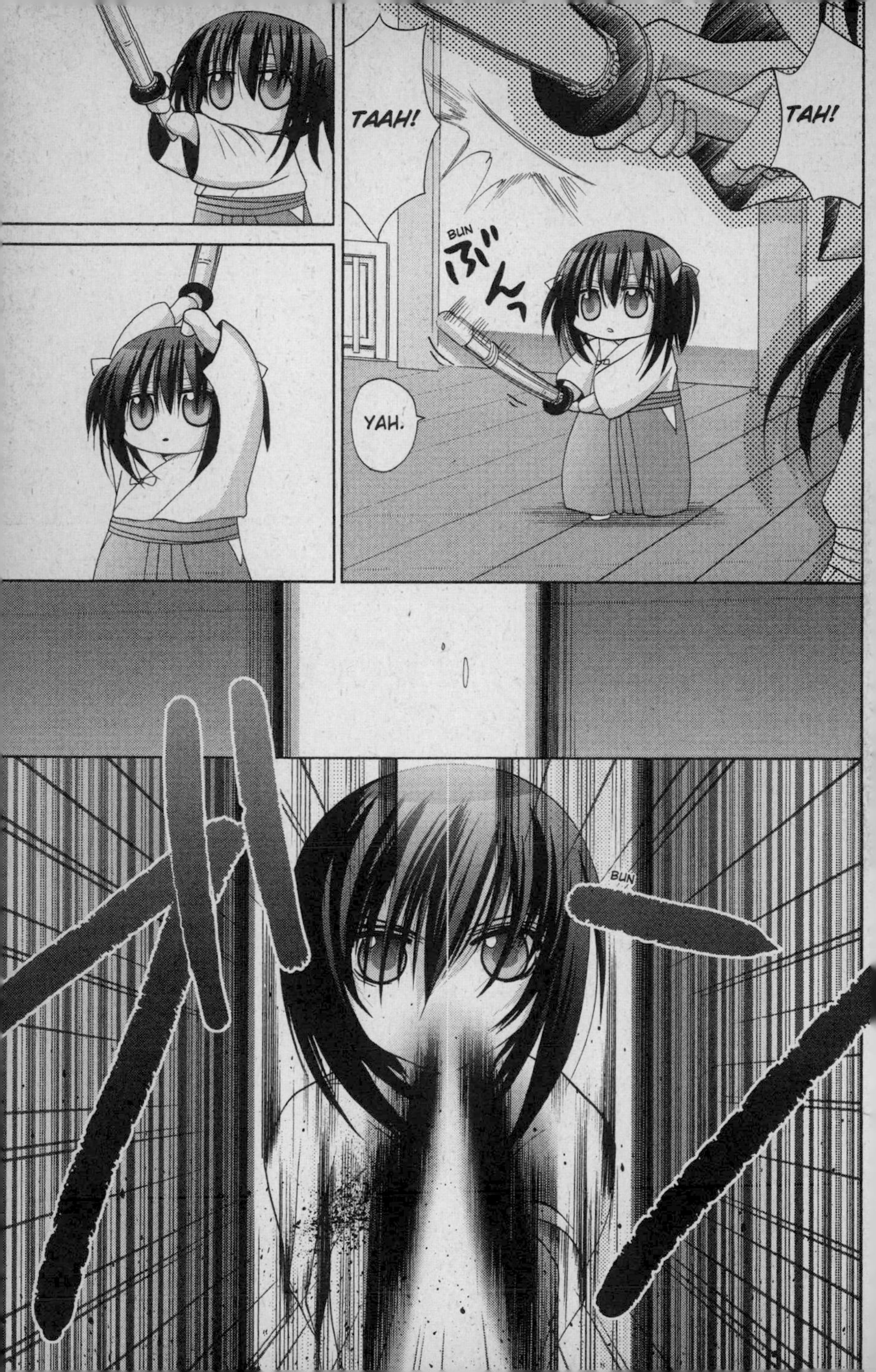
TAH!
TAAH!
BUN
ぶんっ
YAH.
BUN

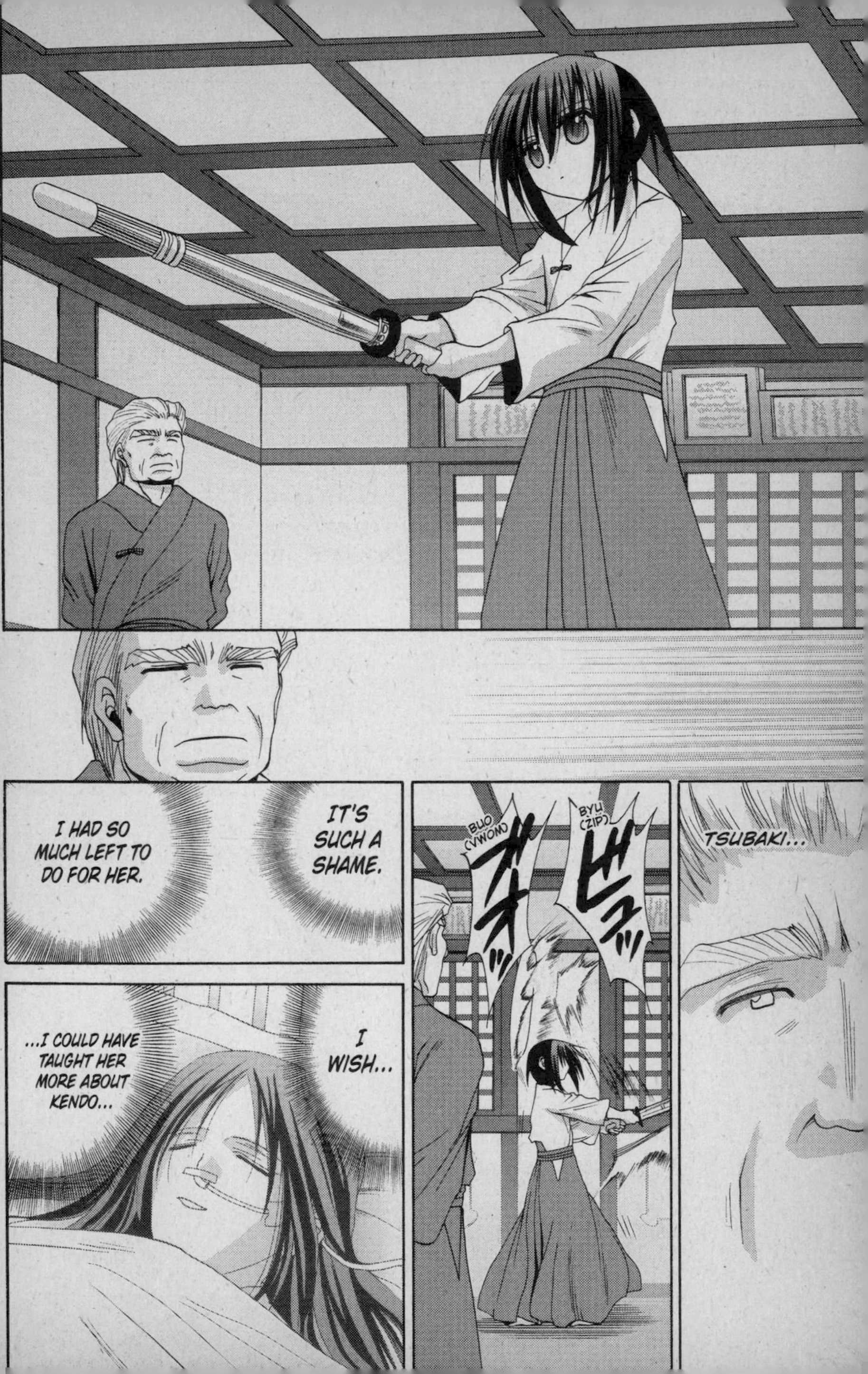
TSUBAKI...
BYU (ZIP)
BUO (VWOM)
IT'S SUCH A SHAME.
I HAD SO MUCH LEFT TO DO FOR HER.
I WISH...
...I COULD HAVE TAUGHT HER MORE ABOUT KENDO...

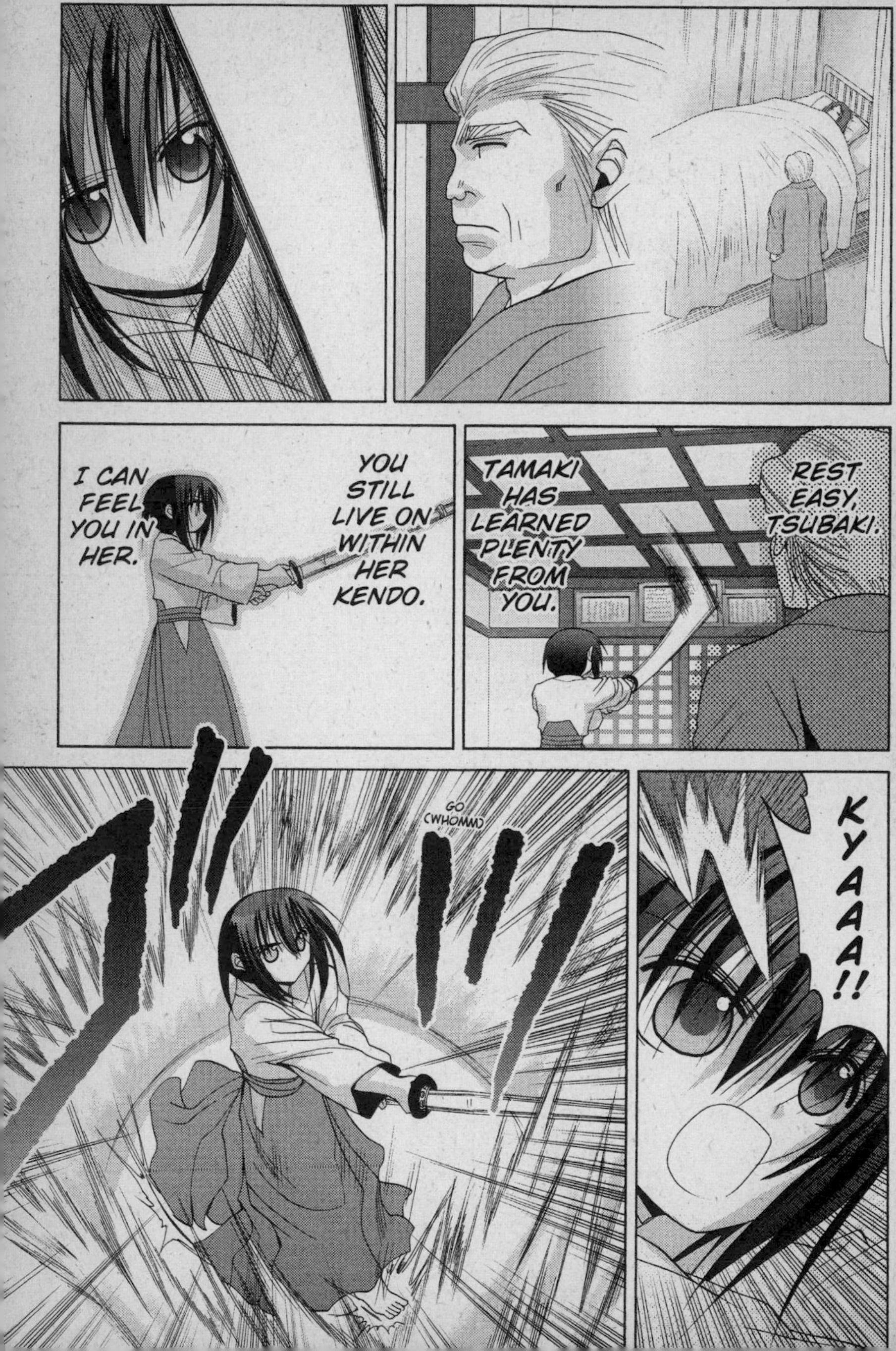
REST EASY, TSUBAKI.
TAMAKI HAS LEARNED PLENTY FROM YOU.
YOU STILL LIVE ON WITHIN HER KENDO.
I CAN FEEL YOU IN HER.
KYAAAA!!
GO (WHOMM)

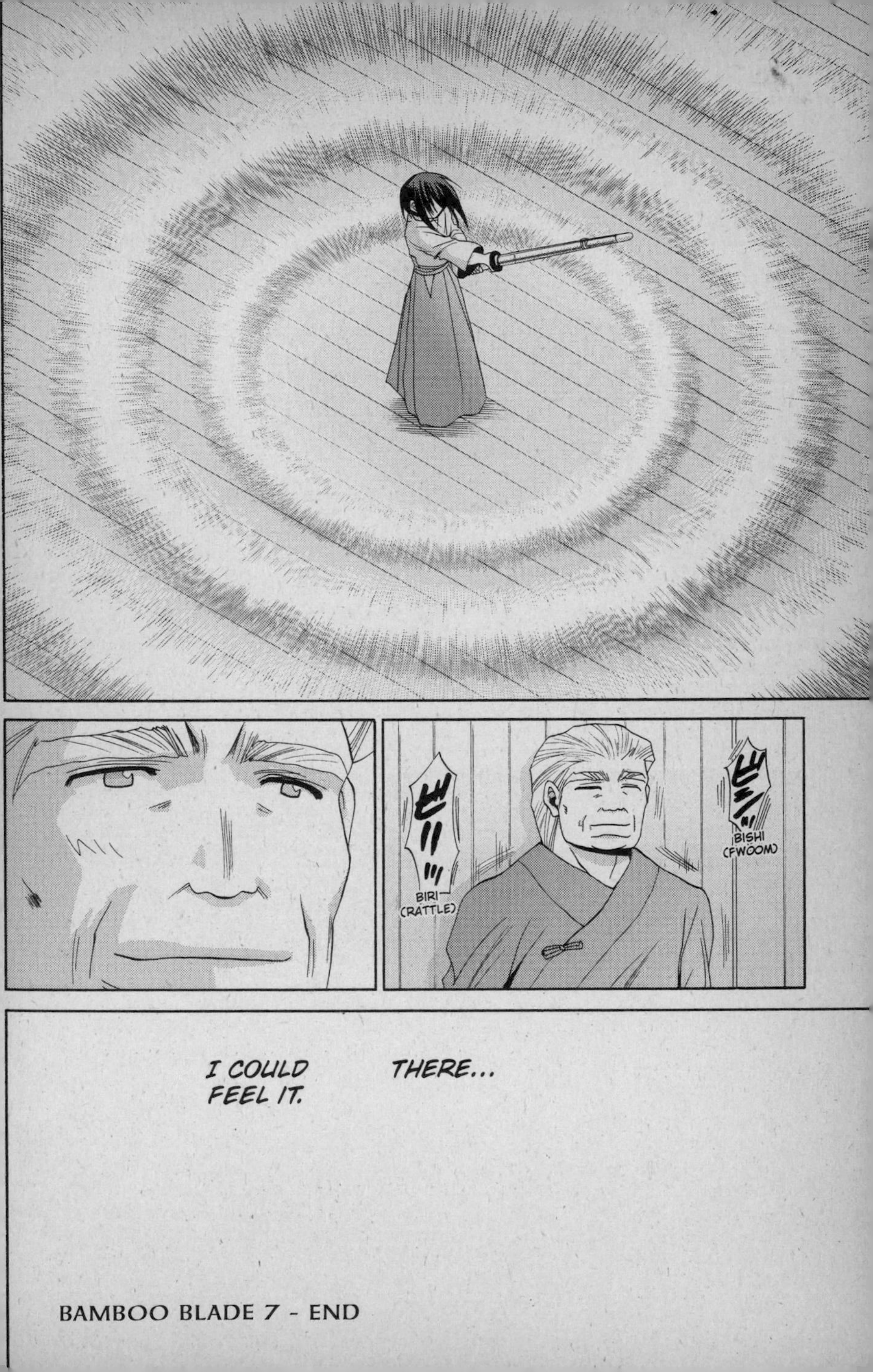
BISHI (FWOOM)
BIRI (RATTLE)
THERE...
I COULD FEEL IT.
BAMBOO BLADE 7 - END

TRANSLATION NOTES

Common Honorifics

No honorific: Indicates familiarity or closeness; if used without permission or reason, addressing someone in this manner would constitute an insult.

-san: The Japanese equivalent of Mr./Mrs./Miss. If a situation calls for politeness, this is the fail-safe honorific.

-sama: Conveys great respect; may also indicate that the social status of the speaker is lower than that of the addressee.

-kun: Used most often when referring to boys, this indicates affection or familiarity. Occasionally used by older men among their peers, but it may also be used by anyone referring to a person of lower standing.

-chan: An affectionate honorific indicating familiarity used mostly in reference to girls; also used in reference to cute persons or animals of either gender.

-senpai: A suffix used in addressing one's upperclassmen.

-sensei: A respectful term for teachers, artists, or high-level professionals.

-dono: A polite, formal honorific used to show respect. Uncommon in modern Japanese.

General Notes

Armor: The guards, or *bogu*, worn in kendo all have their own names: The *men* is the helmet and face mask, the *do* is the breastplate, *tare* refers to the hanging plates worn like a belt, and the *kote* are the gauntlets that protect the hands.

Senpo, Jiho, Chuken, Fukusho, Taisho: These are the five ranks that make up a kendo team and determine the order in which the players appear.

Ari: When a point has been scored, the judge will call out the area struck (*men*, *kote*, *do*, etc.) and then "*ari*," signifying that a point has been scored in the area named.

Shobu ari: The judge calls "*shobu ari*" when the match is over and one combatant has won.

Scoreboard: The letters indicate on which part of the armor the point was scored. The circled letter denotes the first point scored. "F" stands for "foul," and an "X" across the center line means the bout was a draw.

For more information on the formal rules and workings of kendo, see Volume 2 pages 152-154!

Page 20

Hell-Kill Death's Bell: The name written on this sign is lifted from *Bamboo Blade* writer Masahiro Totsuka's prior comedy/fantasy manga series, *Material Puzzle*. In the series, "Hell-Kill Death's Bell" is a forbidden "song" spell that causes those who hear it to commit suicide.

BOOK: BLACK RESURRECTION MANUAL

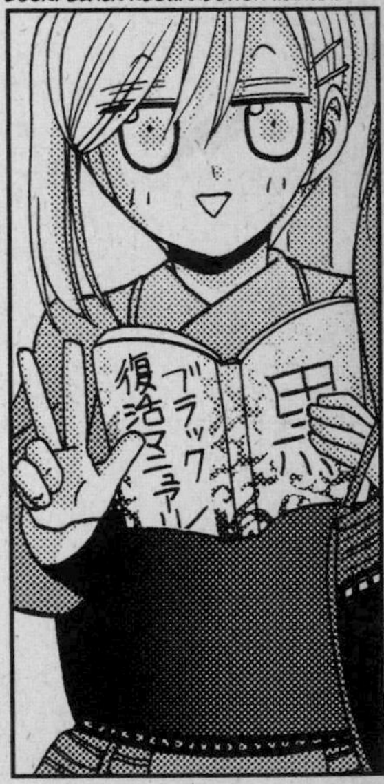
ブラック
復活マニュアル

OMAKE MANGA THEATER ①

MIYAZAKI-SAN AND THE AMAZING○○

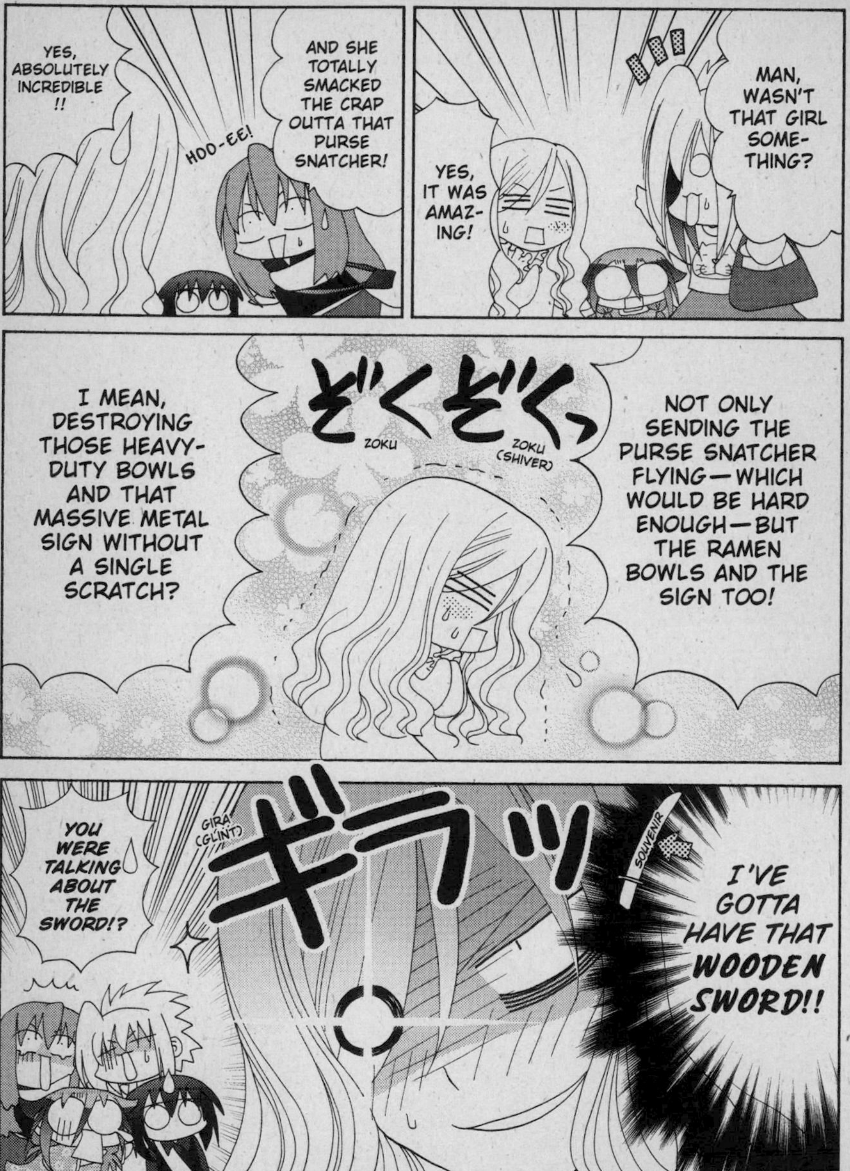
MAN, WASN'T THAT GIRL SOME-THING?
YES, IT WAS AMAZ-ING!
AND SHE TOTALLY SMACKED THE CRAP OUTTA THAT PURSE SNATCHER!
HOO-EE!
YES, ABSOLUTELY INCREDIBLE!!
NOT ONLY SENDING THE PURSE SNATCHER FLYING—WHICH WOULD BE HARD ENOUGH—BUT THE RAMEN BOWLS AND THE SIGN TOO!
ぞくぞくっ
ZOKU
ZOKU (SHIVER)
I MEAN, DESTROYING THOSE HEAVY-DUTY BOWLS AND THAT MASSIVE METAL SIGN WITHOUT A SINGLE SCRATCH?
I'VE GOTTA HAVE THAT WOODEN SWORD!!
SOUVENIR
ギラッ
GIRA (GLINT)
YOU WERE TALKING ABOUT THE SWORD!?

OMAKE MANGA THEATER ②

TAMA-CHAN AND THE FASHION MAGAZINE

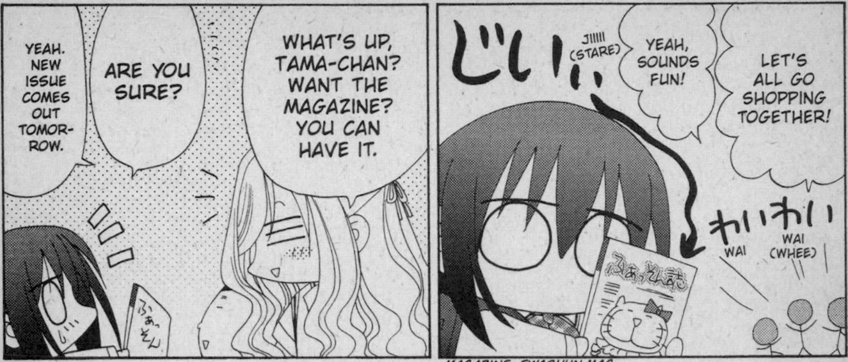
LET'S ALL GO SHOPPING TOGETHER!
YEAH, SOUNDS FUN!
じいー
JIIIII (STARE)
わいわい
WAI WAI (WHEE)
ふぁっそん誌
WHAT'S UP, TAMA-CHAN? WANT THE MAGAZINE? YOU CAN HAVE IT.
ARE YOU SURE?
YEAH. NEW ISSUE COMES OUT TOMORROW.
ふぁっそん

MAGAZINE: FWASHUN MAG

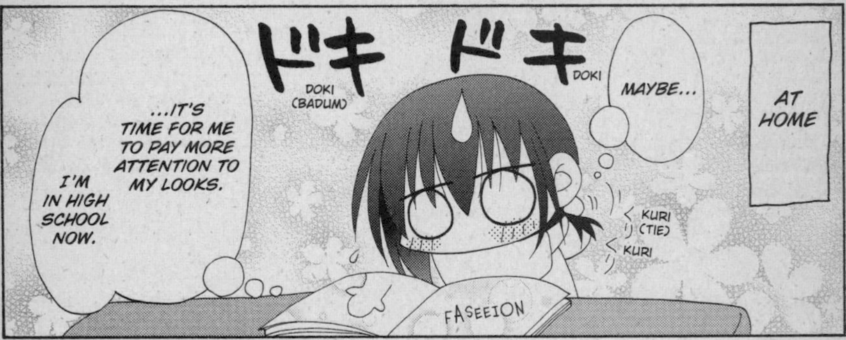
AT HOME
MAYBE...
ドキ
DOKI
ドキ
DOKI (BADUM)
...IT'S TIME FOR ME TO PAY MORE ATTENTION TO MY LOOKS.
I'M IN HIGH SCHOOL NOW.
KURI (TIE)
KURI
FASEEION

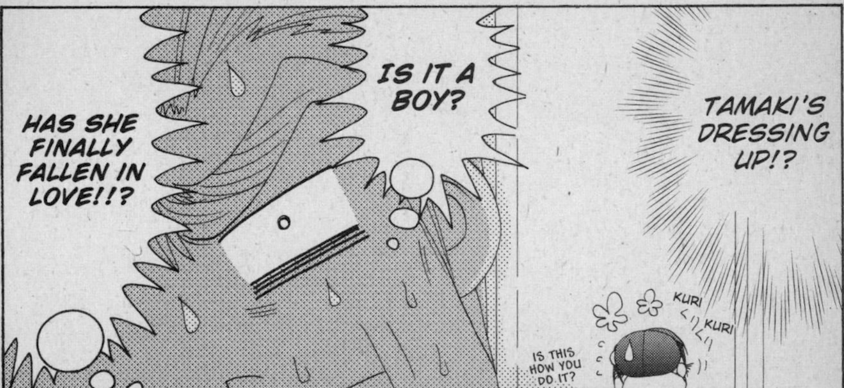
TAMAKI'S DRESSING UP!?
IS IT A BOY?
HAS SHE FINALLY FALLEN IN LOVE!!?
KURI
KURI
IS THIS HOW YOU DO IT?

OMAKE MANGA THEATER ③

SAYAKO-SAN AND THE DESIRE TO PLAY GUITAR

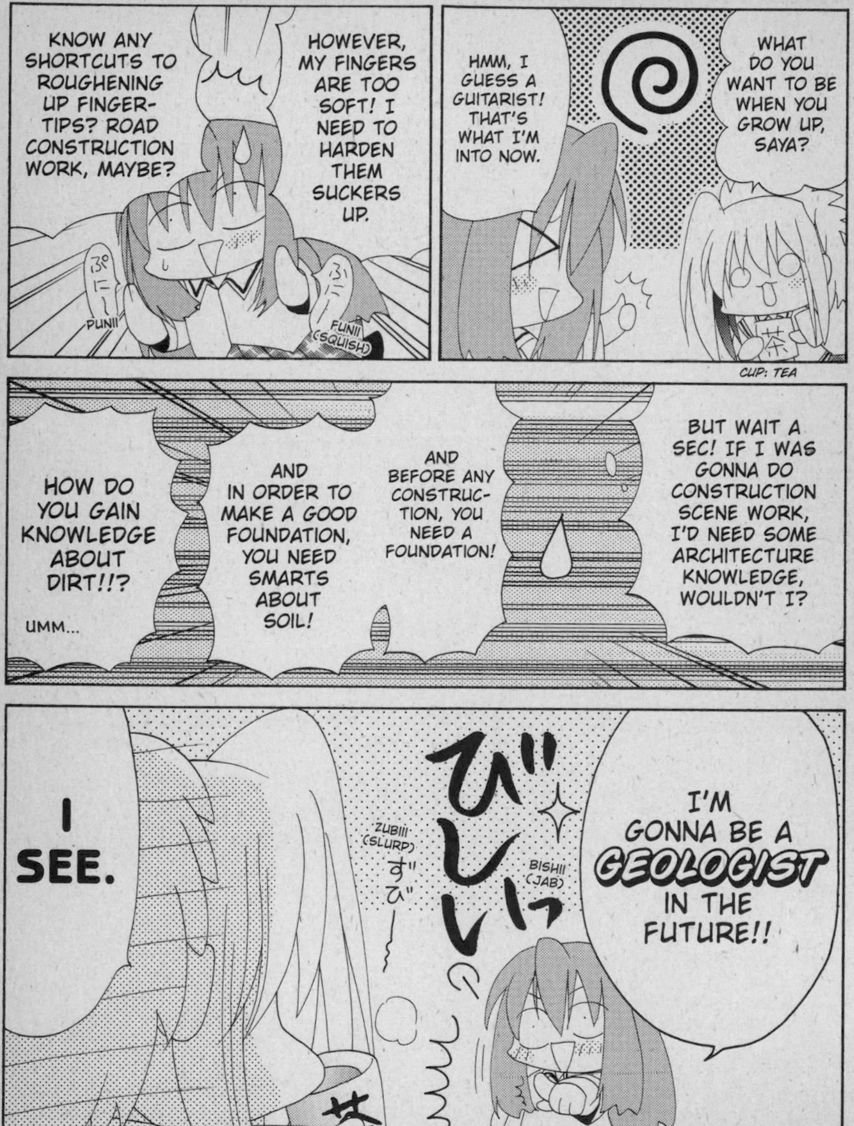
WHAT DO YOU WANT TO BE WHEN YOU GROW UP, SAYA?
HMM, I GUESS A GUITARIST! THAT'S WHAT I'M INTO NOW.
CUP: TEA
HOWEVER, MY FINGERS ARE TOO SOFT! I NEED TO HARDEN THEM SUCKERS UP.
FUNII (SQUISH)
KNOW ANY SHORTCUTS TO ROUGHENING UP FINGER-TIPS? ROAD CONSTRUCTION WORK, MAYBE?
PUNII
BUT WAIT A SEC! IF I WAS GONNA DO CONSTRUCTION SCENE WORK, I'D NEED SOME ARCHITECTURE KNOWLEDGE, WOULDN'T I?
AND BEFORE ANY CONSTRUC-TION, YOU NEED A FOUNDATION!
AND IN ORDER TO MAKE A GOOD FOUNDATION, YOU NEED SMARTS ABOUT SOIL!
HOW DO YOU GAIN KNOWLEDGE ABOUT DIRT!!?
UMM...
I'M GONNA BE A GEOLOGIST IN THE FUTURE!!
BISHII (JAB)
ZUBIII (SLURP)
I SEE.

"BAMBOO BLADE": A LITTLE EXPLANATION
AUTHOR: MASAHIRO TOTSUKA

○ IN THE BEGINNING

"WE'RE STARTING A MAGAZINE CALLED *YOUNG GANGAN*, SO DRAW SOMETHING— ANYTHING!" WELL, I'D ALWAYS WANTED TO DO A MANGA ABOUT A GIRLS' KENDO TEAM, SO THIS WAS MY CHANCE.

HOWEVER, I WAS WORKING ON ANOTHER SERIES, I DIDN'T HAVE TIME, AND THE BOGU WOULD BE ANNOYING TO DRAW, SO I DECIDED TO HAVE ANOTHER ARTIST COME IN TO HANDLE THE HARD WORK. SCHOOL COMEDY IS THE EASIEST GENRE FOR ME TO WRITE, SO, AS I'M SURE YOU CAN TELL WHILE READING, I HAVE A LOT OF FUN WRITING *BAMBOO BLADE*.

AS I'M ALSO DRAWING A SERIES WITH RECURRING SCENES OF DEATH AND BLOODSHED CALLED *MATERIAL PUZZLE* THAT APPEARS IN *MONTHLY SHONEN GANGAN*, IT HELPS BALANCE MY PERSONAL EMOTIONS TO HAVE THIS LIGHT-HEARTED, HAPPY-GO-LUCKY TEEN COMEDY GOING ON AT THE SAME TIME.

I'M THE KIND OF PERSON THAT CAN DRAW OUT A SERIES TO TWENTY OR THIRTY VOLUMES, SO I'M HOPING TO MAKE THIS ONE CLEAN AND SHORT. I'VE HAD THE FINALE PLANNED OUT FROM THE START.

○ FOUNDATION

ONCE I FOUND OUT THAT IGARASHI-SENSEI WOULD BE HANDLING THE ART, I MADE A CONSCIOUS EFFORT TO HELP THE STORY FIT IN WITH THE ART STYLE. FIRST, I CREATED THE CHARACTERS THAT WOULD DRIVE THE STORY. KOJIRO, TAMAKI, AND KIRINO HAD BEEN DESIGNED FROM THE START, BUT YUJI AND DAN WERE ONLY WRITTEN IN WHEN I DISCOVERED THAT I NEEDED THEM—IT WOULD HAVE BEEN HARD TO GET BY WITH JUST GIRLS.

○ MACHIDO HIGH

I JUST DIDN'T HAVE TIME FOR EVERYTHING, SO I LEFT THE DESIGN OF THE TEAM UP TO IGARASHI-SENSEI BEFORE I EVEN HAD PERSONALITIES PICKED OUT FOR THEM.

THE CHARACTERS CAME AFTER THE ART.

I MADE THEM EXAGGERATED BECAUSE I HAD THEM SLATED AS ONE TIME-ONLY GAGS RATHER THAN REPEAT CHARACTERS.

BUT WHEN THE VOICE ACTORS FOR THE MACHIDO HIGH CHARACTERS IN THE ANIME COMPLAINED ABOUT NOT HAVING ENOUGH WORK TO DO, I REGRETTED NOT USING THEM MORE.

I'M SORRY. KURATA-SAN (ANIME SCRIPTWRITER HIDEYUKI KURATA) WROTE A SPECIAL ANIME-ONLY ORIGINAL STORY JUST FOR THEM.

○ TAMAKI'S PART-TIME JOB

THIS WAS A STORY I ALWAYS WANTED TO DO. ONE'S FIRST SUMMER JOB IS ALWAYS A NERVE-WRACKING EXPERIENCE. YOU WORK AND SWEAT AND MAKE MONEY—THE FIRST STEP INTO THE ADULT WORLD.

SOCIALLY INEPT TAMAKI HAS TO OVERCOME HER OWN FAILURES TO HELP THE STORE AND HELP THE CUSTOMERS...AT A KNICKKNACK SHOP, FOR SOME REASON.

AT FIRST, I HAD HER SLATED FOR A BREAD-BAKING FACTORY. IMAGINE ENDLESS ROWS OF BUNS PACKED WITH SWEET BEAN PASTE, BEING POKED IN THE MIDDLE BY TAMAKI. MY EDITOR PUT THE KIBOSH ON THAT ONE PRETTY QUICK.

I'LL HAVE MORE DETAILS ABOUT LATER STORY ARCS ANOTHER TIME.

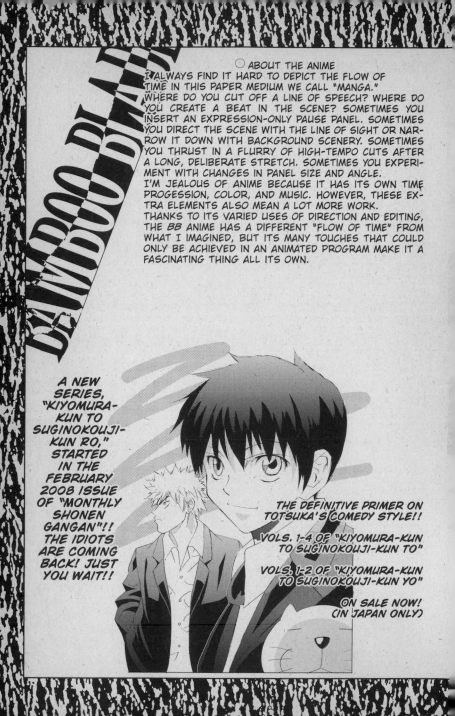

○ ABOUT THE ANIME

I ALWAYS FIND IT HARD TO DEPICT THE FLOW OF TIME IN THIS PAPER MEDIUM WE CALL "MANGA."

WHERE DO YOU CUT OFF A LINE OF SPEECH? WHERE DO YOU CREATE A BEAT IN THE SCENE? SOMETIMES YOU INSERT AN EXPRESSION-ONLY PAUSE PANEL. SOMETIMES YOU DIRECT THE SCENE WITH THE LINE OF SIGHT OR NARROW IT DOWN WITH BACKGROUND SCENERY. SOMETIMES YOU THRUST IN A FLURRY OF HIGH-TEMPO CUTS AFTER A LONG, DELIBERATE STRETCH. SOMETIMES YOU EXPERIMENT WITH CHANGES IN PANEL SIZE AND ANGLE.

I'M JEALOUS OF ANIME BECAUSE IT HAS ITS OWN TIME PROGRESSION, COLOR, AND MUSIC. HOWEVER, THESE EXTRA ELEMENTS ALSO MEAN A LOT MORE WORK.

THANKS TO ITS VARIED USES OF DIRECTION AND EDITING, THE *BB* ANIME HAS A DIFFERENT "FLOW OF TIME" FROM WHAT I IMAGINED, BUT ITS MANY TOUCHES THAT COULD ONLY BE ACHIEVED IN AN ANIMATED PROGRAM MAKE IT A FASCINATING THING ALL ITS OWN.

A NEW SERIES, "KIYOMURA-KUN TO SUGINOKOUJI-KUN RO," STARTED IN THE FEBRUARY 2008 ISSUE OF "MONTHLY SHONEN GANGAN"!! THE IDIOTS ARE COMING BACK! JUST YOU WAIT!!

THE DEFINITIVE PRIMER ON TOTSUKA'S COMEDY STYLE!!

VOLS. 1-4 OF "KIYOMURA-KUN TO SUGINOKOUJI-KUN TO"

VOLS. 1-2 OF "KIYOMURA-KUN TO SUGINOKOUJI-KUN YO"

(ON SALE NOW! (IN JAPAN ONLY)

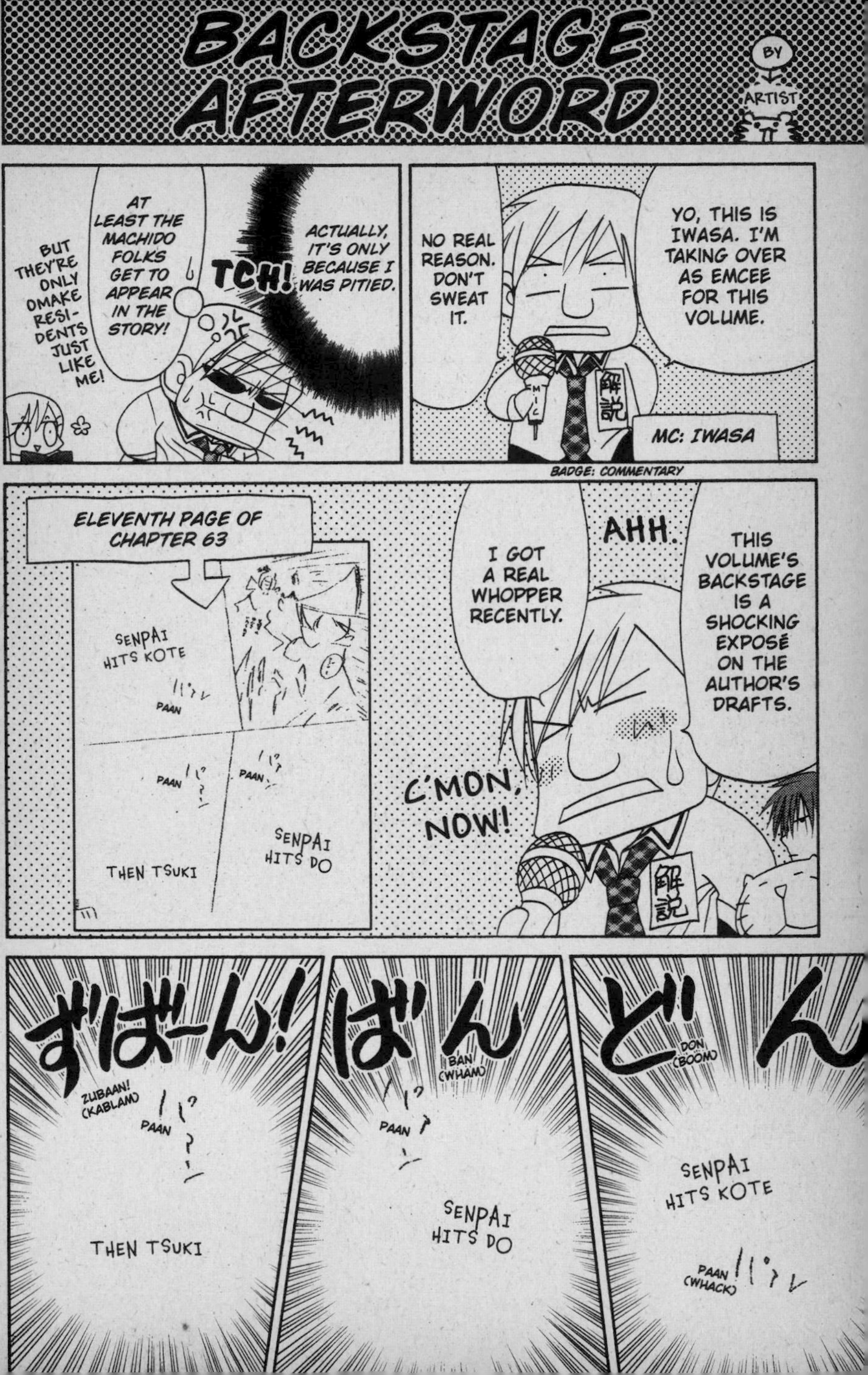
BACKSTAGE AFTERWORD
BY ARTIST
YO, THIS IS IWASA. I'M TAKING OVER AS EMCEE FOR THIS VOLUME.
NO REAL REASON. DON'T SWEAT IT.
MC: IWASA
BADGE: COMMENTARY
ACTUALLY, IT'S ONLY BECAUSE I WAS PITIED.
TCH!
AT LEAST THE MACHIDO FOLKS GET TO APPEAR IN THE STORY!
BUT THEY'RE ONLY OMAKE RESIDENTS JUST LIKE ME!
THIS VOLUME'S BACKSTAGE IS A SHOCKING EXPOSÉ ON THE AUTHOR'S DRAFTS.
AHH.
I GOT A REAL WHOPPER RECENTLY.
C'MON, NOW!
ELEVENTH PAGE OF CHAPTER 63
SENPAI HITS KOTE
PAAN
PAAN
SENPAI HITS DO
PAAN
THEN TSUKI
どん
DON (BOOM)
SENPAI HITS KOTE
PAAN (WHACK)
ばん
BAN (WHAM)
PAAN
SENPAI HITS DO
ずばーん!
ZUBAAN! (KABLAM)
PAAN
THEN TSUKI

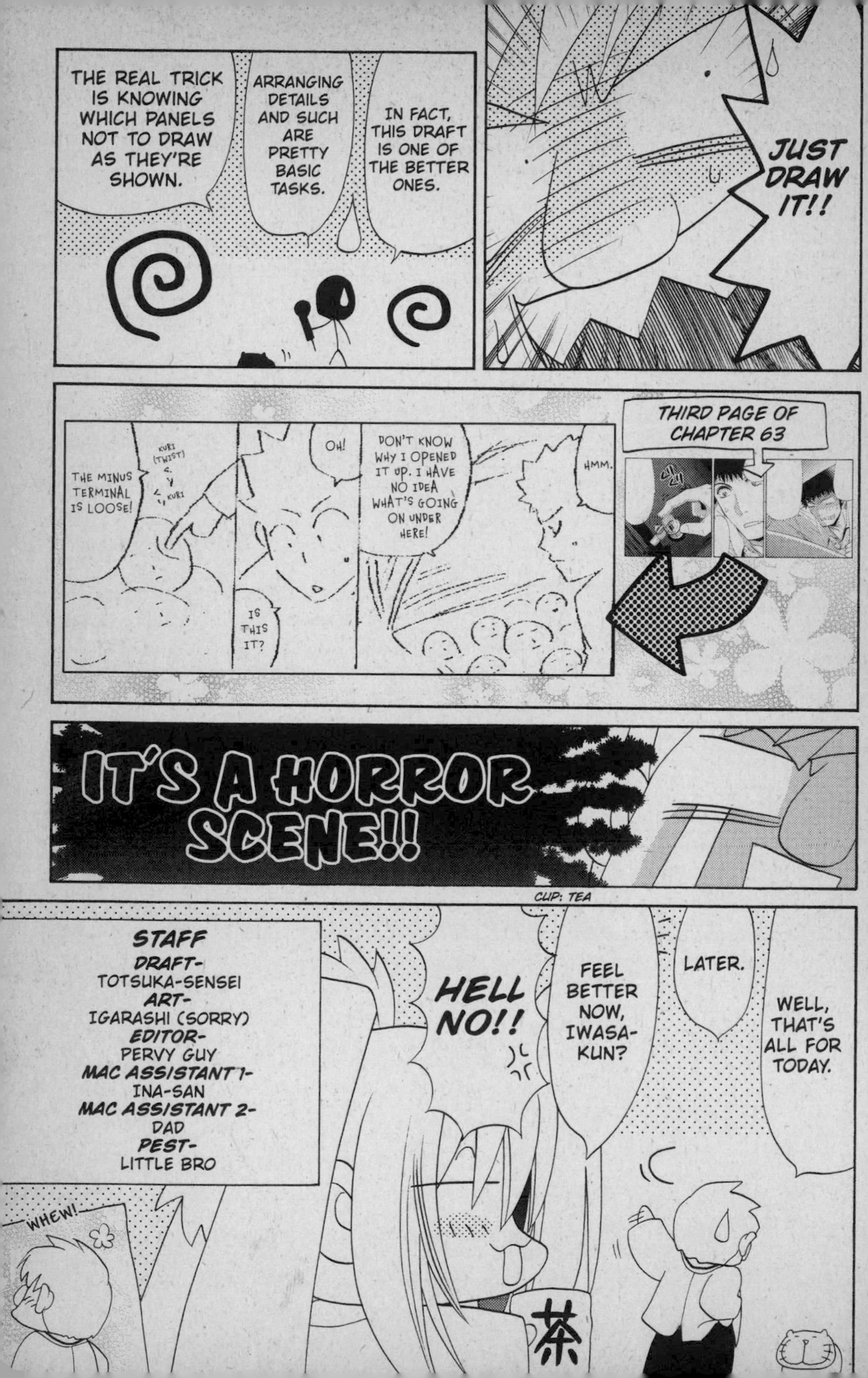
JUST DRAW IT!!
IN FACT, THIS DRAFT IS ONE OF THE BETTER ONES.
ARRANGING DETAILS AND SUCH ARE PRETTY BASIC TASKS.
THE REAL TRICK IS KNOWING WHICH PANELS NOT TO DRAW AS THEY'RE SHOWN.
THIRD PAGE OF CHAPTER 63
HMM.
DON'T KNOW WHY I OPENED IT UP. I HAVE NO IDEA WHAT'S GOING ON UNDER HERE!
OH!
IS THIS IT?
KURI (TWIST) KURI
THE MINUS TERMINAL IS LOOSE!
IT'S A HORROR SCENE!!
WELL, THAT'S ALL FOR TODAY.
LATER.
FEEL BETTER NOW, IWASA-KUN?
HELL NO!!
CUP: TEA
茶
STAFF
DRAFT- TOTSUKA-SENSEI
ART- IGARASHI (SORRY)
EDITOR- PERVY GUY
MAC ASSISTANT 1- INA-SAN
MAC ASSISTANT 2- DAD
PEST- LITTLE BRO
WHEW!

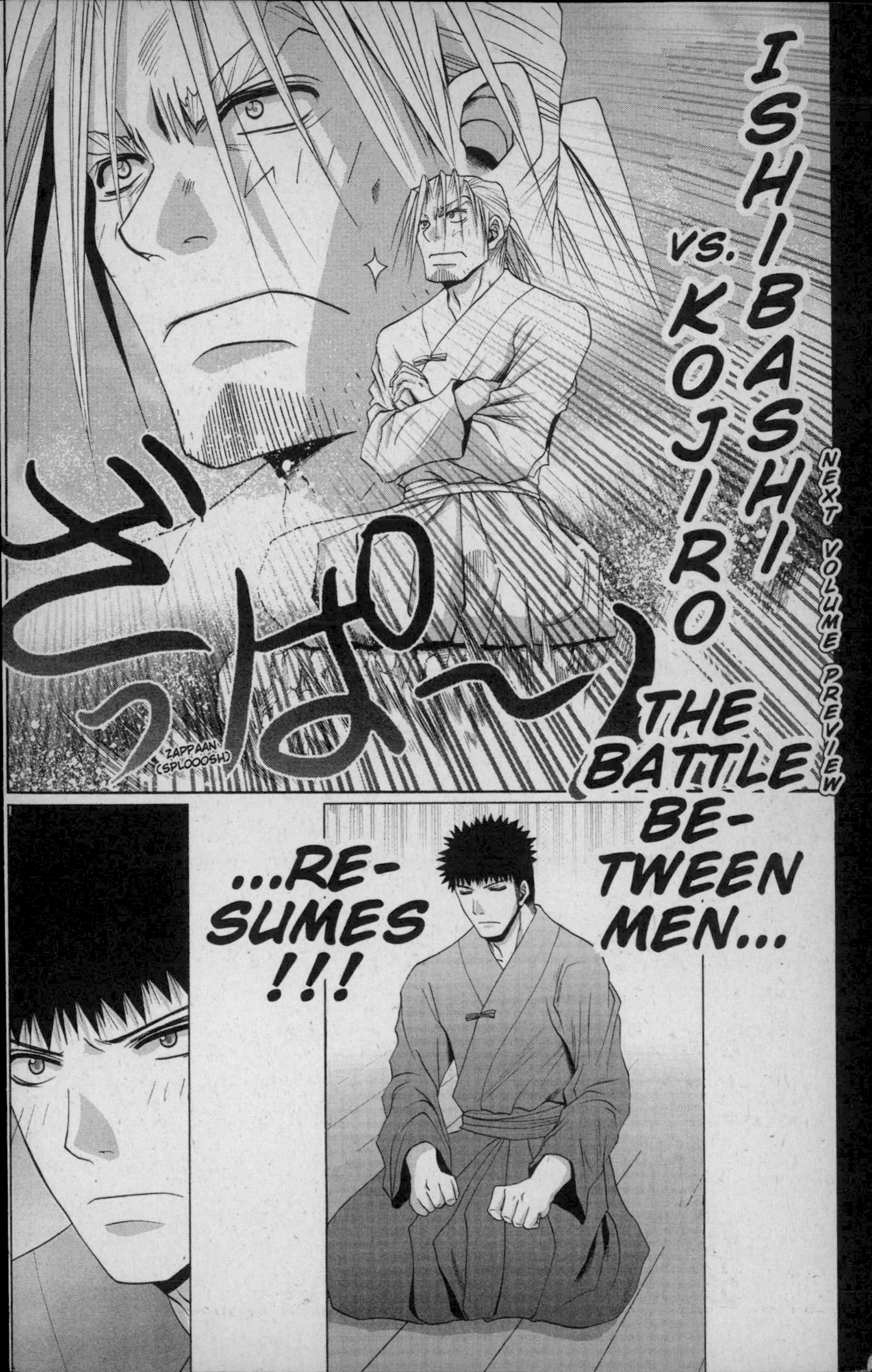
NEXT VOLUME PREVIEW
ISHIBASHI VS. KOJIRO
ZAPPAAN (SPLOOOSH)
THE BATTLE BE-TWEEN MEN...
...RE-SUMES!!!

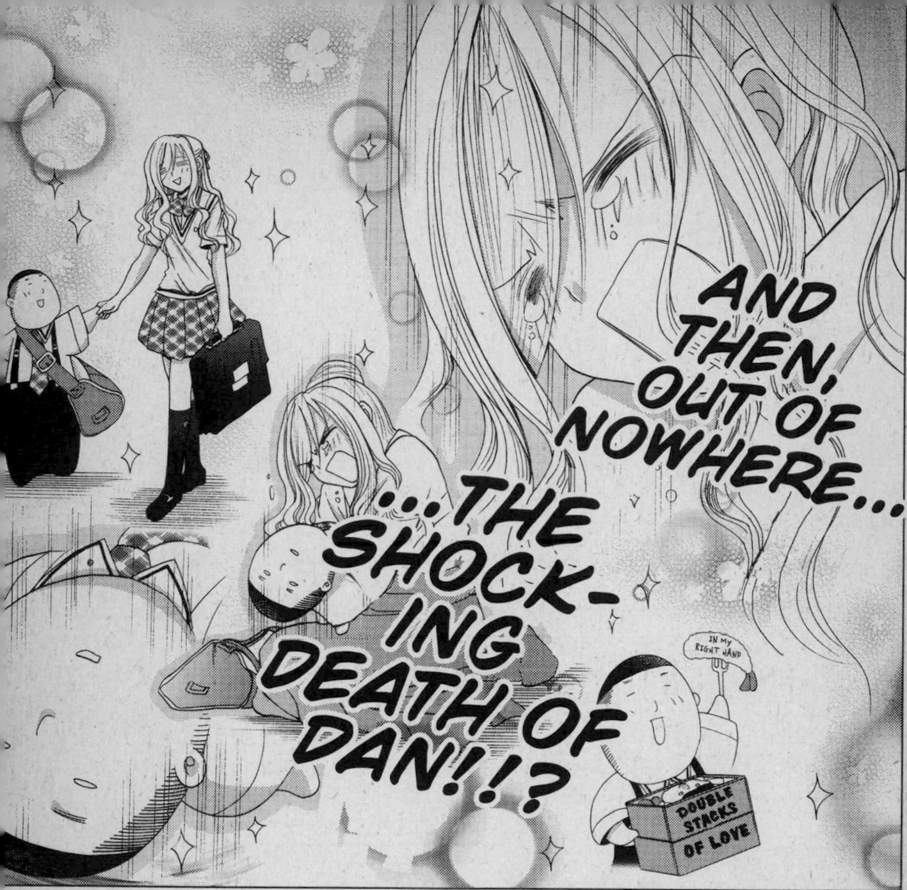
AND THEN, OUT OF NOWHERE...
...THE SHOCKING DEATH OF DAN!!?
IN MY RIGHT HAND
DOUBLE STACKS OF LOVE

DISCOVER THE TRUTH
IN VOLUME 8!
NEW CHARACTERS AS WELL!!
GET READY FOR IT!!!

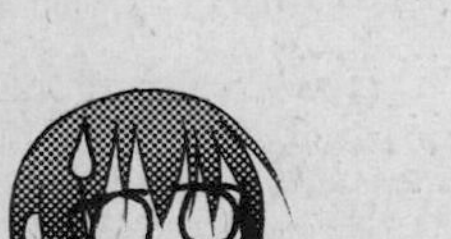

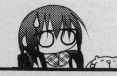

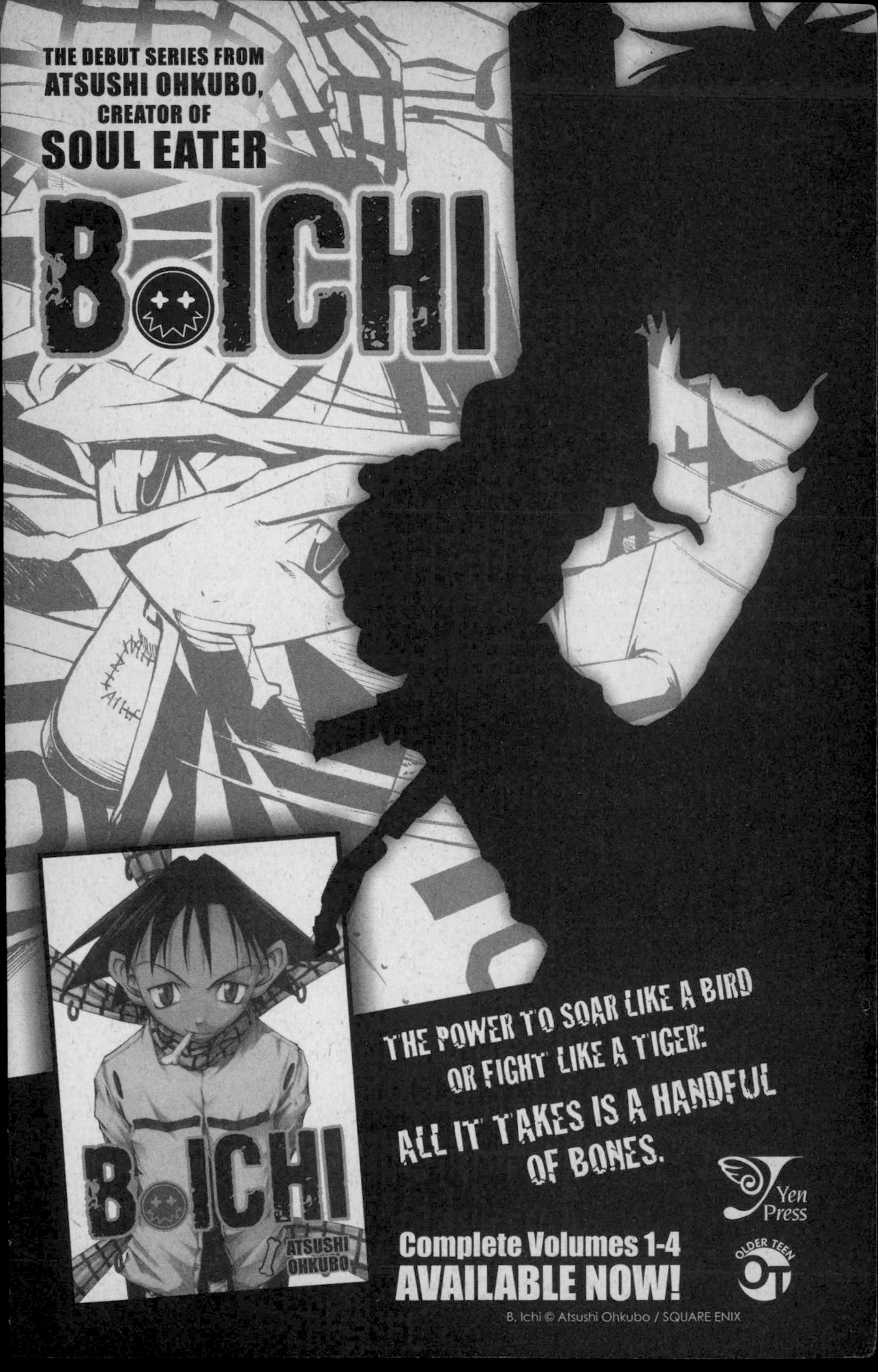
THE DEBUT SERIES FROM
ATSUSHI OHKUBO,
CREATOR OF
SOUL EATER
B.ICHI
B.ICHI
ATSUSHI OHKUBO
THE POWER TO SOAR LIKE A BIRD
OR FIGHT LIKE A TIGER:
ALL IT TAKES IS A HANDFUL
OF BONES.
Yen Press
Complete Volumes 1-4
AVAILABLE NOW!
OLDER TEEN
OT
B. Ichi © Atsushi Ohkubo / SQUARE ENIX

To become the ultimate weapon, one boy must eat the souls of 99 humans...

...and one witch.

Maka is a scythe meister, working to perfect her demon scythe until it is good enough to become Death's Weapon—the weapon used by Shinigami-sama, the spirit of Death himself. And if that isn't strange enough, her scythe also has the power to change form—into a human-looking boy!

 Yen Press

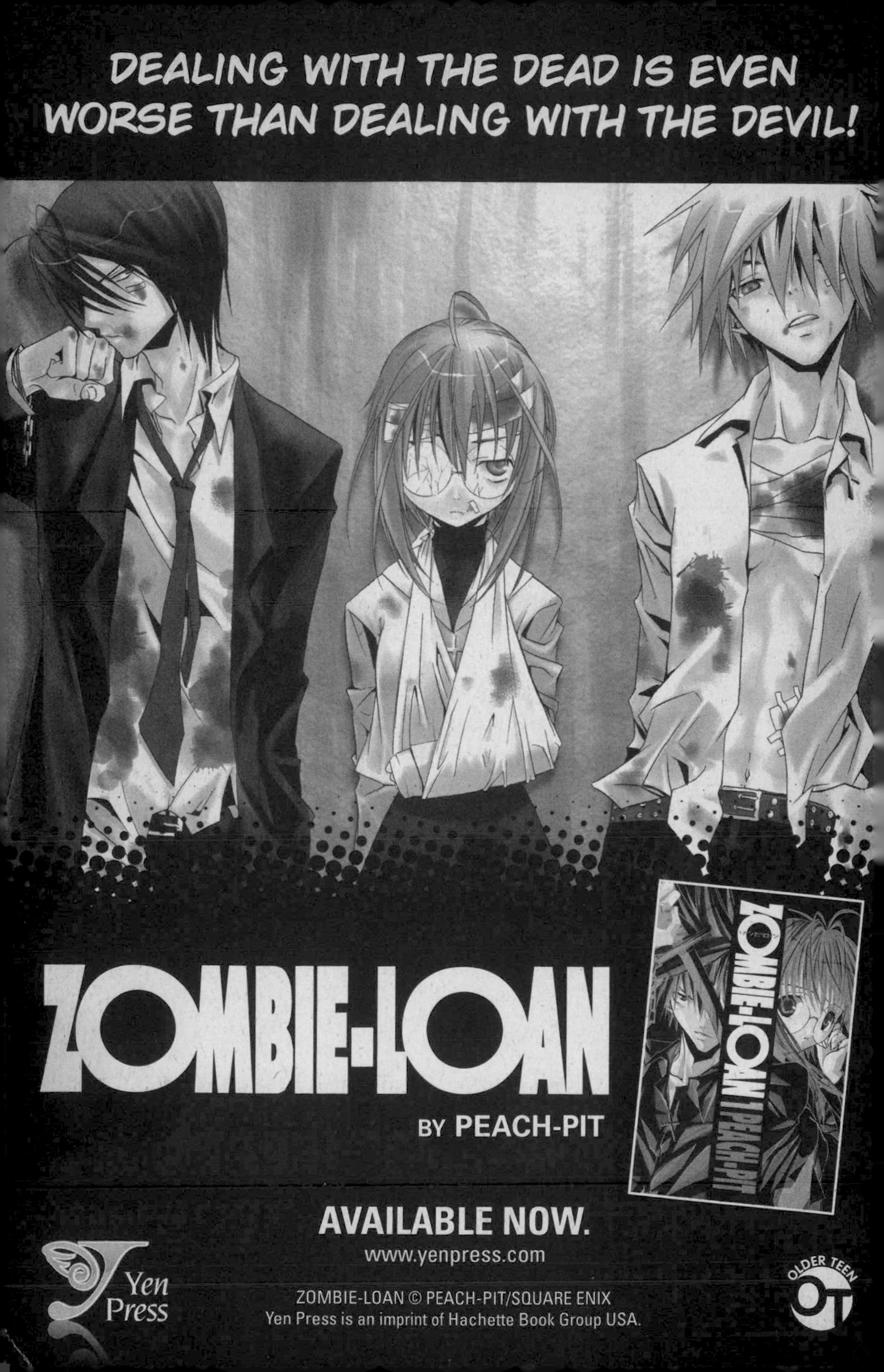
DEALING WITH THE DEAD IS EVEN WORSE THAN DEALING WITH THE DEVIL!
ZOMBIE-LOAN
BY PEACH-PIT
ZOMBIE-LOAN 1 PEACH-PIT
AVAILABLE NOW.
www.yenpress.com
Yen Press
OLDER TEEN OT
ZOMBIE-LOAN © PEACH-PIT/SQUARE ENIX
Yen Press is an imprint of Hachette Book Group USA.

BAMBOO BLADE ⑦

MASAHIRO TOTSUKA
AGURI IGARASHI

Translation: Stephen Paul

Lettering: Terri Delgado

BAMBOO BLADE Vol. 7 © 2008 Masahiro Totsuka, Aguri Igarashi /
SQUARE ENIX CO., LTD. All rights reserved. First published in Japan in
2008 by SQUARE ENIX CO., LTD. English translation rights arranged with
SQUARE ENIX CO., LTD. and Hachette Book Group through Tuttle-Mori
Agency, Inc.

Translation © 2010 by SQUARE ENIX CO., LTD.

Yen Press
Hachette Book Group
237 Park Avenue, New York, NY 10017

www.HachetteBookGroup.com
www.YenPress.com

Yen Press is an imprint of Hachette Book Group, Inc. The Yen Press name
and logo are trademarks of Hachette Book Group, Inc.

First Yen Press Edition: December 2010

ISBN: 978-0-316-07305-9

10 9 8 7 6 5 4 3 2 1

BVG

Printed in the United States of America

JUN 18 2012